International Series in Operations Research & Management Science

Volume 350

The book series **International Series in Operations Research and Management Science** encompasses the various areas of operations research and management science. Both theoretical and applied books are included. It describes current advances anywhere in the world that are at the cutting edge of the field. The series is aimed especially at researchers, advanced graduate students, and sophisticated practitioners.

The series features three types of books:

• Advanced expository books that extend and unify our understanding of particular areas.

• Research monographs that make substantial contributions to knowledge.

• Handbooks that define the new state of the art in particular areas. Each handbook will be edited by a leading authority in the area who will organize a team of experts on various aspects of the topic to write individual chapters. A handbook may emphasize expository surveys or completely new advances (either research or applications) or a combination of both.

The series emphasizes the following four areas:

Mathematical Programming: Including linear programming, integer programming, nonlinear programming, interior point methods, game theory, network optimization models, combinatorics, equilibrium programming, complementarity theory, multiobjective optimization, dynamic programming, stochastic programming, complexity theory, etc.

Applied Probability: Including queuing theory, simulation, renewal theory, Brownian motion and diffusion processes, decision analysis, Markov decision processes, reliability theory, forecasting, other stochastic processes motivated by applications, etc.

Production and Operations Management: Including inventory theory, production scheduling, capacity planning, facility location, supply chain management, distribution systems, materials requirements planning, just-in-time systems, flexible manufacturing systems, design of production lines, logistical planning, strategic issues, etc.

Applications of Operations Research and Management Science: Including telecommunications, health care, capital budgeting and finance, economics, marketing, public policy, military operations research, humanitarian relief and disaster mitigation, service operations, transportation systems, etc.

This book series is indexed in Scopus.

Florian M. Federspiel • Gilberto Montibeller •
Matthias Seifert
Editors

Behavioral Decision Analysis

Foreword by Don N. Kleinmuntz

Springer

Editors
Florian M. Federspiel
INCAE Business School
La Garita, Costa Rica

Gilberto Montibeller
University of Bristol Business School
University of Bristol
Bristol, UK

Matthias Seifert
IE Business School
IE University
Madrid, Madrid, Spain

ISSN 0884-8289 ISSN 2214-7934 (electronic)
International Series in Operations Research & Management Science
ISBN 978-3-031-44423-4 ISBN 978-3-031-44424-1 (eBook)
https://doi.org/10.1007/978-3-031-44424-1

This Springer imprint is published by the registered company Springer Nature Switzerland AG
The registered company address is: Gewerbestrasse 11, 6330 Cham, Switzerland

Foreword

I am writing this foreword from a unique personal perspective: Early in my career, I studied both behavioral decision theory and Bayesian statistics. As a newly minted PhD, I contributed to research in the psychology of judgment and decision making. While doing that, I found myself teaching decision analysis to graduate business students. I became interested both in applying behavioral decision research to decision analysis and in using decision analysis to improve decision making. Eventually, I founded a company that developed and implemented software to improve financial decision making in hospitals and healthcare systems, which was an opportunity to use both psychology and decision analysis in complex organizational settings.

The roots of this book can be related to several distinct strands of research on judgment and decision making that emerged in the mid-twentieth century. First, of course, are the contributions of von Neumann and Morgenstern (1953), which led to wide acceptance of an axiomatic foundation for expected utility theory. Important extensions include incorporating a subjective perspective on probability, embodied in subjective expected utility theory (Savage, 1954), and preferences over multiple criteria (Keeney & Raiffa, 1976). What is shared by these (and related) theories is an explicitly *normative* perspective. In the words of Fishburn (1988, page 26):

> The normative approach is concerned with criteria of coherence, consistency, and rationality in preference patterns that … are often set forth as axioms. It does not necessarily assume that intended or actual choice behavior adheres to the axioms, but it does presume that reasonable people who understand the axioms would want their preferences or implied choices to agree with the axiomatic guidelines.

The field of decision analysis has a direct line of descent from this work: Starting with the normative theory as a base, and working independently, Howard (1966, 1968) and Raiffa (1968), along with their numerous collaborators, developed a *prescriptive* approach to decision making. In the words of Raiffa (1968, p. x): "the approach we take *prescribes* how an individual who is faced with a problem of choice under uncertainty should go about choosing a course of action that is consistent with his personal basic judgments and preferences." This approach must, of necessity, concern itself not just with the normative theory of decision making, but also the methods required to implement that theory, including such pragmatic concerns as how to frame the decision problem, how to assess the decision maker's beliefs and preferences, how to incorporate group opinions, how to convince decision makers that the approach is valid, and a host of other matters familiar to all of us who have ever tried to analyze decisions for individuals, groups, and organizations.

Normative theory also impacted psychologists studying judgment and decision making. The individual responsible was Ward Edwards. He wrote several key papers that had great influence on psychologists, starting with Edwards (1954), in which he introduced psychology to the normative theory of decision making. Very quickly a paradigm for experimental investigations emerged, where actual behavior of experimental subjects was compared to normative rules, which might include the axioms of decision theory and their implications, the rules of probability and statistics, or even basic rules of logic. The predominant finding was that human decision makers often, but not always, deviated from the norms, and did so in a systematic fashion. This paradigm, which became central to the psychological investigation of judgment and decision making, led Edwards (1961) to coin a new name for this descriptive enterprise, *Behavioral Decision Theory*.

Edwards' impact was wide ranging, but also quite close to home: Several key early contributors to Behavioral Decision Theory were graduate students who studied with Edwards at the University of Michigan, including luminaries like Paul Slovic and Amos Tversky. It was Tversky, in collaboration with Daniel Kahneman, who built on and extended the basic paradigm, first examining heuristics and biases in probability judgments (Tversky & Kahneman, 1974), and then focusing on preferences and risky choice (Kahneman & Tversky, 1984). Experimental demonstrations would show systematic deviations from normative theory, and then the researchers would develop alternative theories or explanations to account for the behavior. The result was a proliferation of new accounts of how individuals make judgments and decisions. This work led to explosive growth in research on the psychology of judgment and choice and to efforts to rethink the foundations of adjacent fields like economics, finance, and consumer behavior.

Early on, researchers realized that work on the psychology of judgment and choice also had something to offer to decision analysis. For instance, Hogarth (1975) used Tversky and Kahneman's research on probability judgments to shed light on probability assessment methods. Similarly, Hershey et al. (1982) examined sources of bias in utility function assessments. However, these efforts were relatively few and far between.

In the meantime, Edwards had himself shifted focus from behavioral decision theory to prescriptive and applied efforts to improve judgment and decision-making processes. Notably, Detlof von Winterfeldt, another of Edward's former students, collaborated with Edwards to write what is probably the most important and comprehensive book on decision analysis from a descriptive perspective (von Winterfeldt & Edwards, 1986).

In a chapter that appeared in Edward's Festschrift, von Winterfeldt (1999) argues that these and other published studies show that descriptive research is relevant for the effective practice of decision analysis. However, he also presents a host of open research topics that would further improve the practice of decision analysis. His argument, which I agree with, underscores the opportunity for contributions with descriptive foundations and prescriptive implications. The book you are reading right now is an effort to achieve this confluence of the descriptive and the prescriptive. Calling this endeavor Behavioral Decision Analysis seems appropriate.

Interestingly, there is another stream of research that has great practical relevance and played an important role in the early history of the psychology of judgment and decision making: Paul Meehl created a large and important body of work that compared the effectiveness of intuitive judgment to statistical prediction (Meehl, 1954). The overarching question regards whether to rely upon the intuitive judgment of experts versus statistical formulas built from the same data provided to those experts. Meehl's context was diagnostic and predictive judgments by clinical psychologists, and his unequivocal conclusion was that intuitive judgment of experts was almost always inferior to statistical models. Within psychology, there was a great deal of controversy about this conclusion, but very little empirical evidence to overturn it.

This body of work was particularly salient to me because my father, Benjamin Kleinmuntz, was a psychologist who studied with Meehl at the University of Minnesota and went on to do applied research in judgment and decision making. In an integrative review of this work by Meehl and those who followed him, Benjamin Kleinmuntz (1990) noted that Meehl's result had been extended to encompass a wide range of judgment tasks and settings as well as an equally wide range of formulas (including but not limited to various statistical methods, computerized decision aids, and what we would now call Artificial Intelligence algorithms). He relates the inferiority of intuition relative to models to findings on the inconsistency of expert judgment as well as overconfidence in the accuracy of those judgments. Other useful contributions include research on the robustness of simple approximations to more sophisticated models (Dawes, 1979, 1986) and my own research on error propagation and decomposition in decision analytic models (D. Kleinmuntz, 1990).

In his review, Benjamin Kleinmuntz (1990) also proposes a framework for considering the costs and benefits of intuition and models. These cost-benefit considerations are particularly important since overconfidence in the accuracy of models can be just as damaging as overconfidence in intuitive judgment. For example, in my opinion, the global financial crisis in 2009 was precipitated in large part by the failure of banks and sophisticated investors to properly understand the likelihood of mortgage defaults in the "subprime" segment of the US mortgage market. Banks and investors were relying on the avowed sophistication of financial engineers using quantitative risk assessments to structure mortgage-backed securities. However, neither investors nor engineers considered the flawed information that was being input into the models. Was this a failure of models, a failure of intuition, or both?

What does this have to do with Behavioral Decision Analysis? I think about intuition and models using an idea proposed by Larry Phillips (1982, 1984), another former student of Edwards who is a psychologist turned decision analyst. Phillips proposes the term *requisite decision modeling* to describe the modeling process in decision analysis, where the modeler's intuitive understanding of a problem operates in parallel with the activities of building and using models. The modeler's intuitive understanding and the model's representations evolve through a mutual feedback process, with the modeler's intuition gaining insight from the evolving model and the model benefiting from the modeler's intuitive understanding. Only when the two converge do we have a sense that the modeling process is complete. This is, in essence, a psychological view of building decision analysis models.

The overarching need is for us to develop a psychology of decision analysis tools and tasks that we can rely upon to design better and more effective decision analyses. If this book succeeds in its objectives, it will be a useful step toward this larger end.

Kleinmuntz Associates, LLC Don N. Kleinmuntz
Chicago, IL, USA
January, 2023

References

Dawes, R. M. (1979). The robust beauty of improper linear models in decision making. *American Psychologist, 34*, 571–582.

Dawes, R. M. (1986). Proper and improper linear models. *International Journal of Forecasting, 2*, 5–14.

Edwards, W. (1954). The theory of decision making. *Psychological Bulletin, 41*, 380–417.

Edwards, W. (1961). Behavioral decision theory. *Annual Review of Psychology, 12*, 473–498.

Fishburn, P. C. (1988). *Nonlinear preference and utility theory*. The Johns Hopkins University Press.

Hershey, J. C., Kunreuther, H. C., & Schoemaker, P. J. H. (1982). Sources of bias in assessment procedures for utility functions. *Management Science, 28*, 936–954.

Hogarth, R. M. (1975). Cognitive processes and the assessment of subjective probability distributions. *Journal of the American Statistical Association, 70*(350), 271–289.

Howard, R. A. (1966). Decision analysis: Applied decision theory. In D. B. Hertz & J. Melese (Eds.), *Proceedings of the fourth international conference on operational research* (pp. 55–71). Wiley Interscience.

Howard, R. A. (1968). The foundations of decision analysis. *IEEE Transactions on Systems Science and Cybernetics*, SSC-4, 211–219.

Kahneman, D. & Tversky, A. (1984). Choices, values, and frames. *American Psychologist, 39*(4), 341–350.

Keeney, R. L. & Raiffa, H. (1976). *Decisions with multiple objectives: Preferences and value tradeoffs*. Wiley.

Kleinmuntz, B. (1990). Why we still use our heads instead of formulas: Toward an integrative approach. *Psychological Bulletin, 107*, 296–310.

Kleinmuntz, D. N. (1990). Decomposition and the control of error in decision analytic models. In R. M. Hogarth (Ed.), *Insights in decision making: A tribute to Hillel J. Einhorn* (pp. 107–126). University of Chicago Press.

Meehl, P. E. (1954). *Clinical versus statistical prediction: A theoretical analysis and a review of the evidence*. University of Minnesota Press.

Phillips, L. D. (1982). Requisite decision modelling. *Journal of the Operational Research Society, 33*, 303–312.
Phillips, L. D. (1984). A theory of requisite decision models. *Acta Psychologica, 56*, 29–48.
Raiffa, H. (1968). *Decision analysis: Introductory lectures on choices under uncertainty*. Addison-Wesley.
Savage, L. J. (1954). *The foundations of statistics*. Wiley.
Tversky, A. & Kahneman, D. (1974). Judgment under uncertainty: Heuristics and biases. *Science, 185*, 1124–1131.
von Neumann, J. & Morgenstern, O. (1953). *Theory of games and economic behavior*, 3rd Edition. Princeton University Press.
von Winterfeldt, D. (1999). On the relevance of behavioral decision research for decision analysis. In J. Shanteau, B. A. Mellers, & D. A. Schum (Eds.), *Decision science and technology: Reflections on the contributions of Ward Edwards* (pp. 133–154). Kluwer Academic Publishers.
von Winterfeldt, D. & Edwards, W. (1986). *Decision analysis and behavioral research*. Cambridge University Press.

Contents

Contributors

Saurabh Bansal Smeal College of Business, The Pennsylvania State University (PennState), State College, PA, USA

Manel Baucells Darden School of Business, University of Virginia, Charlottesville, VA, USA

Robin Dillon-Merrill McDonough School of Business, Georgetown University, Washington, DC, USA

Florian M. Federspiel INCAE Business School, La Garita, Costa Rica

Sreyaa Guha Nova School of Business and Economics, Universidade NOVA de Lisboa, Lisbon, Portugal

Jeffery L. Guyse College of Business Administration, California State Polytechnic University, Pomona, CA, USA

Candice H. Huynh College of Business Administration, California State Polytechnic University, Pomona, CA, USA

Richard S. John Department of Psychology, University of Southern California (USC), Los Angeles, CA, USA

Victor Richmond R. Jose McDonough School of Business, Georgetown University, Washington, DC, USA

Konstantinos V. Katsikopoulos University of Southampton Business School, Southampton, England

L. Robin Keller The Paul Merage School of Business, University of California, Irvine, CA, USA

Don N. Kleinmuntz Kleinmuntz Associates, LLC, Chicago, IL, USA

Martin Kocher Vienna Center for Experimental Economics, University of Vienna, Wien, Austria

Sarah A. Kusumastuti Faculty of Economics and Business, Department of Innovation Management and Strategy, University of Groningen, Groningen, The Netherlands

Richard P. Larrick The Fuqua School of Business, Duke University, Durham, NC, USA

Philip Leclerc Brussels Region, Belgium

Michał Lewandowski Institute of Econometrics, Warsaw School of Economics (SGH), Warsaw, Poland

Judit Lienert Eawag: Swiss Federal Institute of Aquatic Science and Technology, Environmental Social Sciences (ESS), Cluster Leader Decision Analysis, Dübendorf, Switzerland

Albert E. Mannes United States Government, Washington, DC, USA

Jason R. W. Merrick Statistical Sciences and Operations Research, Virginia Commonwealth University, Richmond, VA, USA

Gilberto Montibeller University of Bristol Business School, University of Bristol, Bristol, UK

Matthias Praxmarer Max Planck Institute for Research on Collective Goods, Bonn, Germany

Sofía Rodriguez INCAE Business School, La Garita, Costa Rica

Mostafa Sabbaghi Smeal College of Business, The Pennsylvania State University (PennState), State College, PA, USA

Matthias Seifert IE Business School, IE University, Madrid, Spain

Rashmi Sharma Smeal College of Business, The Pennsylvania State University (PennState), State College, PA, USA

Jay Simon Kogod School of Business, American University, Washington, DC, USA

Jack B. Soll The Fuqua School of Business, Duke University, Durham, NC, USA

Matthias Sutter Max Planck Institute for Research on Collective Goods, Bonn, Germany

Canan Ulu McDonough School of Business, Georgetown University, Washington, DC, USA

Detlof von Winterfeldt USC Sol Price School of Public Policy, University of Southern California (USC), Los Angeles, CA, USA

Behavioral Decision Analysis: Past, Present and Future

Florian M. Federspiel, Gilberto Montibeller, and Matthias Seifert

Abstract Decision Analysis has traditionally focused on the design and application of logically consistent tools to support decision makers during the process of structuring problem complexity, modeling uncertainty, generating predictions, eliciting preferences and, ultimately, making better decisions. Two commonly held assumptions are that the decision maker's cognitive belief system is fully accessible and that this system can be understood and formalized by trained analysts. However, in past years, an active line of research has emerged studying instances in which such assumptions may not hold. We aim to unite this community under the common theme of *Behavioral Decision Analysis. We s*uggest a framework, categorizing research based on task focus (prediction or decision) and behavioral level (individual or group). Two theoretical lenses, Descriptive Behavioral Decision Research and Prescriptive Behavioral Decision Research are employed to study these issues. The chapter introduces the taxonomy and subsequent chapters of the book.

Keywords Behavioral Decision Analysis · Prescriptive · Descriptive · History · Evolution

---

F. M. Federspiel (✉)
INCAE Business School, La Garita, Costa Rica
e-mail: Florian.Federspiel@incae.edu

G. Montibeller
University of Bristol Business School, University of Bristol, Bristol, UK

Center for Risk and Economic Analysis of Terrorism Events (CREATE), University of Southern California, Los Angeles, CA, USA
e-mail: Gilberto.Montibeller@bristol.ac.uk

M. Seifert
Operations & Technology, IE Business School, IE University, Madrid, Spain
e-mail: Matthias.Seifert@ie.edu

F. M. Federspiel et al. (eds.), *Behavioral Decision Analysis*, International Series in Operations Research & Management Science 350,
https://doi.org/10.1007/978-3-031-44424-1_1

Research conducted in the domain of Decision Analysis (Howard, 1968; Raiffa, 1968) has traditionally focused on the design and application of logically consistent tools to support decision makers during the process of structuring problem complexity, modeling uncertainty, generating predictions, eliciting preferences and, ultimately, making better decisions.

Importantly, two key assumptions commonly made by scholars in the field of Decision Analysis are that the decision maker's cognitive belief system is fully accessible and that this system can be effectively understood and formalized by trained decision analysts. However, in past years, an active line of research in Decision Analysis has emerged studying instances in which such assumptions may not necessarily hold. For instance, decision makers might struggle to provide quantitative judgments and understand the results of a decision analysis and experts may provide distorted estimates due to cognitive or motivational biases. As a result, descriptive behavior observed in decision or prediction tasks has often been shown to diverge from the one prescribed by normative decision theory.

The behavioral revolution in Decision Sciences began with the pioneering work of Edwards (1954, 1961) and the development of Behavioral Decision Research, which was then followed by Tversky and Kahneman's (1974) seminal work regarding the role of cognitive biases in judgment and decision making. This line of research led to the development of several relevant sub-disciplines, such as Behavioral Economics (Camerer et al., 2004; Thaler, 2016), Behavioral Finance (Hirshleifer, 2015), Behavioral Operations Management (Donohue et al., 2020), and Behavioral Operations Research (Franco et al., 2021; Franco & Hämäläinen, 2016).

Since the 1970s Decision Analysis has recognized the relevance of *Behavioral Decision Research* to the field (von Winterfeldt, 1999). In the 1970s most of the research on this front has been on the estimation of probabilities and consequences of future events, which are required in decision tree analysis and other types of models supporting decision making under uncertainty. For instance, recommendations about debiasing estimates against cognitive biases such as the anchoring and availability bias (Tversky & Kahneman, 1974) were already mentioned in the influential paper about probability encoding by Spetzler and Stael von Holstein (1975). In the same decade, Seaver et al. (1978) were testing different protocols for the expert elicitation of continuous distributions, Fischhoff et al. (1978) were identifying problems in the decomposition of events, among many other relevant developments in the behavioral understanding of decision making under uncertainty since then.

This line of inquiry was then extended to multi-attribute decision analysis (Keeney & Raiffa, 1976) during the 1980s. For instance, Borcherding and von Winterfeldt (1988) and Weber et al. (1988) identified the influence that the value tree structure may exert on attribute weights. Research in this domain also remains healthy with important developments, such as findings about omitted objectives and how to reduce this omitted variable bias, conducted by Keeney and his research associates (Bond et al., 2008, 2010).

In the late 1980s, the landmark book by von Winterfeldt and Edwards, *Decision Analysis and Behavioral Research* then represented a critical milestone towards the consolidation of the field (von Winterfeldt & Edwards, 1986). The book provided closer links between the behavioral findings that had emerged until the mid 1980s and Decision Analysis practice. Significantly, the authors provided insightful recommendations on how to use the former to improve the latter on the main modeling stages of a decision analysis, from the elicitation of input judgments for the decision model to the sensitivity analysis of its results.

To the present day, scholarly investigations into the behavioral implications of practicing Decision Analysis have continued to thrive, for example, regarding the effect of problem representation on the sure thing principle (Keller, 1985), the effect of weighting methods for eliciting multi-attribute models (e.g. Stillwell et al., 1987), judgmental biases in the detection of regime shifts (e.g. Massey & Wu, 2005), individual attitudes towards decision vagueness (Du & Budescu, 2005), the effect of near miss events on subsequent risk taking behavior (e.g. Dillon & Tinsley, 2008; Paine et al., 2020), the role of psychological heuristics for making inferences (Katsikopoulos, 2011), the role of crowd wisdom in judgment aggregation (e.g. Jose et al., 2014; Maciejovsky et al., 2013), cognitive and motivational biases in decision and risk analysis (Montibeller & von Winterfeldt, 2015, 2018), mental accounting and reference price adaptation (e.g. Baucells & Hwang, 2017), uncertainty estimation using judgmental forecasts (e.g. Bansal & Gutierrez, 2020), and more.

At the same time, the role of behavioral research in Decision Analysis has also become increasingly present on the agenda of the INFORMS Decision Analysis Society. This drive has led to, for instance, the *Decision Analysis* Special Issue during the mid-2000s edited by Kleinmuntz and Wu (2006), as well as sponsored sessions on "Behavioral Decision Analysis" that were consistently organized during the Annual Meetings of INFORMS since the year 2013.

Considering these developments, we believe that the time is ripe for consolidating behavioral research more formally within the field of Decision Analysis. It is in this context that the present book aims to unite this thriving decision analysis community under the common theme of *Behavioral Decision Analysis*. The field thereby considers research developments that (i) aim at examining (often experimentally) how human behavior in decision analytic contexts is likely to deviate from model prescriptions, (ii) seek to address potential pitfalls that are likely to induce systematic biases (e.g. during the model building process), (iii) aim to improve the quality of judgments employed by decision analytic models, (iv) seek to improve the interaction between decision makers and decision analytic models.

We define Behavioral Decision Analysis (BDA) as the study of how human behavior affects and informs the design, use, and improvement of decision analytic approaches for supporting individuals and groups in making better choices or predictions in managerially relevant problems. As such, research in this domain focuses on systematic behavioral deviations from decision analytic models both in those environments where the nature of the model could be purely normative or prescriptive.

An explicit intention of improving decisions based on the behavioral evidence presented is essential in our conceptualization of BDA. Relevant research may address issues occurring on the level of the individual decision maker as well as complex social interactions among group members and other decision stakeholders. Furthermore, past BDA studies have been adopting a diverse set of methodological approaches including laboratory and field experiments as well as analytical modeling and we see this rigorous methodological diversity as a strength of the field.

Considering this context, we propose that the influence of descriptive, behavioral research has impacted two major aspects of decision analysis, specifically the normative and prescriptive domain. First, on the *normative-descriptive* interface, previous studies have, for instance, investigated how decision makers' probability and pricing judgments systematically deviate from normative standards, particularly in environments that are characterized by disruptive change (e.g., Seifert et al., 2023). Second, on the *prescriptive-descriptive* interface, research has, for instance, highlighted several biases that may affect judgments required for decision analytic models including propositions for how to debias such judgments (Montibeller & von Winterfeldt, 2015, 2018). In this book we adopt the taxonomy suggested by Montibeller & von Winterfeldt in Chap. 2 and consider research on the normative-descriptive interface as *Descriptive* Behavioral Decision Research and work on the prescriptive-descriptive interface as *Prescriptive* Behavioral Decision Research.

While many behavioral developments are recent in Decision Analysis, our field has a long tradition of considering behavioral issues. An excerpt from a recent analysis by Federspiel and Ramirez Salas (2023) provides evidence of both a long tradition and an ever-increasing growth of this trend. Based on the search term "decision analysis" (DA) the authors compiled the abstracts of over 7700 papers published in *Management Science*, *Operations Research* and *Decision Analysis* (in the latter case evidently covering all articles). After manually classifying a set of these papers and identifying those that form part of BDA as defined here, this data was used to train and validate a suited classifier algorithm. The resultant classifier was then used to classify all the abstracts for further analysis. Figures 1, 2, 3, 4 illustrate the growth and relevance of BDA over time across these three journals.

The results from this analysis show that across all journals, work in the domain of BDA has been present nearly since the very beginning and has recently grown quite dramatically, in particular in *Management Science* (Fig. 1). Expectedly, the participation of BDA remains limited in *Operations Research* (Fig. 2). BDA appears to be a smaller but stable component of papers published in *Decision Analysis* (Fig. 3). On the other hand, BDA has gained considerable relevance within decision analysis in terms of the quantity of articles published in *Management Science* from 2010 onwards (Fig. 1) and there are many citations and downloads of BDA papers for the same journal (Fig. 4).

Taking this impressive growth into account, the field may benefit from a synthesis of previously conducted behavioral research as well as from the development of an axiomatic framework that addresses the role of behavioral insights in decision analysis research. In formally introducing BDA, in Table 1 we suggest a framework for Behavioral Decision Analysis, further decomposing the field into studies that

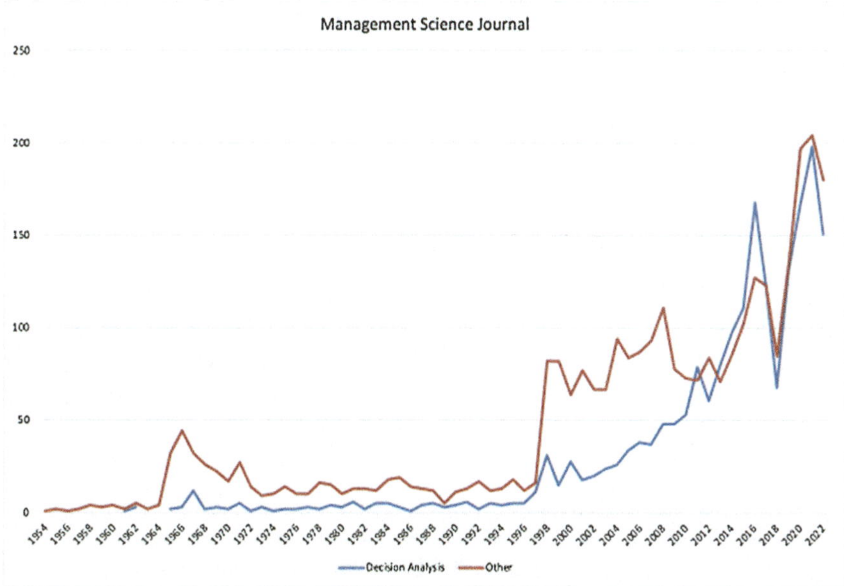

Fig. 1 BDA (blue) vs. DA (red) number of publications over time in *Management Science*

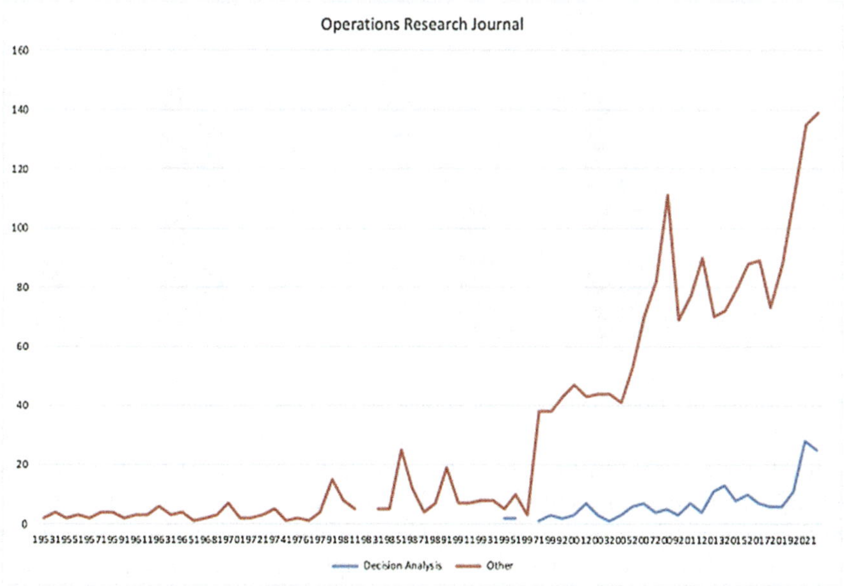

Fig. 2 BDA (blue) vs. DA (red) number of publications over time in *Operations Research*

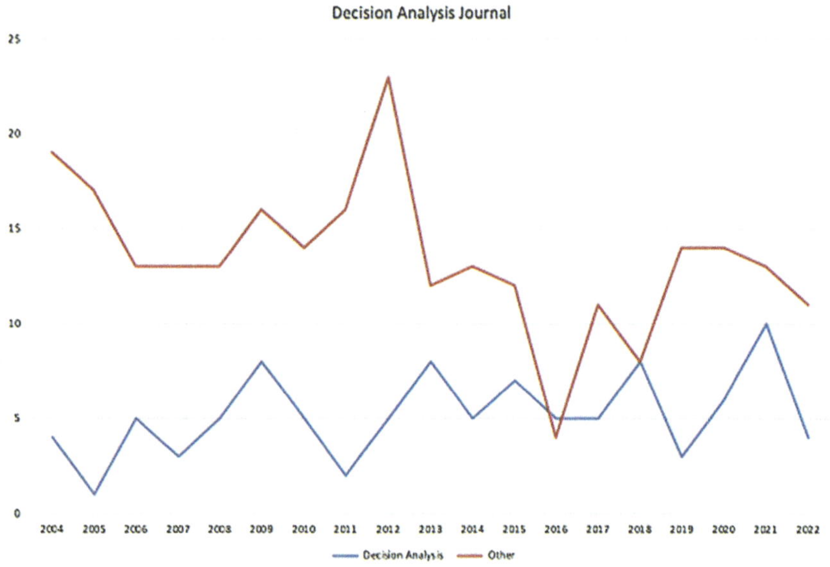

Fig. 3 BDA (blue) vs. DA (red) number of publications over time in *Decision Analysis*

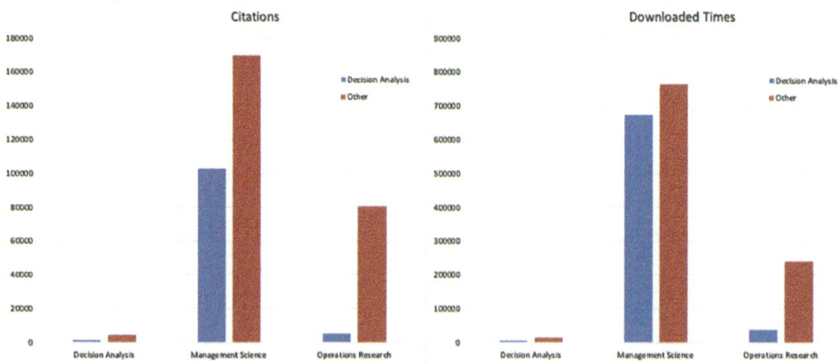

Fig. 4 Number of citations and downloads of BDA (blue) vs. DA (red) publications

either focus on *individual* or *group* decisions at the behavioral level, as well as whether the purpose of the decision analytic intervention is associated with forecasting an uncertain quantity (*prediction* focus) or with deciding (*decision* focus) as task focus. Two theoretical lenses can be employed to research these issues: *Descriptive* Behavioral Decision Research and *Prescriptive* Behavioral Decision Research.

The table also presents the main research aim and some illustrative examples for each dimension (*task focus, behavioral level* and *theoretical lens*). For instance,

Table 1 Dimensions of Behavioral Decision Analysis with example topics of research

Task focus	*Behavioral level*	**Theoretical lenses** **Descriptive behavioral decision research**	**Prescriptive behavioral decision research**
Prediction focus *(Probability judgments, estimations)*	**Individual**	We find that *individual decision makers* deviate from normative estimates • Over precision • System neglect	Incentivize and de-bias *individual decision makers* through targeted interventions • Scoring rules • Debiasing of estimates
	Group	We find that *groups of decision makers* deviate from normative estimates • Group biases in estimates • Boundaries of wisdom of the crowds, trimming	Incentivize and de-bias *groups of decision makers* through targeted interventions • Group aggregation • Group incentives for accuracy • Group elicitation protocols to reduce bias
Decision focus *(Risk taking preferences, resource allocation)*	**Individual**	We find that *individual decision makers* exhibit biases • Near miss events • Algorithm aversion	Incentivize and de-bias *individual decision makers* through targeted interventions • Debiasing in decision tasks
	Group	We find that *groups of decision makers* exhibit biases • Group decision performance	Incentivize and de-bias *groups of decision makers* through targeted interventions • Debiasing in decision tasks

with a *prediction* focus on an *individual* level, *Descriptive* Behavioral Decision Research (BDR) aims to find to which extent individual decision makers deviate from normative estimates. For an example of research in this specific dimension (*prediction* focus, *individual* level, *Descriptive* BDR), behavioral research has shown that subjects suffer from systematic over precision in estimating ranges of impacts, that are typically too narrow in relation to the true value. On the other hand, *Prescriptive* Behavioral Decision Research identifies ways to incentivize accuracy and de-bias individual decision makers. For an example of research in this specific dimension (*prediction* focus, *individual* level, *Prescriptive* BDR), different debiasing tools can be tested and the most effective tool identified against over-precision, as exemplified by the study conducted by Ferretti, Montibeller and von Winterfeldt (2022).

The taxonomy outlined in Table 1 provides a common ground for behavioral research that is of direct relevance for the field of Decision Analysis. The various chapters of this book discuss and provide examples of its relevance, offering a range of innovative works and perspectives of how human judgment and behavior informs and affects both the interfaces between the normative, and prescriptive realms – ultimately as a *necessary* ingredient to enable *better* decision making. We now briefly describe each of the remaining chapters of this book and their contributions to Behavioral Decision Analysis.

In Chap. 2, Montibeller and von Winterfeldt provide a conceptual evolution of Behavioral Decision Research and suggest that the developments of this field can be conceptualized into two perspectives: descriptive and prescriptive. Descriptive Behavioral Decision Research examines deviations from rationality and strives to develop theories or models to explain these deviations. On the other hand, Prescriptive Behavioral Decision Research also starts from observed deviations from rationality, but rather than developing theories or models to explain these deviations, it develops and tests tools or analytical methods to correct these deviations. The chapter also presents a list of major developments in both Descriptive and Prescriptive Behavioral Decision Research. Major developments in Descriptive Behavioral Decision Research are the identification of cognitive and motivational biases in unsupported decision making, the detection of cognitive limitation and adaptive behavior in unsupported decision making, and dysfunctional group behaviors. On the other hand, important developments in Prescriptive Behavioral Decision Research are the identification of relevant biases for prescriptive decision models, the development of effective debiasing strategies for these models, the design of adequate elicitation protocols for eliciting judgments from decision makers and experts, and strategies for the adequate facilitation of groups in decision analysis interventions.

Following, Chaps. 3, 4, 5, 6, 7 are characterized by a common Prediction focus yet encompassing different behavioral levels and theoretical lenses. A summary of each chapter is presented next.

Chapter 3 sheds light on the role of behavioral biases in the process of quantifying uncertainty. This is important, because the process of quantifying uncertainty represents a critical phase in the implementation of most decision analytic interventions. The author of this chapter provides a systematic survey of the different types of biases that may emerge in this context. By doing so, Jose develops a novel process-oriented framework to differentiate between behavioral biases that could occur at each of the major phases of the uncertainty quantification process. In contrast to previous studies, which have typically focused exclusively on biases that may occur during the elicitation phase, the author of this chapter also discusses the implications of these biases for the pre- as well as post-elicitation phase. From a practitioner point of view, the findings of this chapter promise to offer concrete guidance on how decision analysts can potentially avoid, minimize, and correct those behavioral biases that prevail during the multiple stages of the uncertainty quantification process in a more efficient manner.

In Chap. 4, Katsikopoulos focus on decisions under "radical uncertainty", in which meaningful probability distribution cannot be defined as it is typically assumed in Decision Analysis for modeling decisions under uncertainty. The author then provides an instigating and thoughtful discussion on how decisions under this level of uncertainty can be adequately supported. He suggested two main tools, both based on important behavioral insights. First, fast-and-frugal heuristics (Gigerenzer & Gaissmaier, 2011), which are computational models that implement decision rules and are built by utilizing knowledge from human psychology. Their name comes from the fact that they use a few and easily obtainable pieces of information (frugal) and combine those pieces in simple ways (fast). Fast-and-frugal heuristics can prescribe what decisions should be made as computational shortcuts or describe what decisions people actually do make as heuristics in psychology. The chapter provides two fascinating case studies that describe the use of a fast-and-frugal heuristic to improve and explain choices: stopping decisions of incoming cars at military checkpoints in Afghanistan and the best choice for non-urgent operations at the British National Health Service. The second tool he advocates is the use of qualitative scenarios for describing this level of uncertainty, as also promoted in decision analysis by Schoemaker (1993) with a strong behavioral component. From this discussion, he urges Decision Analysis to extend its tools beyond traditional probabilistic models to better cope with higher levels of uncertainty.

In Chap. 5, Bansal, Sharma and Sabbaghi investigate the optimal elicitation of judgments by experts focusing on the calibration process. Specifically, they study whether a decision analyst should share calibration information with experts before eliciting their judgments. While this appears contrary to the usual two-step process of first obtaining judgments for calibrating the experts' judgmental errors before eliciting judgments for the quantities of interest and using the information from the first step to properly adjust them, Bansal et al. find experimental evidence for their approach to improve elicitation under certain circumstances. They find that expert judgment gets worse with increasing task complexity, and that calibration feedback reduces bias and noise in more complex tasks yet does not improve judgments. Further, with numeracy not seeming to play a role, decision makers appear able to judge their performance only in less complex tasks. Overall, this suggests that expert judgments benefit from receiving calibration information for complex tasks.

In Chap. 6, Guha, Seifert and Ulu study probability judgments in environments that are characterized by impending regime shifts. Past research has found evidence for what has been coined as the system neglect hypothesis: In unstable environments with precise signals, DMs exhibit relatively more underreaction in their probability judgments, and in stable environments with noisy signals, they exhibit relatively more overreaction. In this chapter the authors explore the boundaries of system neglect by studying regime shift environments that go beyond the types initially studied in Massey and Wu (2005). In particular, the authors conduct a laboratory experiment, in which regime shifts occur with various levels of transition probabilities that may vary anywhere between 2 and 98 percent. The study reveals that underreaction in probability judgments significantly worsens until regime shifts occur with a 50:50 chance, after which the system neglect pattern is mirrored. The authors conclude by discussing implications for managerial practice in organizational contexts that are characterized by continuous change.

Chapter 7 is a reprint of Larrick et al. (2012), in which the authors build on questions raised by social psychology regarding conformity to examine the wisdom of relying on crowds. Investigating normative questions of optimality or rationality, the authors highlight how classic social psychological experiments such as the famous Asch experiment were misleading, thus calling into question the early conclusion of people yielding too much to the judgment of others. That is, the Asch experiment presented participants with judgments by others that were not representative of their true answers. When instead collecting representative judgments by crowds, how accurate are such judgments? When presented with representative judgments by others, are decision makers able to benefit from group accuracy? The authors argue that to investigate these questions one needs to study the processes by which judgments are elicited and shared with decision makers. Larrick et al. analyze the conditions under which crowds yield accurate judgments and how decision makers use the judgment of others. The authors conclude that, contrary to earlier conclusions, decision makers rely too much on their own judgments and miss an opportunity to learn effectively from others.

Subsequently, Chaps. 8, 9, 10, 11, 12, 13 are characterized by a common Decision focus, while varying regarding the behavioral level and theoretical lens. These chapters are summarized next.

In Chap. 8, Baucells, Leclerc, Lewandowski, and Merrick consider the role of gains and losses, which play a major role in prospect theory to explain risk attitudes against a reference point (Kahneman & Tversky, 1979; Tversky & Kahneman, 1992), in predicting behavior in games. They analyze the descriptive power of different preference models in this context and discuss some advantages and disadvantages of each model as a descriptive tool to predict decisions under uncertainty. The comparative analysis is conducted over two stylized games: a 2x2 game in which a company considers whether to disobey or obey a regulation and the regulator whether to inspect or not; and a 6x6 investment game whereby to firms invest from their endowment to win a reward and the firm with the higher investment wins. The authors provide a proof of concept that one of the descriptive models considered, range utility theory, can represent preferences in games, as well as guarantee the existence without complicating its definition. Furthermore, the theory can also predict observed player behavior with similar parameter values that represent single decision-maker behavior.

In Chap. 9, Kusumastuti and John investigate the consequences of missing objectives in applications of multiattribute utility analysis. In using multiattribute utility analysis (MAU) as a prescriptive model for decision making, identifying all of the relevant objectives of decision makers is critical. Building on earlier research showing that decision makers often fail to consider all relevant objectives and only later recognize missing objectives as important, the authors examine the consequences of missing objective sets in a wide range of MAU applications. In analyzing MAU applications in fields such as energy planning and disaster management, the authors suggest that consequences of incomplete objective sets depend mainly on three factors. They argue that those are the correlation between attributes defining objectives, the completeness of the alternative set considered, and the steepness of assessed weights. The consequences of missing objectives vary significantly. While incomplete objectives do not necessarily lead to utility losses, the authors offer critical insights into what factors lead to situations in which they very well do.

In Chap. 10, Guyse, Huynh, Keller and Simon review the topic of intertemporal choice, an area rife for prescriptive interventions based on the general finding that decision makers usually do not make decisions consistent with a normatively prescribed constant discount rate. After reviewing the classic normative model for intertemporal preferences, Guyse et al. proceed to discuss the consistent anomalies that arise descriptively under different scenarios, which may generally suggest impatience. The authors contrast these findings with evidence to suggest a preference of increasing or constant outcomes over time in particular for non-monetary outcomes suggesting a willingness to wait for improvement. Guyse et al. conclude by prescribing various nudges aimed at maintaining consistency in intertemporal decisions and discuss prescriptive efforts going forward.

In Chap. 11, Federspiel, Dillon-Merrill, Seifert and Rodriguez review the phenomenon of near miss events and their impact on subsequent risk-taking behavior. The authors first synthesize the literature on an interdisciplinary domain of research and offer a refined definition of near miss events based on extant studies and definitions. Behavioral evidence regarding near miss events has shown that events that came close to yet by chance did not result in a loss can lead to both an increase or decrease in risk taking behavior that is often normatively unwarranted. The change in risk taking primarily depends on how the event is perceived and interpreted by the decision maker, which yet predictably depends on a range of factors, which Federspiel et al. proceed to review. As such, the chapter provides a comprehensive overview of how we may define and conceptualize near misses, what normative frameworks dictate in terms of how to respond to these events and their divergence from how people descriptively react to these events, before concluding with which prescriptive interventions have been found to counter the bias.

In Chap. 12, Lienert considers the behavioral challenges of conducting decision analysis for public environmental decision problems with a focus on multi-attribute analysis, a field in which several challenges are relevant for policy analysis (Montibeller, 2018). Her extensive review covers the main challenges for each main stage of a decision analysis in this context: problem structuring, identification of stakeholders, generation of decision objectives, generation of decision alternatives, prediction of consequences for the decision alternatives, elicitation of preferences (value and utility functions), elicitation of attribute weights, and sensitivity analysis. The author emphasizes the importance of further behavioral research on problem structuring, particularly in the selection of relevant stakeholders and in the minimization of the omitted variable bias for both missing fundamental objectives and neglected relevant alternatives. She also highlights the challenges that constructed preferences (Lichtenstein & Slovic, 2006; Slovic, 1995) pose to policy analysis, as different elicitation protocols may lead to distinctive attribute weights and shapes of utility functions (and therefore of risk attitude). Finally, she calls for more BDA research on debiasing tools and adequate modeling of uncertainties in this type of decision analysis application.

Chapter 13 is a reprint of Kocher et al. (2020), in which the authors discuss the role of teams in organizations and their potential for increasing productivity and profitability. The authors work fits well into the scope of this book, because it showcases an additional stream of research that holds important behavioral implications for the practice of decision analysis. Adopting the lens of behavioral and experimental economics, the chapter contains a comprehensive survey of past experimental studies documenting basic differences in decisions taken by individuals and teams. Importantly, the authors review the literature on decisions in the context of uncertainty and time preferences as well as social preferences including bargaining and cooperation, in complex environments that require learning and in moral dilemmas. Moreover, the chapter includes a discussion regarding the important role of self-selection into teams and its potential consequences. Finally, the survey covers relevant field experiments that complement the literature on decision making by looking at how team-based incentive schemes influence productivity and output.

In closing this chapter, we hope that this book acts as a launching platform, to enable further sharing of ideas, exploration of research themes, and engagement in joint research projects under the shared umbrella of Behavioral Decision Analysis. Interdisciplinary research may serve as a bridge to attract more Ph.D. students and senior researchers to our field – as well as provide a stage for more outward growth. Beyond synthesizing behavioral research and providing an axiomatic framework for BDA, building, and expanding our community is a core tenet of our efforts with this book.

References

Bansal, S., & Gutierrez, G. J. (2020). Estimating uncertainties using judgmental forecasts with expert heterogeneity. *Operations Research, 68*(2), 363–380.

Baucells, M., & Hwang, W. (2017). A model of mental accounting and reference price adaptation. *Management Science, 63*(12), 4201–4218.

Bond, S. D., Carlson, K. A., & Keeney, R. L. (2008). Generating objectives: Can decision makers articulate what they want? *Management Science, 54*(1), 56–70. https://doi.org/10.1287/mnsc.1070.0754

Bond, S. D., Carlson, K. A., & Keeney, R. L. (2010). Improving the generation of decision objectives. *Decision Analysis, 7*(3), 238–255.

Borcherding, K., & von Winterfeldt, D. (1988). The effect of varying value trees on multiattribute evaluations. *Acta Psychologica, 68*(1–3), 153–170. https://doi.org/10.1016/0001-6918(88)90052-2

Camerer, C., Loewenstein, G., & Rabin, M. (2004). *Advances in behavioral economics (My DropboxPapers AcrobatBDT for Mng SciBDT on Judgment)*. Princeton University Press.

Dillon, R. L., & Tinsley, C. H. (2008). How near-misses influence decision making under risk: A missed opportunity for learning. *Management Science, 54*(8), 1425–1440.

Donohue, K., Özer, Ö., & Zheng, Y. (2020). Behavioral operations: Past, present, and future. *Manufacturing & Service Operations Management, 22*(1), 191–202. https://doi.org/10.1287/msom.2019.0828

Du, N., & Budescu, D. V. (2005). The effects of imprecise probabilities and outcomes in evaluating investment options. *Management Science, 51*(12), 1791–1803.

Edwards, W. (1954). The theory of decision making. *Psychological Bulletin, 51*(4), 380–417. https://doi.org/10.1037/h0053870

Edwards, W. (1961). Behavioral decision theory. *Annual Review of Psychology, 12*(1), 473–498. https://doi.org/10.1146/annurev.ps.12.020161.002353
Federspiel, F., & Ramirez Salas, R. (2023). The evolution of behavioral decision analysis over time: A text analysis. Working Paper.
Ferretti, V., Montibeller, G., & von Winterfeldt, D. (2022). Testing the effectiveness of Debiasing techniques to reduce Overprecision in the elicitation of subjective continuous probability distributions. *European Journal of Operational Research, forthcoming, 304*(2), 661–675. https://doi.org/10.1016/j.ejor.2022.04.008
Fischhoff, B., Slovic, P., & Lichtenstein, S. (1978). Fault trees: Sensitivity of estimated failure probabilities to problem representation. *Journal of Experimental Psychology: Human Perception and Performance, 4*(2), 330–344. https://doi.org/10.1037/0096-1523.4.2.330
Franco, L. A., & Hämäläinen, R. P. (2016). Behavioural operational research: Returning to the roots of the OR profession. *European Journal of Operational Research, 249*(3), 791–795. https://doi.org/10.1016/j.ejor.2015.10.034
Franco, L. A., Hämäläinen, R. P., Rouwette, E. A. J. A., & Leppänen, I. (2021). Taking stock of behavioural OR: A review of behavioural studies with an intervention focus. *European Journal of Operational Research, 293*(2), 401–418. https://doi.org/10.1016/j.ejor.2020.11.031
Gigerenzer, G., & Gaissmaier, W. (2011). Heuristic decision making. *Annual Review of Psychology, 62*, 451–482. https://doi.org/10.1146/annurev-psych-120709-145346
Hirshleifer, D. (2015). Behavioral finance. *Annual Review of Financial Economics, 7*(1), 133–159. https://doi.org/10.1146/annurev-financial-092214-043752
Howard, R. A. (1968). The foundations of decision analysis. *IEEE Transactions on Systems Science and Cybernetics, 4*(3), 211–219. https://doi.org/10.1109/TSSC.1968.300115
Jose, V. R. R., Grushka-Cockayne, Y., & Lichtendahl, K. C., Jr. (2014). Trimmed opinion pools and the crowd's calibration problem. *Management Science, 60*(2), 463–475.
Kahneman, D., & Tversky, A. (1979). Prospect theory: An analysis of decision under risk. *Econometrica, 47*(2), 263–291. https://doi.org/10.2307/1914185
Katsikopoulos, K. V. (2011). Psychological heuristics for making inferences: Definition, performance, and the emerging theory and practice. *Decision Analysis, 8*(1), 10–29.
Keeney, R. L., & Raiffa, H. (1976). *Decisions with multiple objectives: Preferences and value trade-offs*. Cambridge University Press.
Keller, L. R. (1985). The effects of problem representation on the sure-thing and substitution principles. *Management Science, 31*(6), 738–751.
Kleinmuntz, D. N., & Wu, G. (2006). From the special issue editors... Special issue on psychology and decision analysis. *Decision Analysis, 3*(3), 121–123. https://doi.org/10.1287/deca.1060.0076
Kocher, M. G., Praxmarer, M., & Sutter, M. (2020). Team decision-making. Handbook of labor, human resources and population economics, 1–25.
Larrick, R. P., Mannes, A. E., & Soll, J. B. (2012). The social psychology of the wisdom of crowds. In J. I. Krueger (Ed.), *Social judgment and decision making* (pp. 227–242). Psychology Press.
Lichtenstein, S., & Slovic, P. (Eds.). (2006). *The construction of preference*. Cambridge University Press.
Maciejovsky, B., Sutter, M., Budescu, D. V., & Bernau, P. (2013). Teams make you smarter: How exposure to teams improves individual decisions in probability and reasoning tasks. *Management Science, 59*(6), 1255–1270.
Massey, C., & Wu, G. (2005). Detecting regime shifts: The causes of under-and overreaction. *Management Science, 51*(6), 932–947.
Montibeller, G. (2018). Behavioral challenges in policy analysis with conflicting objectives. In *Recent advances in optimization and modeling of contemporary problems* (Vol. 1–0, pp. 85–108). INFORMS. https://doi.org/10.1287/educ.2018.0182
Montibeller, G., & von Winterfeldt, D. (2015). Cognitive and motivational biases in decision and risk Analysis. *Risk Analysis, 35*(7), 1230–1251. https://doi.org/10.1111/risa.12360

Montibeller, G., & von Winterfeldt, D. (2018). Individual and group biases in value and uncertainty judgments. In L. C. Dias, A. Morton, & J. Quigley (Eds.), *Elicitation* (pp. 377–392). Springer. https://doi.org/10.1007/978-3-319-65052-4_15

Paine, J. W., Federspiel, F., Seifert, M., & Zou, X. (2020). Take a risk or proceed with caution: Prevention motivation moderates responses to near-loss events. *Behavioral Decision Making, 33*(4), 505–522.

Raiffa, H. (1968). *Decision Analysis: Introductory lectures on choices under uncertainty*. Addison-Wesley.

Schoemaker, P. J. H. (1993). Multiple scenario development: Its conceptual and behavioral foundation. *Strategic Management Journal, 14*, 193–213. https://doi.org/10.1002/smj.4250140304

Seaver, D. A., von Winterfeldt, D., & Edwards, W. (1978). Eliciting subjective probability distributions on continuous variables. *Organizational Behavior and Human Performance, 21*(3), 379–391. https://doi.org/10.1016/0030-5073(78)90061-2

Seifert, M., Ulu, C., & Guha, S. (2023). Decision making under impending regime shifts. *Management Science, Articles in Advance, 69*(10), 5695–6415. https://doi.org/10.1287/mnsc.2022.4661

Slovic, P. (1995). The construction of preference. *American Psychologist, 50*(5), 364–371. https://doi.org/10.1037/0003-066X.50.5.364

Spetzler, C. S., & Stael von Holstein, C.-A. (1975). Probability encoding in decision analysis. *Management Science, 22*(3), 340–358.

Stillwell, W. G., Von Winterfeldt, D., & John, R. S. (1987). Comparing hierarchical and nonhierarchical weighting methods for eliciting multiattribute value models. *Management Science, 33*(4), 442–450.

Thaler, R. H. (2016). Behavioral economics: Past, present, and future. *American Economic Review, 106*(7), 1577–1600. https://doi.org/10.1257/aer.106.7.1577

Tversky, A., & Kahneman, D. (1974). Judgment under uncertainty: Heuristics and biases. *Science, 185*(4157), 1124–1131. https://doi.org/10.1126/science.185.4157.1124

Tversky, A., & Kahneman, D. (1992). Advances in prospect theory: Cumulative representation of uncertainty. *Journal of Risk and Uncertainty, 5*(4), 297–323. https://doi.org/10.1007/BF00122574

von Winterfeldt, D. (1999). On the relevance of behavioral decision research for decision analysis. In J. Shanteau, B. A. Mellers, & D. A. Schum (Eds.), *Decision science and technology: Reflections on the contributions of Ward Edwards* (pp. 133–154). Kluwer.

von Winterfeldt, D., & Edwards, W. (1986). *Decision analysis and behavioral research*. Cambridge University Press.

Weber, M., Eisenfuhr, F., & von Winterfeldt, D. (1988). The effects of splitting attributes on weights in multiattribute utility measurement. *Management Science, 34*(4), 431–445.

Behavioral Decision Research: Descriptive and Prescriptive Perspectives

Gilberto Montibeller and Detlof von Winterfeldt

Abstract Behavioral Decision Research has provided a deep understanding of how humans form judgments and make choices, since its emergence in the 1950s. Underlying this body of research is the contrast of actual decision making with the paragons of rationality, which provide the idealized model on how humans should decide. Starting with the Ellsberg and Allais paradoxes and followed by Tversky & Kahneman's seminal research on biases and heuristics in judgments, it has been clear that no real person is fully rational. Exploring deviations from rationality has been a major focus of Behavioral Decision Research. This research has two quite distinct branches: descriptive and prescriptive. Descriptive Behavioral Decision Research examines deviations from rationality and strives to develop theories or models to explain these deviations. Prescriptive Behavioral Decision Research also starts from observed deviations from rationality, but rather than developing theories of models to explain these deviations, it develops and tests tools or analytical methods to correct such deviations. The distinction between the descriptive and prescriptive perspectives in Behavioral Decision Research has often been implicit and blurred in the Decision Sciences literature. In this chapter we aim to address this conceptual lacuna, proposing a taxonomy for these two perspectives in Behavioral Decision Research and describing their main achievements.

Keywords Behavioral Decision Research · Prescriptive normative interface · Descriptive normative interface

G. Montibeller (✉)
University of Bristol Business School, University of Bristol, Bristol, UK

Center for Risk and Economic Analysis of Threats and Emergencies (CREATE), University of Southern California, Los Angeles, California, USA
e-mail: Gilberto.Montibeller@bristol.ac.uk

D. von Winterfeldt
Department of Industrial and Systems Engineering, University of Southern California, Los Angeles, CA, USA

F. M. Federspiel et al. (eds.), *Behavioral Decision Analysis*, International Series in Operations Research & Management Science 350,
https://doi.org/10.1007/978-3-031-44424-1_2

Introduction

Since its emergence in the 1950s, Behavioral Decision Research has provided a deep understanding of how humans form judgments and make choices (see Fischhoff and Broomell (2020) for a recent review). In addition to individual decision making (the traditional focus of Behavioral Decision Research), group-focused behavioral decision research studies how groups perform, combine information, and interact when making decisions (Kerr & Tindale, 2004).

Underlying this body of research is the contrast of actual decision making with the paragons of rationality, which provide the idealized model on how humans should decide. In this chapter we define rationality in a fairly specific sense as adherence to the principles of probability theory, expected utility theory, and multi-attribute utility theory.

Starting with the Ellsberg and Allais paradoxes and followed by Tversky & Kahneman's seminal research on biases and heuristics in judgments, it has been clear that no real person is fully rational. Exploring deviations from rationality has been a major focus of behavioral decision research over the past 50 years. Nonetheless, we can identify two quite distinct branches in Behavioral Decision Research: descriptive and prescriptive.

The distinction between these two perspectives in Behavioral Decision Research, descriptive and prescriptive, has been often implicit and blurred in the Decision Sciences literature. This lack of conceptual clarity has created some confusion and misunderstandings in the field. First, some researchers in the field have claimed that descriptive models should be used for prescriptive purposes, even if they deviate from commonly accepted rationality principles. However, these suggestions may lead to misleading prescriptions and misguided decision advice. Second, many relevant findings from the descriptive perspective have been neglected by researchers and practitioners that want to better support decision making with Decision Analysis. Third, the extensive growth of the descriptive perspective has created an unbalanced agenda on decision making research, focused on showing and finding faults and biases, while disregarding excellence in human judgment and decision making in some tasks and opportunities for decision making improvement and debiasing in others. Fourth, and conversely, the rather slow evolution of the prescriptive perspective has prevented the development of a full body of effective tools and methods that could effectively address the shortcomings and deviations from rationality to help decision makers decide better.

In this chapter we aim to address this conceptual lacuna proposing a taxonomy for these two perspectives in Behavioral Decision Research. We start with a short historic perspective on the evolution of the field, which includes the conceptualizations of rationality, early paradoxes against rationality in the 1950s, the development of behavioral decision research in the 1960s, and the split between the descriptive and prescriptive behavioral decision research in the late 1970s. We then conceptualize the descriptive and prescriptive perspectives and briefly describe some important avenues of research within each perspective. We conclude this chapter with a research agenda following this conceptualization of the field.

Historical Development of Behavioral Decision Research

In 1947 von Neumann and Morgenstern's published "The theory of games and economic behavior" that included (in its second printing of 1948) the axiomatic foundation of expected utility theory (von Neumann & Morgenstern, 2007). While the audience was primarily economists, some psychologists paid attention to this development. Preston and Baratta (1948) examined choices among students' gambles and observed moderate agreement with expected utility (EU) theory. Mosteller and Nogee (1951) conducted similar experiments with some support of EU theory. Edwards, then a student of Mosteller's at Harvard, believed that if people have non-linear utilities for money, they might also have non-linear weights for probabilities. He confirmed this in several experiments (Edwards, 1953, 1954a), and thus the subjective expected utility (SEU) theory was borne. Savage, about the same time, provided the axiomatic rationale for the SEU model (Savage, 1954).

It was not long until critiques of the SEU model appeared. Allais (1953) published his "paradox" which contradicted the SEU model as a description of how people make choices among gambles. The main idea behind the Allais paradox was that people over-value sure thing outcomes over outcomes that are embedded in a gamble. Subsequently, Ellsberg (Ellsberg, 1961) showed that people preferred gambles with a well-defined risk over gambles with ambiguous events. Both criticisms of the SEU model were largely ignored by economists, who began to embrace SEU theory as a viable alternative to expected value theory.

In 1954 and later in 1960, Edwards published two articles that laid the foundation of decision theory as a major topic in psychology: "The Theory of Decision Making" (Edwards, 1954b) and "Behavioral Decision Theory" (Edwards, 1961). His research throughout the early 1960s tested the descriptive validity of the SEU model. Edwards later summarized the results of the early behavioral research as follows: "It is probably fair to say that the SEU model does a very mediocre job of predicting choices among bets, but nothing else does much better."

Some psychologists believed as late as the late 1960s that people generally followed the principles of probability theory and the SEU model in their intuitive thinking. In their article "Man as intuitive statistician" Peterson and Beach (1967) argued that people are generally following probability rules, though sometimes they do so in a suboptimal manner. This point of view was seriously undermined by a series of articles by Tversky and Kahneman, who demonstrated several significant probability biases, concluding that people are not suboptimal Bayesian statisticians, they are not Bayesian at all. Many of the articles supporting this conclusion are compiled in Kahneman et al. (1982) book "Judgment under uncertainty: Heuristics and biases." While this view was not held universally (for example, Gigerenzer (1991)), the current view of most psychologists is that biases such as the availability bias, ignoring base rates, the conjunction fallacy and others are strong and persistent in intuitive unaided probability judgments.

In the later part of the 1970s, Kahneman and Tversky turned their attention to violations of the SEU theory. In 1979 they published the influential paper "Prospect theory: An analysis of decision under risk" (Kahneman & Tversky, 1979), which demonstrated several violations of SEU theory, including the overvaluing of sure things, ambiguity aversion, risk aversion in gains vs. risk seeking in losses, and the dependence of preferences on the definition of the status quo. After overcoming strong resistance by economists, prospect theory is today the best-known descriptive alternative to SEU theory (see Wakker (2010) for details).

In the years following Tversky and Kahneman's seminal work, behavioral researchers have greatly expanded the scope of biases and errors in judgment and decision making, particularly during the 1980s until the 2010s, including biases in problem structuring (e.g. myopic problem representations (Legrenzi et al., 1993; Legrezni & Girotto, 1996)), in model formulation (e.g. omitted variables such as objectives (Bond et al., 2008), alternatives (Butler & Scherer, 1997; Pitz et al., 1980) and uncertainties (Fischhoff et al., 1978; Thomas et al., 2008)), and in multi-attribute utility elicitations (e.g. range insensitivity bias (Gabrielli & von Winterfeldt, 1978; von Nitzsch & Weber, 1993) and proxy bias (Fischer et al., 1987)). However, in the late 1970s, behavioral decision research split into roughly two directions (Luce & von Winterfeldt, 1994; von Winterfeldt, 1999): descriptive research and prescriptive research.

Descriptive behavioral decision research, building on Tversky's & Kahneman's findings, continued to search for additional biases and errors in probability and utility judgments. The descriptive paradigm can be described by four steps (see von Winterfeldt (1999)):

1. Identify a normative model for a judgment or decision-making task (e.g., the multiplication rule for determining the probability of the intersection of two mutually exclusive events).
2. Experimentally demonstrate deviations from the normative model (e.g., the conjunction fallacy (Tversky & Kahneman, 1983)).
3. Develop a descriptive theory or model to explain or predict these deviations (e.g., the representativeness heuristic and support theory).
4. Test the descriptive theory (e.g., to which extent the descriptive theory explains observed judgments that suffer from the conjunction fallacy).

Prescriptive behavioral decision research pursued a different path. Building on the paradigm of engineering psychology, the objective of prescriptive behavioral research has been to improve the quality of judgments, correcting and "debiasing" errors in judgment and decision making. This paradigm can be described by the following steps (see von Winterfeldt (1999)):

1. Identify a normative model for a judgment and decision-making task (e.g., Bayes theorem to revise probabilities in light of data).

2. Observe whether people deviate from the normative model when making judgments (e.g., conservatism, the tendency to insufficiently revise probabilities in comparison with the Bayes theorem (Edwards, 1968; Phillips & Edwards, 1966)).
3. Develop tools and training methods to correct the judgmental error (e.g., by decomposing the task into a prior probability and a likelihood assessment task, then using Bayes theorem to calculate the posterior probability).
4. Test the tools and training methods and implement successful ones when conducting a decision analysis.

Reflecting on this dichotomy between descriptive and prescriptive decision research, Montibeller and von Winterfeldt (2015) observed that many biases and errors in judgment and decision making can easily be corrected with tools or training. An example is the conjunction fallacy described above, which can be corrected by explaining that the intersection of two event cannot be larger than either of the two events and to use the proper calculation of the joint probability. However, a few biases and errors are persistent, hard to correct, and occur in tasks typically required by experts or decision makers when conducting a decision analysis. An example is overprecision, which is the tendency by experts and laypeople to provide credible intervals around a numerical estimate that are much too narrow (see Ferretti et al. (2022)). Based on this observation, prescriptive behavioral decision researchers should primarily focus on biases and errors that are relevant for Decision Analysis (in the sense that they occur in the assessment tasks of the analyses and that are difficult to overcome with tools or training), as well as in improving the quality of judgments that are inputs for decision analysis models.

In this brief historical overview, we have argued that Behavioral Decision Research, while starting from common roots, has bifurcated into two distinctive perspectives since the late 1970s. In the next section we conceptualize those perspectives against a more explicit definition of rationality.

Two Perspectives of Behavioral Decision Research

Economists, psychologists, sociologists, and philosophers have proposed many concepts of rationality. We suggest a relatively narrow definition of rationality for the purpose of this chapter: we consider a person to be rational, if their behavior is consistent with subjective expected utility theory (Savage, 1954), probability theory (Feller, 2009), and multiattribute utility theory (Keeney & Raiffa, 1993).

From this definition of rationality, we can derive several aspects of rational choices and coherent judgments, for example, transitivity of preferences and independence of irrelevant alternatives or events; encoding probabilities consistent with probability theory and updating prior probabilities using Bayesian algorithms; and having preferences that are consistent with one's objectives and tradeoffs.

As described by the brief historical evolution in the previous section, we argue that Behavioral Decision Research has two quite distinct perspectives, which are defined next by taking into account this proposed definition of rationality:

Descriptive Behavioral Decision Research: This perspective examines deviations from rationality and strives to develop theories or models to explain these deviations. An example is the research on hindsight bias (Roese & Vohs, 2012): when decision makers believe that an event is more predictable after it becomes known than it was before the event became known. Descriptive models would describe, for instance, to which extent the estimated probability of an event has been distorted by this bias. Most behavioral decision research in the past 50 years has been descriptive (see Gilovich et al. (2002) and Kahneman and Tversky (2000) for a coverage of this literature). Researchers in this area have typically come from Cognitive or Social Psychology.

Prescriptive Behavioral Decision Research: This perspective also starts from observed deviations from rationality, but rather than developing theories of models to explain these deviations, this line of research develops and tests tools or analytical methods to correct such deviations. An example is the base rate bias: people often tend to ignore base rates, when making probability judgments based on specific evidence. To correct this bias, one can simply split the task of making probability judgments into a part that involves estimating the base rate and a part that involves estimating the conditional likelihood and then use Bayes theorem to calculate the relevant probability. As mentioned previously, a relatively small part of behavioral decision research has been prescriptive (see Montibeller and von Winterfeldt (2015) for a coverage of this literature and Montibeller and von Winterfeldt (2018) for its extension to group decision making). This type of research has been conducted primarily by psychologist, engineers, and statisticians with an interest in improving judgment and decision making, with Decision Analysis or related methodologies.

Having distinguished the two perspectives of Behavioral Decision Research, we now detail some key developments of research within each tradition. We start with the descriptive perspective next.

Descriptive Behavioral Decision Research

Descriptive Behavioral Decision Research studies how judgments are formed and choices are made, examines deviations from rationality in those judgments and choices, and strives to develop theories or models to explain such deviations (see Shafir and LeBoeuf (2002) for a detailed coverage of these deviations). This is a vast field so we organize it here in a way that provides clear links to developments in Prescriptive Behavioral Decision Research (see Weber and Johnson (2009) and Fischhoff and Broomell (2020) for comprehensive reviews of Descriptive Behavioral Decision Research).

One key aspect of this stream of research is a focus on *unsupported* decision making, i.e. on how decision makers form judgments or decide without any decision model, facilitator, or decision analyst providing decision support. In unsupported decision making there is neither support for the *content* of the decision, such as the representation of decision components in prescriptive decision analysis models (Howard, 1968; Keeney & Raiffa, 1993; Raiffa, 1968; von Winterfeldt & Edwards, 1986), nor support for decision making *processes*, such as prescriptive recommendations on how individual, group and organizational decisions should be made (Keeney, 1992; Montibeller, 2022; Spetzler et al., 2016; Tindale et al., 2003).

Decision making models in this stream of research are of a *descriptive* nature: they try to accurately describe how unsupported decisions are made. The quality of these models is assessed in terms of their predictive accuracy, i.e., to which extent the models can predict the choices and behaviors of unsupported decision makers. The field is eminently empirical, with extensive use of behavioral experiments in controlled settings. These experimental conditions range from presenting descriptions of decision situations, in which subjects should provide a judgment or make a choice, to providing simulated environments in which information is experientially provided to subjects before they are asked to exert a judgment or make a choice (Lejarraga & Hertwig, 2021).

One of the most influential descriptive models, which exemplify this descriptive focus, is Prospect Theory (Kahneman & Tversky, 1979; Tversky & Kahneman, 1992; Wakker, 2010). Prospect Theory-based models try to describe two main findings in unsupported decisions under uncertainty. First, that decision makers display different risk attitude if prospects are perceived as gains or as losses against a reference point. Second, that subjective probabilities of events get distorted for low and high probability events. Behavioral laboratory experiments have shown that when subjects are presented with described outcomes as either gains or losses, these subjects show risk averseness behavior for an outcome perceived as a gain and risk seeking behavior for the same outcome perceived as a loss. In addition, events with low probabilities are overestimated and events with high probabilities are underestimated. Prospect Theory models parametrize these findings so unsupported choices under uncertainty could be better predicted.

While Prospect Theory-based models are widely accepted by the scientific community, notice that alternative descriptive models have been proposed to explain different observations of the same phenomenon. For example, in situations in which the uncertainty is experienced, instead of described, researchers have found that subjects underestimate events with low probabilities (Hertwig et al., 2004) and descriptive models have been developed to represent this behavioral finding (Erev et al., 2017). This issue highlights the importance of ecological validity in behavioral lab experiments, which should attempt to replicate actual choices as much as possible, as well as the intrinsic intertwined relationship between experimental design and behavioral findings (Lejarraga & Hertwig, 2021).

The underlying assumption of Behavioral Decision Research is that decision makers present bounded rationality (Simon, 1982), given their inherently limited cognitive capabilities, in contrast with the fully rational model idealized by Decision Theory. The contrast between the paragons of rationality versus the observed behavior in unsupported decision making has provided several research avenues for the field. We cover five of these avenues in the next section, from cognitive and motivational biases to the cognitive limitations and adaptive behavior of decision makers.

Identifying Cognitive Biases in Unsupported Decision Making

The first avenue of Descriptive Behavioral Decision Research is the identification of cognitive biases in unsupported decision making. A cognitive bias in judgment is a systematic deviation from a normative standard that would be expected if said judgment were made by a fully rational decision maker. The bias occurs due to faulty reasoning, typically a simplifying mental heuristic that is inadequate for the judgmental task confronted by the decision maker (see Montibeller & von Winterfeldt, 2015).

One of the earliest biases detected, by Edwards and his associates in the 1960s was conservatism (Edwards, 1968; Phillips & Edwards, 1966). As mentioned previously, this bias occurs when subjects were not revising enough their estimations of probabilities, when receiving new information about events, as they were supposed if they were fully rational and followed the Bayesian rule for probability updating.

The early 1970s saw the emergence of the highly influential research on heuristics-and-bias in Cognitive Psychology by Tversky and Kahneman. In their famous 1974 Science paper they identified and discussed several biases and the role of heuristics in generating those biases (Tversky & Kahneman, 1974). One of these bias is anchoring (Furnham & Boo, 2011), in which an estimation for a variable is anchored by information provided about another unrelated variable. Another cognitive bias is availability (Wänke et al., 1995), in which estimations of probabilities are excessively influenced from factors that happened recently or are easy to recall.

Since then a large number of biases has been identified by behavioral decision researchers (see Gilovich et al. (2002) and Kahneman and Tversky (2000) for useful compilations of papers on specific biases). Indeed, the Wikipedia now lists almost 200 biases,[1] classified as arising from too much information, not enough meaning, need to act fast, and need to recall information. The identification of a large number of cognitive biases in unsupported decision making poses a challenge for Decision Analysis, whose models rely heavily on the elicitation of judgements (for example, those required to define the shape of utility functions, of attribute weights, or of probabilities of events occurring).

The heuristic-and-bias research program and the identification of cognitive biases has been also influential to adjacent disciplines. Examples of such influence is the development of Behavioral Economics with a focus in identifying bias in economic-related decisions (Camerer, 2004; Camerer et al., 2004) and the promotion of choice architectures in Policy Analysis, which can counteract biases observed

[1] See the useful diagram at: https://upload.wikimedia.org/wikipedia/commons/6/65/Cognitive_bias_codex_en.svg.

in public choices (Münscher et al., 2015; Thaler et al., 2013). The latter is an example of a descriptive finding (biases in public choices) leading to prescriptive recommendations (re-designed choice architecture) to improve the outcomes of *unsupported* decision making.

Identifying Motivational Biases in Unsupported Decision Making

The second avenue of research in Descriptive Behavioral Decision Research is the identification of motivational biases in unsupported decision making. A motivational bias in judgment is a systematic deviation from a normative standard that would be expected if said judgment were made by a rational decision maker that would consider all the information and evidence available (see Montibeller & von Winterfeldt, 2015). The bias occurs due to motivated reasoning (Kunda, 1990; Molden & Higgins, 2012), where the outcome being targeted distorts, either conscientiously or sub-conscientiously, the underlying judgment. The reasons for motivational biases range from self-interest, social pressures, or organizational contexts that promote or do not curb such biases.

For example, a prevalent motivational bias is the confirmation bias (Klayman, 1995; Nickerson, 1998), in which decision makers and experts seek only information that favors their pre-selected choice or pre-defined opinion. Another commonly observed motivational bias is wishful thinking (Krizan & Windschitl, 2007; Vosgerau, 2010), that causes excessive optimism in assessing positive consequences of an action under consideration. Inversely, excessive pessimism (Chapin, 2001; Dolinski et al., 1987) may lead decision makers and experts to over-estimate negative consequences of an action under appraisal.

Motivational biases, which are studied in Social Psychology, have attracted perhaps less attention than cognitive biases in Behavioral Decision Research, but are also ubiquitous and highly relevant in affecting unsupported decision making. Experts may suffer from motivational biases if they have a stake in the outcome of the analysis that they are involved with, or in the decisions that results from their expert opinions (Otway & von Winterfeldt, 1992). Decision makers may distort their search of evidence and their appraisal of decision alternatives to favor a pre-selected decision alternative, as the frequent under-estimation costs of major infrastructure projects in cost-benefit analysis illustrate (Flyvbjerg & Bester, 2021). The advent of social media platforms, which favor the clustering of communities with similar values and opinions, has only exacerbated the risks of motivational biases arising from a distorted search and gathering of information (Klayman, 1995; Nickerson, 1998) and may affect unsupported decision making. The identification of several motivational biases also constitutes a challenge for Decision Analysis, as they may distort judgements required by decision models, such as attribute weights or probabilities of events occurring.

Detecting Cognitive Limitations in Unsupported Decision Making

Extensive research in Cognitive Psychology has identified inherent cognitive limitations of subjects in judgment and decision-making tasks. This focus on cognitive limitations in unsupported decision making constitutes the third avenue of research in Descriptive Behavioral Decision Research.

Decision makers are confronted with a large amount of information from the external environment and must be necessarily selective in gathering such information. Another source of information is memory, which must be retrieved to inform judgments and choices. From both sources (the external environment and memory), attention plays a major role and must be selective, given inherent cognitive capacity limitations of humans (see E.U. Weber and Johnson (2009) for a detailed review).

Judgments and choices also require cognitive processing and cognitive effort. There is ample evidence from Descriptive Behavioral Decision Research that both external factors (e.g. problem format, complexity of the task) and the characteristics of decision makers (e.g. numeracy, age, cognitive traits) may affect the formation of judgments and selection of choices (Shafir & LeBoeuf, 2002).

One particularly important aspect of this research on cognitive limitations, for our context, is the research about the complexity of providing judgments (inferences and preferences) in quantitative format, as required by Decision Analysis (Howard, 1968; Keeney & Raiffa, 1993; Raiffa, 1968; von Winterfeldt & Edwards, 1986). The definition of quantitative probabilities of events, quantitative estimations of value or utility of alternatives, and definition of quantitative attribute weights are all classified as cognitively complex operations (see Larichev (1992) for details).

Another relevant behavioral finding in this context is that subjects prefer to provide estimations of probabilities of events employing qualitative labels instead of quantitative judgments (Erev & Cohen, 1990). There is strong behavioral evidence about the ambiguity in employing qualitative labels for this type of judgment (Budescu & Wallsten, 1985; Wallsten & Budescu, 1983), in contrast with their widespread use in risk management practices for unsupported decision making, such as the labels often employed in risk matrices (Cox Jr., 2008; Thomas et al., 2014). Paradoxically, the behavioral evidence is that decision makers prefer receiving quantitative information about uncertain events (Erev & Cohen, 1990; Fischhoff & Davis, 2014), as typically provided by outputs of decision analytic models.

The cognitive complexity in expressing quantitatively preference judgments may explain the difficulties that decision makers often have in reasoning about trade-offs and the conceptual mistakes that are frequently made in decisions that require estimating value trade-offs (Keeney, 2002). For instance, the frequently observed range-insensitivity bias (Fischer, 1995; von Nitzsch & Weber, 1993), in which attribute weights measuring value trade-offs are not adjusted to reflect the ranges of the attributes, may be to some extent caused by the complexity involved in providing such judgments. These cognitive complexities may also explain challenges that decision makers experience in providing quantitative judgments, which are required in decision analysis models.

Investigating Adaptive Behavior in Unsupported Decision Making

The fourth avenue of research in Descriptive Behavioral Decision Research is the finding that judgments involving both predictions of future events (i.e. belief formation) and valuation of outcomes (i.e. preference formation) are *constructed* instead of discovered. Decision makers have a repertoire of methods for developing their beliefs and preferences and adaptive cognitive strategies for selecting options among an option set (Payne et al., 1993).

Descriptive research on this topic has shown, as alluded previously, that information gathering and choice strategies are highly contingent on the task, context, and individual-difference factors (Payne et al., 1992). Task factors are general characteristics of the decision problem, for instance the choice of a single alternative versus the classification of alternatives into categories. Context factors encompass features that are associated with the alternatives under consideration, for example, how similar the alternatives are. Individual-differences factors account for cognitive processing capacity (as previously discussed), knowledge, and experience. Hence, characteristics of the decision problem and of the decision task, coupled with individual characteristics, may affect how judgments are formed.

In addition, the internal trade-off experienced by decision makers in unsupported choices, between maximizing accuracy versus minimizing effort (Johnson & Payne, 1985), plays a role on the construction of judgments and on the choices they made. The adoption of simplified strategies, i.e. heuristics, may be effective in guiding choices and promoting adaptive behavior under certain conditions (Gigerenzer & Gaissmaier, 2011), or may be sources of cognitive biases when compared with normative standards on how choices should be made (Gilovich et al., 2002; Tversky & Kahneman, 1974).

The descriptive research on *preference construction* (Lichtenstein & Slovic, 2006; Slovic, 1995), for instance when decision makers value and choose decision alternatives described by multiple attributes, has shown that two normative conditions are often violated in practice: procedural invariance and descriptive invariance. Procedural invariance requires that normatively equivalent procedures for preference elicitation should provide the same preference order. However, rank reversals have been identified in several situations, in which a change of elicitation protocol causes a reversal of option chosen (Tversky et al., 1990). Descriptive invariance requires that different representations of the same choice problem should yield the same preference for a given option. Yet, the way how a choice is framed, for instance as a loss or a gain against a reference point, has shown to influence the shape of the utility functions of decision makers and their preferred options (Tversky

& Kahneman, 1986). From a constructivist perspective, the failures of these two type of invariance conditions can be explained by three main factors (Payne et al., 1992): the adaptive selection of a simplified choice strategy (Payne et al., 1993), the complexity of the decision task, and the liable nature of values (Fischhoff, 1991).

In the same vein, the descriptive research on belief formation (for example when experts assess the probability of an event occurring or make estimates of a future outcome) shows that people use different modes of probabilistic reasoning which are, again, highly contingent on the task, context, and individual-difference factors (Payne et al., 1992). Several heuristics are employed for probabilistic reasoning, such as availability (Tversky & Kahneman, 1973; Wänke et al., 1995), representativeness (Kahneman & Tversky, 1972), and anchoring and adjustment (Furnham & Boo, 2011; Tversky & Kahneman, 1974). For this type of judgment, again adaptive behavior can employ effective heuristics that support reliable belief formation (Gigerenzer & Gaissmaier, 2011) or these heuristics may lead to distorted beliefs and biased estimates (Gilovich et al., 2002). This fourth line of Descriptive Behavioral Decision Research has major implications for Decision Analysis, both in how to conceptualize and design the inputs of decision analysis models and in how these models should be verified and validated.

Investigating Group Decision Making Behavior

Most relevant organizational decisions are made by groups and there is extensive research in Social Psychology about how groups make decisions. Groups have several advantages when compared with individual decision makers, particularly when the group composition favors diversity of perspectives and representativeness of different interests at stake in the decision. Groups enhance the pooling of relevant and distinctive information, they help in error checking and correction, they can enhance individual task motivation, and they can also improve satisfaction among members (Kerr & Tindale, 2004), as well as increase the commitment to the agreed chosen option (Phillips, 2007).

Group dynamics may present many dysfunctional behaviors and group judgment biases. Relevant dysfunctional behaviors (Kerr & Tindale, 2004, 2011) encompass group pressure on individual members to conform to the majority view; groups that are dominated by a strong, authoritarian, leader; group inattention to novel or unshared information; dysfunctional shared representations about the decision problem; group motivation losses as a result of inefficiencies in the group decision process and disengagement of some members; and group coordination losses as a result of the strains that group work incurs when compared with individual tasks. Group judgment biases (Jones & Roelofsma, 2000; Montibeller & von Winterfeldt, 2018) may exacerbate individual biases (such as groups becoming more overconfident than individual members, see Plous (1995)) or be created at group level (such as groupthink, see (Janis, 1983)).

Summarizing this section, descriptive behavioral studies have identified five main research avenues in Descriptive Behavioral Decision Research. There is extensive evidence that judgments are affected by cognitive and motivational biases, that decision makers and experts have inherent cognitive limitations, and that judgments are constructed instead of discovered. In addition, there is evidence that decision making groups may suffer from dysfunctional behaviors and group judgment biases. We now turn our focus to the second branch of Behavioral Decision Research, prescriptive, and show the implications of these descriptive behavioral findings on this prescriptive front.

Prescriptive Behavioral Decision Research

Prescriptive Behavioral Decision Research also starts from observed deviations from rationality. However, as described previously, rather than developing theories of models to explain these deviations, prescriptive research develops and tests tools or analytical methods to correct such deviations and to improve the quality of judgements and choices.

A major distinction of this research stream, in comparison with Descriptive Behavioral Decision Research, is that decision makers are *supported* by a decision analyst who develops a decision analysis model and facilitates group interactions. We discuss briefly four avenues of research within this prescriptive focus.

Identifying Relevant Biases for Prescriptive Decision Models

A vast number of cognitive biases has been identified by Cognitive Psychology and several motivational biases have been found by Social Psychology in behavioral descriptive studies, as mentioned in the previous section. Hence, a key research questions for Prescriptive Behavioral Decision Research is which biases are the most relevant ones for decision analysis modeling. Such research question drives this first research avenue.

We have argued in a previous article that not all these biases matter for Decision Analysis and have suggested a relatively small sub-set of biases that are the most relevant ones. The most relevant biases are the ones that involve judgments required by decision analysis models, cannot be easily removed with the standard protocols for eliciting judgments or with simple use of logic, and are widespread and resistant to debiasing strategies. Henceforth, these most relevant biases do have significant impact on the quality of decision analysis models (see Montibeller and von Winterfeldt (2015) for details).

We have identified as the most relevant *cognitive biases* for Decision Analysis the following ones (Montibeller & von Winterfeldt, 2015, 2018):

Anchoring: The estimation of a numerical value is based on an initial value (anchor), which is then insufficiently adjusted to provide the final answer (Tversky & Kahneman, 1974).

Availability/Ease of Recall: The probability of an event that is easily recalled is overstated (Bazerman & Moore, 2013; Tversky & Kahneman, 1973).

Certainty Effect: Decision makers prefer sure things to gambles with similar expected utilities; they discount the utility of sure things dramatically, when they are no longer certain (Allais, 1953; Kahneman & Tversky, 1979).

Equalizing Bias: Decision makers allocate similar weights to all objectives (Jacobi & Hobbs, 2007) or similar probabilities to all events (Fox et al., 2005; Fox & Clemen, 2005).

Gain-Loss Bias: Alternative descriptions of a choice and its outcomes (Tversky & Kahneman, 1981), either as gains or as losses, may lead to different answers (Frisch, 1993; Levin et al., 1998; Tversky & Kahneman, 1981).

Myopic Problem Representation: An oversimplified problem representation is adopted (Payne et al., 1999) based on an incomplete mental model of the decision problem (Legrenzi et al., 1993; Legrezni & Girotto, 1996).

Omission of Important Variables: An important variable is overlooked (Jargowsky, 2005), for example, in the definition of objectives (Bond et al., 2008, 2010), identification of decision alternatives (Butler & Scherer, 1997; Pitz et al., 1980), and in hypothesis generation (Fischhoff et al., 1978; Thomas et al., 2008).

Overconfidence: Laypeople and experts provide estimates for a given parameter that are above the actual performance (overestimation) ((Lichtenstein et al., 1982; Lichtenstein & Fischhoff, 1977) or when the range of variation they provide is too narrow (over-precision) (Moore & Healy, 2008).

Proxy Bias: Proxy attributes receive larger weights than the respective fundamental objectives (Fischer et al., 1987).

Range Insensitivity Bias: The weights of objectives are not properly adjusted to changes in the range of attributes (Gabrielli & von Winterfeldt, 1978; von Nitzsch & Weber, 1993).

Scaling Biases: A family of stimulus-response biases (Poulton, 1982, 1989) which comprises: *contraction bias* (underestimating large sizes/differences and overestimating small/size differences); *logarithmic response bias* (using step-changes in the number of digits used in the response, which fit a log scale); *range equalizing bias* (using most of the range of response whatever is the size of the range of the stimuli); *centering bias* (producing a symmetric distribution of responses centered on the midpoint of the range of stimuli); and *equal frequency bias* (using equally all parts of the response scale).

Splitting biases: The way the objectives are grouped affects the weights on objectives (Borcherding & von Winterfeldt, 1988; Pöyhönen et al., 2001; M. Weber et al., 1988); or when the way events in a fault tree are grouped affects the event probabilities.

Similarly, we have argued that the most relevant *motivational biases* for Decision Analysis are the following ones (Montibeller & von Winterfeldt, 2015, 2018):

Affect-Influenced Bias: An emotional predisposition for, or against, a specific outcome or option taints judgments (Finucane et al., 2000; Slovic et al., 2004).

Confirmation Bias: The desire to confirm one's belief, leading to unconscious selectivity in the acquisition and use of evidence (Nickerson, 1998).

Desirability of a positive event or consequence: The desirability of an outcome leads to an increase in the extent to which it is expected to occur (Krizan & Windschitl, 2007, p. 96). It is also called "wishful thinking" (Seybert & Bloomfield, 2009) or "optimism bias" (Weinstein, 1980).

Undesirability of a negative event or consequence: The desire to be cautious, prudent, or conservative in estimates that may be related to harmful consequences (Chapin, 2001; Dolinski et al., 1987).

Desirability of options/choice: The desirability of an option or choice leads to an over- or under-estimation of probabilities, consequences, values, or attribute weights to favor the desired decision alternative (von Winterfeldt, 1999).

The identification of the most relevant biases for Decision Analysis is a prelude to a critical research question for Prescriptive Behavioral Decision Research: how can these biases be removed or minimized? This question has been driving the second prescriptive research direction, which is presented next.

Debiasing Judgments Required by Prescriptive Decision Models

Debiasing refers to attempts to eliminate or at least reduce cognitive or motivational biases. The literature on debiasing judgments required by decision analysis models is rather limited in comparison with the extensive developments in the identification of biases that was conducted by Descriptive Behavioral Decision Research, and almost entirely focused on cognitive biases (see Larrick (2007) for a useful overview). The debiasing tools can be classified into categories of intervention, as follows:

Adequate Elicitation Protocol: This type of debiasing tool is focused on the identification of adequate elicitation protocols for each type of parameter required in a decision analysis model. The choice of an elicitation protocol is an important meta-choice in decision analysis modeling (Ferretti & Montibeller, 2016; Payne et al., 1999), particularly given the constructive nature of judgments and the inherent cognitive limitations of decision makers, which were identified by Descriptive Behavioral Decision Research. While standard protocols for the elicitation of continuous distribution functions are relatively well-established (Morgan, 2014), there are still few systematic comparisons of the effectiveness of alternative elicitation protocols for the many parameters required in decision analysis modeling. Abbas et al. (2008) provide an excellent example of how elicitation protocols can be compared and assessed (in their experiment, they systematically compared two elicitation methods for the estimation of continuous distribution functions).

Effective Elicitation Probes: One distinctive aspect of decision analysis modeling is the role of the decision analyst that supports the decision makers, elicits judgments from them, and facilitates group discussions (Franco & Montibeller, 2010). Decision analysts have developed a set of ad hoc "best debiasing practices", typically with the introduction of elicitation probes. Examples of elicitation probes include the use of counterfactual questions (N. J. Roese, 1999) and hypothetical bets (Morgan & Henrion, 1992) to improve the accuracy of continuous distribution functions by experts, or the use of categories of objectives (Bond et al., 2010; Keeney, 1992) to increase the number of decision objectives generate by decision makers. Research on the effectiveness of these elicitation probes is still rather limited, however Bond et al. (2010) provide a useful example of how to assess the effectiveness of probes for the elicitation of decision objectives performed, while Seaver et al. (1978) and Ferretti, Montibeller and von Winterfeldt (2022) provide possible ways of how alternative probes for the elicitation of continuous probability distributions can be assessed and compared.

Effective Incentives: Incentives are required for experts to provide reliable estimates and for decision makers to provide both reliable estimates and reasoned value judgments. Reliable estimates can be incentivized with the use of adequate scoring rules (Carvalho, 2016) and reasoned value judgments with the employment of adequate preference elicitation protocols (Payne et al., 1999) and cross-checking of preference statements (von Winterfeldt & Edwards, 1986). Other types of incentive involve offering monetary incentives for accuracy or increasing accountability of experts and decision makers (Larrick, 2007).

One additional challenge in this direction of Prescriptive Behavioral Decision Research is that debiasing tools must be designed and employed for each type of parameter required in a decision model. For instance, the elicitation of probabilities of events requires rather specific debiasing tools to reduce the over-precision bias (Ferretti et al., 2022), while the elicitation of attribute weights requires debiasing tools to reduce the range-insensitivity bias (Fischer, 1995; von Nitzsch & Weber, 1993). Therefore, we have previously suggested some debiasing tools for each type of judgment required in a modeling step of decision analysis model (see Montibeller and von Winterfeldt (2015) for details). However, more extensive research on systematically assessing and comparing alternative debiasing tools, as well as designing better tools, for each parameter required in a decision analysis model is needed.

Eliciting Judgments Required by Prescriptive Decision Models

Decision analysis models require expressing quantitative judgments. For example, when eliciting continuous distribution functions, experts should provide a probability estimate for a given level of impact under the fixed-value elicitation method (Morgan & Henrion, 1992). In decisions with multiple objectives, multi-attribute utility based models quantitative preference statements, such as utility functions and attribute weights are required.

However, as discussed in the previous section, Descriptive Behavioral Decision Research has shown that experts and decision makers have intrinsic cognitive limitations in reasoning, and these limitations may impact the elicitation of judgments that are inputs to decision analysis models. As mentioned previously, there is some behavioral evidence that expressing quantitatively preferences is cognitively complex (Larichev, 1992). There is also indication that subjects prefer to provide qualitative statements about probabilities (Payne et al., 1992), despite the inherent ambiguity such labels provide (Budescu & Wallsten, 1985; Wallsten & Budescu, 1983).

Hence elicitation protocols may have to be adapted to accommodate such cognitive limitations, and this constitutes the third direction of prescriptive behavioral decision research. Indeed, many of the interesting developments in Europe in multicriteria analysis have been exactly trying to address these limitations, with a larger number of preference relations being available to decision makers (Figueira et al., 2010), methods that try to reduce cognitive demands in the elicitation of preferences (Larichev & Brown, 2000), and several methods that can deal with incomplete information (M. Weber, 1987). Methods that try to reduce the cognitive burden of eliciting probability estimates or probability density functions share the same type of behavioral concern (e.g. Jaspersen and Montibeller (2015)).

Furthermore, the findings from Descriptive Behavioral Decision Research that judgments are constructed has important implications for Decision Analysis. First, when judgments are constructed (Lichtenstein & Slovic, 2006; Slovic, 1995), the choice of an elicitation protocol and problem representation must be carefully considered by the decision analyst. Second, the development of clearer preferences and reliable estimations should be seen as a major benefit of any decision analysis intervention (Montibeller, 2018; Payne et al., 1999). Third, the adoption of a constructivist paradigm alters the way that decision analysis models are conceptualized and validated, as there are no "true preferences" or "right estimates" for future events. Under this paradigm, modeling is focused on learning about preferences and beliefs (Payne et al., 1999; Roy, 1993).

Facilitating Decision Making Groups with Decision Analysis

Thus far in this section we have considered issues related to individual decision making. The fourth Prescriptive Behavioral Decision research direction extends the issues that have been discussed so far in this section and is focused on how better facilitate decision making groups with decision analysis modeling.

As mentioned in the previous section, groups have several advantages when compared with individual decision makers, particularly when the group composition favors diversity of perspectives and representativeness of different interests at stake in the decision. In supporting group decision making, what decision analysts seek to develop are requisite models (Phillips, 1984), which are not "perfect" but only rich enough to help the group solving the problem that it is dealing with.

On the other hand, group dynamics may present many dysfunctional behaviors and group biases. Decision processes that are adequately facilitated and well-designed elicitation techniques, such as Delphi (Linstone & Turoff, 1975), may help to minimize these behaviors in decision making groups. Relevant group biases need to be dealt with when dealing with groups, as there is evidence that they affect group judgments. Montibeller and von Winterfeldt (2018) suggest five main biases, based on reviews of forecasting elicitation (Kerr & Tindale, 2011) and of team-based decision making (Jones & Roelofsma, 2000):

False consensus: an individual group member overestimates the similarities between his or her judgment and the other members, leading to judgments using incorrect assumptions about the decision problem (Ross et al., 1977).

Groupthink: members of very cohesive groups are focused on getting consensus on the agreed solution (Janis, 1983), disregarding other decision alternatives, objectives, or limiting information search (Jones & Roelofsma, 2000).

Group polarization: group discussions enhance the initial position or opinion of the majority of its members (Lamm, 1988). This bias may affect the choice, if the group had an initial inclination for a given policy option, as well as the group's risk attitude, which may become more risk seeking/averse than those of its individual members as discussions progress (Isenberg, 1986).

Group escalation of commitment: a group supports a course of action that is clearly failing, which is exacerbated by groupthink and group polarization (Jones & Roelofsma, 2000).

Group overconfidence: groups suffer from overconfidence levels that move beyond the overconfidence of its individual members (Plous, 1995).

The available debiasing tools against group biases encompass the use of multiple experts with different perspectives of the decision problem, encouragement of expressions of multiple perspectives and opinions, use of structured elicitation protocols, and employment of facilitated decision processes. However, this is an under-researched but relevant area for further developments in Prescriptive Behavioral Decision Research.

In addition, as also mentioned in the previous section, preferences are constructed instead of discovered; that is, they are developed during the decision-aiding process instead of predefined in the decision makers' minds (Roy, 1993; Slovic, 1995). Facilitated decision analysis interventions require an effective management of decision-making processes, which can promote information sharing among members of the group, supports negotiation of their different perspectives and stakes, and enables the group to reach a joint agreement on the chosen option. The design of adequate decision making processes (Montibeller, 2022; Spetzler et al., 2016) and the adequate facilitation of decision making groups (Franco & Montibeller, 2010) are core concerns of this avenue of research.

Conclusions and Directions for Further Research

In this chapter we have explored the developments of Behavioral Decision Research and argued that, historically, the field has bifurcated into two distinctive perspectives: descriptive and prescriptive. Descriptive Behavioral Decision Research examines deviations from rationality and strives to develop theories or models to explain these deviations. On the other hand, Prescriptive Behavioral Decision Research also starts from observed deviations from rationality, but rather than developing theories of models to explain these deviations, this research stream develops and tests tools or analytical methods to correct such deviations and improve the quality of judgments.

We have described here some important developments within each perspective. Specifically, Descriptive Behavioral Decision Research has identified a large number of cognitive biases in unsupported decision making, as well as some equally relevant motivational biases that may affect decision makers. There is also relevant research on cognitive limitations, in which decision makers must trade-off accuracy and effort when choosing, and on adaptive behavior when decision makers are confronted with complex decision settings. In addition, from Social Psychology, there are important findings about group decision making, including group judgment biases and dysfunctional group dynamics.

Similarly, we have discussed some relevant developments from Prescriptive Behavioral Decision Research. The definition of relevant biases for Decision Analysis, among the plethora of biases that have been identified in unsupported decision making, is the starting point for systematic efforts for debiasing judgments required in decision analysis models. Beyond debiasing, there are also other aspects of eliciting judgments required by these models, such as adequate elicitation protocols and methods that require less information about preferences and inferences. Finally, issues of group facilitation in facilitated decision modeling have also been researched within this perspective.

Despite these advances, the full split of the field that we described here is rather unfortunate, as it has prevented the full development of Prescriptive Behavioral Decision Research. Furthermore, this split has led to a rather pessimistic agenda from Descriptive Behavioral Decision Research, focused on doubting the ability of decision makers in choosing well and making sound judgements (see also the discussion by Kahneman and Klein (2009) on the conditions for when experts can make accurate unsupported decisions).

Hence, an important direction for further research is extending the four avenues of Prescriptive Behavioral Decision Research that we have described in this chapter. Specifically, more systematic research about suitable elicitation protocols, efficient debiasing tools, and adequate facilitated modeling is needed. Conversely, Descriptive Behavioral Decision Research would benefit, in our opinion, from an effort in trying to improve decision making, moving beyond simply identifying biases and error in judgments. Finally, we hope that the taxonomy presented here can provide a clear framework for the use of behavioral evidence in sound prescriptive advice.

References

Abbas, A. E., Budescu, D. V., Yu, H.-T., & Haggerty, R. (2008). A comparison of two probability encoding methods: Fixed probability vs. fixed variable values. *Decision Analysis, 5*(4), 190–202. https://doi.org/10.1287/deca.1080.0126

Allais, M. (1953). Le comportement de l'Homme Rationnel devant le risque: Critique des postulats et axiomes de l'Ecole Americaine. *Econometrica, 21*(4), 503–546. https://doi.org/10.2307/1907921

Bazerman, M. H., & Moore, D. A. (2013). *Judgment in managerial decision making* (8th ed.). John Wiley & Sons.

Bond, S. D., Carlson, K. A., & Keeney, R. L. (2008). Generating objectives: Can decision makers articulate what they want? *Management Science, 54*(1), 56–70. https://doi.org/10.1287/mnsc.1070.0754

Bond, S. D., Carlson, K. A., & Keeney, R. L. (2010). Improving the generation of decision objectives. *Decision Analysis, 7*(3), 238–255.

Borcherding, K., & von Winterfeldt, D. (1988). The effect of varying value trees on multiattribute evaluations. *Acta Psychologica, 68*(1–3), 153–170. https://doi.org/10.1016/0001-6918(88)90052-2

Budescu, D. V., & Wallsten, T. S. (1985). Consistency in interpretation of probabilistic phrases. *Organizational Behavior and Human Decision Processes, 36*(3), 391–405. https://doi.org/10.1016/0749-5978(85)90007-X

Butler, A. B., & Scherer, L. L. (1997). The effects of elicitation aids, knowledge, and problem content on option quantity and quality. *Organizational Behavior and Human Decision Processes, 72*(2), 184–202. https://doi.org/10.1006/obhd.1997.2737

Camerer, C. (2004). Prospect theory in the wild: Evidence from the field. In *Advances in behavioral economics (my DropboxPapers AcrobatBDT for Mng SciBDT on judgment)* (pp. 148–161). Princeton University Press.

Camerer, C., Loewenstein, G., & Rabin, M. (2004). *Advances in behavioral economics (my DropboxPapers AcrobatBDT for Mng SciBDT on judgment)*. Princeton University Press.

Carvalho, A. (2016). An overview of applications of proper scoring rules. *Decision Analysis, 13*(4), 223–242. https://doi.org/10.1287/deca.2016.0337

Chapin, J. (2001). Self-protective pessimism: Optimistic bias in reverse. *North American Journal of Psychology, 3*(2), 253–262.

Cox, L. A., Jr. (2008). What's wrong with risk matrices? *Risk Analysis, 28*(2), 497–512. https://doi.org/10.1111/j.1539-6924.2008.01030.x

Dolinski, D., Gromski, W., & Zawisza, E. (1987). Unrealistic pessimism. *The Journal of Social Psychology, 127*(5), 511–516. https://doi.org/10.1080/00224545.1987.9713735

Edwards, W. (1953). Probability-preferences in gambling. *The American Journal of Psychology, 66*(3), 349–364. https://doi.org/10.2307/1418231

Edwards, W. (1954a). Probability-references among bets with differing expected values. *The American Journal of Psychology, 67*(1), 56–67. https://doi.org/10.2307/1418071

Edwards, W. (1954b). The theory of decision making. *Psychological Bulletin, 51*(4), 380–417. https://doi.org/10.1037/h0053870

Edwards, W. (1961). Behavioral decision theory. *Annual Review of Psychology, 12*(1), 473–498. https://doi.org/10.1146/annurev.ps.12.020161.002353

Edwards, W. (1968). Conservatism in human information processing. In B. Kleinmuntz (Ed.), *Formal representation of human judgment* (pp. 17–52). Wiley.

Ellsberg, D. (1961). Risk, ambiguity, and the savage axioms. *The Quarterly Journal of Economics, 75*(4), 643–699. https://doi.org/10.2307/1884409

Erev, I., & Cohen, B. L. (1990). Verbal versus numerical probabilities: Efficiency, biases, and the preference paradox. *Organizational Behavior and Human Decision Processes, 45*(1), 1–18. https://doi.org/10.1016/0749-5978(90)90002-Q

Erev, I., Ert, E., Plonsky, O., Cohen, D., & Cohen, O. (2017). From anomalies to forecasts: Toward a descriptive model of decisions under risk, under ambiguity, and from experience. *Psychological Review, 124*(4), 369–409. https://doi.org/10.1037/rev0000062

Feller, W. (2009). *An introduction to probability theory and its applications* (Vol. Vol. 1, 3rd ed.). Wiley.

Ferretti, V., & Montibeller, G. (2016). Key challenges and meta-choices in designing and applying multi-criteria spatial decision support systems. *Decision Support Systems, 84*, 41–52. https://doi.org/10.1016/j.dss.2016.01.005

Ferretti, V., Montibeller, G., & von Winterfeldt, D. (2022). Testing the effectiveness of Debiasing techniques to reduce Overprecision in the elicitation of subjective continuous probability distributions. *European Journal of Operational Research, forthcoming, 304*(2), 661–675. https://doi.org/10.1016/j.ejor.2022.04.008

Figueira, J. R., Greco, S., Roy, B., & Słowiński, R. (2010). ELECTRE methods: Main features and recent developments. In *Handbook of multicriteria analysis* (pp. 51–89). Springer. https://doi.org/10.1007/978-3-540-92828-7_3

Finucane, M. L., Alhakami, A., Slovic, P., & Johnson, S. M. (2000). The affect heuristic in judgments of risks and benefits. *Journal of Behavioral Decision Making, 13*(1), 1–17. https://doi.org/10.1002/(SICI)1099-0771(200001/03)13:1<1::AID-BDM333>3.0.CO;2-S

Fischer, G. W. (1995). Range sensitivity of attribute weights in multiattribute value models. *Organizational Behavior and Human Decision Processes, 62*(3), 252–266. https://doi.org/10.1006/obhd.1995.1048

Fischer, G. W., Damodaran, N., Laskey, K. B., & Lincoln, D. (1987). Preferences for proxy attributes. *Management Science, 33*(2), 198–214.

Fischhoff, B. (1991). Value elicitation: Is there anything in there? *American Psychologist, 46*(8), 835–847. https://doi.org/10.1037/0003-066X.46.8.835

Fischhoff, B., & Broomell, S. B. (2020). Judgment and decision making. *Annual Review of Psychology, 71*(1), 331–355. https://doi.org/10.1146/annurev-psych-010419-050747

Fischhoff, B., & Davis, A. L. (2014). Communicating scientific uncertainty. *Proceedings of the National Academy of Sciences, 111*(Supplement_4), 13664–13671. https://doi.org/10.1073/pnas.1317504111

Fischhoff, B., Slovic, P., & Lichtenstein, S. (1978). Fault trees: Sensitivity of estimated failure probabilities to problem representation. *Journal of Experimental Psychology: Human Perception and Performance, 4*(2), 330–344. https://doi.org/10.1037/0096-1523.4.2.330

Flyvbjerg, B., & Bester, D. W. (2021). The cost-benefit fallacy: Why cost-benefit analysis is broken and how to fix it. *Journal of Benefit-Cost Analysis, 12*(3), 395–419. https://doi.org/10.1017/bca.2021.9

Fox, C. R., Bardolet, D., & Lieb, D. (2005). Partition dependence in decision analysis, resource allocation, and consumer choice. In R. Zwick & A. Rapoport (Eds.), *Experimental business research, Vol. III: Marketing, accounting, and cognitive perspectives* (pp. 229–251). Springer.

Fox, C. R., & Clemen, R. T. (2005). Subjective probability assessment in decision analysis: Partition dependence and bias toward the ignorance prior. *Management Science, 51*(9), 1417–1432.

Franco, L. A., & Montibeller, G. (2010). Facilitated modelling in operational research. *European Journal of Operational Research, 205*(3), 489–500. https://doi.org/10.1016/j.ejor.2009.09.030

Frisch, D. (1993). Reasons for framing effects. *Organizational Behavior and Human Decision Processes, 54*(3), 399–429. https://doi.org/10.1006/obhd.1993.1017

Furnham, A., & Boo, H. C. (2011). A literature review of the anchoring effect. *Journal of Socio-Economics, 40*(1), 35–42. https://doi.org/10.1016/j.socec.2010.10.008

Gabrielli, W. F., & von Winterfeldt, D. (1978). Are importance weights sensitive to the range of alternatives in multiattribute utility measurement? (No. 78–6; Research Report). Los Angeles, CA.

Gigerenzer, G. (1991). How to make cognitive illusions disappear: Beyond "Heuristics and Biases". *European Review of Social Psychology, 2*(1), 83–115. https://doi.org/10.1080/14792779143000033

Gigerenzer, G., & Gaissmaier, W. (2011). Heuristic decision making. *Annual Review of Psychology, 62*(1), 451–482. https://doi.org/10.1146/annurev-psych-120709-145346

Gilovich, T., Griffin, D. W., & Kahneman, D. (2002). *Heuristics and biases: The psychology of intuitive judgement*. Cambridge University Press.

Hertwig, R., Barron, G., Weber, E. U., & Erev, I. (2004). Decisions from experience and the effect of rare events in risky choice. *Psychological Science, 15*(8), 534–539. https://doi.org/10.1111/j.0956-7976.2004.00715.x

Howard, R. A. (1968). The foundations of decision analysis. *IEEE Transactions on Systems Science and Cybernetics, 4*(3), 211–219. https://doi.org/10.1109/TSSC.1968.300115

Isenberg, D. J. (1986). Group polarization: A critical review and meta-analysis. *Journal of Personality and Social Psychology, 50*(6), 1141–1151. https://doi.org/10.1037/0022-3514.50.6.1141

Jacobi, S. K., & Hobbs, B. F. (2007). Quantifying and mitigating the splitting bias and other value tree-induced weighting biases. *Decision Analysis, 4*(4), 194–210. https://doi.org/10.1287/deca.1070.0100

Janis, I. L. (1983). *Groupthink: Psychological studies of policy decisions and fiascoes*. Houghton Mifflin.

Jargowsky, P. A. (2005). Omitted variable bias. In *Encyclopedia of social measurement* (Vol. 2, pp. 919–924). Elsevier.

Jaspersen, J. G., & Montibeller, G. (2015). Probability elicitation under severe time pressure: A rank-based method. *Risk Analysis, 35*(7), 1317–1335. https://doi.org/10.1111/risa.12357

Johnson, E. J., & Payne, J. W. (1985). Effort and accuracy in choice. *Management Science, 31*(4), 395–414.

Jones, P. E., & Roelofsma, P. H. M. P. (2000). The potential for social contextual and group biases in team decision-making: Biases, conditions and psychological mechanisms. *Ergonomics, 43*(8), 1129–1152. https://doi.org/10.1080/00140130050084914

Kahneman, D., & Klein, G. (2009). Conditions for intuitive expertise: A failure to disagree. *American Psychologist, 64*(6), 515. https://doi.org/10.1037/a0016755

Kahneman, D., Slovic, P., & Tversky, A. (1982). *Judgment under uncertainty: Heuristics and biases*. Cambridge University Press.

Kahneman, D., & Tversky, A. (1972). Subjective probability: A judgment of representativeness. *Cognitive Psychology, 3*(3), 430–454. https://doi.org/10.1016/0010-0285(72)90016-3

Kahneman, D., & Tversky, A. (1979). Prospect theory: An analysis of decision under risk. *Econometrica, 47*(2), 263–291. https://doi.org/10.2307/1914185

Kahneman, D., & Tversky, A. (2000). *Choices, values, and frames*. Cambridge University Press.

Keeney, R. L. (1992). *Value-focused thinking: A path to creative decision making*. Harvard University Press.

Keeney, R. L. (2002). Common mistakes in making value trade-offs. *Operations Research, 50*(6), 935–945.

Keeney, R. L., & Raiffa, H. (1993). *Decisions with multiple objectives: Preferences and value trade-offs* (2nd ed.). Cambridge University Press.

Kerr, N. L., & Tindale, R. S. (2004). Group performance and decision making. *Annual Review of Psychology, 55*(1), 623–655. https://doi.org/10.1146/annurev.psych.55.090902.142009

Kerr, N. L., & Tindale, R. S. (2011). Group-based forecasting?: A social psychological analysis. *International Journal of Forecasting, 27*(1), 14–40. https://doi.org/10.1016/j.ijforecast.2010.02.001

Klayman, J. (1995). Varieties of confirmation bias. In J. Busemeyer, R. Hastie, & D. Medin (Eds.), *Psychology of learning and motivation: Vol. 32. Decision making from a cognitive perspective: Volume 32* (pp. 365–418). Academic Press.

Krizan, Z., & Windschitl, P. D. (2007). The influence of outcome desirability on optimism. *Psychological Bulletin, 133*(1), 95–121. https://doi.org/10.1037/0033-2909.133.1.95

Kunda, Z. (1990). The case for motivated reasoning. *Psychological Bulletin, 108*(3), 480–498. https://doi.org/10.1037/0033-2909.108.3.480

Lamm, H. (1988). A review of our research on group polarization: Eleven experiments on the effects of group discussion on risk acceptance, probability estimation, and negotiation positions. *Psychological Reports, 62*(3), 807–813. https://doi.org/10.2466/pr0.1988.62.3.807

Larichev, O. I. (1992). Cognitive validity in design of decision-aiding techniques. *Journal of Multi-Criteria Decision Analysis, 1*(3), 127–138. https://doi.org/10.1002/mcda.4020010303

Larichev, O. I., & Brown, R. V. (2000). Numerical and verbal decision analysis: Comparison on practical cases. *Journal of Multi-Criteria Decision Analysis, 9*(6), 263–273. https://doi.org/10.1002/1099-1360(200011)9:6<263::AID-MCDA280>3.0.CO;2-W

Larrick, R. P. (2007). Debiasing. In D. J. Koehler & N. Harvey (Eds.), *Blackwell handbook of judgment and decision making* (pp. 316–338). Blackwell.

Legrenzi, P., Girotto, V., & Johnson-Laird, P. N. (1993). Focusing in reasoning and decision making. *Cognition, 49*(1–2), 37–66. https://doi.org/10.1016/0010-0277(93)90035-T

Legrezni, P., & Girotto, V. (1996). Mental models in reasoning and decision making. In J. Oakhill & A. Garnham (Eds.), *Mental models in cognitive science: Essays in honour of Phil Johnson-Laird* (pp. 95–118). Psychology Press.

Lejarraga, T., & Hertwig, R. (2021). How experimental methods shaped views on human competence and rationality. *Psychological Bulletin, 147*(6), 535–564. https://doi.org/10.1037/bul0000324

Levin, I. P., Schneider, S. L., & Gaeth, G. J. (1998). All frames are not created equal: A typology and critical analysis of framing effects. *Organizational Behavior and Human Decision Processes, 76*(2), 149–188.

Lichtenstein, S., & Fischhoff, B. (1977). Do those who know more also know more about how much they know? *Organizational Behavior and Human Performance, 20*(2), 159–183. https://doi.org/10.1016/0030-5073(77)90001-0

Lichtenstein, S., Fischhoff, B., & Phillips, L. D. (1982). Calibration of probabilities: The state of the art to 1980 (D. Kahneman, P. Slovic, & A. Tversky, Eds., pp. 306–334). Cambridge University Press.

Lichtenstein, S., & Slovic, P. (Eds.). (2006). *The construction of preference*. Cambridge University Press.

Linstone, H. A., & Turoff, M. (1975). *The Delphi method: Techniques and applications*. Addison-Wesley Pub. Co., Advanced Book Program.

Luce, R. D., & von Winterfeldt, D. (1994). What common ground exists for descriptive, prescriptive, and normative utility theories? *Management Science, 40*(2), 263–279. https://doi.org/10.1287/mnsc.40.2.263

Molden, D. C., & Higgins, E. T. (2012). Motivated thinking. In K. J. Holyoak & R. G. Morrison (Eds.), *The Oxford handbook of thinking and reasoning* (pp. 390–409). Oxford University Press.

Montibeller, G. (2018). Behavioral challenges in policy analysis with conflicting objectives. In *Recent advances in optimization and modeling of contemporary problems* (Vol. 1–0, pp. 85–108). INFORMS. https://doi.org/10.1287/educ.2018.0182

Montibeller, G. (2022). Decision making for enhanced health security: Managing emerging health threats, making reasoned choices, and allocating scarce resources (Vol. 328). Springer International Publishing. https://doi.org/10.1007/978-3-030-98132-7.

Montibeller, G., & von Winterfeldt, D. (2015). Cognitive and motivational biases in decision and risk analysis. *Risk Analysis, 35*(7), 1230–1251. https://doi.org/10.1111/risa.12360

Montibeller, G., & von Winterfeldt, D. (2018). Individual and group biases in value and uncertainty judgments. In L. C. Dias, A. Morton, & J. Quigley (Eds.), *Elicitation* (pp. 377–392). Springer. https://doi.org/10.1007/978-3-319-65052-4_15

Moore, D. A., & Healy, P. J. (2008). The trouble with overconfidence. *Psychological Review, 115*(2), 502–517. https://doi.org/10.1037/0033-295X.115.2.502

Morgan, M. G. (2014). Use (and abuse) of expert elicitation in support of decision making for public policy. *Proceedings of the National Academy of Sciences, 111*(20), 7176–7184. https://doi.org/10.1073/pnas.1319946111

Morgan, M. G., & Henrion, M. (1992). *Uncertainty: A guide to dealing with uncertainty in quantitative risk and policy analysis*. Cambridge University Press.

Mosteller, F., & Nogee, P. (1951). An experimental measurement of utility. *Journal of Political Economy, 59*(5), 371–404. https://doi.org/10.1086/257106

Münscher, R., Vetter, M., & Scheuerle, T. (2015). A review and taxonomy of choice architecture techniques: Choice architecture techniques. *Journal of Behavioral Decision Making, 29*(5), 511–524. https://doi.org/10.1002/bdm.1897

Nickerson, R. S. (1998). Confirmation bias: A ubiquitous phenomenon in many guises. *Review of General Psychology, 2*(2), 175–220. https://doi.org/10.1037/1089-2680.2.2.175

Otway, H., & von Winterfeldt, D. (1992). Expert judgment in risk analysis and management: Process, context, and pitfalls. *Risk Analysis, 12*(1), 83–93. https://doi.org/10.1111/j.1539-6924.1992.tb01310.x

Payne, J. W., Bettman, J. R., & Johnson, D. E. J. (1993). *The adaptive decision maker*. Cambridge University Press.

Payne, J. W., Bettman, J. R., & Johnson, E. J. (1992). Behavioral decision research: A constructive processing perspective. *Annual Review of Psychology, 43*, 87–131. https://doi.org/10.1146/annurev.ps.43.020192.000511

Payne, J. W., Bettman, J. R., & Schkade, D. A. (1999). Measuring constructed preferences: Towards a building code. *Journal of Risk and Uncertainty, 19*(1–3), 243–270.

Peterson, C. R., & Beach, L. R. (1967). Man as an intuitive statistician. *Psychological Bulletin, 68*(1), 29–46. https://doi.org/10.1037/h0024722

Phillips, L. D. (1984). A theory of requisite decision models. *Acta Psychologica, 56*(1–3), 29–48. https://doi.org/10.1016/0001-6918(84)90005-2

Phillips, L. D. (2007). Decision conferencing. In W. Edwards, R. F. Miles, & D. von Winterfeldt (Eds.), *Advances in decision analysis: From foundations to applications* (pp. 375–399). Cambridge University Press.

Phillips, L. D., & Edwards, W. (1966). Conservatism in a simple probability inference task. *Journal of Experimental Psychology, 72*(3), 346–354. https://doi.org/10.1037/h0023653

Pitz, G. F., Sachs, N. J., & Heerboth, J. (1980). Procedures for eliciting choices in the analysis of individual decisions. *Organizational Behavior and Human Performance, 26*(3), 396–408. https://doi.org/10.1016/0030-5073(80)90075-6

Plous, S. (1995). A comparison of strategies for reducing interval overconfidence in group judgments. *Journal of Applied Psychology, 80*(4), 443–454. https://doi.org/10.1037/0021-9010.80.4.443

Poulton, E. C. (1982). Biases in quantitative judgements. *Applied Ergonomics, 13*(1), 31–42. https://doi.org/10.1016/0003-6870(82)90129-6

Poulton, E. C. (1989). *Bias in quantifying judgements*. Erlbaum.

Pöyhönen, M., Vrolijk, H., & Hämäläinen, R. P. (2001). Behavioral and procedural consequences of structural variation in value trees. *European Journal of Operational Research, 134*(1), 216–227. https://doi.org/10.1016/S0377-2217(00)00255-1

Preston, M. G., & Baratta, P. (1948). An experimental study of the auction-value of an uncertain outcome. *The American Journal of Psychology, 61*(2), 183–193. https://doi.org/10.2307/1416964

Raiffa, H. (1968). *Decision analysis: Introductory lectures on choices under uncertainty*. Addison-Wesley.

Roese, N. J. (1999). Counterfactual thinking and decision making. *Psychonomic Bulletin & Review, 6*(4), 570–578. https://doi.org/10.3758/BF03212965

Roese, N. J., & Vohs, K. D. (2012). Hindsight bias. *Perspectives on Psychological Science, 7*(5), 411–426. https://doi.org/10.1177/1745691612454303

Ross, L., Greene, D., & House, P. (1977). The "false consensus effect": An egocentric bias in social perception and attribution processes. *Journal of Experimental Social Psychology, 13*(3), 279–301. https://doi.org/10.1016/0022-1031(77)90049-X

Roy, B. (1993). Decision science or decision-aid science? *European Journal of Operational Research, 66*(2), 184–203. https://doi.org/10.1016/0377-2217(93)90312-B

Savage, L. J. (1954). *The foundations of statistics*. John Wiley & Sons. https://onlinelibrary.wiley.com/doi/10.1002/nav.3800010316

Seaver, D. A., von Winterfeldt, D., & Edwards, W. (1978). Eliciting subjective probability distributions on continuous variables. *Organizational Behavior and Human Performance, 21*(3), 379–391. https://doi.org/10.1016/0030-5073(78)90061-2

Seybert, N., & Bloomfield, R. (2009). Contagion of wishful thinking in markets. *Management Science, 55*(5), 738–751. https://doi.org/10.1287/mnsc.1080.0973

Shafir, E., & LeBoeuf, R. A. (2002). Rationality. *Annual Review of Psychology, 53*(1), 491–517. https://doi.org/10.1146/annurev.psych.53.100901.135213

Simon, H. A. (1982). *Models of bounded rationality*. MIT Press.

Slovic, P. (1995). The construction of preference. *American Psychologist, 50*(5), 364–371. https://doi.org/10.1037/0003-066X.50.5.364

Slovic, P., Finucane, M. L., Peters, E., & MacGregor, D. G. (2004). Risk as analysis and risk as feelings: Some thoughts about affect, reason, risk, and rationality. *Risk Analysis, 24*(2), 311–322. https://doi.org/10.1111/j.0272-4332.2004.00433.x

Spetzler, C., Winter, H., & Meyer, J. (Eds.). (2016). *Decision quality value creation from better business decisions*. John Wiley & Sons,. https://doi.org/10.1002/9781119176657

Thaler, R. H., Sunstein, C. R., & Balz, J. P. (2013). Choice architecture. In E. Shafir (Ed.), *The behavioral foundations of public policy* (pp. 428–439). Princeton University Press.

Thomas, P., Bratvold, R. B., & Bickel, J. E. (2014). The risk of using risk matrices. *SPE-166269-PA, 6*(02), 56–66. https://doi.org/10.2118/166269-PA

Thomas, R. P., Dougherty, M. R. P., Sprenger, A. M., & Harbison, J. I. (2008). Diagnostic hypothesis generation and human judgment. *Psychological Review, 115*(1), 155–185. https://doi.org/10.1037/0033-295X.115.1.155

Tindale, R. S., Kameda, T., & Hinsz, V. B. (2003). Group decision making. In J. Cooper & M. Hogg (Eds.), *Handbook of social psychology* (pp. 381–403). Sage.

Tversky, A., & Kahneman, D. (1973). Availability: A heuristic for judging frequency and probability. *Cognitive Psychology, 5*(2), 207–232. https://doi.org/10.1016/0010-0285(73)90033-9

Tversky, A., & Kahneman, D. (1974). Judgment under uncertainty: Heuristics and biases. *Science, 185*(4157), 1124–1131. https://doi.org/10.1126/science.185.4157.1124

Tversky, A., & Kahneman, D. (1981). The framing of decisions and the psychology of choice. *Science, 211*(4481), 453–458. https://doi.org/10.1126/science.7455683

Tversky, A., & Kahneman, D. (1983). Extensional versus intuitive reasoning: The conjunction fallacy in probability judgment. *Psychological Review, 90*(4), 293–315. https://doi.org/10.1037/0033-295X.90.4.293

Tversky, A., & Kahneman, D. (1986). Rational choice and the framing of decisions. *The Journal of Business, 59*(4), S251–S278.

Tversky, A., & Kahneman, D. (1992). Advances in prospect theory: Cumulative representation of uncertainty. *Journal of Risk and Uncertainty, 5*(4), 297–323. https://doi.org/10.1007/BF00122574

Tversky, A., Slovic, P., & Kahneman, D. (1990). The causes of preference reversal. *The American Economic Review, 80*(1), 204–217.

von Neumann, J., & Morgenstern, O. (2007). *Theory of games and economic behavior (60th anniversary ed)*. Princeton University Press.

von Nitzsch, R., & Weber, M. (1993). The effect of attribute ranges on weights in multiattribute utility measurements. *Management Science, 39*(8), 937–943.

von Winterfeldt, D. (1999). On the relevance of behavioral decision research for decision analysis. In J. Shanteau, B. A. Mellers, & D. A. Schum (Eds.), *Decision science and technology: Reflections on the contributions of Ward Edwards* (pp. 133–154). Kluwer.

von Winterfeldt, D., & Edwards, W. (1986). *Decision analysis and behavioral research*. Cambridge University Press.

Vosgerau, J. (2010). How prevalent is wishful thinking? Misattribution of arousal causes optimism and pessimism in subjective probabilities. *Journal of Experimental Psychology: General, 139*(1), 32–48. https://doi.org/10.1037/a0018144

Wakker, P. P. (2010). *Prospect theory: For risk and ambiguity*. Cambridge University Press.

Wallsten, T. S., & Budescu, D. V. (1983). Encoding subjective probabilities: A psychological and psychometric review. *Management Science, 29*(2), 151–173.

Wänke, M., Schwarz, N., & Bless, H. (1995). The availability heuristic revisited: Experienced ease of retrieval in mundane frequency estimates. *Acta Psychologica, 89*(1), 83–90. https://doi.org/10.1016/0001-6918(93)E0072-A

Weber, E. U., & Johnson, E. J. (2009). Mindful judgment and decision making. *Annual Review of Psychology, 60*(1), 53–85. https://doi.org/10.1146/annurev.psych.60.110707.163633

Weber, M. (1987). Decision making with incomplete information. *European Journal of Operational Research, 28*(1), 44–57. https://doi.org/10.1016/0377-2217(87)90168-8

Weber, M., Eisenfuhr, F., & von Winterfeldt, D. (1988). The effects of splitting attributes on weights in multiattribute utility measurement. *Management Science, 34*(4), 431–445.

Weinstein, N. D. (1980). Unrealistic optimism about future life events. *Journal of Personality and Social Psychology, 39*(5), 806–820. https://doi.org/10.1037/0022-3514.39.5.806

Behavioral Biases in the Uncertainty Quantification Process

Victor Richmond R. Jose

Abstract Humans play important roles in the process of quantifying uncertainty. The participation of humans in this important exercise opens the process to behavioral biases. In this paper, we examine the different types of biases that may occur when quantifying uncertainty using a process-oriented framework. In particular, we examine the potential biases in each of the major phases of the uncertainty quantification process. Traditionally, most of the literature has focused on biases that occur in the elicitation phase, but we discuss how these can also permeate in the pre- and post-elicitation phases. The recognition of biases in these different phases allows practitioners to potentially avoid, minimize, and correct behavioral biases that result in the multiple stages of the uncertainty quantification process.

Keywords Uncertainty quantification · Behavioral biases · Pre-elicitation · Elicitation · Post-elicitation

Introduction

Methods for quantifying uncertainty has grown in recent years with newer methods and techniques that leverage the use of data and multiple sources of information. Over the years, humans have played an important role in this process and the knowledge held by experts are too valuable for companies and individuals to simply ignore or discard. In certain contexts, subject matter experts are the only viable source of uncertainty information.

The inclusion of humans however has also made this process prone to behavioral biases – irrational behavior that unconsciously affect our ability to perform tasks

V. R. R. Jose (✉)
McDonough School of Business, Georgetown University, Washington, DC, USA
e-mail: vrj2@georgetown.edu

F. M. Federspiel et al. (eds.), *Behavioral Decision Analysis*, International Series in Operations Research & Management Science 350,
https://doi.org/10.1007/978-3-031-44424-1_3

and make decisions (Gilovich et al., 2002). Biases affect the quality of gathered information and may impact decisions we later make using this information.

There has been some recent push for data-driven methods to be used in uncertainty quantification (e.g., Deshpande et al., 2019). The main driving force here is data availability and ease of access but another perhaps more salient force is that data-driven methods appear to have an *illusion of objectivity* (Berger & Berry, 1988; Jose, 2011). However, this illusion quickly wanes as individuals and organizations recognize the increasing amount of empirical evidence surrounding successful expert elicitation and uncertainty quantification. In addition, many data-driven approach can still exhibit biases similar to biases associated with humans such as overconfidence and overfitting (Grushka-Cockayne et al., 2017).

When humans are involved in the uncertainty quantification, experience has shown that appropriately chosen experts can provide invaluable information that may not be easily accessible through other data sources. Quantifying uncertainty through experts can take on many forms from simple questions directly asking for probabilities to assessments of more complex models that require estimation of multiple related parameters and quantities. Regardless of the task, experts often find these tasks cognitively challenging, because quantities such as probabilities, quantiles, and distributions are by nature abstract and concepts that people often do not directly assess in daily life. Similarly, exploring these concepts linguistically through words instead of numerical quantities is also a non-trivial ask for most people. This had led to the famous theory by Amos Tversky and Daniel Kahneman that when asked to quantify these uncertainties, human experts tend to use *heuristics* that simplify and speed up the task but inadvertently introduce error and bias into their judgments (Kahneman et al., 1982).

Since Tversky and Kahneman (1974) seminal work, numerous studies have emerged studying specific cognitive biases and methods to minimize these biases. Some recent reviews related to these are provided by Camerer (1995) and Della Vigna (2009). Some recent reviews such as O'Hagan et al. (2006) and Kynn (2008) have focused on these biases in the context of elicitation, while Montibeller and von Winterfeldt (2015) examine these general cognitive and motivational biases from a broader decision and risk analysis lens.

These biases perhaps are unavoidable but there has been a significant amount of work that studies how we can reduce, eliminate, and correct biases. The first step however requires identifying these possible biases and locating where they could be avoided or minimized. In this paper, we focus on behavioral biases in the context of uncertainty quantification by looking at the entire process from its earlier stages as well as stages beyond the formal elicitation phase. In terms of behavioral biases, we mostly discuss *cognitive biases*, which refer to systematic deviations in thinking and judgment that results to different outcomes when subjected to a set of normative rules compared to when the individual is left to their own devices (von Winterfledt & Edwards, 1993). We do also include a few other forms of biases such as *motivational and emotional biases* as they relate to the process of uncertainty quantification.

The aim of this piece is to help interested parties in uncertainty quantification to identify which biases are likely to occur at each of the stages in the uncertainty quantification process. This will hopefully allow practitioners to redesign steps, set safeguards and checks, and perhaps make adjustments in real time as well as after the fact. For researchers, this hopefully will highlight areas and stages in the uncertainty quantification process that still has significant gaps that need to be studied and examined.

The remainder of this paper is organized as follows: Sect. "The Elicitation Process" discusses the uncertainty quantification process focusing on the different phases and stages as well as the roles humans have in this process. The next three sections discuss how the different behavioral biases occur in each of these phases (pre-elicitation, elicitation, and post-elicitation), highlighting their effect in the process of uncertainty quantification. The last section concludes.

The Elicitation Process

Depending on the nature of the uncertainty, the elicitation process can become complex, involved, and challenging. Recognizing the importance of expert information in decision analysis, numerous decision analysts have structured this process into stages in an elicitation protocol (Merkhofer, 1987; Morgan et al., 1990; Phillips, 1999; O'Hagan et al., 2006). In many of these protocols, the elicitation procedure focuses on a specific method or context. For example, Garthwaite et al. (2005) discuss a four-stage approach that details the construction of a joint distribution across beliefs for elicitation, while Veen et al. (2017) suggests a 5-step method for eliciting expert judgment by decomposing the procedure into smaller steps with adjustable outcomes.

In terms of applications, we can also see varying set-ups and proposed processes. Walls and Quigley (2001), for example, detail a 5-stage process in the context of reliability growth modeling. Shephard and Kirkwood (1994) describe another specific sequence of steps in videotaping and post-production processing interview assessments.

In this chapter, we discuss a 9-step elicitation process that heavily borrows from the 7-step process detailed in Clemen and Reilly (2013). In this structure, we group the steps into 3 general phases which are *pre-elicitation*, *elicitation*, and *post-elicitation phases*. Table 1 lists these phases and summarizes the steps in each of these.

To begin disentangling where behavioral biases can possibly occur in this process, we briefly describe these three phases below and identify how humans participate in this process.

- ***Pre-elicitation***. In the pre-elicitation phase, the "User" (or End-User or Client) of uncertainty information begins the formulation stage in which key uncertainties are identified and sources for this information could be collected. To some

Table 1 The uncertainty quantification process using experts: three phases and nine stages

Phase 1: Pre-elicitation	
(1)	Background and set-up
(2)	Identification and recruitment of experts
Phase 2: Elicitation	
(3)	Motivating experts
(4)	Knowledge exploration
(5)	Assessment training
(6)	Assessment/estimation
Phase 3: Post-elicitation	
(7)	Verification
(8)	Aggregation of information
(9)	Reporting and usage

extent, this phase includes the design of the elicitation instrument and protocol. In this process, the initial decision on what to collect and how to collect the information is determined. Typically, this process may include individuals beyond the user. The design for example of the elicitation instrument may require a "Designer," another individual or team who have expertise in collecting information on subsections of the instrument.

In this stage, a "Recruiter" (who again may or may not be distinct from the User and Designer) begins the process of sourcing experts. Sourcing often is done internally in many organizations. In other cases, it may require the use of a Recruiter's connections, an external firm, or some online platform. Here, we refer to the recruited individuals as sources of information as "Experts."

- ***Elicitation***. The elicitation phase is often viewed narrowly as the actual assessment or estimation step. However this phase actually involves a sequence of steps that prepares Experts in assessing and estimating the uncertainties of interest. The task often begins by motivating Experts and building trust as well as confidence in the elicitation process. This process can be performed by the Recruiter but is often done by the "Elicitor," the individual who eventually will conduct the formal assessment step. The process continues through structuring and decomposition where knowledge is explored and the initial thoughts about the instrument may be modified. The last preparatory stage is training where instructions are provided and some assessments that often are not used in the final output are performed.

Once the Experts are prepared for the assessment stage, the formal process of elicitation is performed by the Elicitor after which Experts are debriefed and generally allowed to leave the process. In many instances, researchers and practitioners often focus on this phase as the singular focus of elicitation protocols. This process is naturally challenging because when Experts are exposed to the elicitation instrument and begin the formal assessment, serious errors are likely difficult to correct and often the recourse for such errors is to require a complete reboot of the elicitation process which will likely cost the User both time and money.

- ***Post-elicitation*** In this last phase, three things are often done. First, elicited information is verified by the Elicitor. The Elicitor would perform logical and coherence checks such as: do probabilities add up to 1, are Experts logically consistent with their estimates, and so on. When issues arise, a decision has to be made whether this elicited information is to be excluded, corrected, or kept. After verification, the process can proceed to an aggregation phase where multiple source of information are combined by the Elicitor for easier use by the User. In the rare instance that only limited amounts of information is collected or assessments are singular, the aggregation phase is discarded.

Finally, the User utilizes all the information into a reported quantity that the User incorporates in their analysis and decision. In some cases, this information is reported to a targeted "Audience" or other "Stakeholders" in the decision context.

This process (summarized in Fig. 1) can sometimes involve iteration within each phase or across phases. In addition, additional human participants can be involved in the process but these are likely not as significant as the individuals who we have explicitly mentioned. It may also be possible that some of these roles are played by the same individual (e.g., same person who recruits and elicits) or some of these roles are fulfilled by non-human participants such as an online platform, algorithm, or program. Hanea et al. (2022) provides a similar discussion of the uncertainty quantification process, detailing the actors in the process and the current challenges

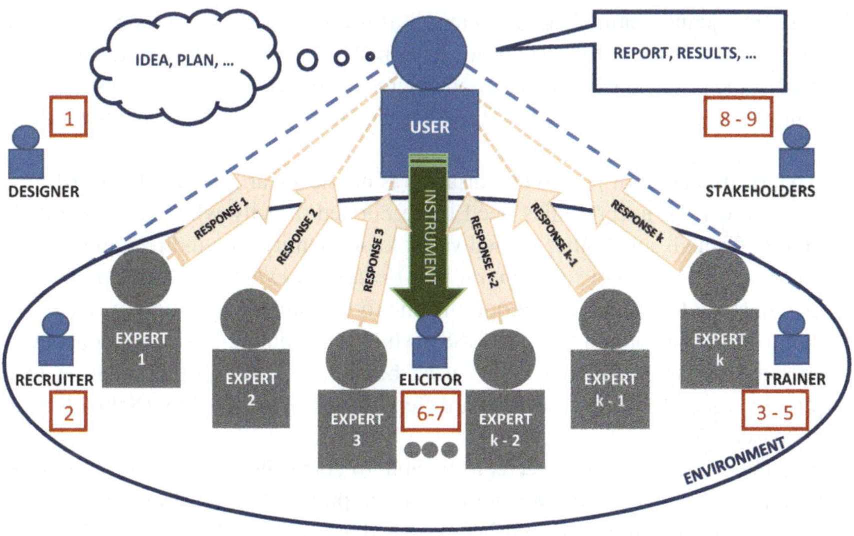

Fig. 1 The uncertainty quantification process: A simplified diagram. Number in boxes refer to the stages listed in Table 1

in practice. We complement this work by identifying the behavioral biases that exist in this process.

Behavioral Biases in the Pre-Elicitation Phase

Behavioral biases refer to "a variety of deviations from rational choice theory" made by individuals in their decision-making process (Gigerenzer, 2018). The literature has often interpreted these biases as systematic flaws in thinking that persistently occurs in many setting and is often replicable in experimental settings. In the pre-elicitation phase, bias is likely to come from three possible sources – (i) actions made by a User in setting up and framing the uncertainty quantification research questions, (ii) choices made by the Designer in the initial assessment/elicitation instrument, and (iii) decisions made by the Recruiter in gathering Experts for the elicitation process.

We examine these three possible areas briefly by highlighting the most common types of behavioral biases that both directly and indirectly result from choices made in these three areas. The discussion provided here is by no means exhaustive however it highlights behavioral biases that are likely to exist in this phase of the uncertainty elicitation process.

Background and Framing

Uncertainty quantification begins in numerous ways but when a User recognizes the need to consult Experts, the User needs to formally think about the nature and background of the problem being considered. Clemen and Reilly (2013) suggest that this step may involve teasing out what variables need to be elicited and what limitations need to be recognized in this study.

The identification of important variables is not necessarily straightforward for a User since certain uncertainties need to be elicited directly while some are done indirectly through some other related variable or quantity. The indirect approach is often *prone to the selective perception bias* or *status quo bias*. Selective perception is the tendency to ignore certain options due to discomfort or difficulty caused by thinking of such an option (Walsh, 1988), while status quo refers to the tendency to simply use variables that have been used before even though the situation may require another approach or tackles a different type of uncertainty (Samuelson & Zeckhauser, 1988).

In addition, the User also needs to be able to correctly rank variables based on importance since some variables will not be important in the estimation process. Depending on the number of items being ranked or analyzed, the User may be prone to additional biases. For example, when faced with a problem with hundreds of variables, the decision on which subset to choose as critical in an elicitation may lead to an overload of choices. The *choice overload bias* may create issues in the selection process but may also have repercussions down the process when Users who ruminate over choices may experience higher amounts of regret when issues occur (Chernev et al., 2015).

Lyles and Thomas (1988) also discuss a general framework in problem formulation that may be applicable to uncertainty quantification. In this framework, depending on the criterion used, the problem formulation process can be narrowed down and biases related to this process can then be identified. For example, when the problem formulation criterion used is political, a User may encounter biases such as *social pressures*, *escalating commitment*, and *illusion of control*. While if the process were described to be as decisive, the User may be prone to biases such as *social pressure*, *emotional stress*, or the *prior hypothesis bias* (Hambrick & Snow, 1977).

Initial Design

Once variables and quantities of interests are determined, a User with the help perhaps of the Designer and Elicitor would start conceptualizing the elicitation instrument – the primary tool that would be used to collect information (e.g., questionnaire, platform, interface, sequence of questions, design, etc.). Though the design may be revisited in later stages (e.g., during the knowledge exploration stage), this initial design often has a domino effect. It affects who will be included as Experts, how Experts will be motivated, and perhaps how they will be trained.

In this stage, there are many design choices a Designer can make. Here we examine several important elements in the design of the instrument. In particular, we examine three basic design elements: (i) format, (ii) length, and (iii) encoding.

- **Format**. In terms of format, elicitations can be grouped into three big subcategories – individual, semi-moderated groups, and moderated groups. In individual assessments, an Expert has no contact with other experts and provide assessments directly to the Elicitor or the interface. Semi-moderated group assessments allow for Experts to interact with a moderator and other experts in an unstructured or semi-structured manner, while moderated groups follow a very structured format (e.g., Delphi groups where Experts minimally interact with each other and mostly with the Elicitor acting as a moderator). Cooke (1991) discusses these multiple formats in eliciting uncertainty and provides the benefits and disadvantages of each in greater detail.

Individual tasks tend to preserve independence and uncorrelatedness among experts, but group tasks may benefit from improved shared knowledge (Phillips, 1999). Moderated groups aim to be somewhere in between, i.e., increase information sharing yet still retain some form of independence among experts. Groups can also be challenging and issues such as *assembly costs*, *game theoretic participant behavior*, and *consensus failure* (Chesley, 1975).

The interactions are also interesting in this context from a behavioral point of view. Some biases that may occur are *herding*, *social influence*, and *conversational norms*. Herding refers to the gravitation of opinions to a particular point of view for reasons not associated with learning or proper updating of information. Often in group settings, it may be due effects such as the loudest voice effect in the room or exhaustion from not reaching a consensus. In uncertainty quantification group discussions, social influence bias occurs when an expert asymmetrically treats positive and negative information learned from the group, e.g., overamplify positive information and underweigh negative information shared by others (Muchnik et al., 2013).

Conversational norms bias refers to the tendency of individuals engaging in conversation to trade off accuracy for informativeness (Yaniv & Foster, 1995). As an example, instead of providing an accurate location (such as a GPS position) a person may provide a description based on the nearest large city (e.g., close to Washington DC). In an elicitation context, it may be simply transforming a known estimate to the expert such as 23.45% to a statement such as roughly 1 in 5 or perhaps referring to such as a low chance event.

- **Length**. The number of tasks faced by each Expert is a decision that the User or Designer of the instrument makes. This will have an impact on cost and the type of Elicitor needed in the elicitation phase. Psychologically, the biggest issues associated with length are *motivation loss* and *expert fatigue* (Speirs-Bridge et al., 2010; Hemming et al., 2018). Motivation loss refers to a decrease in effort and interest in the elicitation exercise, while expert fatigue occurs when an expert is cognitively overburdened by a series of tasks in a short period of time. Research shows that these can easily affect memory recall and accuracy (James et al., 2010).

If the number of elicitation tasks increase, it may be better to spread them over multiple sessions or perhaps divide the tasks among other experts. Beyond the formal assessment, the Designer needs to take into account the time needed to perform training such as calibrating with seed questions and comprehension tasks (Rossi et al., 2019). When tasks are done offline, it may be useful to provide Experts sufficient time to complete the assessment as well as provide nudges to guarantee that tasks are not performed haphazardly.

A related issue with length is sequencing of tasks. Depending on the context, an Expert maybe exposed to a *sequence bias* or *question-order effect* (Boyle et al., 1993). This phenomenon is related to a general class of biases known as *anchoring*, a tendency to rely too heavily on a few pieces of information (Jacowitz & Kahneman, 1995; Furnham & Boo, 2011). The sequence bias may be perhaps easily addressed by a randomization process but this may be challenging in group settings or scenarios with a small number of experts.

- **Encoding**. Information or variable encoding refers to how we collect and capture the information about the uncertainties and variables we are eliciting (Wallsten & Budescu, 1983). Methods can be direct, indirect or some combination of the two. Direct methods record judgments of uncertainty directly from the Expert such as interviews and probability-scale questionnaires, while indirect methods estimate judgments of uncertainty from related assessment tasks such as gamble-like and probability-wheel methods (Chesley, 1975; Renooij, 2001). Typically, indirect methods require Experts to perform simpler tasks (e.g., making comparisons or selecting between a finite set of lotteries), but Experts may be suspicious about the process and wary of how their responses might be misused.

Among different encoding methods, individual accuracy may also widely vary even for the same uncertainty being examined. Abbas et al. (2008) compared two probability encoding methods – one that fixes the probability (e.g., quantile estimation) and one that fixes the variable value (e.g., probability estimation). They show that individuals have a harder time estimating quantiles since individuals are often more exposed to likelihood estimation (e.g., what is the chance of having more than 1 inch of snow?) rather than estimating values (e.g., what is the minimum amount of snow that exceeds 90% of all the snow days?)

Alternatively, Experts could be asked to provide estimates in the form of probability distributions. In some instances, Experts may be asked to provide an actual distribution or enough information to generate a distribution, e.g., in the 2014 Global Energy Forecasting Competition, experts were asked to provide 99 quantiles for various quantities in the areas of load, price, wind and solar forecasting (Hong et al., 2016). Alternatively, experts may be asked to provide parameters for a chosen (or reported) distribution family (Perry & Greig, 1975; Kadane, 1980; Garthwaite et al., 2005). Requiring significant amounts of information from an Expert (e.g., more than 3 quantiles) can be cognitively challenging and will likely make these Experts rely on computing technology, while asking for parameters might be cognitively easier but may corner Experts into a distribution that are not consistent with their beliefs.

To relieve the cognitive burden of assessing distributions and provide some middle ground, a common strategy is to provide Experts partitions. This does not fix the distribution while still reducing the assessment burden for an Expert. For example, in the US Survey of Professional Forecasters (SPF), Experts are asked to provide probability estimates say for inflation in the following percentage point categories: Less Than 0, Between 0 and 0.9, Between 1 and 1.9, etc. This survey of experts has been one of the longest and impactful group forecasting elicitation exercise in macroeconomic forecasting (Croushore & Stark, 2019).

The partition choice however provides some form of anchor for Experts, which may be construed as a form of public information shared by the Elicitor or User. Fox and Clemen (2005) and See et al. (2006) explain that the *partition dependence bias* tends to pull an Expert's belief closer toward an ignorance prior (i.e., equal likelihood for each category in a partition). In the US SPF, we see that there have been significant and systematic changes in the reporting behavior in the periods immediately after the partitions were changed. Similarly, another partition-related bias called *extremeness aversion* may be in play (Lewis et al., 2019). In uncertainty quantification with partitions, extremeness aversion refers to dislike the categories in the extreme ends of a partition and assigning them even less probability compared to the case when they were not exposed to the partition.

Beyond numerical and mathematical representations of uncertainty, Experts may also be able to provide meaningful information when asked to provide more qualitative assessments. These can often be done in addition to quantitative questions related to the uncertainty (Pye et al., 2018; Padilla et al., 2021). These however can also lead to challenges in interpretation from the side of the User. Mauboussin and Mauboussin (2018) perfectly illustrate this challenge by providing response distributions to commonly used terms. They illustrate that common words like "always" or "never" still has some variability when interpreted by people. Regardless of such, it is still possible to measure the vague meaning of such words but this often require great effort on the part of the Elicitor (Wallsten et al., 1986).

In practice, there are likely other design elements that could be studied and may be prone to behavioral biases. These three represent the most common elements that all instrument design problems consider.

Recruitment

The last stage of the pre-elicitation phase is the recruitment of experts. In this stage, the critical decision is made by the Recruiter in the method by which she seeks and selects experts. When the User and Recruiter are the same person, there may be no misalignment of incentives unless the same person explicitly makes an effort to wear different hats in these different roles. When the two roles are not filled by the same person, the User may have to consider on how to properly incentivize the Recruiter (e.g., payment based on performance, increased likelihood of reusing their service, etc.).

Selection bias is likely the most common bias encountered in this phase. This bias refers to the tendency of the Recruiter to favor the choice of certain experts over others based on factors associated to the Recruiter rather than the problem at hand. For example, a recruiter may be using the same online platform to gather large number of participants in an election as well as a financial market risk study. Depending on the platform, the participant base may be broad enough say for an election type study but not technical enough for the market risk study.

Diversity is another challenge a Recruiter has to manage. For groups of Experts, diversity is needed beyond expertise in order to harness the *wisdom-of-the-crowds effect* (Budescu & Chen, 2015). In addition, there may be unintended consequences when the pool is dominated by a single subgroup based on factors such as sex, age, race, or cultural background. For example, numerous studies show how cross-cultural and cross-national differences have an effect on the forecasting accuracy and calibration on similar tasks (Phillips & Wright, 1977; Yates et al., 1989; Whitcomb et al., 1995).

Finally, two additional biases have also been reported in the literature related to this setting – *confirmation* and *correlation biases*. Confirmation bias occurs "when there is a desire to confirm one's belief, leading to an unconscious selectivity in the acquisition and use of evidence" (Montibeller & von Winterfeldt, 2015). In expert recruitment, the acquisition of evidence can be reflected in the choice of which experts to include and exclude from the study. A correlation bias occurs when experts selected tend to excessively share common points of view reducing their independence. This can be attributed to similar training, exposure to the same sets of information, close professional networks, and the likes (Broomell & Budescu, 2009).

Behavioral Biases in the Elicitation Phase

Elicitation is a well-studied field of research and practice. Being a fundamental step in the decision analysis cycle, it is unsurprising that many of the well-known biases in uncertainty quantification has been identified in this stage. In this section, we cluster the stages into two areas: (i) motivating and exploring and (ii) assessment training and estimation. This grouping is based on when Experts begin the task of assessment. We provide some discussion of Kahneman and Tversky's (1977, 2013) classic treatment of heuristic and biases in the context of uncertainty quantification and add as well some other non-cognitive biases that may appear in this phase.

Motivating and Exploring

We begin the elicitation phase by looking at the basic life cycle of Experts in the process. They often enter after the recruitment stage and often leave after the formal assessment process. In some cases, they are kept until the verification stage especially when access to these experts are easy, e.g., Experts that are internally sourced.

Depending on the Expert's exposure to uncertainty quantification methods, Experts are often suspicious of the process. In addition, some technical experts often have hesitancy in providing assessments related to uncertainty since expertise are often viewed as a way to resolve uncertainty. For example, empirical studies have shown that scientists often display hesitancy in reporting uncertainty in public policy settings (Fischhoff, 2012; Broomell & Kane, 2017). This can be attributed to multiple reasons such as the view that expressing uncertainty is misplaced imprecision or that end users are likely to misinterpret these assessments.

Beyond trust, one of the most common ways to motivate Experts is through incentives. Often Experts participate because of monetary as well as non-monetary incentives. Direct monetary incentives refer to payments that are given to Experts. As economic theory predicts, Trautmann and van de Kuilen (2015) provide empirical evidence that beliefs from monetary incentivized methods are more predictive than beliefs from non-incentivised introspection. This benefit diminishes with more complex monetary incentive mechanisms.

To add another layer to this, payments may also be performance or non-performance-based (e.g., fixed payments for participation). The literature on incentives suggest that a higher performance-based reward will likely lead to better forecasting accuracy (Lazear, 2000; Chen et al., 2015). The caveat in this is that the reward typically needs to be significantly higher than the payment for participation to mentally create a distinction between a low-power versus a high-power incentive for Experts. Gneezy and Rustichini (2000) show that in some settings Experts' performance is better when they are not paid compared to being insufficiently paid.

With respect to non-monetary incentives, the Elicitor also needs to be aware of these since these may signal the quality of expert information provided (Della Vigna & Pope, 2018). As an example, Experts may behaviorally show *altruism* and *prosocial motivation* as a participant (Andreoni, 1989). Altruism in this setting may mean that Experts expend a lot of effort because they believe the problem is important; they care about the Stakeholders of this problem; or perhaps they simply want the exercise to succeed. Alternatively, the Expert may react antagonistically to the problem depending on the nature of the exercise and the topic. Another important set of behavioral considerations are *reputation* and *recognition*. Both of which can play an important role in some of these quantification exercises (Collins & Evans, 2008; Benoit et al., 2022). Experts who value these may behave in a completely different manner when their reputation for example is at stake. Lichtendahl and Winkler (2007) show that when competition is high among Experts, forecasts are likely to be exaggerated. If a monetary prize or a larger share of a prize is associated with ranking, Experts are likely to trade truthful reporting for a better chance of being ranked highly to receive the monetary prize and perhaps to be recognized by other peers and Experts (Gaba et al., 2004).

Elicitation in group settings can also be prone to many cognitive and motivational biases. Montibeller and von Winterfeldt (2018) discuss these in addition to individual biases and provide some excellent suggestions on how to debias when gathering value and uncertainty judgments. This also plays an important role in the next stage of knowledge exploration.

In the knowledge exploration stage, the initial design in the pre-elicitation phase is reconsidered. Clemen and Reilly (2013) describes this process as *structuring and decomposition* since the quantity of interests are often complex and need to be broken down into smaller digestible components. This process is often difficult and prone to bias if fully done in the pre-elicitation stage. Experts in this stage provide information to properly build a general model, e.g., using an influence diagram. Since the design is reconsidered, the initial biases mentioned in the pre-elicitation stage are likely to persist in this stage if left unattended.

Exploration-related biases may also occur, in particular, the *omitted variable* and *naïve representation biases*. Omitted variable bias occurs when important pieces of information are inadvertently or deliberately overlooked (Manzi & Forster, 2019). On the other hand, naïve representation bias refers to the psychological effect when individuals oversimplify problems to reduce the cognitive burden of complex problems (Johnson-Laird et al., 1999).

In addition to the interaction among Experts in the process, a new interaction also emerges that may be prone to some behavioral considerations. Shephard and Kirkwood (1994) explain that interpersonal and communication skills of the Elicitor will play an important role in this stage. Problems may arise with poor interpersonal skills such as Experts feeling attacked or needing to be defensive when pressed to explain a point or provide reasoning for an opinion. In addition, the appropriate use of language and level of technical terminology is critical in motivating Experts to properly think about the uncertainty being considered.

Assessment: Training and Implementation

Despite our best efforts to pre-empt and reduce biases, we do not have full control on how Experts will react to the actual elicitation instrument when the formal assessment and estimation procedure begins. To reduce some of these possible issues, training has often been suggested as an excellent opportunity to debias and prepare Experts for the formal assessment step (Keeney & von Winterfeldt, 1991; Adame, 2016).

Perhaps no work on behavioral biases exist that does not recognize the seminal contributions of the *heuristic-bias framework* of Tversky and Kahneman (1974). This influential body of work created the framework of thinking about how the complex challenge of elicitation is broken down by most individuals into smaller, simpler, and more primitive tasks through rules of thumbs known as heuristics. This act of simplification then opens up to the possibility of cognitive biases, which subconsciously and systematically affect the way we respond to the initial task.

The three main classes of heuristics that they find are: (i) *anchoring*, (ii) *availability*, and (iii) *representativeness*. We discuss each of them briefly in the context of uncertainty quantification. Kahneman et al. (1982) and Gilovich et al. (2002) provide detailed reviews and analysis about these different biases in uncertainty quantification as well as other more general settings, for interested readers.

- **Anchoring**. The anchoring heuristic refers to the tendency to rely too heavily on specific pieces of information. Though adjustments are often made afterwards, the anchor often prohibits individuals from adjusting enough away from the anchor. As an example, an Elicitor asking an Expert for multiple quantiles. If an Expert is first asked about the median then asked about say the 0.05 and 0.95 quantiles, an Expert may potentially use the initial estimate for the median as an anchor and not adjust appropriately.

The scale of an elicitation question or instrument can also play the role of an anchor (Hora et al., 1992; Hora, 2007). In the US SPF example mentioned earlier, the partition provided some scale information on the lowest and highest amounts of growth, which provided an anchor. Another form of anchor is the assessment format, which can lead to the *law of the instrument bias*. This bias suggests that Experts who are often used to certain elicitation formats may treat elements from those past activities as something applicable to the present (Hill & Fowles, 1975; Kaplan, 2017). For example, an Expert used to the Delphi method may tend to adjust their beliefs to something that they believe would be closer to a consensus even when the group assessment task does not require Experts to reach a consensus.

Unsurprisingly, certain pieces of information can also provide an anchor and lead to biases such as *conservatism* and *incidental environmental anchoring* (Kynn, 2008; Critcher & Gilovich, 2008; Benjamin, 2019). In conservatism, individuals tend to heavily rely on prior information and not update probability judgment based on new information accordingly. On the other hand, incidental environmental anchoring refers to using irrelevant information that coincidentally appears in the scenario or setting to adjust one's estimate of uncertainty.

- **Availability**. This heuristic is a simplification scheme where individuals assessing the uncertainty of an event uses the ease of recall of similar events as a way to assess the uncertainty (Tversky & Kahneman, 1973). As an example, suppose an Expert had previously experienced flooding in their house, an availability-related bias may lead the Expert to believe that the likelihood of floods is higher when conducting an environmental assessment study.

The ease of recall can often be driven by multiple factors. For example, if the similar events being recalled tend to be more prominent or emotionally striking, a *salience bias* may occur. Guerin (1982) demonstrated how current and recent world news related to revolutions, troop movements and deaths tend to overestimate the probabilities of related geopolitical events. As another example, events that survive over time provide additional visibility and perceptions of success to Experts and may distort their assessment of likelihoods. This *survivorship bias* can occur when an individual is asked to assess the likelihood that a product made by a company that was founded 200 years ago will outlast a similar product made by a newer, not-so-well known company.

- **Representativeness**. When asked to assess the likelihood of an event, one heuristic that some individuals may use is representativeness. Here an individual imagines the category this event may belong to and assess its likelihood by using information about the representative object in that category (Olson, 1976). For example, if an expert was asked to assess the durability of a new German household appliance, the representativeness heuristic is being applied if the assessment of this new product was made by thinking of the quality of another popular German product that the Expert may be more familiar with.

Similarly, this heuristic has been used in explaining several well-known biases such as *base-rate neglect*, *insensitivity to sample sizes*, and *insensitivity to prior information* (Hamill et al., 1980; Pennycook & Thompson, 2016). In these cases, the assessment of probabilities is done incorrectly by assuming that the sample evidence is representative of the population and relevant pieces of information are ignored. Consider the following example: an Expert was informed that two companies (one large and one small) both have an average daily defect rate of 3% and that on a specific day one company had a defect rate of 5%. When asked which company was likelier to have had the defect rate of 5%, base-rate neglect would have led individuals to say that it was equally likely when probability theory will suggest that deviations from the average are likelier to occur for the company that produces a smaller number of items.

Many more behavioral biases may arise in the elicitation phase. For example, *affect-related* (or *emotion-based*) biases may affect an Expert but unlike the other cognitive biases that we discuss, this affect-related bias may not be systematic across all participating Experts. Persistent biases in the elicitation phase, however, can also occur beyond the heuristic-biases framework. Caverni et al. (1990) provides some discussion of cognitive biases based on other psychological theories and framework.

Behavioral Biases in the Post-Elicitation Phase

Biases in the post-elicitation phase are often warily examined primarily because the search for these biases are often seen as a post-mortem exercise. This sometimes leads to issues about confidence and trust in the uncertainty quantification process. Practitioners however have realized that recognizing these biases at this stage is equally important since there are remedies and corrective approaches that can still be done. The hope is that these corrective steps do not necessarily involve re-doing a significant portion of the process or do not require significant amounts of additional resources.

Verification is the first post-elicitation stage. It is an important step that prepares elicited information for post-processing, i.e., encoding, converting, and aggregating them into a more suitable form for reporting and use. In this stage, the most common type of verification is an *internal consistency check* also known as *coherence checks*. These refer to tests that inspects whether or not assessments follow rules of probability and logic. For example, do probabilities add up to one? Are the conditional probabilities consistent with the marginal and joint probability assessments? Are distributions defined on reasonable ranges or intervals?

In some cases, these can easily be verified during the elicitation phase and Experts can be notified immediately so that they can re-assess their reports. If left unchanged, the Elictor and User may have to choose either to modify, exclude, or include the incoherent assessment. Caution however i.e. required since choosing one of these options may inadvertently lead to a *confirmation bias*, where the decision to say exclude is dependent on whether or not the observation supports some initial hypotheses of the User. In other cases, some of these internal consistency properties and checks provide ways to debias forecasts. For example, Clemen and Ulu (2008) exploit the property of interior additivity of subjective probabilities to reduce the partition dependence bias when assessing continuous quantities.

Beyond internal consistency, biases can result from external inconsistencies by Experts when dealing with probabilistic statements (Kynn, 2008). As an example when an uncertainty of interest is categorical in nature and reports are expressed probabilistically, it may be possible that the actual reports often do not align with the uncertainties' categorical nature unless an expert always provides forecasts of 0 or 1. In this case, calibration is often a check for external consistency. Lichtenstein and Fischhoff (1980) would say that an expert is *well-calibrated* if their probability forecasts match with the long run proportion of events happening, e.g., if we examine all the occasions an expert says 25% then we expect perfect calibration to show us that only 25% of these events happening.

Poor calibration is often associated with an overconfidence bias. As an umbrella term, Moore and Schatz (2017) disentangles this bias in three ways: *overprecision*, *overestimation*, and *overplacement*. Overprecision is often the most common bias that is seen in uncertainty estimation (Brenner et al., 1996; Hora, 2004). The classic paradigm for overprecision is to examine experts' ability to provide variability estimates through the use of confidence intervals or variance estimates. In this setting for example, overconfidence often lead to narrower than expected confidence intervals and smaller than expected variance estimates (Soll & Klayman, 2004).

On the other hand, overestimation has to do with the belief that one is better than they actually are. Unlike overprecision, this does not require knowledge about the truth but rather focuses on one's perception of one's expertise. In the context of uncertainty quantification, this is often difficult to disentangle from overprecision. Lastly, overplacement is an Expert's belief that they are better than others. In this context, we often see this when the pool of experts is heterogenous in terms of expertise and specialty and often get amplified in group assessment settings.

Problems with calibration can also be seen in the opposite direction. In particular, *underconfidence* is another common issue that lead to wider than expected confidence intervals and larger than expected variance estimates. For example, in examining growth and inflation forecasts in the European Survey of Professional Forecasters, Jose et al. (2014) find that on average, forecasters exhibit overconfidence when estimating output growth but underconfidence when estimating inflation. In both cases, some statistical approaches to debiasing and addressing the calibration concern are available and can provide improvements in forecast accuracy.

In some settings, comfort and rationale may also be verified. In this step, experts may be asked follow-up questions to determine whether they are satisfied with their assessment (Merkhofer, 1987). Alternatively, subjects may have also provided feedback explaining how they were able to create the forecasts or a description of their methodology. For example, in some of the M-Competitions, participants were asked to provide code and descriptions of the methodology that they used to predict the thousands of time series provided (Makridakis et al., 2022). This provides the Elicitor and User some insights on the thought process used for the uncertainty quantification.

In the next stage, biases are less likely to occur in aggregation when the combination mechanism is set in advance. However in some contexts, the User may have some flexibility in choosing the mechanism for aggregation. Numerous methods are available for such and some methods might likely provide evidence to a pre-existing hypothesis leading to some form of confirmation bias (Genest & Zidek, 1986; Clemen & Winkler, 1999; Winkler et al., 2019; Petropoulos et al., 2022). In addition, aggregation mechanisms need to be chosen with care since these mechanism may retain or even amplify existing biases such as overconfidence in the final estimate (Grushka-Cockayne et al., 2017).

To close out the process, we also mention some issues that may exist in the reporting stage. Here, new individuals may appear, namely the Stakeholders (as well as an "Audience" for the report). Depending on the relationship between the User and these new individuals, the way in which uncertainty is reported may be exposed to additional biases, particularly motivational ones. *Conflicts of interests* are also another strong bias that has been heavily documented in the literature and is something that could also have been encountered by other actors in the process such as the Recruiter and Elicitor (Bojke et al., 2021).

When the uncertainty being reported is deemed to be a negative event, a bias might also occur in order to increase caution and conservatism due to the undesirability of an outcome (Chapin, 2001; Harris & Hahn, 2011,). Conversely, desirable outcomes can also have an effect of being over- or under-estimated by the User depending on what type of reaction the User may want to invoke on the Audience or the Stakeholders (King & Bruner, 2000; Krumpal, 2013). These motivational biases are harder in general to check because the User no longer provides checks on another individual, but rather has to be self-aware of the choices she makes and the likelihood that she may be prone to these forms of biases.

Ending Remarks

The fact that humans play multiple roles in the process of uncertainty quantification has led to the identification of numerous potential behavioral biases. From experience, these biases can distort and reduce the quality of information that we collect. At the same time, the information Experts provide in this process is valuable and often critical in many applications.

In this paper, we have highlighted how biases appear in the different stages of the uncertainty quantification process. An important task that we have not done here is to talk about methods to correct for biases, i.e., debiasing methods for the uncertainty quantification process. Though some were discussed in passing, the topic of debiasing requires another full paper to properly give it justice. We note that despite the fact that there are some recommendations for debiasing certain well-known biases, these approaches are never universally valid. The debiasing approach is going to be contingent on many factors such as the scenario, setting, composition of experts, and so on. Larrick (2004) provides an excellent overview of debiasing methods for the interested reader. Montibeller and von Winterfeldt (2015, 2018) also provide excellent detailed discussions of debiasing in the context of decision and risk analysis.

The literature has generated numerous debiasing strategies that can be employed on experts. These can involve simple things such as creating nudges and increasing the amount of training time to more complex strategies such as designing proper incentives and employing strategic combination of simpler debiasing strategies. In addition, recruiters, elicitors, and other humans on the "eliciting" side of the process may also be prone to bias and may require bias reduction training. And many of these debiasing techniques and training will require considerable resources such as time, talent, or monetary resources.

Though we may not necessarily eliminate all possible biases, we often have to remember that the presence of bias does not make our assessments and elicited values completely unusable and problematic. In many instances, bias can be corrected without needing extensive amounts of resources poured into debiasing. Depending on the context and problem, the efforts to reduce bias may also be unequal with more attention given to stages and phases that are critical to the problem at hand and the decision that needs to be made.

Though a lot of attention has already been given to the study of biases, there are still a lot of new avenues to study and explore. A significant chunk of existing work has focused on biases mainly in the elicitation phase and the design stage. In examining the entire process, we see that there are more things that can be studied in the pre-elicitation and post-elicitation phases. In fact, one can potentially argue that addressing and understanding biases in the pre-elicitation phase prior to the design stage can be impactful to both research and practice. The argument for such is that these biases in such an early stage can potentially have a bullwhip effect in the later stages.

There is also some interesting challenges and questions that can be explored in the post-elicitation phase. Though there is some natural hesitancy for post hoc analysis, it may be an important step to perform. The hesitancy often stems from an avoidance of experiencing regret or an incentive not to expose problems in the pre-elicitation and elicitation phases. Finally, we note that additional empirical work and case studies are much needed in this area. Though the practice of uncertainty quantification is enriched by the discovery of newer fallacies and biases, it is equally enriched by best practices and successful accounts of complex and meaningful quantifications.

References

Abbas, A. E., Budescu, D. V., Yu, H. T., & Haggerty, R. (2008). A comparison of two probability encoding methods: Fixed probability vs. fixed variable values. *Decision Analysis, 5*(4), 190–202.

Adame, B. J. (2016). Training in the mitigation of anchoring bias: A test of the consider-the-opposite strategy. *Learning and Motivation, 53*, 36–48.

Andreoni, J. (1989). Giving with impure altruism: Applications to charity and Ricardian equivalence. *Journal of Political Economy, 97*(6), 1447–1458.

Benjamin, D. J. (2019). Errors in probabilistic reasoning and judgment biases. *Handbook of Behavioral Economics: Applications and Foundations, 2*, 69–186.

Benoit, J. P., Dubra, J., & Romagnoli, G. (2022). Belief elicitation when more than money matters: Controlling for "control". *American Economic Journal: Microeconomics, 14*(3), 837–888.

Berger, J. O., & Berry, D. A. (1988). Statistical analysis and the illusion of objectivity. *American Scientist, 76*(2), 159–165.

Bojke, L., Soares, M., Claxton, K., Colson, A., Fox, A., Jackson, C., …, Taylor, A. (2021). Reviewing the evidence: Heuristics and biases. In *Developing a reference protocol for structured expert elicitation in health-care decision-making: A mixed-methods study*. NIHR Journals Library.

Boyle, K. J., Welsh, M. P., & Bishop, R. C. (1993). The role of question order and respondent experience in contingent-valuation studies. *Journal of Environmental Economics and Management, 25*(1), S80–S99.

Brenner, L. A., Koehler, D. J., Liberman, V., & Tversky, A. (1996). Overconfidence in probability and frequency judgments: A critical examination. *Organizational Behavior and Human Decision Processes, 65*(3), 212–219.

Broomell, S. B., & Budescu, D. (2009). Why are experts correlated? Decomposing correlations between judges. *Psychometrika, 74*(3), 531–553.

Broomell, S. B., & Kane, P. B. (2017). Public perception and communication of scientific uncertainty. *Journal of Experimental Psychology: General, 146*(2), 286–304.

Budescu, D. V., & Chen, E. (2015). Identifying expertise to extract the wisdom of crowds. *Management Science, 61*(2), 267–280.

Camerer, C. (1995). Individual decision making. In *Handbook of experimental economics* (pp. 587–703). Princeton University Press.

Caverni, J. P., Fabre, J. M., & Gonzalez, M. (1990). *Cognitive biases*. North Holland.

Chapin, J. (2001). Self-protective pessimism: Optimistic bias in reverse. *North American Journal of Psychology, 3*(2), 253–262.

Chen, C. X., Rennekamp, K. M., & Zhou, F. H. (2015). The effects of forecast type and performance-based incentives on the quality of management forecasts. *Accounting, Organizations and Society, 46*, 8–18.

Chernev, A., Böckenholt, U., & Goodman, J. (2015). Choice overload: A conceptual review and meta-analysis. *Journal of Consumer Psychology, 25*(2), 333–358.

Chesley, G. R. (1975). Elicitation of subjective probabilities: A review. *The Accounting Review, 50*(2), 325–337.

Clemen, R. T., & Reilly, T. (2013). *Making hard decisions with decision tools*. Cengage Learning.

Clemen, R. T., & Ulu, C. (2008). Interior additivity and subjective probability assessment of continuous variables. *Management Science, 54*(4), 835–851.

Clemen, R. T., & Winkler, R. L. (1999). Combining probability distributions from experts in risk analysis. *Risk Analysis, 19*(2), 187–203.

Collins, H., & Evans, R. (2008). *Rethinking expertise*. University of Chicago Press.

Cooke, R. M. (1991). *Experts in uncertainty. Opinion and subjective probability in science*. Oxford University Press.

Critcher, C. R., & Gilovich, T. (2008). Incidental environmental anchors. *Journal of Behavioral Decision Making, 21*(3), 241–251.

Croushore, D., & Stark, T. (2019). Fifty years of the survey of professional forecasters. *Economic Insights, 4*(4), 1–11.

Della Vigna, S. (2009). Psychology and economics: Evidence from the field. *Journal of Economic Literature, 47*(2), 315–372.

Della Vigna, S., & Pope, D. (2018). What motivates effort? Evidence and expert forecasts. *The Review of Economic Studies, 85*(2), 1029–1069.

Deshpande, G., Arora, C., & Ruhe, G. (2019). Data-driven elicitation and optimization of dependencies between requirements. Proceedings of IEEE 27th International Requirements Engineering Conference, 416–421.

Fischhoff, B. (2012). Communicating uncertainty fulfilling the duty to inform. *Issues in Science and Technology, 28*(4), 63–70.

Fox, C. R., & Clemen, R. T. (2005). Subjective probability assessment in decision analysis: Partition dependence and bias toward the ignorance prior. *Management Science, 51*(9), 1417–1432.

Furnham, A., & Boo, C. H. (2011). A literature review of the anchoring effect. *The Journal of Socio-Economics, 40*(1), 35–42.

Gaba, A., Tsetlin, I., & Winkler, R. L. (2004). Modifying variability and correlations in winner-take-all contests. *Operations Research, 52*(3), 384–395.
Garthwaite, P. H., Kadane, J. B., & O'Hagan, A. (2005). Statistical methods for eliciting probability distributions. *Journal of the American Statistical Association, 100*(470), 680–701.
Genest, C., & Zidek, J. V. (1986). Combining probability distributions: A critique and an annotated bibliography. *Statistical Science, 1*(1), 114–135.
Gigerenzer, G. (2018). The 'bias' bias in behavioral economics. *Review of Behavioral Economics, 5*(3–4), 303–336.
Gilovich, T., Griffin, D., & Kahneman, D. (2002). *Heuristics and biases: The psychology of intuitive judgment*. Cambridge University Press.
Gneezy, U., & Rustichini, A. (2000). Pay enough or don't pay at all. *The Quarterly Journal of Economics, 115*(3), 791–810.
Grushka-Cockayne, Y., Jose, V. R. R., & Lichtendahl, K. C. (2017). Ensembles of overfit and overconfident forecasts. *Management Science, 63*(4), 1110–1130.
Guerin, B. (1982). Salience and hindsight biases in judgements of world events. *Psychological Reports, 50*(2), 411–414.
Hambrick, D. C., & Snow, C. C. (1977). A contextual model of strategic decision making in organizations. Proceedings of the 1977 Academy of Management, 109–112.
Hamill, R., Wilson, T. D., & Nisbett, R. E. (1980). Insensitivity to sample bias: Generalizing from atypical cases. *Journal of Personality and Social Psychology, 39*(4), 578–589.
Hanea, A. M., Hemming, V., & Nane, G. F. (2022). Uncertainty quantification with experts: Present status and research needs. *Risk Analysis, 42*(2), 254–263.
Harris, A. J., & Hahn, U. (2011). Unrealistic optimism about future life events: A cautionary note. *Psychological Review, 118*(1), 135–154.
Hemming, V., Burgman, M. A., Hanea, A. M., McBride, M. F., & Wintle, B. C. (2018). A practical guide to structured expert elicitation using the IDEA protocol. *Methods in Ecology and Evolution, 9*(1), 169–180.
Hill, K. Q., & Fowles, J. (1975). The methodological worth of the Delphi forecasting technique. *Technological Forecasting and Social Change, 7*(2), 179–192.
Hong, T., Pinson, P., Fan, S., Zareipour, H., Troccoli, A., & Hyndman, R. J. (2016). Probabilistic energy forecasting: Global energy forecasting competition 2014 and beyond. *International Journal of Forecasting, 32*(3), 896–913.
Hora, S. C. (2004). Probability judgments for continuous quantities: Linear combinations and calibration. *Management Science, 50*(5), 597–604.
Hora, S. C. (2007). Eliciting probabilities from experts. In W. Edwards, R. F. Miles, & D. von Winterfeldt (Eds.), *Advances in decision analysis*. Cambridge University Press.
Hora, S. C., Hora, J. A., & Dodd, N. G. (1992). Assessment of probability distributions for continuous random variables: A comparison of the bisection and fixed value methods. *Organizational Behavior and Human Decision Processes, 51*(1), 133–155.
Jacowitz, K. E., & Kahneman, D. (1995). Measures of anchoring in estimation tasks. *Personality and Social Psychology Bulletin, 21*(11), 1161–1166.
James, A., Choy, S. L., & Mengersen, K. (2010). Elicitator: An expert elicitation tool for regression in ecology. *Environmental Modelling & Software, 25*(1), 129–145.
Johnson-Laird, P. N., Legrenzi, P., Girotto, V., Legrenzi, M. S., & Caverni, J. P. (1999). Naive probability: A mental model theory of extensional reasoning. *Psychological Review, 106*(1), 62–88.
Jose, V. R. R. (2011). Assessing probability distributions from data. In *Wiley Encyclopedia of operations research and management science* (Vol. 1, pp. 183–190). John Wiley and Sons.
Jose, V. R. R., Grushka-Cockayne, Y., & Lichtendahl, K. C., Jr. (2014). Trimmed opinion pools and the crowd's calibration problem. *Management Science, 60*(2), 463–475.
Kadane, J. B. (1980). Predictive and structural methods for eliciting prior distributions. In *Bayesian analysis in econometrics and statistics* (pp. 89–93). North Holland Publishing.
Kahneman, D., Slovic, P., & Tversky, A. (1982). *Judgment under uncertainty: Heuristics and biases*. Cambridge University Press.

Kahneman, D., & Tversky, A. (1977). *Intuitive prediction: Biases and corrective procedures*. Decisions and Designs Inc.

Kahneman, D., & Tversky, A. (2013). Prospect theory: An analysis of decision under risk. In *Handbook of the fundamentals of financial decision making: Part I* (pp. 99–127).

Kaplan, A. (2017). *The conduct of inquiry: Methodology for behavioral science*. Routledge.

Keeney, R. L., & von Winterfeldt, D. (1991). Eliciting probabilities from experts in complex technical problems. *IEEE Transactions on Engineering Management, 38*(3), 191–201.

King, M. F., & Bruner, G. C. (2000). Social desirability bias: A neglected aspect of validity testing. *Psychology & Marketing, 17*(2), 79–103.

Krumpal, I. (2013). Determinants of social desirability bias in sensitive surveys: A literature review. *Quality & Quantity, 47*(4), 2025–2047.

Kynn, M. (2008). The 'heuristics and biases' bias in expert elicitation. *Journal of the Royal Statistical Society: Series A, 171*(1), 239–264.

Larrick, R. P. (2004). Debiasing. In *Blackwell handbook of judgment and decision making* (pp. 316–338).

Lazear, E. P. (2000). The power of incentives. *American Economic Review, 90*(2), 410–414.

Lewis, J., Gaertig, C., & Simmons, J. P. (2019). Extremeness aversion is a cause of anchoring. *Psychological Science, 30*(2), 159–173.

Lichtendahl, K. C., & Winkler, R. L. (2007). Probability elicitation, scoring rules, and competition among forecasters. *Management Science, 53*(11), 1745–1755.

Lichtenstein, S., & Fischhoff, B. (1980). Training for calibration. *Organizational Behavior & Human Performance, 26*(2), 149–171.

Lyles, M. A., & Thomas, H. (1988). Strategic problem formulation: Biases and assumptions embedded in alternative decision-making models. *Journal of Management Studies, 25*(2), 131–145.

Makridakis, S., Spiliotis, E., & Assimakopoulos, V. (2022). The M5 competition: Background, organization, and implementation. *International Journal of Forecasting, 38*(4), 1325–1336. In Press.

Manzi, G., & Forster, M. (2019). Biases in bias elicitation. *Communications in Statistics-Theory and Methods, 48*(18), 4656–4674.

Mauboussin, A., & Mauboussin, M. J. (2018). If you say something is "likely," how likely do people think it is. Harvard business review Online. Retrieved October 1, 2022, from https://hbr.org/2018/07/if-you-say-something-is-likely-how-likely-do-people-think-it-is

Merkhofer, M. W. (1987). Quantifying judgmental uncertainty: Methodology, experiences, and insights. *IEEE Transactions on Systems, Man, and Cybernetics, 17*(5), 741–752.

Montibeller, G., & von Winterfeldt, D. (2015). Cognitive and motivational biases in decision and risk analysis. *Risk Analysis, 35*(7), 1230–1251.

Montibeller, G., & von Winterfeldt, D. (2018). Individual and group biases in value and uncertainty judgments. In *Elicitation* (pp. 377–392). Springer.

Moore, D. A., & Schatz, D. (2017). The three faces of overconfidence. *Social and Personality Psychology Compass, 11*(8), e12331.

Morgan, M. G., Henrion, M., & Small, M. (1990). *Uncertainty: A guide to dealing with uncertainty in quantitative risk and policy analysis*. Cambridge University Press.

Muchnik, L., Aral, S., & Taylor, J. S. (2013). Social influence bias: A randomized experiment. *Science, 341*(6146), 647–651.

O'Hagan, A., Buck, C. E., Daneshkhah, A., Eiser, J. R., Garthwaite, P. H., Jenkinson, D. J., Oakley, J. E., & Rakow, T. (2006). *Uncertain judgements: Eliciting experts' probabilities*. Wiley.

Olson, C. L. (1976). Some apparent violations of the representativeness heuristic in human judgment. *Journal of Experimental Psychology: Human Perception and Performance, 2*(4), 599–608.

Padilla, L. M., Powell, M., Kay, M., & Hullman, J. (2021). Uncertain about uncertainty: How qualitative expressions of forecaster confidence impact decision-making with uncertainty visualizations. *Frontiers in Psychology, 11*, 579267.

Pennycook, G., & Thompson, V. A. (2016). Base-rate neglect. In *Cognitive illusions* (pp. 44–61). Psychology Press.

Perry, C., & Greig, I. D. (1975). Estimating the mean and variance of subjective distributions in PERT and decision analysis. *Management Science, 21*(12), 1477–1480.

Petropoulos, F., Apiletti, D., Assimakopoulos, V., Babai, M. Z., Barrow, D. K., …, Ziel, F.. (2022). Forecasting: Theory and practice. *International Journal of Forecasting, 38*(3), 705–871.

Phillips, L. D. (1999). Group elicitation of probability distributions: Are many heads better than one? In J. Shanteau, B. Mellers, & D. Schum (Eds.), *Decision science and technology: Reflections on the contributions of Ward Edwards* (pp. 313–330). Springer.

Phillips, L. D., & Wright, C. N. (1977). Cultural differences in viewing uncertainty and assessing probabilities. In *Decision making and change in human affairs* (pp. 507–519). Springer.

Pye, S., Li, F. G., Petersen, A., Broad, O., McDowall, W., Price, J., & Usher, W. (2018). Assessing qualitative and quantitative dimensions of uncertainty in energy modelling for policy support in the United Kingdom. *Energy Research & Social Science, 46*, 332–344.

Renooij, S. (2001). Probability elicitation for belief networks: Issues to consider. *The Knowledge Engineering Review, 16*(3), 255–269.

Rossi, S. H., Blick, C., Nathan, P., Nicol, D., Stewart, G. D., & Wilson, E. C. (2019). Expert elicitation to inform a cost-effectiveness analysis of screening for renal cancer. *Value in Health, 22*(9), 981–987.

Samuelson, W., & Zeckhauser, R. (1988). Status quo bias in decision making. *Journal of Risk and Uncertainty, 1*(1), 7–59.

See, K. E., Fox, C. R., & Rottenstreich, Y. S. (2006). Between ignorance and truth: Partition dependence and learning in judgment under uncertainty. *Journal of Experimental Psychology: Learning, Memory, and Cognition, 32*(6), 1385–1402.

Shephard, G. G., & Kirkwood, C. W. (1994). Managing the judgmental probability elicitation process: A case study of analyst/manager interaction. *IEEE Transactions on Engineering Management, 41*(4), 414–425.

Soll, J. B., & Klayman, J. (2004). Overconfidence in interval estimates. *Journal of Experimental Psychology: Learning, Memory, and Cognition, 30*(2), 299–314.

Speirs-Bridge, A., Fidler, F., McBride, M., Flander, L., Cumming, G., & Burgman, M. (2010). Reducing overconfidence in the interval judgments of experts. *Risk Analysis, 30*(3), 512–523.

Trautmann, S. T., & van de Kuilen, G. (2015). Belief elicitation: A horse race among truth serums. *The Economic Journal, 125*(589), 2116–2135.

Tversky, A., & Kahneman, D. (1973). Availability: A heuristic for judging frequency and probability. *Cognitive Psychology, 5*(2), 207–232.

Tversky, A., & Kahneman, D. (1974). Judgment under uncertainty: Heuristics and biases. *Science, 185*(4157), 1124–1131.

Veen, D., Stoel, D., Zondervan-Zwijnenburg, M., & Van de Schoot, R. (2017). Proposal for a five-step method to elicit expert judgment. *Frontiers in Psychology, 8*(2110), 1–11.

von Winterfeldt, D., & Edwards, W. (1993). *Decision analysis and behavioral research*. Cambridge University Press.

Walsh, J. P. (1988). Selectivity and selective perception: An investigation of managers' belief structures and information processing. *Academy of Management Journal, 31*(4), 873–896.

Walls, L., & Quigley, J. (2001). Building prior distributions to support Bayesian reliability growth modelling using expert judgement. *Reliability Engineering & System Safety, 74*(2), 117–128.

Wallsten, T. S., & Budescu, D. V. (1983). State of the art—Encoding subjective probabilities: A psychological and psychometric review. *Management Science, 29*(2), 151–173.

Wallsten, T. S., Budescu, D. V., Rapoport, A., Zwick, R., & Forsyth, B. (1986). Measuring the vague meanings of probability terms. *Journal of Experimental Psychology: General, 115*(4), 348–365.

Whitcomb, K. M., Onkal, D., Curley, S. P., & George Benson, P. (1995). Probability judgment accuracy for general knowledge: Cross-national differences and assessment methods. *Journal of Behavioral Decision Making, 8*(1), 51–67.

Winkler, R. L., Grushka-Cockayne, Y., Lichtendahl, K. C., & Jose, V. R. R. (2019). Probability forecasts and their combination: A research perspective. *Decision Analysis, 16*(4), 239–260.

Yaniv, I., & Foster, D. P. (1995). Graininess of judgment under uncertainty: An accuracy-informativeness trade-off. *Journal of Experimental Psychology: General, 124*(4), 424–432.

Yates, J. F., Zhu, Y., Ronis, D. L., Wang, D. F., Shinotsuka, H., & Toda, M. (1989). Probability judgment accuracy: China, Japan, and the United States. *Organizational Behavior and Human Decision Processes, 43*(2), 145–171.

Analyzing Decisions Under Uncertainty: Simple Tools of the Heathens

Konstantinos V. Katsikopoulos

Abstract A major obstacle for engaging with standard decision analysis is that one must reduce uncertainty to risk. This chapter contributes to situations where uncertainty cannot be meaningfully reduced to risk. I synthesize findings and perspectives of behavioural scientists who have ventured outside the lab and into the wild. Psychologist Gerd Gigerenzer and colleagues' fast-and-frugal-heuristics program provides transparent and accurate, simple quantitative rules for laypeople and experts; and the radical-uncertainty thesis of economists Mervyn King and John Kay shows that important organizations and groups can make truly rational decisions by employing rich, coherent qualitative narratives. I speculate on the way forward for these ideas in decision analysis, and more generally connect to "soft" and "behavioral" operations research.

Keywords Uncertainty · Risk · Fast-and-frugal heuristics · Rich and coherent narratives

In a very enjoyable piece, one of the fathers of decision analysis, Ron Howard (1992) describes the "religious spectrum of decision aiding". Howard calls standard decision analysis the old-time religion, and beyond it, he names heretics, cults, and heathens. Wait… Is this serious? Yes, it is. And it actually helps understand the landscape of (behavioral) decision analysis, and how the present chapter fits into it and also into this book.

Howard's heretics follow the general ideas of standard decision analysis but may, and do, change it to achieve greater alignment with behavioral research. This includes behavioral decision analysis as in the classic text of von Winterfeldt and Edwards (1986), which is revisited here. Such work is occupied with how human

K. V. Katsikopoulos (✉)
Centre for Operational Research, Management Science and Information Systems and Centre for Behavioural Action and Research, University of Southampton Business School, Southampton, UK
e-mail: K.Katsikopoulos@soton.ac.uk

F. M. Federspiel et al. (eds.), *Behavioral Decision Analysis*, International Series in Operations Research & Management Science 350,
https://doi.org/10.1007/978-3-031-44424-1_4

behavior, unaided or aided, diverges from the prescriptions of standard models such as the maximization of expected value/utility, the revision of probabilistic beliefs according to Bayes rule, and so on.

Furthermore, again in Howard's terms, cults are willing to bend standard decision analysis practice. The soft OR (operations/operational research; Rosenhead & Mingers, 2001) and behavioral OR (Kunc et al., 2016) approaches can be placed in the cult category. The interpretation of behavioral decision analysis used here includes ideas from soft and behavioral OR.

And who are the *heathens*? That would be those of us who pursue methods that have different underlying philosophies than standard decision analysis. Ron Howard gives the example of Saaty's (1980) analytic hierarchy process that relies on paired comparisons between options and does not compute utilities, and easily dismisses it because it can violate axioms of internal logical consistency. Plenty of researchers and practitioners, however, stick to such, and simpler, methods (Frey et al., 2009). For example, in product design, Pugh's (1990) convergence process does not output a numerical measure of the worth of design options, only which design should be chosen. Across multi-attribute choice, classification, and forecasting tasks, after decades of heathen work, a theory is emerging guiding the employment of methods significantly simpler than standard decision and risk analysis (Katsikopoulos et al., 2018).

Why are the heathens so persistent? What methods do they use, formal models or verbal techniques? Do these methods work? Or do they lead to wrong decisions unless one gets lucky? If in fact heathen decision making is systematically right, under what conditions is that the case? Here I provide some answers to such questions. The answers rely on conceptual arguments and empirical evidence from the behavioral sciences, such as economics and psychology. Crucially, the arguments and the evidence refer to decisions under *uncertainty*, as opposed to decisions under risk, which is the province of standard decision analysis. The paradigm of decision making under uncertainty is a recurrent one in behavioral decision research, even though it is regularly swept under the rug. It fits well with the prediction/individual cell of the taxonomy employed in the book (Chap. 1).

The chapter is structured as follows. In the first section I discuss what distinguishes uncertainty from risk, according to a definition by economist Frank Knight. In the next two sections, I provide two examples of simple tools for analyzing decisions under uncertainty: Psychologist Gerd Gigerenzer, of the Max Planck Institute for Human Development and colleagues' *fast-and-frugal-heuristics* program provides transparent and accurate, simple quantitative models for laypeople and experts; and the radical uncertainty thesis of economists Mervyn King (now in the UK House of Lords) and John Kay suggests that consequential decisions can be made rationally by employing rich and coherent *narratives*, aimed at making decision situations more clear. Throughout, some underpinnings of the two approaches are also discussed. In the final section, I offer some thoughts on the way forward for such ideas in the theory and practice of behavioral decision analysis, and more generally connect to soft and behavioral OR.

The Distinction Between Risk and Uncertainty

More than a hundred years ago, founder of the Chicago School of Economics Frank Knight wrote (1921, p. 233, emphasis added):

> The practical difference between the two categories, *risk and uncertainty*, is that in the former the distribution of the outcome in a group of instances is known (either through calculation a priori or from statistics of past experience), while in the case of uncertainty this is not true, the reason being in general that it is impossible to form a group of instances, because the situation dealt with is in a high degree unique.

In decision analysis terms, if we know the probabilities of all outcomes that may result from choosing an option, then we are making a decision under risk. If we do not know some of these probabilities, we are making a decision under uncertainty. One can of course imagine other categories—for example, in a radical version, uncertainty could come from not knowing some of the possible outcomes to begin with, let alone their probabilities.

A premise of standard decision analysis is that we can always assume that we are dealing with decisions under risk. There is considerable appreciation in practice of how challenging it might be to estimate or elicit probabilities, but, ultimately, there is a conviction that it can be done. There is a multitude of methods, including tests and checks for ensuring that the provided probabilities 'make sense'. This could mean that the probabilities obey standards of internal logical consistency, such as summing to one, or are being assigned a score via a quantitative rule (Matheson & Winkler, 1976).

I have the utmost respect for the work that has gone into building, applying, and revising models of decision analysis under risk. But I also believe that there is something important in emphasizing that one *cannot always* meaningfully reduce uncertainty to risk, and it might be a mistake to insist on forcing what might sometimes turn out to resemble a straitjacket. A 2020 book, written by two authorities in real-world, extremely consequential decision making, but not necessarily likely to be read by many operations researchers and management scientists, has made this case vividly.

Mervyn King is an economist and the former governor of the Bank of England from 2003 to 2013, amidst the "Great Recession". John Kay is also an economist who has been the inaugural dean of Oxford's Said School of Business and director of several public companies. Together they wrote the compelling *Radical Uncertainty: Decision Making for an Unknowable Future* (Kay & King, 2020). Besides paying homage to Frank Knight, and others, who have resisted "the lure of probabilities", the authors continuously invite readers to simply reflect on whether decisions are made under risk or under uncertainty. Consider the following example.

Kay and King discuss President Obama's decision of approving, or not, a raid on the Abbottabad compound in Pakistan where Osama Bin Laden was believed to be hiding. A failed operation would have greatly undermined faith in Obama's presidency, with all the important cascading effects that such developments have. In the risk paradigm, Obama's decision hinges on the probability that bin Laden was indeed hiding in the compound. According to Kay and King, however, the estimates of the probability provided to the President ranged wildly, from 30% to 95%. Obama did not demand convergence to a consensus value or interval, nor did he seek guarantees that the probability exceeded some threshold, critical for switching from one decision to another. Rather, he took the courageous step of acknowledging that this decision had to be made under irreducible uncertainty. Kay and King identify and emphasize a concise and essential statement made by Obama in taking this step (from Bowden, 2012, p. 160, emphasis added):

> In this situation what you started getting was probabilities that *disguised* uncertainty as opposed to actually providing you with more useful information.

One could say that most decision makers do not face probabilities that are as hard to pin down as what Obama was facing. Perhaps. This is ultimately an empirical question, and I am happy to trust that decision analysts exhibit diligence in ascertaining whether in a particular scenario probabilities can be elicited or estimated or they cannot. The point of my allusion to Kay and King's book is to build the case that some extremely consequential decisions are made under uncertainty, and it does not really make sense to view them otherwise. For instance, with some reflection, it is clear that the fields of technology and business spawn an abundance of decisions under uncertainty. In fact, where there is potential for innovation, there is a lack of knowledge of possible outcomes in the future, and of course any associated probabilities. In 2000, how could anyone predict and make management decisions about smartphone sales in 2020, when we did not know what smartphones were? Or which company's scenario planning in 2019 included outcomes caused by a global pandemic, and can you really blame them for not doing so? And so on.

Are we splitting hairs? Even if a situation is nominally one under uncertainty, this does not mean that good, or excellent, or even the best decisions could not be reliably made by reducing the uncertainty to risk. The science and engineering of decision making has been elaborating this very notion since Blaise Pascal in the middle of the seventeenth century used probability theory to 'prove' that one should believe in God, and we must be getting quite good at it by now. And anyway, except for probability theory, what other tools do we have to tame uncertainty? Even if there are other such tools, how good can they be when it is obviously probability that reigns? There are no blanket answers to such questions, but the next two sections do provide some answers, and in fact surprising ones. There are two types of tools—other than probability theory—developed by heathens, that are effective in analyzing decisions under uncertainty.

First Tool: Fast-and-Frugal Heuristics

Optimization, a standard approach in hard OR, is often not possible to apply in practice because the calculation of the 'optimal' solution is computationally intractable or requires information that cannot be obtained. *Heuristics* are a traditional way of circumventing such problems; they are computational shortcuts that allow to "quickly [find] good feasible solutions" (Hillier & Lieberman, 2001, p. 624). That is, hard OR analyzes heuristics formally and emphasizes their usefulness. A second meaning of heuristics, well known in soft and behavioral OR, comes from psychology and behavioral economics, and refers to shortcuts that people use when making judgments and choices; in one of behavioral science's celebrated papers those shortcuts have been said to be "in general... quite useful but sometimes lead to severe and systematic errors" (Tversky & Kahneman, 1974, p. 1124). That is, this psychological meaning of heuristics is informal (verbal) and emphasizes their shortcomings.

The present chapter refers to a third, interdisciplinary, meaning of heuristics, which is a hybrid of the two meanings above. *Fast-and-frugal* heuristics (Gigerenzer et al., 1999) are computational models as in hard OR, that are built by utilizing knowledge from human psychology as in soft/behavioral OR. Their name comes from the fact that they use a few and easily obtainable pieces of information (frugal), and combine those pieces in simple ways (fast). Fast-and-frugal heuristics can prescribe what decisions should be made as computational shortcuts in hard OR do, or describe what decisions people actually do make as heuristics in psychology and behavioral OR do. In this chapter, the focus is more on the prescriptive power of fast-and-frugal heuristics, including the conditions under which they are successful and under which they are not; for a synthesis of the descriptive power of fast-and-frugal heuristics, see Katsikopoulos (2023).

One of the major strengths of fast-and-frugal heuristics is that they are successful *and* transparent to end users (i.e., easy for them to understand, apply, and explain to others), a combination that decision models from machine learning, data science, and OR often struggle to achieve (Ward et al., 1991; Rudin, 2019; Katsikopoulos et al., 2020; Gigerenzer, 2022). The reader *Heuristics: The Foundations of Adaptive Behavior* (Gigerenzer et al., 2011) presents a number of classic fast-and-frugal heuristics, as well as their underlying theory and successful applications (across a number of fields, notably medicine and finance). For article-length reviews see Martignon and Hoffrage (2002), Katsikopoulos (2011), Gigerenzer and Gaissmaier (2011), and Katsikopoulos et al. (2018).

This section provides two concrete applications in OR, aiming to illustrate the approach of fast-and-frugal heuristics in the context of behavioral decision analysis, and to highlight some basics of the theory of heuristic success. The heuristics presented here do not require probabilities as input, and hence are applicable to decisions under uncertainty. The material presented builds on and extends a similar review in a chapter (Katsikopoulos, 2016) in the inaugural collection *Behavioral Operational Research: Theory, Methodology, and Practice* (Kunc et al., 2016).

Application: Friend or Foe?

Niklas Keller, one of my early PhD students and later a co-founder of the decision consulting firm *Simply Rational*, has a strong intrinsic interest in decisions made by important institutions, such as the military. This passion serendipitously led him to stumble upon a data treasure—the real decisions made by NATO forces at checkpoints in Afghanistan between 2004 and 2009, as those were, for a very brief period of time, revealed by *Wikileaks*. The soldiers have to classify a car approaching a checkpoint as a friend or a foe, and decide how to make the car stop, so that it can be respectively searched or neutralized. These decisions can mean no less than the difference between life and death for the civilians who are in a car as well as the soldiers. How are soldiers making these decisions? Is it working? Can research help them do better? I present the main empirical answers here; for more context, formal theory and details see Keller and Katsikopoulos (2016) and Katsikopoulos et al. (2020).

The Wikileaks data consists of 1160 reports, 7 of which refer to suicide attackers and 1053 to civilians. All suicide attacks resulted to all car occupants and soldiers dying. Unfortunately, there were casualties in the civilian incidents as well, and 204 people were injured or killed. The research question is whether researchers can construct a decision aid that improves upon the accuracy of unaided soldiers, and at the same is transparent to them.

Framing the decision as one under risk and then applying standard OR techniques is tempting, but does not work. The issue is that the estimate of the probability of a hit (i.e., soldiers classify a car with suicide attackers as a foe) is zero. There are two problems with this estimate—first it cannot be true, and second if it is plugged in an OR approach—such as game theory or the statistical induction of a decision tree, it leads to extreme solutions such as classifying all cars as friends (Keller & Katsikopoulos, 2016; Katsikopoulos 2023). As in Obama's case, it might be better to acknowledge that we do not have the necessary information to treat this decision as one under risk; rather it is a decision under uncertainty.

In order to prescribe to someone what they should do, it often helps if you first figure out what they actually do. It seems that soldiers rely almost exclusively on a heuristic (use of the heuristic is consistent with soldier decision making in 1020 out of 1053, or 97%, of incidents) that uses one attribute, *compliance*:

> If an approaching car appears to comply with soldier instructions—for example, if it slows down—then classify it as a friend and ensure peacefully that it stops so that it can be searched; If the car does not appear to comply—for example, if it speeds up—then classify it as a foe and ensure that it is neutralized, for example by shooting at it.

Niklas Keller asked experts on checkpoint decisions, such as experienced military personnel and teachers in military academies, their insights about how to classify an approaching car as friend or foe, and tried to establish if those insights could be combined with the compliance attribute. He performed a *cognitive task analysis* (Vicente, 1999), where he worked with experts to integrate compliance into a slightly more complicated, but still transparent structure. This structure is a called a *fast-and-frugal tree* (Martignon et al., 2008), and is shown below in Fig. 1 (in the tree, threat cues refer to any information that could make an approaching car seem suspicious, such as intelligence information).

The aid of Fig. 1 is a *decision tree*, which is a popular type of model in statistics and machine learning (Breiman et al., 1984), commonly viewed as 'interpretable'

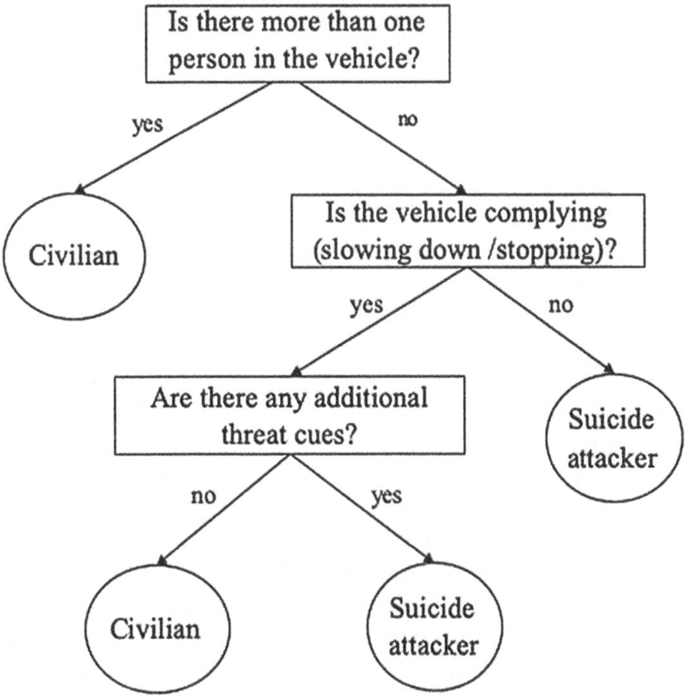

Fig. 1 A fast-and-frugal decision tree for classifying cars approaching a checkpoint as friend or foe (adapted from Keller & Katsikopoulos, 2016); see text for details

(Bertsimas et al., 2019). This particular decision tree is especially constrained to be easy to understand: It asks only a few questions, it asks those questions one at a time, and each time it asks a question it is possible that a decision is made immediately (regardless of the answers to subsequent questions). These properties ensure that the tree is fast and frugal. Is it also accurate?

It turns out that the Fig. 1 tree is much more accurate than soldiers; when applied to the *Wikileaks* dataset, it leads to 78 casualties. In fact, this number is likely an overestimate because it assumes that everyone identified as a suicide attacker would be injured or killed, but the soldiers are able to sometimes neutralize a car without hurting its occupants (Katsikopoulos et al., 2020).

This application of a fast-and-frugal heuristic to an operational decision was an example of *integration of intuition and analysis*: The soldiers' intuition of using the compliance attribute was enhanced by working with experts in a cognitive task analysis, producing a simple decision tree that includes the compliance attribute and also other attributes. This integration was pursued by a qualitative method of facilitated interviewing. The next application also integrated intuition and analysis, but did so by using quantitative modeling, and also looked at the issue of integration in a more abstract and more general way. I present the main concepts and empirical results here; for the mathematical analyses see Katsikopoulos et al. (2022).

Application: Knowledge and Thinking

In the remainder, by intuition I mean the strong feeling of 'knowing' that a decision is right without being able to articulate why (Koopman, 1977; Klein, 2015). Gigerenzer (2007) has suggested that intuition may be operating via the use of heuristics that are particularly fast and frugal. Analysis refers to deliberate thinking that allows putting forth reasons for making a decision. Kahneman's (2011) System 1/2 metaphor is capturing this division of labor between intuition and analysis (for origins of such ideas, see Schneider & Schiffrin, 1977). The point of the exercise described below is how should decision makers implement this division. Can it be made 'optimally'? Does an optimality theory work in practice?

To answer, we first need to define the research question more precisely. Consider a set of *interrelated* decision tasks. If you are first comparing decision options *A* and *B*, and subsequently options *B* and *C*, then your choice of intuition or analysis for the first task might affect your choice for the second task. This is so because if you analyzed options *A* and *B* in order to evaluate and compare them, then it seems odd to 'forget' this analysis and use intuition to evaluate *A* when comparing it with *C* (the reverse path of first using intuition and then analysis appears to be more plausible, although there would have to be a reason for changing one's approach).

Now we are very close to defining the research question. We can capture the above interrelation by modeling intuition as a *single-cue* (single-attribute) heuristic, such as the *recognition heuristic* (Goldstein & Gigerenzer, 2002): Options are either 'recognized' or not, and in a choice where one option is recognized and the other is not, intuition dictates that the recognized option is chosen; but if both options are recognized, then analysis is used to make a choice (if neither option is recognized, then a choice is made randomly). Recognition of an option could be literal—I have been to or heard of this restaurant but not of the other one—or an umbrella term for 'knowing' that I prefer this restaurant… because… I cannot say why, but I know I do. This model allows to capture interrelations in the use of analysis and intuition. For instance, if I recognize *A* and *B* and thus used analysis to choose between them, this also implies, according to the model, that I cannot use intuition to choose between *A* and another recognized option *C*.

So now, assuming that there is a correct choice in each paired comparison, one can ask the following research question:

> How should recognition be distributed across a set of options, so that accuracy, over the set of all paired comparisons between two options, is maximized?

It is interesting to ask if this 'optimal' distribution reflects the substantial use of intuition or not. What does that mean? Say that there are four options *A*, *B*, *C*, and *D*, and accuracy is maximized when *A* and *B* are recognized, and *C* and *D* are not; then intuition would be used in 67% of all paired comparisons (4 out of 6—between *A* and *C* or *D* as well as between *B* and *C* or *D*). A scenario in which this distribution would be optimal is if *A* and *B* are equally good for the decision maker and better than *C* and *D*; then, the maximum would equal 88% (5.5 out of 6—the random choice between *C* and *D* would produce an error half of the time).

Together with Martin Egozcue and Luis Fuentes Garcia, we derived a necessary and sufficient condition for the *positive* use (i.e., in more than zero paired comparisons) of intuition to be optimal, and then investigated empirically how often was this condition met in datasets. Note that, in the above model, this proportion is capped at approximately 50%. We also checked what is the *benefit* in accuracy in using the theoretically 'optimal' mix over using analysis alone. We used both synthetic and natural datasets. There were two natural datasets, one in which the task was to forecast the ranking of male tennis players in the 2007 Wimbledon tournament (for details on the dataset see Scheibehenne & Bröder, 2007); and another in which the task was to choose the 'best' (as judged by *NHS* experts in a King's Fund study; for details on the dataset see Fasolo et al., 2010) London hospital for a serious, non-urgent operation. The main results are summarized below in Table 1. A substantial amount of intuition should be used, and the resulting benefits can be quite large, especially in domains where large numbers of choices are made such as for health and wealth.

Theory: The Role of Sparsity

The two studies sampled above suggest that intuitive, transparent heuristics such as fast-and-frugal trees and single-cue heuristics can be accurate as well. Furthermore, decades of competitions among such simple models and more complex optimization models such as linear regressions (including regularized versions), Bayesian networks, decision trees, random forests, and support vector machines, spread across disciplines such as psychology, economics, engineering design, statistics, and machine learning, have again and again shown that the differences in predictive accuracy between these two model families are not that large, and that each family enjoys a region of superior performance. In other words, heuristics can be *robust*.

For example, in a book authored by an interdisciplinary team including psychologists, machine learning specialists, and workers in behavioral OR (Katsikopoulos et al., 2020), my co-authors and I found that, over 64 classification studies, the average *out of sample* accuracy of fast-and-frugal trees and *tallying* (i.e.,

Table 1 Summary of empirical results on intuition in the 'optimal' mix of intuition and analysis, for a set of interrelated decision tasks (adapted from Katsikopoulos et al., 2022); see text for details

Dataset	Prevalence of 'optimal' positive proportion of intuition (%)	'Optimal' proportion of intuition (%)	Accuracy benefit of 'optimal' mix over analysis alone (%)
Synthetic	95	52	24
Wimbledon	100	36	3
King's fund	48	25	8

a linear model that weights each predictor by one) lagged by just 0.5% from classification and regression trees—79.1% for both heuristics vs. 79.6% for the more complex model. Note that the book also provides an array of examples where heuristics were consistently more accurate in *out of population* tasks. How come? Are there theoretical explanations for such results?

In many ways, this is an open research problem, but we also have some quite satisfactory answers (for reviews, see for example Martignon & Hoffrage, 2002 and Katsikopoulos et al., 2018). A good one-word answer is *sparsity*. A model is sparse if only a (very) small proportion of its parameters are different from zero, and thus only a (very) small proportion of attributes are used. For example, regularization techniques push regressions towards sparsity. It is well known that the right kind of sparsity can make a model more predictively accurate because it does not use unnecessary parameters to fit data in the training sample and overfit in the training set (Geman et al., 1992; Rudin, 2019).

The fast-and-frugal tree of Fig. 1 is a sparse version of the full-blown decision trees that could be constructed by relaxing the constraint that after each question an exit is always possible, and having the same three attributes. Tallying is also sparse. And the recognition heuristic is as sparse as they come. While there is consensus that such transparent models can also be accurate, there are more than one approaches to deriving them. For example, Bertsimas et al. (2019) and Rudin (2019) suggest that sparse models be derived as solutions to carefully crafted optimization problems, whereas workers in the fast-and-frugal heuristics tradition have set up such models by first deeply observing human decision making (Gigerenzer et al., 2011; Gigerenzer, 2022; Katsikopoulos et al., 2020).

Second Tool: Rich and Coherent Narratives

Concerns about the over-mathematization of OR are recurrent (Ackoff, 1979; Rosenhead & Mingers, 2001; Mingers, 2011). John Kay and Mervyn King embark on a similar exercise for economics and finance, and more generally about decisions under uncertainty, and provide an alternative to building complex mathematical models to support such decisions.

Among other models, these authors take on the popular *value at risk* (VaR) models, used for risk management in banks. The objective of the VaR approach is to compute the monetary amount that an investment will lose at most over a specified period of time and with an acceptable probability. For example, one may compute that a security will lose at most 6% of its value over a day with a probability of 95%. Such computations are meant to provide some ascertainment about the consequences of worst-case scenarios. The idea is to manage risk by predicting it.

Of course, as financial crises like the 2008 Great Recession have demonstrated, it is very challenging, to say the least, to predict economic developments. Why? Approaches such as VaR make simplifying assumptions that do not hold in practice—such as stationarity: the future will, in a probabilistic sense, be like the past—and often require much more and much better data than is available. As Kay and King point out (2020, pp. 366–367):

> But how were the crucial parameters—the means, variances and covariances—of the returns on these portfolios to be determined? The only possible answer was to look to historic data series. Thus an assumption of stationarity was built into the modeling. Of course, these historic data series were of necessity drawn from a period in which the banks that provided the data had not suffered crippling losses. So they were derived in a way which almost inevitably underestimated the variances of the underlying probability distribution.

Such effects show that over-mathematized approaches can provide a false sense of stability, with devastating consequences (legendary investor Warren Buffet has called them *weapons of mass destruction*; for more discussion see Katsikopoulos et al., 2020). For instance, asset management company Northern Rock collapsed even though until the day it ran out of money, quantitative risk assessment instruments suggested that it was well capitalized. Former trader and subsequent best-selling author Nassim Taleb (2007, 2020) has been a vehement critic of approaches such as VaR, and has consistently advocated for simple, robust principles such as making sure that bankers have "skin in the game". There are parallels between such principles and fast-and-frugal heuristics, but it is important to note that Taleb does not propose models. Similarly, John Kay and Mervyn King embrace a qualitative approach.

Instead of indulging in computing what might actually be un-computable (such as probabilistic risks), and blindly trusting the results, Kay and King insist that it is much more reasonable to ask a simple question: *What is going on here?* They draw from their extensive experience, and put forth the argument that deep reflection should precede modeling, and, often in the messy real world of high stakes, actually replace it. Crucially, individual reflection should be coupled with group discussion, and lots of it. In an insightful paragraph, Kay and King (2020, pp. 185–186) juxtapose decisions about health and wealth:

> Jerome Groopman, writer and practising physician, has attempted to discover *How Doctors Think* in a book with that title. Groopman describes mistakes he and his colleagues have made in diagnosis, attributing many to the standard list of 'biases' familiar to readers of behavioral economics. But most are in fact the result of excessive attention to prior probabilities – 'he looked healthy when he walked into the surgery', 'there is a lot of it about', 'most of my patients with symptom x have disease y'. The good doctor listens, tests, asks questions, and only then arrives at a provisional diagnosis, treading a fine line between correctly identifying the symptoms which support a provisional diagnosis and being too quick to identify what he or she expects to find. That is why good doctors discuss difficult cases with their colleagues, and many groups of clinicians institutionalize that practice.

When the Bank of England's monetary policy committee members discuss "what is going on here", they ponder *rich* questions such as how would a particular setting of the interest rate affect market sentiment and financial investment, and then they decide and act on the basis of this discussion. Now, richness does not suffice for a narrative to qualify as effective. When a team led by Timo Ehrig interviewed investment and central bankers about how they communicate, it was found that winning narratives must also be *coherent*. Proposed decisions are scrutinized for their reasoning, as the following quote from a senior economist at a central bank illustrates (Ehrig et al., 2021, p. 1757):

> [The first] story predicts that by the end of [the year], inflation is back to under 2%, the second story was that inflation will be closer to 3%, […] the first story was that the significant slack in labor market should put pay pressure down and this should lead to low inflation. [the second story was:] If you believe that inflation will be down to 1.8%, then you have to believe that other components in the consumer basket will go down by unusual amounts.

We have now completed our brief tour of simple tools for analyzing decisions under uncertainty. The tools are alternatives to standard decision analysis, including its heretic versions. These tools of the heathens draw from the behavioral sciences, and might be unknown to workers in the management sciences and hard OR, as well as soft and behavioral OR, including this book's proposal for behavioral decision analysis. Can they be integrated with the mainstream? If yes, how? The next, concluding section of the chapter offers some thoughts.

Ways Forward

The importance, or even the necessity, of reflection and discussion in decision analysis has not escaped OR theory and practice. For example, there is work on how decision analysis can be married with scenario-based planning (Montibeller et al., 2006; Montibeller & Franco, 2011). The whole, quite influential, approach of facilitated modeling (Franco & Montibeller, 2010) is a broader conception of the same idea. In such approaches, narratives support and make quantitative modeling more convincing and useful. It seems to me that what this chapter's heathen tools might naturally lead to is the reverse relationship: *Quantitative modeling supports and makes narratives more convincing and useful.* Simple, yet precise, models such as heuristics à la Gigerenzer can make the kind of narratives put forth by King and Kay richer, more coherent, and ultimately more convincing and useful.

Such relationships could articulate and push forward a new paradigm in behavioral decision analysis. In old-time religion, heretic, or cult decision analysis paradigms, human behavior is often viewed as something to control, improve, or even eliminate. In this chapter's heathen decision analysis paradigm, human behavior can lead to transparent and accurate heuristics, which in turn can lead to narratives that put decision analysts and decision makers on the same page, and also bring success. This chapter would have served its purpose if it inspired more research, on the blackboard and on the job, in developing heathen decision analysis.

Other heathen decision analysis paradigms can exist too, and in fact already do exist, although less in OR. In engineering and product design, Pugh's (1990) convergence process continues to have strong appeal and enjoy considerable success. The late Don Clausing and I had begun to draw parallels between such methods and fast-and-frugal heuristics (Clausing & Katsikopoulos, 2008), but a lot remains to be done.

And what about soft and behavioral OR? Is there room for heathens there? I said in the Introduction that Ron Howard would have called those cults. Perhaps it might have been more precise to have said that soft and behavioral OR are quite big and broad, so that there is room for heathens as well. For instance, Jonathan Rosenhead has consistently drawn attention to the importance of robustness in decision making, especially in the face of uncertainty (Rosenhead et al., 1972; Rosenhead, 2002). While Rosenhead did not discuss explicitly heuristics or narratives, there might be such connections lurking.

In conclusion, I am very thankful that Ron Howard offered the incisive metaphor of the old-time religion, heretics, cults, and heathens, around which this chapter was framed. *Oxford Languages* via *Google* seem to suggest that the word 'heathen' is primarily derogatory, expressing how a member of a widely held religion regards someone who does not belong to the religion. But, to continue in the same motif, *to every thing there is a season*; and I would like to think that (behavioral) decision analysis has moved on, and that now the time has come when heathens can contribute to the old-time religion.

References

Ackoff, R. L. (1979). The future of operational research is past. *Journal of Operational Research Society, 30*, 93–104.

Bertsimas, D., Dunn, J., & Mundru, N. (2019). Optimal prescriptive trees. *INFORMS Journal on Optimization, 1*(2), 164–183.

Bowden, M. (2012). *The finish: The killing of Osama bin Laden*. Atlantic Books.

Breiman, L., Friedman, J. H., Olshen, R. A., & Stone, C. J. (1984). *Classification and regression trees*. Chapman and Hall.

Clausing, D., & Katsikopoulos, K. V. (2008). Rationality in systems engineering: Beyond calculation or political action. *Systems Engineering, 11*(4), 309–328.

Ehrig, T., Katsikopoulos, K. V., Jost, J., & Gigerenzer, G. (2021). An exploratory study of heuristics for anticipating prices. *Management Decision, 59*(7), 1750–1761.

Fasolo, B., Reutskaja, E., Dixon, A., & Boyce, T. (2010). Helping patients choose: How to improve the design of comparative scorecards of hospital quality. *Patient Education and Counseling, 78*(3), 344–349.

Franco, L. A., & Montibeller, G. (2010). Facilitated modelling in operational research. *European Journal of Operational Research, 205*(3), 489–500.

Frey, D. D., Herder, P. M., Wijnia, Y., Subrahmanian, E., Katsikopoulos, K. V., & Clausing, D. P. (2009). The Pugh controlled convergence method: Model-based evaluation and implications for design theory. *Research in Engineering Design, 20*(1), 41–58.

Geman, S., Bienenstock, E., & Doursat, R. (1992). Neural networks and the bias/variance dilemma. *Neural Computation, 4*(1), 1–58.

Gigerenzer, G. (2007). *Gut feelings: The intelligence of the unconscious*. Penguin.

Gigerenzer, G. (2022). *How to stay smart in a smart world*. Penguin.

Gigerenzer, G., & Gaissmaier, W. (2011). Heuristic decision making. *Annual Review of Psychology, 62*, 451–482.

Gigerenzer, G., Hertwig, R., & Pachur, T. (Eds.). (2011). *Heuristics: The foundations of adaptive behavior*. Oxford University Press.

Gigerenzer, G., Todd, P. M., & The ABC Research Group. (1999). *Simple heuristics that make us smart*. Oxford University Press.
Goldstein, D. G., & Gigerenzer, G. (2002). Models of ecological rationality: The recognition heuristic. *Psychological Review, 109*(1), 75–90.
Hillier, F. S., & Lieberman, G. J. (2001). *Introduction to operations research*. McGraw Hill.
Howard, R. A. (1992). Heathens, heretics, and cults: The religious spectrum of decision aiding. *Interfaces, 22*(6), 15–27.
Kahneman, D. (2011). *Thinking, fast and slow*. Macmillan.
Katsikopoulos, K. V. (2011). Psychological heuristics for making inferences: Definition, performance, and the emerging theory and practice. *Decision Analysis, 8*(1), 10–29.
Katsikopoulos, K. V. (2016). Behavior with models: The role of psychological heuristics in operational research. In *Behavioral operational research* (pp. 27–45). Palgrave Macmillan.
Katsikopoulos, K. V., Durbach, I. N., & Stewart, T. J. (2018). When should we use simple decision models? A synthesis of various research strands. *Omega: The International Journal of Management Science, 81*, 17–25.
Katsikopoulos, K. V. (2023). *Cognitive operations: Models that open the black box and predict our decisions*. Palgrave Macmillan.
Katsikopoulos, K. V., Egozcue, M., & Garcia, L. F. (2022). A simple model for mixing intuition and analysis. *European Journal of Operational Research, 303*(2), 779–789.
Katsikopoulos, K. V., Şimşek, Ö., Buckmann, M., & Gigerenzer, G. (2020). *Classification in the wild: The science and art of transparent decision making*. MIT Press.
Kay, J. A., & King, M. A. (2020). *Radical uncertainty. Decision-making beyond the numbers*. Bridge Street Press.
Keller, N., & Katsikopoulos, K. V. (2016). On the role of psychological heuristics in operational research; and a demonstration in military stability operations. *European Journal of Operational Research, 249*(3), 1063–1073.
Klein, G. (2015). A naturalistic decision making perspective on studying intuitive decision making. *Journal of Applied Research in Memory and Cognition, 4*(3), 164–168.
Knight, F. H. (1921). *Risk, uncertainty and profit*. Houghton Mifflin.
Koopman, B. O. (1977). Intuition in mathematical operations research. *Operations Research, 25*(2), 189–206.
Kunc, M., Malpass, J., & White, L. (Eds.). (2016). *Behavioral operational research: Theory, methodology and practice*. Springer.
Martignon, L., & Hoffrage, U. (2002). Fast, frugal, and fit: Simple heuristics for paired comparison. *Theory and Decision, 52*(1), 29–71.
Martignon, L., Katsikopoulos, K. V., & Woike, J. K. (2008). Categorization with limited resources: A family of simple heuristics. *Journal of Mathematical Psychology, 52*(6), 352–361.
Matheson, J. E., & Winkler, R. L. (1976). Scoring rules for continuous probability distributions. *Management Science, 22*(10), 1087–1096.
Mingers, J. (2011). Soft OR comes of age—But not everywhere! *Omega, 39*(6), 729–741.
Montibeller, G., & Franco, L. A. (2011). Raising the bar: Strategic multi-criteria decision analysis. *Journal of the Operational Research Society, 62*(5), 855–867.
Montibeller, G., Gummer, H., & Tumidei, D. (2006). Combining scenario planning and multi-criteria decision analysis in practice. *Journal of Multi-Criteria Decision Analysis, 14*(1–3), 5–20.
Pugh, S. (1990). *Total design*. Addison-Wesley.
Rosenhead, J. (2002). *Robustness analysis*. Newsletter of the European Working Group.
Rosenhead, J., Elton, M., & Gupta, S. K. (1972). Robustness and optimality as criteria for strategic decisions. *Journal of the Operational Research Society, 23*(4), 413–431.
Rosenhead, J., & Mingers, J. (Eds.). (2001). *Rational analysis for a problematic world revisited: Problem structuring methods for complexity, uncertainty and conflict*. John Wiley and Sons.
Rudin, C. (2019). Stop explaining black box machine learning models for high stakes decisions and use interpretable models instead. *Nature Machine Intelligence, 1*(5), 206–215.
Saaty, T. (1980). *The analytic hierarchy process*. McGraw-Hill.

Scheibehenne, B., & Bröder, A. (2007). Predicting Wimbledon 2005 tennis results by mere player name recognition. *International Journal of Forecasting, 23*(3), 415–426.
Schneider, W., & Schiffrin, R. M. (1977). Automatic vs controlled processing. *Psychological Review, 84*, 1–64.
Taleb, N. N. (2007). *The black swan: The impact of the highly improbable*. Random house.
Taleb, N. N. (2020). *Skin in the game: Hidden asymmetries in daily life*. Random House Trade Paperbacks.
Tversky, A., & Kahneman, D. (1974). Judgment under uncertainty: Heuristics and biases. *Science, 185*(4157), 1124–1131.
Vicente, K. J. (1999). *Cognitive work analysis: Toward safe, productive, and healthy computer-based work*. CRC Press.
Von Winterfeldt, D., & Edwards, W. (1986). *Decision analysis and behavioral research*. Cambridge University Press.
Ward, S. C., Chapman, C. B., & Klein, J. H. (1991). Theoretical versus applied models: The newsboy problem. *Omega, 19*(4), 197–206.

Should an Analyst Share Calibration Information with Experts?

Saurabh Bansal, Mostafa Sabbaghi, and Rashmi Sharma

Abstract Many times, expert judgment is used in a two-step procedure: (i) obtain judgments for calibration quantities for which true/empirical values are available to calibrate the expert's judgmental errors, and then (ii) obtain judgments for focal quantities (quantities of interest but without historical data), adjust them using the calibration information, and then use the adjusted judgments to assist decision making. In such situations, should a decision analyst share the calibration information with the expert before the expert provides judgments for focal quantities? We answer this question using laboratory experiments. We specifically investigate the role of task complexity, numeracy, and self-awareness on the use of calibration information by the expert. We find that: (a) Expert judgment tends to be of a worse quality as task complexity increases, (b) Calibration feedback does not improve managerial judgments in a less complex task, but it does reduce the bias and (especially) noise in a more complex task, (c) Numeracy does not impact the use of calibration information by experts regardless of task complexity, and (d) Individuals are able to directionally discern whether they are doing well in less complex tasks, but not in more complex tasks. As such these results suggest that when faced with complex tasks experts do benefit from receiving calibration information. However, this benefit comes at the expense of rendering this information inapplicable for the decision analyst to adjust the focal judgments provided by an expert. In contrast, experts do not benefit from receiving calibration information for simple tasks, allowing decision analysts to continue to use the calibration information to adjust managerial judgments.

S. Bansal (✉) · R. Sharma
The Pennsylvania State University, Pennsylvania, PA, USA
e-mail: sub32@psu.edu; ros5253@psu.edu

M. Sabbaghi
The Pennsylvania State University, Pennsylvania, PA, USA

California State University, Sacramento, CA, USA
e-mail: mzs1252@psu.edu

F. M. Federspiel et al. (eds.), *Behavioral Decision Analysis*, International Series in Operations Research & Management Science 350,
https://doi.org/10.1007/978-3-031-44424-1_5

Keywords Expert judgement · Calibration · Task complexity · Numeracy · Self-awareness

Introduction

Consider a manager who provides judgments for business situations under uncertainty, e.g., forecasting demand or prices, determining inventory levels etc. Prior literature suggests a two-step process to obtain and use these judgments effectively (Fig. 1). The first step is a calibration process in which a decision analyst (she) requests a manager or expert (he) to provide judgments for a set of phenomena for which empirical data (for forecasting type judgments) or true values (for problem solving situations) are available. A comparison of managerial judgments with empirical data or true values provides the errors for the calibration quantities. From these judgmental errors the analyst obtains the bias and consistency in the manager's judgments. The bias is the average error in the manager's judgments. Consistency refers to the dispersion in the judgmental errors, with a high variability in the judgmental errors implying a low consistency. Subsequently, in the second step, the decision analyst requests the manager to provide judgments for a second set of quantities, the *focal quantities*, for which historical data are not available. She then uses the information collected during the calibration procedure to process these second set of judgments by (i) debiasing these judgments, and (ii) accounting for consistency. These processed judgments are then used for decision making in situations involving the focal quantities.

Now suppose that the manager requests that he is provided with the outcome of the calibration procedure before he gives his judgments for the focal quantities.

> Should the decision analyst provide this calibration information to the manager?

The manager's request may be driven by pure curiosity or by a belief that this information will help him improve his performance for the focal judgments. The decision analyst, however, would worry about at least three issues that may arise from providing this information to the manager. The first issue is whether the bias in the manager's judgments would indeed reduce after the manager receives the calibration information. The second issue is whether the manager's judgments would exhibit a lower or higher consistency after the feedback. While a manager may anticipate that the calibration information might improve his judgment process, it is also possible that the manager may not be able to carefully revisit, diagnose, and

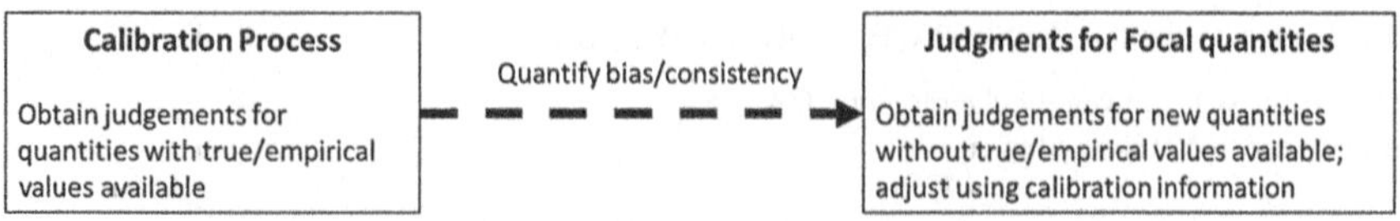

Fig. 1 Two-step process to use expert judgments

improve his judgment process. This may lead to a deterioration rather than an improvement in the consistency of his judgments. A third related issue is whether providing this information will render the calibration information unusable. That is, the bias and consistency information collected during calibration may not continue to be accurate after the manager has access to the calibration information. In this paper we investigate these three issues using laboratory experiments. We next illustrate these issues with an example that also forms the basis of our experimental studies.

Consider the case where the analyst requests the manager to provide judgments, and the firm's profit is a strictly concave function of the manager's judgment. A classical example is that of the newsvendor problem (Petruzzi & Dada, 2010; Whitin, 1955), where the manager chooses an inventory order quantity q under uncertain demand, in order to maximize expected profit. The solid line in Fig. 2(a) illustrates the typical concave nature of the expected profit function $F(q)$ as a function of the inventory level. Suppose that the analyst uses a calibration procedure and obtains the information shown in Fig. 2(a) for three calibration judgments, e.g., suggested inventory levels for three different products with similar cost/revenue profiles. This information shows that the manager's judgments on average exceed the optimal choice and have a spread around the average judgment.

Now suppose that the decision analyst shares this calibration information with the manager, before obtaining the manager's judgments for focal quantities. These focal quantities are inventory levels for new products for which the firm does not have historical demand data, but the manager has a subjective understanding of the likely demand scenarios. Figures 2(b) and 2(c) illustrate two of many possible scenarios of how the manager might adjust his judgments for focal quantities. In both Figs. 2(b) and 2(c), the manager's judgments have become unbiased, and he chooses the optimal quantity on average in both cases. However, the variance in the order quantities is lower in Fig. 2(b) than in Fig. 2(c). As a result, the firm's expected profit is lower in the case with Fig. 2(c). Furthermore, in both instances, the decision analyst should not debias judgments based on the calibration information collected earlier, as it is no longer accurate for focal judgments.

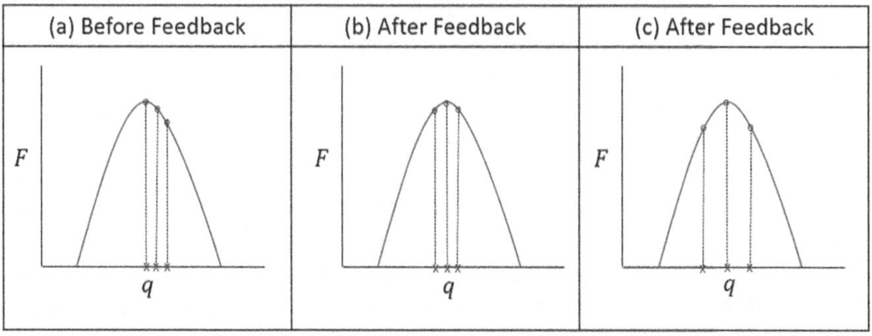

Fig. 2 (**a**) Judgmental error for three calibration quantities, (**b**) Complete bias removal after feedback with small variability, (**c**) Complete bias removal after feedback with large variability

The above example illustrates the importance of studying the impact of providing calibration information to managers. Accordingly, in this chapter we seek to understand the effect of providing calibration information to managers on their subsequent performance where, (i) managers provide quantitative judgments, and (ii) performance is evaluated in terms of both the bias and the consistency in judgments. We will refer to the process of providing the information generated during the calibration process to the manager as *calibration feedback*.

We first focus on understanding the changes in bias and consistency of judgments when calibration feedback is provided. Then, we investigate how the effect of calibration feedback depends on managers' ability (measured as in-task performance before receiving any feedback and numeracy) and the complexity of the decision task. We generate data for these analyses using a laboratory experiment with two well-known decision tasks. The first task is an *Estimation* task, in which subjects observe historical demand data for a product and estimate the value corresponding to a specified percentile of the demand distribution. The second task is an *Optimization* task based on the classical newsvendor problem in which subjects observe historical demand data for a product and determine how much inventory to order given the unit cost and selling price for the product. The optimization task is more complex than the estimation task because it involves performing a tradeoff between too much and too little inventory. As we discuss later, these two tasks are closely connected since the solution to the newsvendor problem is a critical fractile of the demand distribution. We exploit this feature in our experiment design to develop treatments in which normative decisions are identical.

The remainder of this chapter is organized as follows. We first review the related literature, followed by experiment design and protocol, results, and conclusion.

Literature Review

Our focus is related to two streams of literature, (i) calibration of managerial judgments, and (ii) effect of feedback on subsequent performance. Prior literature on calibration of expert judgments is motivated by the notion that experts typically synthesize various phenomena in their domain of expertise and can convert this mental synthesis into numerical estimates in a consistent manner. Expert judgments are naturally useful in contexts where historical data are not available to provide an estimate or a probability distribution of the outcome of an uncertain event. However, it is also important to quantify the performance and trends of these judgments so that they can be used prudently for decision making. To this end, many calibration protocols have been developed. Typically, in these protocols experts provide judgments for quantities for which true or empirical values (of distributions) are available. The protocols vary based on what data are collected during the calibration process and how they are processed. In some instances, it is possible to identify calibration quantities that are in the same domain as the focal quantity. In some other instances, calibration quantities are from related but not the same domain as the focal quantity (Cooke, 1991). The specific judgment sought during calibration can be different based on expert preference, competency, and problem focus. Prior literature has focused on calibrating point judgments for binary variables (Cooke, 1991), point judgments from multiple experts for most likely outcomes with quantities with continuous outcomes (Bansal & Gutierrez, 2020), fractile judgments (Bansal et al., 2017), cumulate probability judgments (Bansal & Palley, 2017), and full probability distributions using a visual tool (Andre, 2016).

A substantial body of literature has also studied the relative performance of these approaches (see, e.g., Abbas et al., 2008; Budescu & Du, 2007). A salient theme in this body of work is that calibration often involves a trusting relationship between the expert and the decision analyst. Identification of factors or protocols that build or hamper this trust, therefore, is naturally useful for decision analysis. In our calibration experiences, experts have almost always been curious about how well they perform during the calibration process. We have typically shared this information with them after obtaining focal judgments. Many times, they try to visit each calibration judgment and conjecture about why their judgmental error was large (or small) for a specific judgment. The frequency of the request received to share the calibration information before they provide the focal judgments is high and suggests a potential avenue to strengthen the relationship between the expert and the analyst.

As such, this calibration information is a type of feedback provided to experts. There is a related body of work that seeks to understand types of feedback and their efficacy on subsequent human judgments. Kluger and DeNisi (1996) provides a meta-analytic review of this literature. The dimensions of feedback studied in this literature include (i) type of feedback (e.g., Doherty & Balzer, 1988; Hammond et al., 1973), (ii) timing of feedback (e.g., Daley & Wang, 2018; Lurie & Swaminathan, 2009), (iii) content of feedback (e.g., Hogarth et al., 1991; Wooten & Ulrich, 2017), and (iv) presentation format of feedback (e.g., Atwater & Brett, 2006; Brutus, 2010). This literature reports mixed findings on the efficacy of feedback.

In terms of type of feedback, this literature studies three main types, namely, outcome feedback, performance feedback, and cognitive feedback (Lawrence et al., 2006). Outcome feedback conveys the outcome of the uncertainty to the decision-maker (e.g., for demand forecasting the outcome feedback consists of the actual demand realization after forecast). Performance feedback involves the communication of metrics that measure performance such as the accuracy and the consistency of the decisions. Cognitive feedback offers information about the process that the manager uses to make the decisions. For example, cognitive feedback in a newsvendor task could include the underage cost implied by the quantity ordered. Of these three types, outcome feedback is generally the least effective because it leads to overreaction on part of a decision maker. Both performance and cognitive feedback tend to be more effective because they tend to induce a stronger cognitive reflection (Hammond et al., 1973; Lawrence et al., 2006). The conventional decision analysis use of expert calibration is consistent with performance feedback, where the decision analyst has the information for the bias and dispersion of the manager's judgments and can share this information with the manager as feedback, before obtaining focal judgments.

A second source of variation in the effectiveness of feedback is the frequency and/or timing of feedback. Chhokar and Wallin (1984) found that changing the frequency at which feedback was provided did not alter the safety performance in a manufacturing plant. More recent literature cautions against providing too frequent feedback as it can lead to an increased emphasis on more recent outcomes which are noisy (Lam et al., 2011; Lurie & Swaminathan, 2009). In the literature on content and specificity of feedback, Goodman et al. (2004) find that more specific feedback leads to less learning. Hogarth et al. (1991) and Wooten and Ulrich (2017) also study the role of specificity and penalty for judgmental errors on the efficacy of feedback.

In the context of this literature, we focus on issues that are of general interest for decision analysts: Does a manager's performance before receiving the feedback and task complexity impact how much he benefits from the calibration information? We measure this benefit both as (i) the average impact on performance consistent with prior literature, and (ii) variability in judgmental error as it directly translates into loss of profit for a firm (as shown in Fig. 2). The variance in managerial decisions can take two forms, namely, heterogeneity and consistency. The focus of this study in on the consistency of decisions. To clarify, suppose that multiple managers make a series of decisions. The variance of these decisions has two components. The first is due to the heterogeneity between managers. The second component, which is the focus of the present study, is the variance in the decisions made by a specific manager. This second form of variance is a measure of the (in)consistency of a manager's decisions.

Experiment

Experiment Design

The experiment had two dimensions with a 2 (*Task*: Estimation, Optimization) by 2 (*Feedback*: Feedback, No Feedback) design. Figure 3 shows this design with the four treatments. In the task dimension, we asked participants to provide their judgments for (i) the 80th quantile of various probability distributions, and (ii) the optimal order quantity for the newsvendor problem when the demand is uncertain, the cost of acquiring one unit is $1 and the selling price is $5. The solution for this newsvendor problem is that an expected profit maximizer should consistently choose the 80th quantile of the demand distribution (see, Petruzzi & Dada, 2010). Therefore, on this dimension the two tasks are normatively equivalent. Behaviorally, the difference between the two tasks is that the Estimation task requires a direct assessment of a specific part of the probability distribution of uncertain demand. In contrast, the Optimization task involves the tradeoff between ordering too much

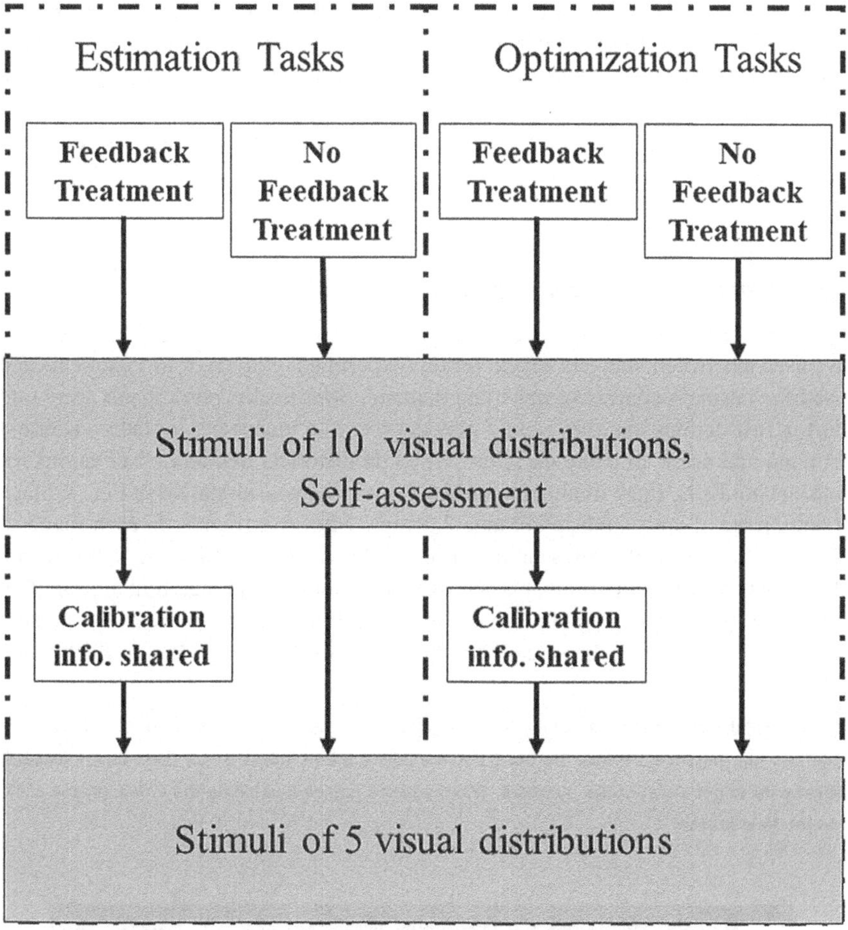

Fig. 3 Experimental design with four treatments

inventory (with the cost of $1 if the demand exceeds supply) and too little inventory (with the loss of net revenue by $4) under uncertain demand. As a result, the Optimization task is more complex when compared to Estimation task. The second difference in these two tasks is the set of recorded behavioral biases in providing these values. An extensive body of prior work suggests a robust presence of a pull to center effect in the newsvendor Optimization task (see, Lau et al., 2014). Due to this effect, human decision makers tend to choose a lower than optimal inventory level when the profit margin exceeds 50%. Behavioral biases have also been documented for uncertainty estimation tasks, with a similar finding that individuals tend to provide lower estimates of quantiles for probability values that are close to one (see, e.g. Gonzalez & Wu, 1999). The results for lower values such as the 80th quantile are not clear.

In the second dimension (*Feedback)* of the experiment, we either provided a participant with feedback on their performance (in "Feedback" treatment) or did not provide this feedback (in "No Feedback" treatment). The specific form of feedback we provided was: (i) a histogram of their judgmental errors, and (ii) the average value of judgmental error, across multiple calibration distributions. More details and experimental protocol follow next.

Experiment Details and Protocol

We used a between-subjects design for this experiment with the four treatments and used the business context of uncertain demand. Specifically, participants were told during instructions that they would play the role of a manager who faces uncertain demand and needs to make decisions based on historical demand observations for various products. Each treatment consisted of two stages, as shown in Fig. 3. Stage 1 comprised of ten rounds, and Stage 2 comprised of five rounds. In each round of Stage 1, a member of the research team played a video projected onto a big screen that was visible to all participants. In the video, numbers in black font appeared on a white background, stayed on screen for 2 s, and then faded, followed by the next number. A snapshot of the screen with this video is provided in Fig. 4. Each video

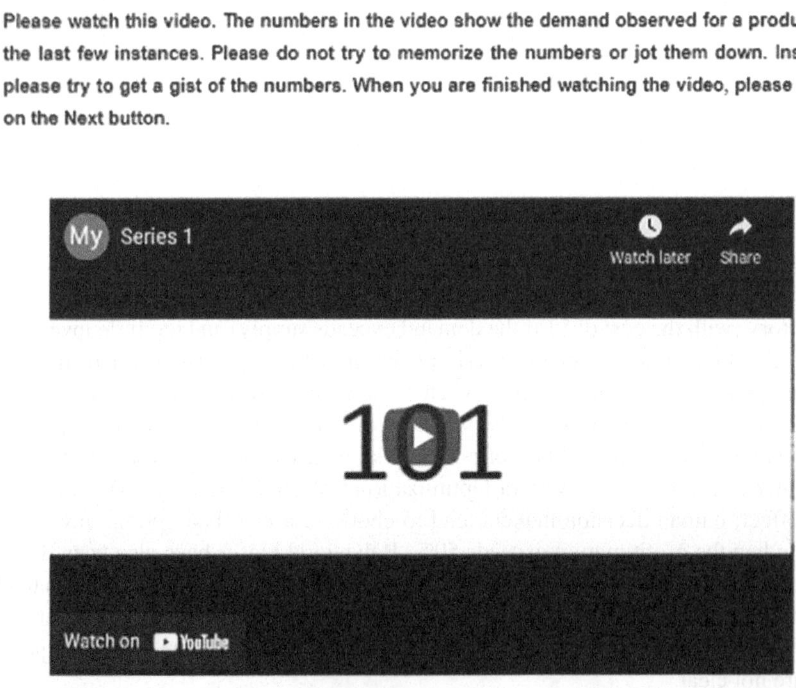

Fig. 4 Videos shown in each round of the experiment

showed 25 numbers. These numbers were random realizations from Normal probability distributions with a specific mean and standard deviation. Participants were told that these numbers represented historical demand scenarios for a product and that their magnitude and variability also represented future outcomes. Prior research such as Haran (2011) has used such videos to study probability elicitation in laboratory experiments.

The participants were encouraged to construct a sense of the distribution in their minds as they watched the video. They were advised against noting down the numbers and in each round the video was played just once to minimize this possibility. After the video ended, participants' screen showed a response box in which they would type their responses. Figure 5 shows this response boxes for the Estimation task. Sessions were separately run for the four treatments, with the same set of 15 videos. In the two treatments with the Estimation task, participants were asked to provide their best judgment for the 80th quantile. In the two treatments with the Optimization task, participants were asked to provide the order quantity that would maximize expected profit. This expected profit was described to them as the quantity that would maximize the profit across all demand scenarios shown in the video when each scenario was equally likely. We also considered alternative stimuli and quantities used in the prior decision analysis literature such as questions about ages of individuals with specific names or local temperatures (Bansal & Palley, 2017). However, the newsvendor task was not intuitive over such quantities and the use of videos appeared to provide a real and fitting context both for Estimation and Optimization tasks.

Stage 2 of a treatment varied based on the Feedback type. In the "Feedback" treatments at the beginning of Stage 2 the participants went through two items. First, we asked them to specify on a Likert scale of 1 to 7, how well they believed they were doing. Second, we provided them with calibration feedback based on their performance in the ten rounds in Stage 1. To determine this feedback to a participant, the embedded code in the experiment software first determined the percentage judgmental error in each round as:

$$\text{Percentage Judgmental Error} = \frac{\text{Response} - \text{True Value}}{\text{True Value}} \text{x} 100$$

The true value here denotes the 80th quantile of the underlying probability distribution for that round. The participant was provided with a histogram representation of the ten judgmental error values from the Stage 1 rounds obtained using this calculation. Figure 6 shows a sample histogram. The top part of the histogram also

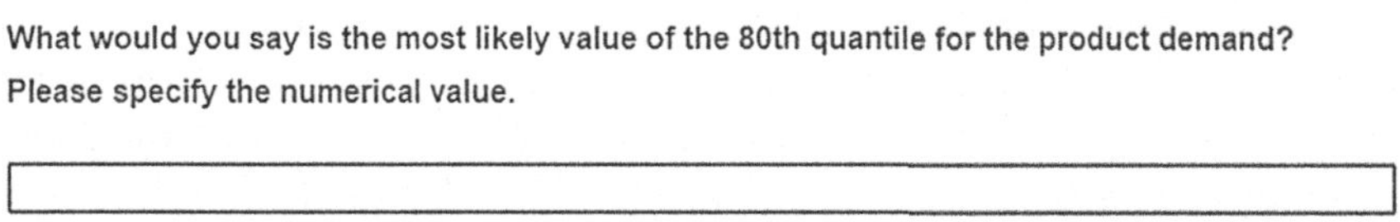

Fig. 5 Screen for participants' response in Estimation Task

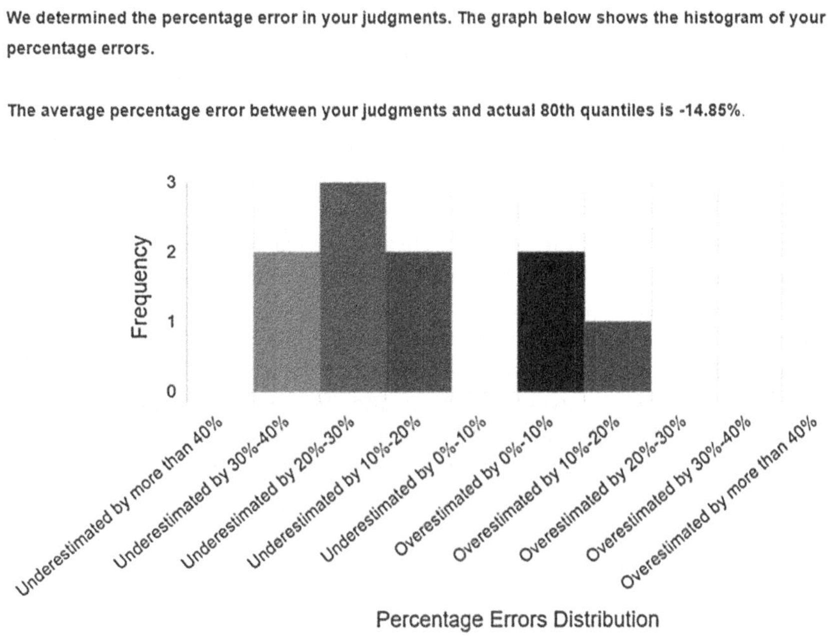

Fig. 6 Calibration feedback provided to participants in the feedback treatments

showed the average judgmental error in Stage 1. Note that in this quantification, a positive error (negative) error represents a response that is higher (lower) than the normative value. Participants in the "Feedback" treatment were explained this detail at the beginning of the experiment. Participants were given 2 min to study and process this calibration feedback on their screen. Subsequently, they provided their responses in five more rounds. In the "No Feedback" treatment participants provided a response to the Likert scale question and then continued to the next five rounds.

In all treatments, at the end of Stage 2, we administered a numeracy questionnaire with seven questions. Table 1 shows these questions. This questionnaire was adopted from Govindarajan (2016) and its use is consistent with the prior research on investigating the impact of numeracy on decision making.

The experiment protocol was as follows. The experiment was conducted at a dedicated behavioral research lab, the LEMA[1]lab, at the Pennsylvania State University. We recruited participants from a pool of self-enrolled students. A majority of the participants in the pool were undergraduate students, with some graduate students and staff members. In each session, participants entered the lab and were seated at individual computers. They were provided with written instructions for their specific treatment. The researcher played a video describing these instructions for that session using a power point presentation. The video also contained payment

[1] Laboratory for Economics, Management and Auctions, www.lema.psu.edu.

Table 1 Numeracy questionnaire

Numeracy score: list of questions
1. Imagine that we flip a fair coin 1000 times. What is your best guess about how many times the coin would come up heads in 1000 flips?
2. In the BIG BUCKS LOTTERY, the chance of winning a $10 prize is 1%. What is your best guess about how many people would win a $10 prize if 1000 people each buy a single ticket to BIG BUCKS?
3. In ACME PUBLISHING SWEEPSTAKES, the chance of winning a car is 1 in 1000. What percent of tickets to ACME PUBLISHING SWEEPSTAKES win a car?
4. Imagine we are throwing a five-sided die 50 times. On average, out of these 50 throws how many times would this five-sided die show an odd number (1, 3 or 5)?
5. Imagine we are throwing a loaded die (6 sides). The probability that the die shows a 6 is twice as high as the probability of each of the other numbers. On average, out of these 70 throws how many times would the die show the number 6?
6. Out of 1000 people in a small town 500 are members of a choir. Out of these 500 members in a choir 100 are men. Out of the 500 inhabitants that are not in a choir 300 are men. What is the probability that a randomly drawn man is a member of the choir? Please indicate the probability in percent
7. In a forest 20% of mushrooms are red, 50% brown and 30% white. A red mushroom is poisonous with a probability of 20%. A mushroom that is not red is poisonous with a probability of 5%. What is the probability that a poisonous mushroom in the forest is red?

details. This video-based instruction format ensured a uniformity of experimental protocol across all sessions. Subsequently, the researcher started the experiment. Participants looked at the main screen for the videos and provided responses on their individual screen. They finished the numeracy questionnaire at the end of the experiment at their own pace. Their payment was composed of two parts: a fixed payment of $10, plus an amount that varied between $0 to $10. To determine this amount, we computed the average percentage judgmental error in the last five rounds for each participant. Each 10% increase in this percentage error reduced the additional payment by $1. The average payment was $17.

Metrics

We use three metrics to analyze the experimental data. Let $\hat{x}^k_{i,j}$ denote the stated response by participant i in round j for treatment $k = \{1,2,3,4\}$ where $k = 1,2,3,4$ represent the treatments: Estimation with Feedback; Estimation with No Feedback; Optimization with feedback; and Optimization with No feedback, respectively. The normative value of the response in round j is denoted as x_j.

The first metric measures the judgmental bias using signed percentage error. For each response $\hat{x}^k_{i,j}$, this metric is determined using the judgmental error $\hat{x}^k_{i,j} - x_j$ as

$$\Delta^k_{i,j} = \frac{\hat{x}^k_{i,j} - x_j}{x_j} \times 100.$$

At the participant level, we denote the average percentage error from Stage 1 (rounds 1–10) and Stage 2 responses (rounds 11–15), as $\bar{\Delta}^k_{i,j\in S_1} = \frac{\sum_{j=1}^{10} \Delta^k_{i,j}}{10}$, and as $\bar{\Delta}^k_{i,j\in S_2} = \frac{\sum_{j=11}^{15} \Delta^k_{i,j}}{5}$ respectively. At the treatment level the average percentage error across all participants from all Stage 1 and Stage 2 responses are equal $\bar{\Delta}^k_{j\in S_1} = \frac{\sum_i \bar{\Delta}^k_{i,j\in S_1}}{I_k}$ and $\bar{\Delta}^k_{j\in S_2} = \frac{\sum_i \bar{\Delta}^k_{i,j\in S_2}}{I_k}$ respectively, where I_k denotes the number of participants in treatment k.

The second metric quantifies the variability in judgmental errors. Judgmental errors in participants responses are composed of two parts:[2] bias and noise. We seek to specifically understand the impact of calibration feedback on the noise. The second metric – the absolute percentage debiased error – measures this noise. To determine this metric, we first compute the debiased judgmental errors. For each response $\hat{x}^k_{i,j}$ we first obtain the absolute percentage debiased error by subtracting the participant specific bias in Stage 1 and Stage 2, as:

$$\Delta^{ku}_{i,j\in S_1} = \left|\Delta^k_{i,j\in S_1} - \bar{\Delta}^k_{i,j\in S_1}\right|, \text{and } \Delta^{ku}_{i,j\in S_2} = \left|\Delta^k_{i,j\in S_2} - \bar{\Delta}^k_{i,j\in S_2}\right|,$$

where u denotes unbiased state of judgmental errors after the debiasing. At the treatment level the average absolute percentage debiased error across from all Stage 1 and Stage 2 responses are $\bar{\Delta}^{ku}_{j\in S_1} = \frac{\sum_i \Delta^{ku}_{i,j\in S_1}}{I_k}$ and $\bar{\Delta}^k_{j\in S_2} = \frac{\sum_i \Delta^{ku}_{i,j\in S_2}}{I_k}$ respectively.

An alternate way to quantify the noise is to measure the variance (or the standard deviation) of the debiased errors. The absolute percentage debiased error provides some natural advantages for our purposes. Absolute errors tend to be more stable and robust. Under most parametric models, absolute errors and variances tend to move in the same direction as data dispersion increases. Finally, in the specific domain of operations management, the quality of managerial forecasts is often measured using a mean absolute percentage error (MAPE), which is similar to the second metric.

The third metric is MAPE. For each response $\hat{x}^k_{i,j}$, this metric is determined as

$$\Delta^{ka}_{i,j} = \# \frac{\hat{x}^k_{i,j} - x_j}{x_j} \# \times 100,$$

where a denotes the absolute error. At participant level, the MAPE from Stage 1 (rounds 1–10) and Stage 2 responses (rounds 11–15) is determined as $\bar{\Delta}^{ka}_{i,j\in S_1} = \frac{\sum_{j=1}^{10} \Delta^{ka}_{i,j}}{10}$, and as $\bar{\Delta}^{ka}_{i,j\in S_2} = \frac{\sum_{j=11}^{15} \Delta^{ka}_{i,j}}{5}$ respectively. At the treatment level the

[2] We ignore the effect of sampling variability for the purposes of this analysis.

MAPE is determined as $\overline{\Delta}^{ka}_{j\in S_1} = \frac{\sum_i \overline{\Delta}^{ka}_{i,j\in S_1}}{I_k}$ and $\overline{\Delta}^{ka}_{j\in S_2} = \frac{\sum_i \overline{\Delta}^{ka}_{i,j\in S_2}}{I_k}$ respectively.

MAPE is used extensively to measure forecast accuracy but has the drawback that it measures the aggregated effect of bias and variability in judgments. In data analysis, we largely rely on the first two metrics as they directly help us understand the impact of calibration feedback on the bias and noise on managerial decisions and engage the third metric for robustness checks.

We denote the Likert scale responses by participants and their numeracy scores as L_i^k and D_i^k, respectively. The numeracy score was determined as the number of correct responses provided by a participant for the seven questions shown in Table 1.

Summary Statistics and Preliminary Analysis

The number of participants in each treatment was: 40 in Estimation with Feedback; 37 in Estimation with No Feedback; 35 in Optimization with Feedback; and 33 in Optimization with No Feedback. All participants provided a complete set of responses. We discarded the responses of three participants after a validation check. A total of 40, 37, 35, 30 participants provided usable responses. Figure 7(a) shows the treatment level performance on the first metric of average percentage error; Fig. 7(b) shows the treatment level performance on the second metric of average absolute percentage debiased error; Fig. 7(c) shows the treatment level values of MAPE. In each Figure, the vertical line shows the 95% confidence intervals.

Focusing on Fig. 7(a), we observe a consistent trend: In each treatment and in each of the two Stages, participants on average reported values that were lower than normative values. This trend is reflected in the negative values of all bars. This trend aligns with prior literature. The forecasting literature has reported that individuals are likely to report a lower quantile than normative values when the requested quantile is to the right of the mode (which in our case of the Normal distribution is the 50th quantile). The newsvendor literature has reported that individuals on average choose a lower (than normative) inventory level when the profit margin exceeds 50%. The Figure also shows that the bias in the optimization task is more acute than the estimation task. Specifically, the confidence intervals for the Optimization treatments, both with and without feedback, do not overlap with the confidence intervals for the Estimation treatments.

At the aggregated level, this visual inspection also suggests that calibration feedback did not improve the bias in a statistically significant manner. We draw this conclusion based on the overlapping confidence intervals for Stage 1 and Stage 2 rounds, within the two treatments: Estimation with Feedback, and Optimization with Feedback. We also observe in the Figure that there was no difference in performance in Stage 1 of the two Estimation treatments; and the two Optimization treatments. This result suggests that there was no systematic difference between the participants' responses for Stage 1 questions of the two Estimation treatments; and

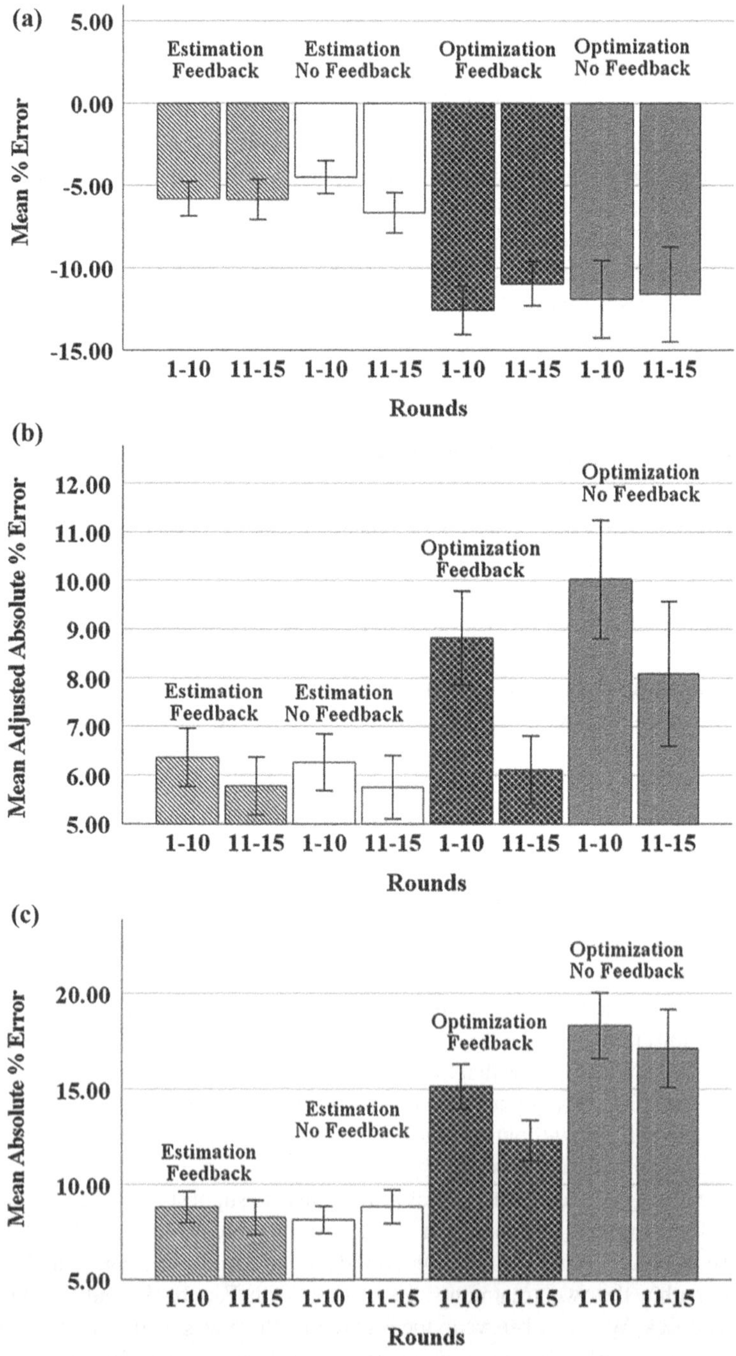

Fig. 7 (**a**) Summary of average percentage errors, (**b**) Summary of average absolute debiased percentage error, (**c**) Summary of average absolute percentage error

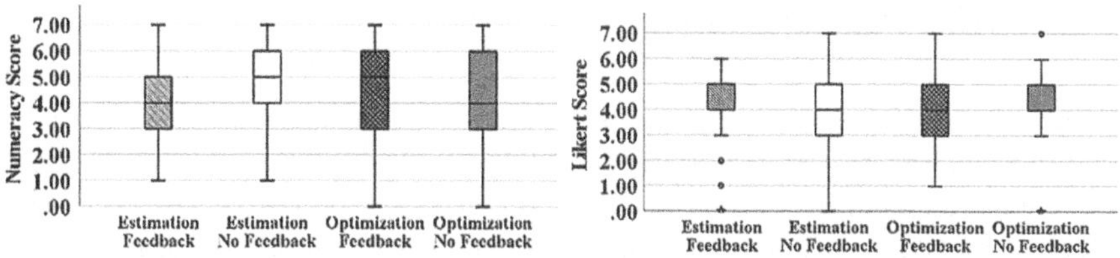

Fig. 8 (**a**) Numeracy scores in four treatments, (**b**) Self-assessment scores in the four treatments

of the two Optimization treatments. Any differences in their performance in Stage 2 questions are therefore attributable to role of task complexity and calibration feedback.

Figure 7(b) provides a complementary perspective based on noise in the judgments. In general, the noise in Stage 1 in the two Optimization treatments was statistically higher than in the two Estimation treatments. This difference in performance due to task complexity is consistent with the observation above for the bias. As such, this difference confirms that the participants' performance was worse in the Optimization task. The Figure also shows that the noise level did not change after calibration in the Estimation task. Specifically, the noise levels in the Stages 1 and 2 in each of the two Estimation treatments are not statistically different. They are also not different between the two treatments. The two Optimization treatments present a contrasting picture. The average noise in Stage 1 of the two treatments is statistically similar. However, the noise in Stage 2 rounds decreases significantly when calibration feedback is provided. Infact, the noise in rounds 11–15 in the treatment Optimization with Feedback reduces to the levels observed in the two Estimation treatments.

Figure 7(c) provides a confirmation to these general trends. The MAPE for the two Estimation treatments is consistently lower than the Optimization treatments. Within the Estimation treatments, the average performance before and after calibration feedback is not statistically different. Within the Optimization treatments, the performance after calibration feedback is clearly better as shown by a statistically lower MAPE in the Stage 2 rounds in the treatment Optimization with feedback.

Figures 8(a) and (b) show the Likert scores and numeracy scores for the four treatments, respectively. They show overlapping scores on numeracy and self-assessment for the participants in the four treatments showing no substantial differences in the participants in the four treatments on these dimensions.

Detailed Analysis and Results

We next answer specific questions regarding the impact of various factors on participants' performance and quantify these effects, using econometric models.

Does Task Complexity Matter?

In order to determine whether complexity impacted participants' judgments, we ran two models. The first mixed-effects model maps into Fig. 7(a) and regresses the percentage judgmental error in participants' responses on (i) the task-feedback-Stage combination, (ii) possible learning effects, while controlling for participant level random effects:

$$\text{Model}(\text{A}): \quad \Delta_{i,j}^{k} = \beta_0 + (\beta_1 + \gamma_{1i})t + \beta_2(\textbf{Task;Feedback;Stage}) + \gamma_{0i} + \epsilon_{i,j}$$

In this equation, β_0 denotes the constant; $\beta_1 + \gamma_{1i}$ denote the aggregated learning effects; $\boldsymbol{\beta}_2$ denotes the vector of task-feedback-Stage combinations; γ_{0i} denotes the participant level random effects, and $\epsilon_{i,j}$ is the noise. For learning effects, we use the superlinear form $t = \sqrt{j}$ representing a tapering effect of learning. We use the word "learning" to denote a potential improvement in the quality of responses on account of practice, better focus, and other such factors during the experiment. The vector $\boldsymbol{\beta}_2$ contains seven binary (dummy) variables. Each of the four treatments has two Stages: Stage 1 and Stage 2. A response in the experimental data can belong to any of these eight categories. In our analysis we use the category: Estimation-Feedback-Stage 1 to be the base dummy variable. Seven dummy variables capture the marginal impact of each of the remaining seven categories.

The second mixed-effects model maps into Fig. 7(b), and it regresses the absolute debiased percentage errors on the same set of independent variables. The equation is:

$$\text{Model}(\text{B}): \quad \Delta_{i,j}^{ku} = \beta_0' + (\beta_1' + \gamma_{1i}')t + \beta_2'(\textbf{Task;Feedback;Stage}) + \gamma_{0i}' + \epsilon_{ij}'$$

with a similar interpretation as above.

Table 2 shows the estimation results of both models. To study the effect of complexity alone, we focus on the base dummy variable and the three Stage 1 dummy variables. Focusing on Model (A) we observe that the coefficient for the dummy variable for the Estimation task (Estimation-Feedback-Stage 1) is not statistically significant. In contrast, the coefficients for each of the two dummy variables for the Optimization tasks (Optimization-No Feedback-Stage 1 and Optimization-Feedback-Stage 1) are statistically significant at 1% level. This trend suggests that participants' performance in the optimization task, on average, was worse than in the Estimation task. When compared to the Stage 1 responses in the Estimation task, their responses had a higher bias. They underestimated the normative value by an additional 6.850% to 7.769%. Focusing on Model (B) we observe an identical trend. On average, the variability in the participants' decision was higher in the optimization treatments by 2.722% to 3.881%. We also ran alternate models, e.g., with fixed effects only, with different level of aggregations, and obtained similar trends. This analysis shows that task complexity has a detrimental effect on managerial decisions. We conclude:

Table 2 Results for impact of complexity and feedback on performance

	Model (A)	Model (B)
Intercept	−2.967 (1.754)	5.092*** (0.907)
Feedback in context		
Estimation-no feedback-stage 1	–	–
Estimation-no feedback-stage 2	−1.388 (1.026)	−1.156 (0.667)
Estimation-feedback-stage 1	−1.293 (2.134)	0.157 (0.955)
Estimation-feedback-stage 2	−0.553 (2.279)	−1.086 (1.028)
Optimization-NoFeedback-stage 1	−6.850** (2.303)	3.881*** (1.032)
Optimization-NoFeedback-stage 2	−5.713* (2.463)	1.237 (1.102)
Optimization-feedback-stage 1	−7.769*** (2.206)	2.722** (0.987)
Optimization-feedback-stage 2	−4.832* (2.359)	−0.672 (1.060)
Learning		
Adjusted round	−0.735 (0.389)	0.489 (0.249)
Conditional R^2	0.503	0.275

"-" indicates the reference category for each of the dummy variables. Significance at the 5%, 1%, and 0.1% levels is indicated by *, **, and ***, respectively

A higher decision complexity leads to judgmental errors with a higher bias and a higher variability.

Does Feedback Improve Performance?

We next seek to understand if calibration feedback improves the quality of focal judgments that were obtained in Stage 2. Focusing on the bias, we consider the results in Model (A). In the estimation task, the coefficients for Estimation-Feedback-Stage 1 and Estimation-Feedback-Stage 2 are −1.293 and −0.553, respectively. The standard deviations for these two coefficients are 2.134 and 2.279 respectively. The correlation coefficient between these estimates is equal to 0.366 (we do not report the complete pairwise correlation matric for brevity). From these values we obtain the p-value of the difference between the two coefficient values (Wald Statistic) to be equal to 0.384, indicating that feedback had no significant impact on the bias in managerial judgments in the Estimation task. The results for the Optimization task point to an opposite direction. Specifically, the dummy variables of Stage 1 and Stage 2 have coefficients of −7.769 and −4.832 respectively, with a correlation coefficient of 0.458. The Wald test provides a p-value of 0.108, suggesting that feedback was somewhat able to reduce the bias in the Optimization task.

Focusing next on the noise in judgmental errors, we consider the results in Model (B). Following a similar process as above, we conclude that feedback does not affect the noise in the judgments for the Estimation task. However, the noise does drop down after feedback in this task in a statistically significant manner at p-value of 1%. In fact, the results for this Model confirm that feedback in the Optimization task reduces the noise to the level of Estimation task. We conclude:

> Calibration feedback does not improve managerial judgments in a less complex task, but it does reduce the bias and (especially) noise in a complex task.

Does Numeracy Matter?

We next focus on understanding the impact of numeracy on performance. To this end, we first investigate if individuals with higher numeracy scores tend to perform better at the two tasks. We ran separate models for the Estimation task and Optimization task in order to identify the differential impact of numeracy on the two tasks. For each of these tasks, the first regression was on the average percentage error from the Stage 1 rounds:

$$\text{Model}(C): \quad \Delta_{i,j}^{k} = \beta_0 + (\beta_1 + \gamma_{1i})t + \beta_2 D_i^k + \gamma_{0i} + \epsilon_{i,j}$$

Note that we combined the data from the two treatments of feedback (Feedback: "Feedback", and "No Feedback"). The results did not change when data were separated by the feedback type. The second regression was on the average absolute debiased percentage error:

$$\text{Model}(D): \quad \Delta_{i,j}^{ku} = \beta_0^{'} + (\beta_1^{'} + \gamma_{1i}^{'})t + \beta_2^{'} D_i^k + \gamma_{0i}^{'} + \epsilon_{ij}^{'}$$

Table 3 Effect of numeracy on estimation tasks

	Model (C)	Model (D)
Intercept	−8.816*** (2.180)	5.953*** (1.081)
Numeracy score	0.697 (0.426)	−0.198 (0.183)
Learning		
Adjusted round	1.002 (0.426)	0.546 (0.295)
Conditional R^2	0.346	0.131

Table 4 Effect of numeracy on optimization tasks

	Model (C)	Model (D)
Intercept	0.698 (3.782)	8.131*** (2.070)
Numeracy score	−0.990 (0.766)	−0.443 (0.365)
Learning		
Adjusted round	−3.711*** (0.777)	1.393** (0.499)
Conditional R^2	0.557	0.260

Table 5 Effect of numeracy on the learning from calibration feedback in estimation task

	Model (E)	Model (F)
Intercept	1.987 (1.723)	1.064 (0.997)
Numeracy score	−0.428 (0.400)	−0.120 (0.232)
Conditional R^2	0.880	0.877

Tables 3 and 4 show the results for the Estimation task and Optimization task respectively. The coefficients of the Numeracy score in these results are statistically insignificant suggesting that Numeracy did not significant impact the quality of the judgments for the two tasks. A Wald test also revealed no systematic differences in the role of Numeracy on the quality of judgments.

Our experimental design also enables us to understand if individuals with a higher numeracy improved their performance using calibration feedback to a greater extent. To understand this feature, we focused only on the two treatments in which calibration feedback was provided. For the Estimation task, we ran the following ordinary least squares model for the average percentage error:

$$\text{Model}(\text{E}): \quad \overline{\Delta}^{k}_{i,j\in S_1} - \overline{\Delta}^{k}_{i,j\in S_2} = \beta_0 + \beta_1 D_i^k + \epsilon_i$$

This model regresses the participant level difference in average percentage error between Stage 1 and Stage 2 on the participant's numeracy score. A similar model is applicable for the variability measure:

$$\text{Model}(\text{F}): \quad \overline{\Delta}^{ku}_{i,j\in S_1} - \overline{\Delta}^{ku}_{i,j\in S_2} = \beta_0' + \beta_1' D_i^k + \epsilon_i'$$

Tables 5 and 6 show the results for the Estimation task and Optimization task respectively. These results show that numeracy did not moderate the effect of participants' learning from the calibration feedback. From this discussion, we conclude:

Numeracy does not impact the use of calibration information by experts, regardless of task complexity.

Table 6 Effect of numeracy on the learning from calibration feedback in optimization task

	Model (E)	Model (F)
Intercept	0.406 (3.340)	0.547 (2.003)
Numeracy score	0.362 (0.691)	0.483 (0.415)
Conditional R^2	0.880	0.881

Table 7 Relationship between self-assessment and actual performance on estimation task

	Model (G)	Model (H)
Intercept	−11.531*** (2.461)	7.098*** (1.181)
Self-awareness	1.368* (0.517)	−0.478* (0.224)
Learning		
Adjusted round	0.270 (0.458)	0.546 (0.299)
Conditional R^2	0.338	0.135

Are Individuals Self-Aware?

Do participants know how well they have done on the calibration tasks? We used an analysis similar to the previous section to understand this feature. For Estimation and Optimization tasks separately, we first regressed the average percentage error from the Stage 1 rounds on the participants' response for their performance:

$$\text{Model}(\text{G}): \quad \Delta_{i,j}^{k} = \beta_0 + (\beta_1 + \gamma_{1i})\text{t} + \beta_2 S_i^k + \gamma_{0i} + \epsilon_{i,j}$$

In the second regression, we used the average absolute debiased percentage error as the dependent variable:

$$\text{Model}(\text{H}): \quad \Delta_{i,j}^{ku} = \beta_0' + (\beta_1' + \gamma_{1i}')t + \beta_2' S_i^k + \gamma_{0i}' + \epsilon_{ij}'$$

Tables 7 and 8 show the results for the Estimation task and Optimization task respectively. Focusing on Table 7 we observe that the coefficients for Self-awareness are marginally significant. On average, on the Estimation task an increase of 1 unit on the Likert scale of self-assessment decreases the bias by 1.368% and the average absolute percentage error by 0.478%. This effect is not present for the Optimization task. We observe in Table 8 that these coefficients are not significant, leading to the conclusion:

> Individuals can directionally discern whether they are doing well in less complex tasks, but not in more complex tasks.

Table 8 Relationship between self-assessment and actual performance on optimization task

	Model (G)	Model (H)
Intercept	2.186 (5.260)	8.337*** (2.693)
Self-awareness	−1.348 (1.151)	−0.496 (0.544)
Learning		
Adjusted round	−3.721*** (0.783)	1.391** (0.499)
Conditional R^2	0.565	0.259

Discussion

In light of the experimental results, we now revisit the three concerns that a decision analyst may have regarding sharing calibration feedback with an expert. First, calibration feedback does not seem to affect the bias in simple tasks such as forecasting and direct estimation. However, experts are able to use the calibration information to reduce their managerial bias for more complex tasks such as optimization. Second, the same affect is present for noise. Calibration feedback helps an expert reduce the noise in her judgments for complex tasks but not simple ones. As such these results suggest that when faced with simple tasks human decision makers are able to focus and reach their cognitive potential. In contrast, when faced with complex tasks they are often more tentative. Calibration feedback provides them with information needed to streamline their thought process, make amends, and improve the quality of decisions.

While these improvements naturally serve an expert or decision maker, they do pose problems to decision analysts. Decision analysts often rely on calibration information to quantify the bias and noise in an expert's decisions. They use this information to systematically adjust or process the expert's decisions for new uncertainties or quantities. Our results suggest that for simple tasks, an analyst can share the calibration information with the expert without rendering the calibration information inapplicable. This is not the case for complex tasks where calibration information is no longer accurate after it has been shared with an expert. For situations where the analyst must share the calibration information with the expert, a better approach might be to adopt a three step process in which, (i) calibration information is collected for a first set of calibration quantities and shared with the expert, (ii) calibration information is collected on a second set of calibration quantities (to enable the expert to react to the calibration information and for the decision analyst to update the calibration information), and (iii) obtain focal judgments and adjust/process them using the second set of calibration information. Future research should quantify the benefits of this three-step approach.

References

Abbas, A. E., Budescu, D. V., Yu, H. T., & Haggerty, R. (2008). A comparison of two probability encoding methods: Fixed probability vs. fixed variable values. *Decision Analysis, 5*(4), 190–202.

Andre, Q. (2016). Distbuilder v 1.1.0. https://doi.org/10.5281/zenodo.166736

Atwater, L., & Brett, J. (2006). Feedback format: Does it influence manager's reactions to feedback? *Journal of Occupational and Organizational Psychology, 79*(4), 517–532.

Bansal, S., & Gutierrez, G. J. (2020). Estimating uncertainties using judgmental forecasts with expert heterogeneity. *Operations Research, 68*(2), 363–380.

Bansal, S., Gutierrez, G. J., & Keiser, J. R. (2017). Using experts' noisy quantile judgments to quantify risks: Theory and application to agribusiness. *Operations Research, 65*(5), 1115–1130.

Bansal, S., & Palley, A. (2017). Is it better to elicit quantile or probability judgments? A comparison of direct and calibrated procedures for estimating a continuous distribution. *A Comp. Direct Calibrated Proced. Estim. a Contin. Distrib. (6 June 2017). Kelley Sch. Bus. Res. Pap. Bloom. Indiana Univ.*, 17–44.

Brutus, S. (2010). Words versus numbers: A theoretical exploration of giving and receiving narrative comments in performance appraisal. *Human Resource Management Review, 20*(2), 144–157.

Budescu, D. V., & Du, N. (2007). Coherence and consistency of investors' probability judgments. *Management Science, 53*(11), 1731–1744.

Chhokar, J. S., & Wallin, J. A. (1984). A field study of the effect of feedback frequency on performance. *The Journal of Applied Psychology, 69*(3), 524.

Cooke, R. (1991). *Experts in uncertainty: Opinion and subjective probability in science*. Oxford University Press on Demand.

Daley, B., & Wang, R. (2018). When to release feedback in a dynamic tournament. *Decision Analysis, 15*(1), 11–26.

Doherty, M. E., & Balzer, W. K. (1988). Cognitive feedback. *Advances in Psychology (Elsevier), 54*, 163–197.

Gonzalez, R., & Wu, G. (1999). On the shape of the probability weighting function. *Cognitive Psychology, 38*(1), 129–166.

Goodman, J. S., Wood, R. E., & Hendrickx, M. (2004). Feedback specificity, exploration, and learning. *The Journal of Applied Psychology, 89*(2), 248.

Govindarajan, S. (2016). *Effects of numeracy and financial literacy on undesirable financial and related academic outcomes in college students*. The University of Texas at Arlington.

Hammond, K. R., Summers, D. A., & Deane, D. H. (1973). Negative effects of outcome-feedback in multiple-cue probability learning. *Organizational Behavior and Human Performance, 9*(1), 30–34.

Haran, U. (2011). *Subjective probability interval estimates: A simple and effective way to reduce overprecision in judgment*. Carnegie Mellon University.

Hogarth, R. M., Gibbs, B. J., McKenzie, C. R., & Marquis, M. A. (1991). Learning from feedback: Exactingness and incentives. *Journal of Experimental Psychology. Learning, Memory, and Cognition, 17*(4), 734.

Kluger, A. N., & DeNisi, A. (1996). The effects of feedback interventions on performance: A historical review, a meta-analysis, and a preliminary feedback intervention theory. *Psychological Bulletin, 119*(2), 254.

Lam, C. F., DeRue, D. S., Karam, E. P., & Hollenbeck, J. R. (2011). The impact of feedback frequency on learning and task performance: Challenging the "more is better" assumption. *Organizational Behavior and Human Decision Processes, 116*(2), 217–228.

Lau, N., Hasija, S., & Bearden, J. N. (2014). Newsvendor pull-to-center reconsidered. *Decision Support Systems, 58*, 68–73.

Lawrence, M., Goodwin, P., O'Connor, M., & Önkal, D. (2006). Judgmental forecasting: A review of progress over the last 25 years. *International Journal of Forecasting, 22*(3), 493–518.

Lurie, N. H., & Swaminathan, J. M. (2009). Is timely information always better? The effect of feedback frequency on decision making. *Organizational Behavior and Human Decisión Processes, 108*(2), 315–329.

Petruzzi, N. C., & Dada, M. (2010). Newsvendor models. In *Wiley encyclopedia of operations research and management science*.

Whitin, T. M. (1955). Inventory control and price theory. *Management Science, 2*(1), 61–68.

Wooten, J. O., & Ulrich, K. T. (2017). Idea generation and the role of feedback: Evidence from field experiments with innovation tournaments. *Production and Operations Management, 26*(1), 80–99.

The Role of Environmental Instability in Detecting and Responding to Signals of Impending Regime Shifts

Sreyaa Guha, Matthias Seifert, and Canan Ulu

Abstract Regime shifts caused by disruptive technologies, legislative changes, pandemics, climate change and terrorist threats affect our lives considerably. In the face of impending change, we are often required to both make accurate predictions about when a regime shift occurs and to change our decisions in response to these shifts. Past research has suggested that people exhibit a systematic bias when it comes to estimating the probability of a regime shift, which is known as the system neglect hypothesis (Massey & Wu, 2005, *Management Science, 51*, 932–947): decision makers primarily react to signals they observe rather than the underlying environmental system that generated the signal. As such, in unstable environments with precise signals, decision makers have been found to exhibit relatively more under-reaction in their probability judgments, whereas in stable environments with noisy signals, they tend to exhibit relatively more overreaction. More recently, Seifert et al. (2023, *Management Science*, in press) demonstrated that under- and overreaction in decisions when there is an impending regime shift can be accurately described as the result of an interplay between prospect theory and system neglect. Specifically, under- and overreaction in pricing decisions mimics under-and overreaction in probability judgments predicted by system neglect only when the decision maker's prior probability of a regime shift is low. In contrast, the effect of system neglect is dampened by changes in the decision makers' risk attitude when prior probabilities are high. In the present chapter we study the extent to which these previously found patterns of under- and overreaction in probability judgments and pricing decisions

S. Guha (✉)
Nova School of Business and Economics, Universidade NOVA de Lisboa, Carcavelos, Lisbon, Portugal
e-mail: sreyaa.guha@novasbe.pt

M. Seifert
Operations & Technology, IE Business School, IE University, Madrid, Spain
e-mail: Matthias.Seifert@ie.edu

C. Ulu
McDonough School of Business, Georgetown University, Washington, DC, USA
e-mail: canan.ulu@georgetown.edu

F. M. Federspiel et al. (eds.), *Behavioral Decision Analysis*, International Series in Operations Research & Management Science 350,
https://doi.org/10.1007/978-3-031-44424-1_6

hold for various levels of environmental instability which go beyond the ones studied in past research. In particular, the authors conduct a laboratory experiment, in which regime shifts occur with various levels of transition probabilities that may vary anywhere between 2% and 98%. The study reveals that underreaction in probability judgments significantly worsens until regime shifts occur with a 50:50 chance, after which the system neglect pattern is mirrored. Furthermore, a series of local regression analyses indicate that under- and overreaction in pricing decisions for low versus high prior probabilities held by the decision makers seems to be generally consistent with previous research as the behavioral pattern persists across various levels of environmental instability.

Keywords System neglect · Probability judgments · Pricing decisions · Overreaction · Change detection

Introduction

Organizations frequently face the challenge of coping with disruptive changes in the environment they operate in. Doing so effectively is complicated, because it requires managers to not only accurately predict the timing of when the shift is likely to occur, but also to decide on an appropriate response to mitigate risk. For example, according to a recent McKinsey survey (Heineke et al., 2021), there exists broad consensus regarding the view that the automotive sector is subject to an impending regime shift towards the commercialization of autonomous vehicles. Technological trends in autonomous driving as well as early pilot projects testing consumer responses to robotaxi services or the efficiency of driverless trucks on selected highways in China and the US signal this potential shift. However, predictions regarding the timing of when autonomous driving may be commercialized at scale pose a difficult task, because of uncertainty regarding the success of necessary technological advancements, the granting of regulatory approvals and the availability of necessary capital. Moreover, this uncertainty creates a complex strategic decision problem as players in the automotive industry need to decide on how to adapt their business processes in order to maintain competitiveness. Another example of a regime shift can be observed on Wall Street: the year 2022 has seen growing concerns among economists and investment professionals about an impending recession. In addition to rising inflation rates caused by the Russia-Ukraine conflict and the Fed's announcement to aggressively increase interest rates, the US government bond market has also shown what is known as a yield curve inversion- a situation where short-term Treasury yields exceed long-term ones- which, in the past, has often signalled an upcoming economic downturn (McKeever, 2022)., While moving into a recession would result in fundamental changes in the decision making of investors and businesses, substantial disagreement persists as to how imminent this regime shift really is and what the appropriate response should be (Rosenbaum, 2022; Winck, 2022).

Examples like these suggest that impending regime shifts are ubiquitous and may result from technological market disruptions, economic downturns, pandemics, regulatory drug approvals, political elections, natural disasters, terrorist threats and more. Importantly, what they have in common is that they pose a fundamental problem to businesses and consumers alike; they typically require decision makers to accurately assess the timing of the shift when only imperfect information is available as well as to effectively act upon such information.

Past research has suggested that people exhibit a systematic bias when it comes to estimating the probability of a regime shift, which is known as the system neglect hypothesis (Massey & Wu, 2005): decision makers primarily react to signals they observe rather than the underlying environmental system that generated the signal. Consequently, in unstable environments (where the transition probability from one regime to the other is high) with precise signals, decision makers tend to underreact in their judgments regarding the likelihood of a regime shift, whereas in stable environments with noisy signals, they overreact. In a similar vein, Kremer et al. (2011) show that forecasters are likely to overreact to demand forecasting errors in relatively stable environments but underreact to errors in relatively unstable environments. The system neglect hypothesis thus lays out a comprehensive account of those biases that individuals are likely to exhibit in their probability judgments when processing signals indicative of regime shifts.

From the perspective of behavioral decision theory, system neglect is grounded in the distinction between the strength and weight of evidence (Griffin & Tversky, 1992). In particular, past research has shown that decision makers differ in their responses to the strength, or magnitude of an observed effect, and to the weight of evidence, which describes the predictive validity or reliability of the information source. For example, participants in coin-flipping experiments systematically overweight the proportion of heads observed in a sequence of coin flips (i.e., the strength of evidence), whereas they tend to underweight the length of the coin flip sequence (i.e., the weight of evidence). One could argue that a sequence of five heads out of six coin tosses would have high strength but a low weight of evidence, whereas a sequence of 40 heads out of 70 flips would be associated with low strength but a high weight of evidence. Based on these findings, Massey and Wu (2005) examined how decision makers respond to the strength and weight of evidence in dynamic environments where there is an impending regime shift. In unstable environments with precise signals, the weight of evidence that is indicative of a regime shift is high. In contrast, in stable environments with noisy signals, the weight of evidence that is indicative of a regime shift is low. Consequently, given the same initial prior beliefs and a signal indicative of a regime shift, the updated belief that the regime shift has occurred should be higher in unstable environments with precise signals than in stable environments with noisy signals. However, individuals behave similarly across these systems in that they do not pay attention to the weight of the signal, which ultimately results in system neglect. When the weight of the evidence is strong (as in unstable environments with precise signals), system neglect predicts relatively more underreaction in probability judgments. However, when the weight of evidence is weak (as in stable environments with noisy signals), system neglect predicts relatively more overreaction in probability judgments. Following Massey and Wu's (2005) work, past research has examined the implications of system neglect for forecasting approaches and applications (Glaser et al., 2007; Watson & Zheng, 2008; Ketter et al., 2009; Kremer et al., 2011; Grushka-Cockayne et al., 2016), Bayesian learning (Li et al., 2014; Moreno & Rosokha, 2016), change detection in nonstationary systems with unknown parameters (Brown & Steyvers, 2009), random support theory (Brenner et al., 2005), strategic interactions in games (Kareev et al., 2014), demand censoring in newsvendor decision making (Rudi & Drake, 2014), narrow bracketing of qualitative judgments (Simonsohn & Gino, 2013) and the value of information (Ambuehl & Li, 2018). Furthermore, it seems to be difficult to overcome the behavioral pattern of under- and overreaction in probability judgments through learning (see, for example, Li et al., 2014). A recent study by Seifert et al. (2023) has focused on the implications of system neglect on pricing decisions in environments with shifting regimes. Using a model that combines predictions from prospect theory and the system neglect hypothesis, the authors compare changes in empirical pricing decisions that occur in response to observing a signal indicative of regime shift to those of a Bayesian risk-neutral agent. The pattern of under- and overreaction found in pricing decisions is consistent with system neglect only when the decision maker's prior probability of a regime shift is low. When the decision maker's prior probability of a regime shift is high, the effect of system neglect is dampened by the changes in the decision maker's risk attitude.

To date, only a few studies have explored the boundaries of under- and overreaction in probability judgments and pricing decisions when there is an impending regime shift that go beyond the experimental parameters used in Massey and Wu's (2005) original work. Among the rare existing studies, Seifert et al. (2023) have varied the role of the decision maker (i.e., buyer versus seller), the decision domain (i.e., gains versus losses) and the desirability of the regime shift (i.e., desirable versus dreaded shifts) and generally found supporting evidence for their predicted behavioral pattern. However, further studies that test the robustness of previously reported findings in regime shift contexts with varying levels of environmental stability have yet to be conducted. Doing so promises to provide further insights into the generalizability and severity of under- and overreaction in regime shift detection.

The objective of the present chapter is to directly address this gap. Using Massey and Wu's (2005) original study context as a starting point, we explore how variations in the likelihood of the regime shift affect subsequent under- and overreaction in probability judgments and pricing decisions when compared to a Bayesian risk-neutral agent.

Method

In the present study, we begin with a systematic analysis of how transition probabilities affect regime shift judgments when maintaining the signal diagnosticity at the levels used by Massey and Wu (2005). Specifically, Massey and Wu (2005) originally tested the system neglect hypothesis with various levels of transition probabilities viz., 2%, 5%, 10% and 20%. By doing so, they interpreted 2% as a low transition probability of shifting from one regime to another and 20% as a high transition probability. Taking this into account, the objective of our study was to extend this setup by considering environments in which transition probabilities were associated with values of 2%, 20%, 50%, 80% and 98%. At the same time, we relied on the same values for signal diagnosticity as in Massey and Wu (2005) such that a ratio of (60%)/(40%) was associated with a low, and (90%)/(10%) with a high level of diagnosticity, respectively. In total, we thus created ten separate experimental conditions; that is, we combined two levels of signal diagnosticity with five levels of transition probability.

In addition, we study whether the desirability of the regime shift influences probability judgments. In particular, we distinguish between dreaded and desirable shifts by manipulating whether the environment transitions into a regime with "Good" or "Bad" outcome characteristics. In the case of a dreaded regime shift, losses are incurred only after the shift has taken place. In contrast, in the case of a desirable regime shift, losses accumulate only prior to the shift. Generally, decision makers can be expected to show patterns of pessimism and optimism in their probabilistic beliefs (e.g. Hartzmark et al., 2021) that could potentially interfere with the effect of system neglect. Consistent with Seifert et al. (2023), we study both probability judgments and pricing decisions of buyers of insurance contracts which would cover any losses incurred in the current period if the prevailing regime was "Bad". In our experiment, decision makers only learn about whether a regime shift has occurred in a given period by observing signals that are either indicative or regime shift or not. However, they are left uncertain about the actual underlying state of the world until probability judgments and pricing decisions for all periods have been elicited.

We rely on the same statistical process outlined in Massey and Wu (2005) to operationalize regime shift environments: In particular, regimes are represented by two urns containing different combinations of red and green balls. The process is illustrated in Fig. 1. Over several rounds, decision makers observe signals generated by one of the two regimes. The system starts in one of the regimes and can switch to the second one with transition probability q, where the second regime represents an absorbing state in that the system remains in that regime until the end. Consistent with Seifert et al. (2023), we study two conditions in the stochastic process: a dreaded shift condition where the system starts in the "Good" regime represented by the Green urn and can switch to the "Bad" regime represented by the Red urn, and a desirable shift condition, where the system starts in the "Bad" regime represented by the Red bin and can switch to the "Good" regime represented by the Green bin.

In each time period, buyers in the experimental insurance market face the decisions depicted in Figs. 2 and 3 when contemplating their pricing judgments for the single-period insurance contract in a given round. In the dreaded shift condition, the probability that the regime has switched (p_t both in Figs. 2 and 3) is equal to the probability that the "Bad" regime prevails whereas in the desirable shift condition

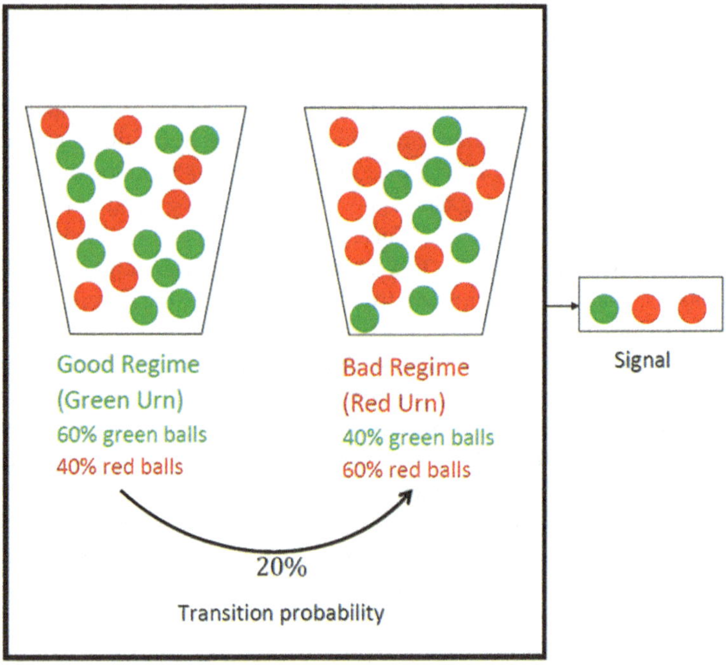

Fig. 1 Statistical process

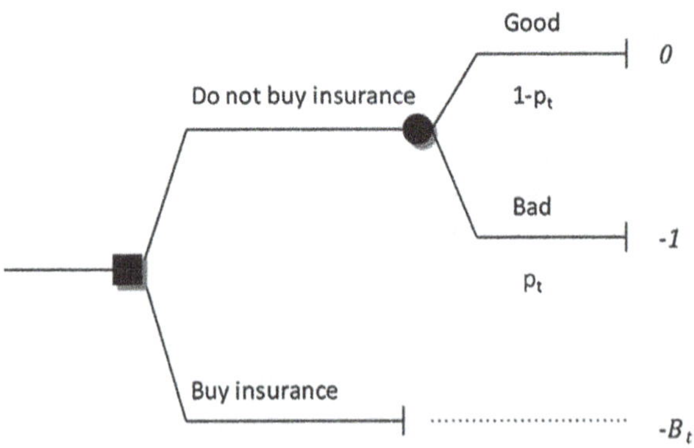

Fig. 2 Insurance buying decision under Dreaded Regime Shift

the probability that the regime has switched is equal to the probability that the "Good" regime prevails.

Given this setup, we consider a lottery with zero loss in the "Good" regime and a sure loss of $1 in the "Bad" regime. Payment B_t in Figs. 2 and 3 denotes the price the decision maker is willing to pay in period t for an insurance contract that will eliminate the risk entirely. Thus, buyers in the insurance market face a lottery in the domain of losses.

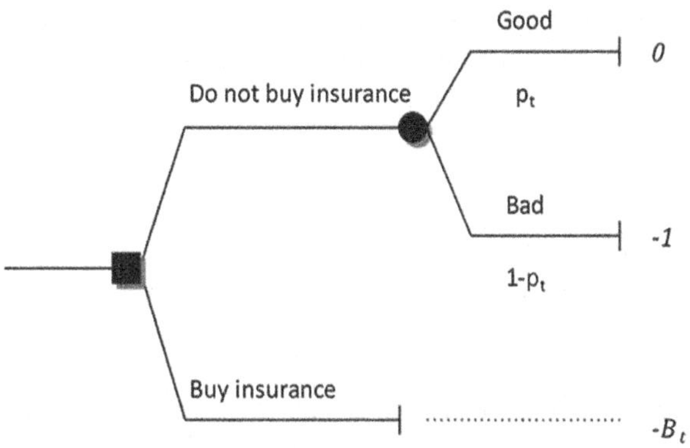

Fig. 3 Insurance buying decision under Desirable Regime Shift

In each period, a ball is sampled with replacement from one of the two regimes; the "Bad" regime produces red balls more often (with probability $p_B > 0.5$) than the "Good" regime (with probability $p_G < 0.5$). As in Massey and Wu (2005), we assume that $p_B = 1 - p_G$. Following this logic, d= $\frac{p_B}{p_G}$ can be interpreted as a measure of signal diagnosticity such that environments with higher values for *d* generate more precise, and thus more informative, signals. Given this setup, decision makers' probability judgment that the regime has switched, p_t^e, and their willingness to pay, B_t^e, can be elicited. Using p_t^e we compute the under- and overreaction in probability judgments as described in Massey and Wu (2005). In particular, our dependent measure compares changes in empirical probability judgments when a signal indicative of regime shift is observed against a normative, Bayesian standard. Furthermore, using both p_t^e and B_t^e, we build a model and compute the under- and overreaction in pricing decisions as a combination of system neglect and change in risk premium. Our measure of under- and overreaction in pricing decisions thereby compares changes in the empirical willingness to pay for an insurance contract that result from observing a signal indicative of regime shift to those that would be made by a Bayesian, risk neutral agent (for a detailed derivation of the model, please see Seifert et al., 2023).

Experiment

For our study we recruited 315 subjects on the online platform Amazon Mechanical Turk. Participants read through the instructions, in which they were informed about both the task as well as the payoff scheme used to determine their final compensation. In the study, we randomly assigned participants to either the dreaded or desirable shift condition, where they remained for the duration of the experiment. Participants provided responses under ten different decision environments, each of which differed in terms of its underlying transition probability of shifting from one regime to another as well as in terms of the diagnosticity of signals. As described above, we chose five different transition probabilities ($q = 2\ \%$, $q = 20\ \%$, $q = 50\ \%$, $q = 80\ \%$ *and* $q = 98\ \%$) and two different levels of signal diagnosticity ($d = \frac{60\%}{40\%}$ and $d = \frac{90\%}{10\%}$). Parameter values underlying each decision environment were displayed on the task screen throughout all rounds. There were 10 rounds in each environment; one signal (i.e., red/green ball) was sampled and shown to participants in each round. Signal and state sequences were randomly generated from the underlying statistical process. In each decision environment buyers were endowed with an initial budget of 100 experimental currency units (ECUs), which they could use to bid for an insurance contract across the 10 rounds. Buyers faced the lotteries shown in Figs. 2 and 3 with the magnitude of loss equal to −10 ECUs. In the instructions, we emphasized that the insurance would only be worth bidding for in case the buyer indeed believed that the observed signal had originated from the "Bad" regime. Participants were informed that any remaining ECUs, after subtracting all insurance purchasing costs as well as any uninsured losses incurred during any round, would be used to calculate their final payoff. At the end of each round, participants obtained information about whether or not they had successfully purchased the insurance but were left uninformed about the underlying state. In every round, the participants started out by observing a signal and subsequently provided a judgment regarding the probability (between 0% and 100%) that the regime had shifted as well as how much they would be willing to pay for the insurance contract (between 0 and 10 ECUs). We employed a BDM mechanism (Becker et al., 1964) to elicit true valuations for the insurance contract. Following this mechanism, a number was randomly drawn from the price list between 0 and 10, which represented the market price for a given round. Any transaction was successful if their willingness to pay was at least as much as the generated market price.

Results

Under- and overreaction in probability judgments: Fig. 4 displays the pattern of under- and overreaction in probability judgments for desirable and dreaded regime shift conditions. Negative values on the y-axis indicate a tendency to underestimate the likelihood of a regime shift in response to observing signals (i.e., underreaction), whereas positive values indicate that decision makers overestimate the probability of a shift when compared to a Bayesian model (i.e., overreaction). Wilcoxon signed-rank tests exhibit significantly more underreaction in unstable environments with precise signals than in stable environments with noisy signals. We studied the probability judgments across ten different environments characterized by five different levels of transition probabilities. Following Massey and Wu (2005), we consider 2% to be representative of a low transition probability (and, hence, stable environment), whereas the remaining probabilities lie above 20% and can therefore be considered as high transition probabilities that are representative of an unstable environment.

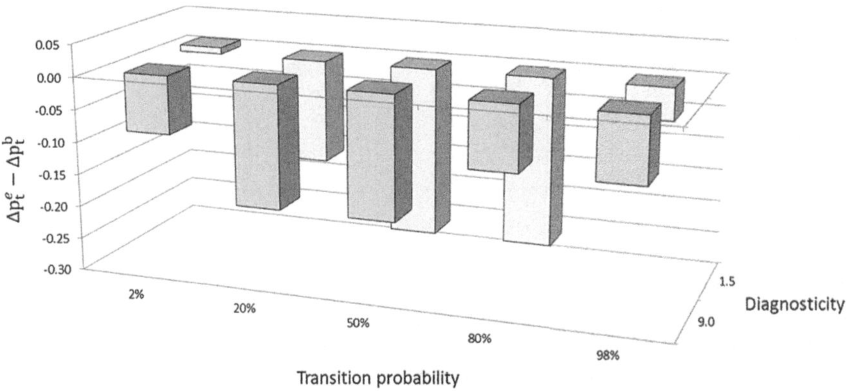

Fig. 4 Median under- and overreaction in probability judgments (y-axis) in the desirable regime shift condition

Our main aim was to explore the extent to which the predictions of the system neglect hypothesis would hold for transition probability that go beyond the values that were originally used in Massey and Wu (2005). Taking this into account, our findings show that for desirable regime shifts, an increase in the transition probability up to a value of 50% results in more underreaction in probability judgments. However, transition probabilities that exceed 50% appear to result in a reversal of the underreaction pattern in that participants' judgments suffered to a lesser extent from an underestimation of the regime shift probability. Specifically, we observe progressively more underreaction for unstable environments, $q = 20\%$ (M = −0.2) and $q = 50\%$ (M = −0.26) with precise signals than in stable environments with noisy signals (M = 0, Kruskal-Wallis chi-squared = 126.78, $p < 0.001$). For the environments with transition probabilities above 50%, the underreaction for unstable environments, $q = 80\%$ (M = −0.19) and $q = 98\%$ (M = −0.1) with precise signals reduces, although it is relatively more than in stable environments with noisy signals (M = 0, Kruskal-Wallis chi-squared = 99.527, $p < 0.001$).

We observe a similar behavioral pattern in the dreaded regime shift condition. In particular, when the transition probability is smaller than 50%, we initially observe relatively more underreaction in unstable environments, $q = 20\%$ (M = −0.19) and $q = 50\%$(M = −0.19) with precise signals than in stable environments with noisy signals (M = 0.01, Kruskal-Wallis chi-squared = 105.45, $p < 0.001$). However, for environments with transition probabilities above 50%, underreaction in probability judgments is substantially reduced for unstable environments, $q = 80\%$ (M = −0.1) and $q = 98\%$(M = −0.1) with precise signals (d = 9), although we observe relatively more underreaction compared to stable environments with noisy signals (M = 0, Kruskal-Wallis chi-squared = 81.594, $p < 0.001$) (Fig. 5).

In addition to studying under- and overreaction in probability judgments, we also examined under- and overreaction in the pricing decisions. For this purpose, we conducted a series of local regression analyses (Loader, 2006) as well as nonparametric tests between regime shift conditions. Further details on this analysis are provided in Seifert et al. (2023). As mentioned above, our measure of under- and

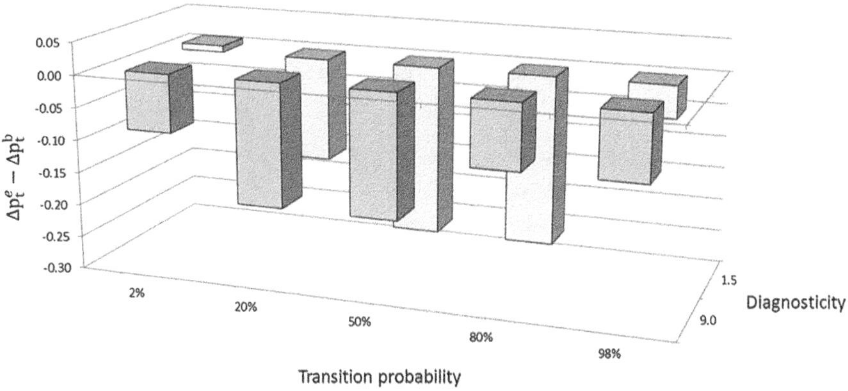

Fig. 5 Median under- and overreaction in probability judgments (y-axis) in the dreaded regime shift condition

overreaction compares changes in the empirical willingness to pay for an insurance contract that result from observing a new signal of regime shift to those that would be made by a Bayesian, risk neutral agent (denoted in the following figures as $\Delta B_t^e - \Delta B_t^b$ on the y-axis).

When plotting our under- and overreaction measure against the prior probability of the decision makers, we obtain a pattern of pricing decisions in which we find relatively more underreaction in insurance pricing decisions in unstable environments with precise signals than in stable environments with noisy signals, particularly when the decision maker's prior probability of a regime shift is low. This prior probability represents the DM's probability judgment regarding the regime shift before observing a new signal. The underreaction in pricing decisions, however, diminishes for higher prior probabilities of regime shifts. Note that in the case of dreaded regime shifts, positive values of $\Delta B_t^e - \Delta B_t^b$ indicate overreaction, whereas negative values indicate underreaction in pricing decisions. The reverse is true for desirable regime shifts.

We find that in environments with precise signals and transition probabilities of 20% and above, the pattern of relative underreaction (i.e., with pronounced underreaction for low prior probabilities) generally persists. This pattern is robust across buyers' insurance pricing decisions in both dreaded and desirable regime shift environments.

Figures 6, 7, 8, 9, 10 show the outcome of our local regression analyses in the case of dreaded regime shift environments. Specifically, they exhibit the pattern of under- and overreaction in buyers' insurance pricing decisions (y-axis) when plotted against various levels of prior probabilities held by the decision makers (x-axis). On the left panel (Fig. 6) we show the under- and overreaction pattern in pricing decisions when the environment is stable (i.e. $q = 2\%$) and signals are noisy. Figs. 7, 8, 9, 10 exhibit the behavioral patterns under various levels of environmental instability i.e., $q = 20\ \%$, $50\ \%$, $80\ \%$ and 98% with precise signals. For all unstable environments with precise signals, we find relative underreaction in pricing

Fig. 6 q = 2%, d = 1.5

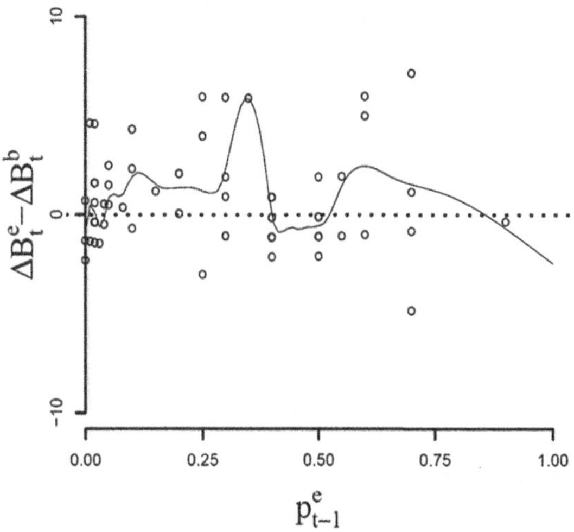

Fig. 7 q = 20%, d = 9

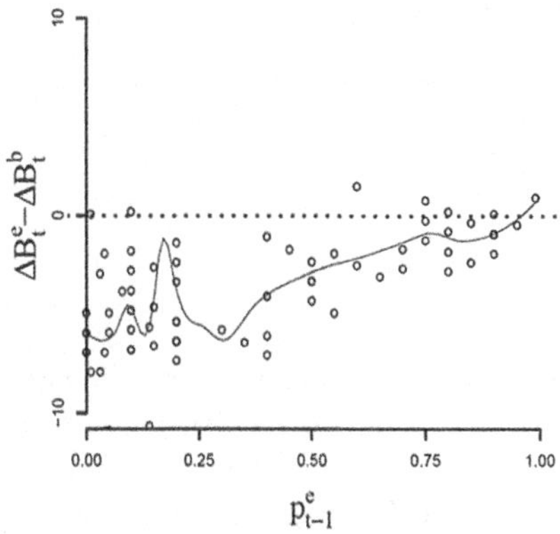

Fig. 8 q = 50%, d = 9

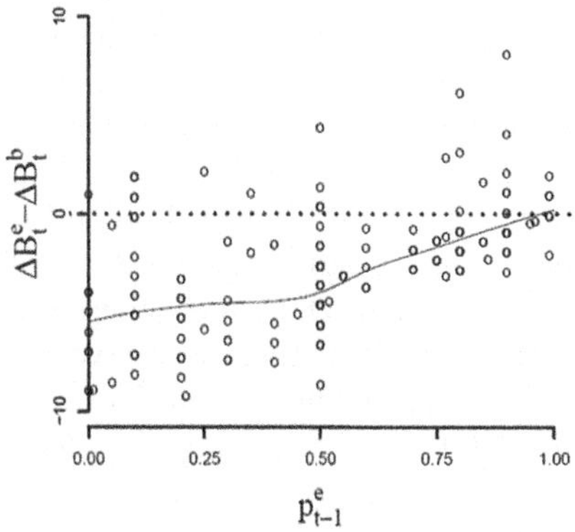

Fig. 9 q = 80%, d = 9

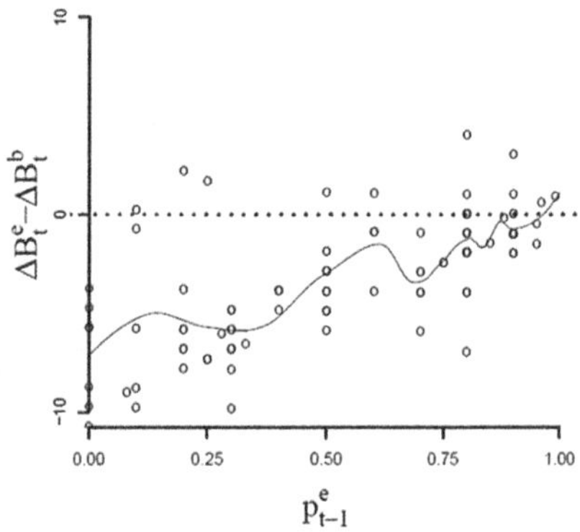

Fig. 10 q = 98%, d = 9

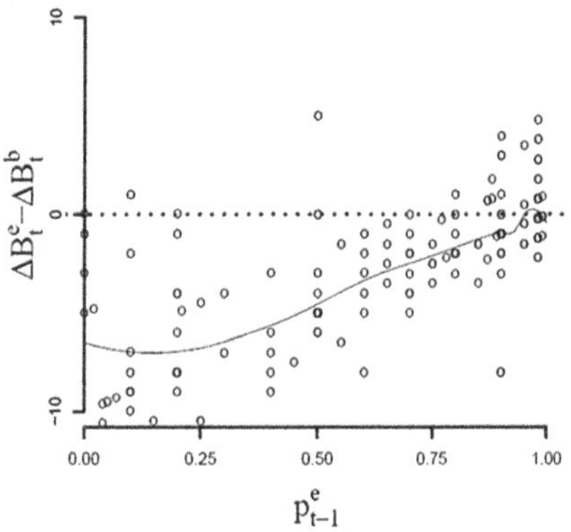

decisions compared to the reaction under a stable environment with precise signals. We next conducted a series of nonparametric tests to support our local regression results. Our results show that compared to a stable environment with noisy signals ($M = -0.12$), there is significantly more underreaction in pricing decisions in the all the unstable environments with precise signals; for $q = 20\%$ ($M = -3.19$, $W = 8977$, $p < 0.001$); $q = 50\%$ ($M = -2.87$, $W = 20108$, $p < 0.001$); $q = 80\%$ ($M = -1.95$, $W = 8781$, $p < 0.001$); $q = 98\%$ ($M = -1.49$, $W = 15998$, $p < 0.001$).

Figures 11, 12, 13, 14, 15 exhibit the behavioral pattern of under- and overreaction in buyers' pricing decisions when the regime shift is desirable. While Fig. 11 exhibits under- and overreaction in pricing decisions when the environment is stable and signals are noisy, Figs. 12, 13, 14, 15 exhibit the behavioral patterns under various levels of environmental instability with precise signals. When the regime shift is desirable, positive values of $\Delta B_t^e - \Delta B_t^b$ indicate underreaction and negative values indicate overreaction (see Seifert et al., 2023 for details). Similar to the dreaded regime shift condition, we observe relative underreaction in pricing decisions for all unstable environments with precise signals; for $q = 20\%$ ($M = 3.35$, $W = 3439$, $p < 0.001$); $q = 50\%$ ($M = -3.68$, $W = 5557$, $p < 0.001$); $q = 80\%$ ($M = 1.95$,

Fig. 11 q = 2%, d = 1.5

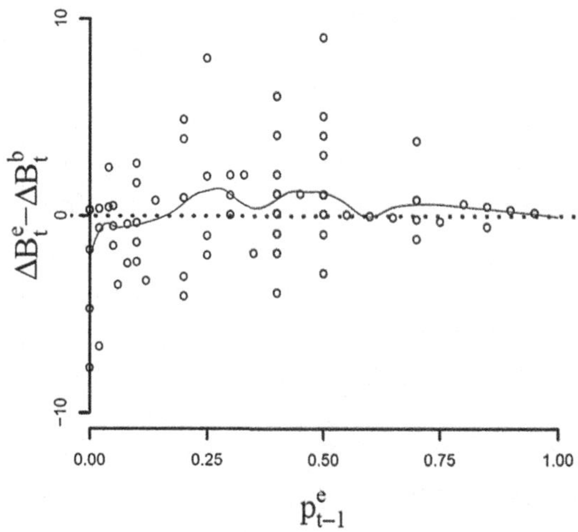

Fig. 12 q = 20%, d = 9

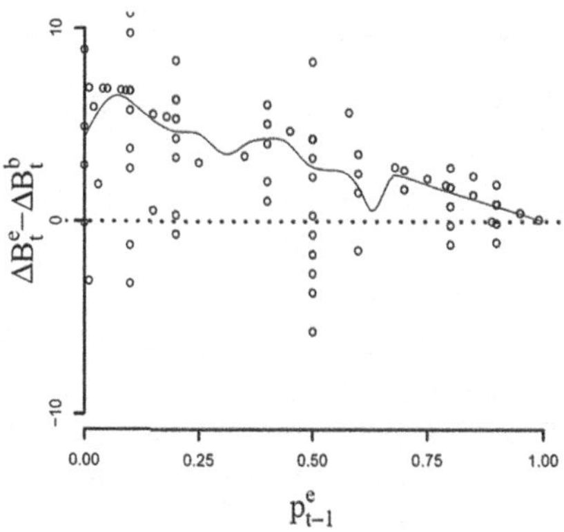

Fig. 13 q = 50%, d = 9

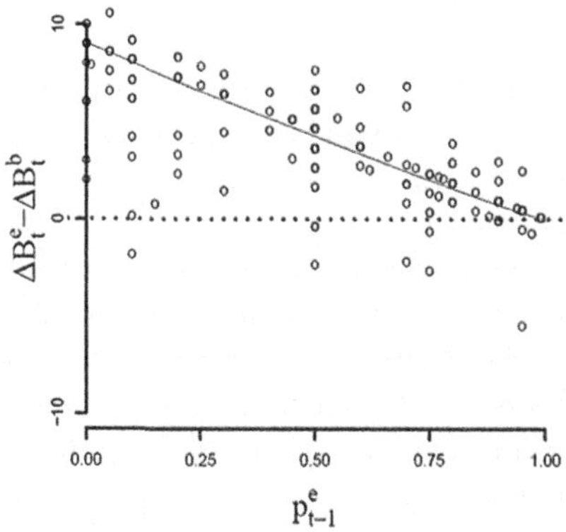

Fig. 14 q = 80%, d = 9

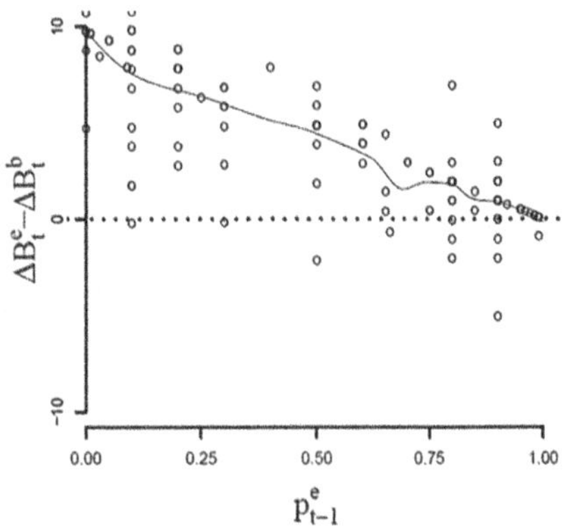

Fig. 15 q = 98%, d = 9

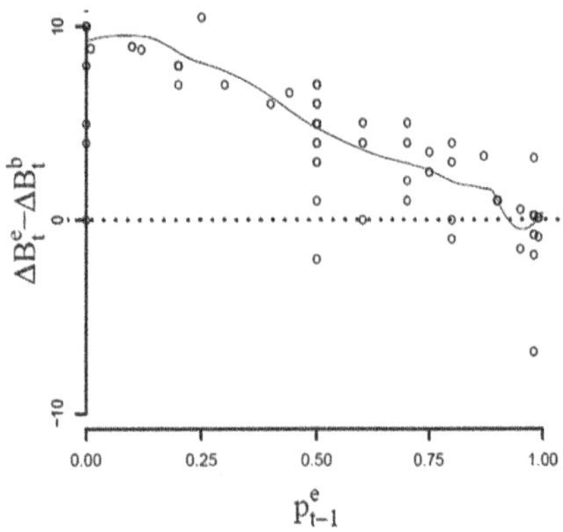

$W = 3791$, $p < 0.001$); $q = 98\%$ ($M = 2.98$, $W = 4375$, $p < 0.001$) compared to that under stable environment with precise signals ($M = 0.29$).

Discussion and Conclusion

In this book chapter, we studied how environmental instability influences probability judgments and decision making in the face of impending regime shifts. Based on the experimental design for studying regime shift environments that was originally adopted by Massey and Wu (2005), we explored the robustness of previously reported under- and overreaction patterns when varying the transition probability underlying the environmental system. Analyzing over 12,000 decisions provided by 315 participants recruited on the online platform Amazon Mechanical Turk, we found that system neglect significantly increases underreaction in probability judgments up to a level at which regime shifts occur with a 50:50 chance. Beyond this point, underreaction in probability judgments begins to decrease and diminishes when the regime changes almost with certainty. The fact that a transition probability of 50% serves as an inflection point as well as the symmetry of the underreaction pattern before and after this point suggest that system neglect affects probability judgments regardless of the order in which the odds of the regime shift are presented (e.g., 40:60 or 60:40). In other words, when detecting regime change, decision makers do not appear to make a cognitive distinction between the focal regime to which the environment shifts and the starting regime when it comes to judging the general probability of change.

In addition to under- and overreaction in probability judgments, we used this setup to study the impact of environmental instability on pricing decisions in experimental insurance markets. Using the same experimental setup as in Seifert et al. (2023), we elicited decision makers' willingness to pay for an insurance that could protect them from losses that could be incurred either before or after the regime shift takes place. Our findings generally provide supporting evidence for the under- and overreaction pattern in pricing decisions that was initially reported in Seifert et al. (2023). Specifically, we show that the desirability of shift from "Good" to "Bad" urn (or vice versa) does not appear to influence the pricing decisions across environments with varying degrees of transition probabilities. Furthermore, our local regression analyses indicate that the magnitude of under- and overreaction that decision makers show when their perceived prior probability of regime shift is low versus high seems to be robust across various levels of environmental instability.

Regime shifts caused by disruptive technologies, legislative changes, pandemics, climate change and terrorist threats affect our lives considerably. In the face of impending change, we are often required to both make accurate predictions about when a regime shift occurs and to change our decisions. Our research provides additional experimental evidence that engaging in these two tasks is not trivial as judgments for both tasks can be systematically flawed. We outline the magnitude of under- and overreaction for various levels of environmental instability, which could be informative for organizations that try to avoid common behavioral pitfalls in the face of impending change.

Acknowledgements This work was funded by Fundação para a Ciência e a Tecnologia (UIDB/00124/2020, UIDP/00124/2020 and Social Sciences DataLab – PINFRA/22209/2016), POR Lisboa and POR Norte (Social Sciences DataLab, PINFRA/22209/2016). Furthermore, it was supported by the Ministerio de Ciencia e Innovación España [10.13039/501100011033, Grants ECO2014-52925-P, PID2019-111512RB-I00-HMDM, and HDL-HS-280218].

References

Ambuehl, S., & Li, S. (2018). Belief updating and the demand for information. *Games and Economic Behavior, 109*, 21–39.

Brenner, L., Griffin, D., & Koehler, D. J. (2005). Modeling patterns of probability calibration with random support theory: Diagnosing case-based judgment. *Organizational Behavior and Human Decision Processes, 97*(1), 64–81.

Brenner, L. A., Griffin, D. W., & Koehler, D. J. (2012). A case-based model of probability and pricing judgments: Biases in buying and selling uncertainty. *Management Science, 58*(1), 159–178.

Brown, S. D., & Steyvers, M. (2009). Detecting and predicting changes. *Cognitive Psychology, 58*(1), 49–67.

Glaser, M., Langer, T., & Weber, M. (2007). On the trend recognition and forecasting ability of professional traders. *Decision Analysis, 4*(4), 176–193.

Griffin, D., & Tversky, A. (1992). The weighing of evidence and the determinants of confidence. *Cognitive Psychology, 24*(3), 411–435.

Grushka-Cockayne, Y., Jose, V. R. R., & Lichtendahl, K. C., Jr. (2016). Ensembles of overfit and overconfident forecasts. *Management Science, 63*(4), 1110–1130.

Hartzmark, S. M., Hirshman, S. D., & Imas, A. (2021). Ownership, learning, and beliefs. *The Quarterly Journal of Economics, 136*(3), 1665–1717.

Heineke, K., Heuss, R., Kelkar, A., & Kellner, M. (2021). *What's next for autonomous vehicles?* McKinsey Center for Future Mobility, McKinsey & Company.

Kareev, Y., Avrahami, J., & Fiedler, K. (2014). Strategic interactions, affective reactions, and fast adaptations. *Journal of Experimental Psychology General, 143*(3), 1112.

Ketter, W., Collins, J., Gini, M., Gupta, A., & Schrater, P. (2009). Detecting and forecasting economic regimes in multi-agent automated exchanges. *Decision Support Systems, 47*(4), 307–318.

Kremer, M., Moritz, B., & Siemsen, E. (2011). Demand forecasting behavior: System neglect and change detection. *Management Science, 57*(10), 1827–1843.

Li, Y., Massey, C., & Wu, G. (2014). Learning to detect change. Chicago Booth School of Business Research Paper, (09-03), Chicago.

Massey, C., & Wu, G. (2005). Detecting regime shifts: The causes of under-and overreaction. *Management Science, 51*(6), 932–947.

McKeever, V. (2022). Is a recession on the way? These unconventional economic indicators may provide some clues. CNBC. https://www.cnbc.com/2022/04/08/recession-signals-these-unusual-indicators-may-be-worth-monitoring.html

Moreno, O. M., & Rosokha, Y. (2016). Learning under compound risk vs. learning under ambiguity: An experiment. *Journal of Risk and Uncertainty, 53*(2–3), 137–162.

Rosenbaum, E. (2022). Main street is convinced that a recession will hit the U.S. economy this year. CNBC. https://www.cnbc.com/2022/05/05/main-street-is-more-sure-than-wall-street-a-recession-is-coming.html

Rudi, N., & Drake, D. (2014). Observation bias: The impact of demand censoring on newsvendor level and adjustment behavior. *Management Science, 60*(5), 1334–1345.

Seifert, M., Ulu, C., & Guha, S. (2023). Decision making under impending regime shifts. *Management Science, 69*(10), 6165–6180.

Simonsohn, U., & Gino, F. (2013). Daily horizons: Evidence of narrow bracketing in judgment from 10 years of MBA admissions interviews. *Psychological Science, 24*(2), 219–224.

Watson, N., & Zheng, Y. S. (2008). Over-reaction to demand changes due to subjective and quantitative forecasting. Working paper, Harvard Business School, Cambridge, MA.

Winck, S. (2022). The next recession isn't here yet. Here's when you should really start worrying about the economy. Business Insider. https://www.businessinsider.com/economic-outlook-recession-odds-when-start-worrying-indicators-spending-employment-2022-5

The Social Psychology of the Wisdom of Crowds (with a New Section on Recent Advances)

Richard P. Larrick, Albert E. Mannes, and Jack B. Soll

Abstract This chapter reviews the "wisdom of crowds" through the lens of social psychology. Early research on social influence cast a pessimistic light on whether collectives can be wise. The famous Asch (1955) studies left the impression that collective judgment is easily harmed since individuals conform too readily to what others say. Research on the wisdom of crowds, of course, demonstrates the benefits of collective judgment over individual judgment. This raises the practical question of how and when collectives will be more accurate than individuals. After briefly reviewing social influence research, the chapter describes the basic logic of the wisdom of crowds: Independent errors are more likely to bracket the truth, which cancel each other out when averaged together. The chapter then turns to conditions that foster better individual inputs to collective judgment by ensuring diverse perspectives through group composition and processes that preserve independence. It also discusses the attraction of relying on single experts and the challenges of reliably identifying them. Finally, the chapter reviews research on the degree to which people understand the benefits of listening to others and evidence that they often fail to learn enough from others. The original chapter was published in 2011. The new chapter ends with an update that explores recent work on the benefits of discussion and analytical techniques for finding the more expert members within a crowd.

Keywords Crowd composition · Elicitation process · Crowd vs. individual · Judgment aggregation

R. P. Larrick · J. B. Soll (✉)
The Fuqua School of Business, Duke University, Durham, NC, USA
e-mail: rick.larrick@duke.edu; jsoll@duke.edu

A. E. Mannes
Data Scientist, Washington, DC, USA

F. M. Federspiel et al. (eds.), *Behavioral Decision Analysis*, International Series in Operations Research & Management Science 350,
https://doi.org/10.1007/978-3-031-44424-1_7

Picture yourself taking part in a classroom psychology experiment on perception. You and nine other subjects are being asked to judge the lengths of lines in a vision test. The experimenter holds up a large card that contains three lines of different lengths, marked A, B, and C, and a target line. The subjects are asked: Which of A, B, or C is the same length as the target? For each card, all subjects take turns reporting which line matches the target. The first few sets of cards are unremarkable. Everyone states what is clear to the eye. On the fifth trial, the obvious answer to you is B, but the first person says C (you find this mildly amusing). However, the second person also says C. The third says C, and then the fourth. Everyone says C. When it is your turn to answer, what do you say? Before hearing the response of others, you thought the answer was obviously B. But the unanimous opinion of others is C.

All students of social psychology recognize the famous Asch (1955) experiment, and most remember that three of four subjects at some point conform to a group answer that defies their own perceptions. Deutsch and Gerard (1955) introduced the term *normative social influence* to characterize the tendency for people to give public responses that allow them to fit in with others even when they privately disagree. However, Asch's classic study has come to symbolize more. In its own time—an era of totalitarian governments that repressed individualism and McCarthyite pressures in the United States that did likewise—Asch's study reinforced a suspicion of groups and a celebration of the lone, independent individual.

Early conformity research was criticized for leaving the widely held but misleading impression that people yield too much to the judgments of others, thereby harming themselves. Some authors (Allen, 1965; Campbell, 1961) suggested that this pessimistic conclusion is misleading because it was foreordained by the experimental design. In the Asch study, the other nine group members were only pretending to be subjects and had been planted to give consistently false answers before the true subject responded. Allen observed, "[M]ost psychological experiments in this area have been designed in such a manner that conformity was by necessity maladaptive: factually incorrect, detrimental to the group and the individual, or simply dishonest" (1965, p. 136).

In response, some authors stressed the adaptive value of conformity. Under uncertainty, people look to others for information (Deutsch & Gerard, 1955; Festinger, 1954), and groups are usually a valid source of information (Campbell, 1961). Allen observed that "a person may go along with beliefs expressed by most of the other people around him because he realizes that opinions shared by many are often more likely to be correct than the opinions held by a single individual. In some situations conformity is constructive and appropriate; in other situations it is not" (1965, pp. 136–137). (See Kameda & Tindale, 2006, and Krueger & Massey, 2009, for recent analyses of the adaptiveness of conformity.)

This chapter builds on the questions raised by classic social psychology experiments on conformity to examine the wisdom of relying on crowds. We review two general sets of questions. The normative questions ask what is rational or optimal: How accurate are the judgments of collectives? When individuals disagree with the judgments of others, should they change their judgment or hold firm to their initial opinion (Bell et al., 1988)? The descriptive questions ask what people actually do when they have access to the judgments of others: Do individuals understand why they should listen to others? Do they effectively decide when to listen to others (Bell et al., 1988)?

To address these questions, we build on a research tradition that differs markedly from the Asch tradition. The Asch situation was by nature misleading. In more mathematical terms, the answers from the false group members were unrepresentative of true answers. Brunswik (1955) famously argued that decision makers need to be presented with representative stimuli to assess how well they use information (Dhami et al., 2004). To understand whether groups yield accurate answers and whether subjects are able to benefit from group accuracy, one needs to study processes in which representative judgments are elicited and shared with decision makers.

The remainder of the chapter is divided into two main sections. First, we describe recent research on the wisdom of crowds. This innovative literature combines decades of research in different fields showing the benefits of combining information across people. We analyze the conditions that make crowds effective to answer the normative questions of how and when crowds are wise. We then examine the descriptive question of how people use the judgments of others. We review a growing body of research showing that people are egocentric in their use of judgments: They rely too much on their own judgments and miss the opportunity to learn from others.

The Wisdom of Crowds

Some of the earliest studies in social psychology examined whether groups were fundamentally different from individuals. In the 1920s, researchers examined whether groups were smarter than individuals (see Larrick & Soll, 2006, for a historical review). In one early study students estimated the temperature in a classroom. When the estimates were averaged, the result was more accurate than the estimate of a typical group member. It should be noted that individual members of this "group" never interacted with one another. Where did the benefits come from? Early authors were surprised by this result and attributed it to some mysterious group property. As one writer put it, "In every coming together of minds … [t]here is the Creative Plus, which no one mind by itself could achieve" (Overstreet, as cited by Watson, 1928). In time, researchers recognized that the power of groups came from something much simpler but still elegant: Combining judgments takes individual imperfection and smoothes the rough edges to isolate the collective's view of the truth. Or, to put it more mathematically and mundanely, averaging cancels error.

Subsequent research in the forecasting literature demonstrated that simple combination methods that weight people equally, such as averaging judgments, often perform as well as more sophisticated statistical methods of combination (Armstrong, 2001; Clemen, 1989). The power and simplicity of averaging was summed up in the title of James Surowiecki's (2004) best-selling book, *The Wisdom of Crowds*.

Consider a brief example that illustrates the power of averaging. Imagine two professors estimating the number of students who are likely to apply to a program in neuroscience. Their goal is to get as close to the truth as possible. Being too high or too low is equally bad (e.g., being 5 high or 5 low will be treated as a miss of 5). Professor L estimates 40. Professor H estimates 60. Their average guess is 50. If the truth turns out to be 47, the judges have missed by 7 and 13, respectively, and their average miss is 10. But the average of the judges' guesses, 50, missed the true value of 47 by only 3—a substantially smaller error than the average miss of 10. Why does this happen? The judgments of 40 and 60 "bracket" the truth: The high error and low error offset each other. It is bracketing that gives averaging its power (Larrick & Soll, 2006; Soll & Larrick, 2009).

Now suppose that the truth is 37. Both professors have overestimated (by 3 and 23, respectively), and the average performance of the professors has missed by (3 + 23)/2 = 13. The average guess of 50 also misses by 13. In cases like this—where both judges fall on the same side of the truth—averaging "locks in" the average individual error. This is the worst case scenario for averaging. With bracketing, averaging will be more accurate than the average individual error.

Of course, Professor L is more accurate than Professor H in both examples. Picking Professor L's lone judgment would have done well in the second scenario although fallen short of the average in the first scenario. It is tempting to declare Professor L smarter than the average. Research on groups frequently compares group performance to the performance of the "best member." It is important to point out, however, that in judgments under uncertainty the best member standard can be misleading when defined post hoc. Even when there is skill in judgment, there is luck as well, and it takes a large sample to know whether one judge is truly more accurate than another. The critical questions are whether (a) one judge is *reliably* better than another judge by *a substantial margin* over time and (b) whether the difference in ability is *detectable* from available cues in advance. In this example, could one know anything in advance about Professors L and H (or their answers) that would lead one to heavily favor the judgment of one over the other before knowing the outcome? Averaging is powerful, because, thanks to bracketing, it must perform better than the average judge and can often perform much better. This performance makes it superior to choosing individual judges when judges are roughly similar in ability or when it is hard to distinguish their ability in advance.

The idea of bracketing generalizes to larger crowds.[1] To illustrate, the *Wall Street Journal* surveys a panel of about 50 economists every 6 months to make macroeconomic forecasts about inflation, unemployment, and so forth. The resulting diagram of forecasts often looks like a reasonable approximation of a normal distribution (see three hypothetical examples in Fig. 1). When the truth is added to the plot 6 months later, it is often the case that the crowd of economists is roughly centered on

[1] One can conceive of bracketing in a group as the rate at which randomly selected pairs bracket the truth or as a ratio of the proportion of the crowd falling on each side of the truth. For example, if 60% of the crowd is high and 40% low, the pairwise bracketing rate is $1 - [(.6 \times .6) + (.4 \times .4)] = .48$, and there is a 1.5 (.6/.4) ratio.

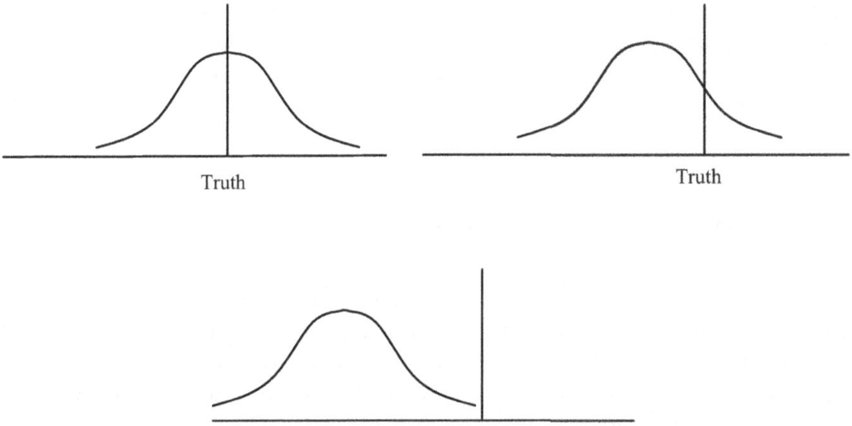

Fig. 1 Three distributions of individual judgments in which judgments are evenly distributed around the truth (top left panel), bracket the truth (top right panel), or are biased below the truth (bottom panel)

the truth (top left panel). Even when the distribution is not centered on the truth, it often brackets the truth (top right panel). Given some degree of bracketing, the average of the crowd is by mathematical necessity more accurate than the average individual.[2] When there is no bracketing—that is, the whole crowd is biased strictly

[2]This mathematical necessity can be proven by applying Jensen's inequality. Let Judge *i*'s estimate on quantity *j* be represented as $X_{ij} = T_j + D_{ij}$, where T_j is the correct answer and D_{ij} is the deviation, $i = 1, 2, \ldots, n$, and $j = 1, 2, \ldots, m$. Let $w_1, w_2, \ldots, w_n$ be the weights assigned to *n* judgments, where $W_i = 1$. Accuracy on a given estimate is a function of the deviation, $f(D)$. Typically, $f(D)$ is increasing in $|D|$, so higher scores reflect lower accuracy. For a quantity *j*, the deviation for a weighted average is the weighted average of the deviations of the individual estimates:

$$f\left(w_1x_{1j} + w_2x_{2j} + \ldots + w_nx_{nj} - T_j\right) = f\left(\sum_{i=1}^{n} w_iD_{ij}\right).$$

The right-hand side of the preceding equation gives the accuracy of a weighted average. If f is a convex function, then Jensen's inequality states that

$$\sum_{i=1}^{n} w_i f\left(D_{ij}\right) \geq f\left(\sum_{i=1}^{n} w_iD_{ij}\right).$$

In this chapter, we focus on absolute error as our accuracy standard because it is neutral in punishing larger versus small errors. Past forecast research has focused on squared error as the loss function, which implies that larger errors are worse than smaller ones. When squared error is used as the loss function, averaging is more accurate than the average judge even when there is no bracketing.

Aggregation also improves judgment using other criteria for accuracy, such as correlations with the truth.

above or below the truth as in the bottom panel—the average of the crowd is still as accurate as the average individual. Averaging the answers of a crowd, therefore, ensures a level of accuracy no worse than the average member of the crowd and, in some cases, a level better than nearly all members.

Conditions for Crowds to be Wise

Crowds, of course, are not always wiser than individuals. The degree to which crowds are more accurate than individuals is a function of two factors: expertise and diversity. First, the crowd needs to consist of individuals with some knowledge or expertise about the issue in question. This could be based on past education or past experience. In quantitative judgments, expertise allows individuals to use imperfect evidence to make predictions that will fall close to the truth over many judgments.

Second, the crowd needs to hold diverse perspectives on the judgment in question. As a result of holding diverse perspectives, different individuals will bring different areas of expertise to bear on a judgment and therefore make different mistakes. For example, imagine two professors predicting the academic ability of graduate school applicants. One professor tends to focus on past research experience; the other focuses on grades. Both cues are valid—both cues are predictive of future performance. Moreover, the cues are not perfectly correlated, so over many cases, they often lead to conflicting conclusions. Thus, when one professor is optimistic about a student who has a good deal of research experience and the second professor is pessimistic because the student has low grades, their average assessment is more complete and likely to be more accurate than their individual assessments. Relying on a subset of cues introduces errors that can be offset by including the additional valid cues used by other judges.

To appreciate the effect of diversity on judgment, consider its absence. Imagine a marketing team evaluating the revenue potential of new possible products. If all of the marketers have worked in the same company on the same past products at the same period of time, they have developed a shared set of experiences that guide their judgment about which new products are best. As a result, they are likely to hold shared opinions such as "customizability is more attractive to people under 40 than to people over 40." The consequence is that they share the same expertise—and the same blind spots. Forecasting researchers term this pattern "positively correlated forecast errors" and show mathematically that it reduces the value of aggregating judgments across people because similar errors cannot cancel each other. Sociologists who study social networks refer to shared patterns of knowledge as *redundant* (Burt, 1992, 2004). The word redundant evokes the right image: In the extreme, the knowledge of one person is a pretty good substitute for another person's. From a wisdom-of-crowds perspective, it is as if you do not have a crowd; your crowd is effectively one.

There are two ways to foster diversity. Differences in perspective are created through who is in the group (composition) and how they share information (process).

Composition

Research in the forecasting literature (Clemen & Winkler, 1986) has demonstrated the value of combining forecasts from different econometric models based on different economic schools of thought. The organizational literature has emphasized cross-functional teams as the best source for new ideas (Cronin & Weingart, 2007). A company does not want a new product designed by marketers alone—marketers will give it a fantastic look with many features but may pay less attention to the cost of production. The company needs expertise in other areas (finance, engineering, etc.) to ensure that the product meets a more optimal set of objectives.

Network sociologists propose enhancing diversity by finding gaps in the social network (Burt, 1992). The premise is that in tightly knit groups, people talk a great deal, and come to know and value the same things. They become redundant. From a group's vantage point, new ideas and new perspectives lie outside their own boundaries—even in other closely knit groups. The beauty of separation is that separated groups are likely to have evolved different views that are redundant *within* a group but nonredundant *between* them (Burt, 2004).

Creating diversity through composition can be challenging. One obstacle is that in-groups that share a similar perspective often look down on out-groups (DiDonato et al., 2011). Members of the marketing group suspect that members of the finance group are just bean counters who will stifle creativity. A second obstacle is that real differences in language and thinking impede collaboration between groups (Cronin & Weingart, 2007). These obstacles tend to lead people to associate with similar others. Sociologists term this tendency *homophily*; informally, it is the tendency for birds of a feather flocking together. Thus, when people assemble teams, they often select members based on common experience, common training, and common attitudes. This facilitates harmony but limits diversity.

Process

The second source of diversity is the process a group or collective uses to elicit judgments. A good group process ensures that individuals think independently before sharing their judgments. Why is independence important? Imagine being in an experiment in which you are asked to estimate the years in which important events happened. Imagine also that before you see a question, you see the real answer from another subject. For example, you see 1300 followed by the question "In what year was the Magna Carta written?" To what extent is your answer influenced by first seeing the answer of another subject? Koehler and Beauregard (2006) found that when answers were given without seeing other answers—that is, when answers were independent—they were typically 50 years apart (median value). When answers were given after seeing someone else's answer, however, they differed by only 10 years from the answer that was seen. Cognitive psychologists have called this general phenomenon *anchoring* (Tversky & Kahneman, 1974). Anchoring occurs because people start with a number, such as the year 1300, and unconsciously recruit evidence consistent with it (Chapman & Johnson, 1999; Mussweiler & Strack, 1999) and then fail to adjust sufficiently from it (Epley & Gilovich, 2001).

Whether a deliberate strategy or an unconscious anchoring process, people rely on others to form their judgments. Deutsch and Gerard (1955) called this tendency *informational influence* and contrasted it with the *normative influence* illustrated in the Asch study. Recall that participants in the Asch experiment would often publicly report an answer with which they disagreed privately. Informational influence, on the other hand, occurs when people use the judgments of others to reduce their own uncertainty. It results in a new opinion—public and private—that incorporates the beliefs of others.

Because of anchoring and informational influence, single judgments in a group can propagate through the judgments of others if the others have not first formed an opinion. For example, having one person start a discussion with an opinion ("we should increase inventory by 20%") tends to lead others to think in small variations of that opinion. The result is that both the initial accuracy and the initial error in the first judgment are spread to those who hear it (economists have studied this phenomenon under the name *information cascades*; see Krueger & Massey, 2009, for a review). Anchoring and informational influence produce *positively correlated error* and *redundancy*, which amount to reducing the effective sample size.

Better group processes ensure that members think independently to form their judgments before sharing them. Research on brainstorming has found that working independently leads to a bigger and better pool of ideas than working face to face (Girota et al., 2010; Paulus & Yang, 2000). This effect occurs, in part, because independent ideas are generated in parallel, whereas face-to-face conversations require taking turns. But some of the effect is due to groups developing a common way of thinking about a question due to anchoring and informational influence. The danger of anchoring during group discussion has led one forecasting expert (Armstrong, 2006) to propose that many decisions would be better made if groups shared information without ever meeting.

Crowds Versus Individual Experts

To say that a crowd is wise invites the question, "Compared to what?" The implicit comparison in these examples has been to the average individual in the crowd. Indeed, for quantitative judgments, the average of the crowd can never be worse than the average individual in the crowd. With a high rate of bracketing, averaging will be far superior to the average individual. However, the average individual is not the only standard by which to judge a crowd. One can also ask how well averaging performs compared with the best member of the crowd (Luan, Katsikopoulos, & Reimer, 2012). For this comparison to be informative, it is important to predict beforehand who the best judge will be. As noted earlier, it is always possible to determine the best performer after the fact.

There can be significant barriers to accurate identification of expertise. If there is no reliable track record of performance, one needs to rely on other cues. In a group discussion, members often rely on confidence and verbosity as cues to expertise (Littlepage et al., 1997). Unfortunately, cues like confidence often correlate weakly with actual accuracy (Burson et al., 2006). Consequently, group members often inaccurately rank order the expertise of the members of their group (for example, Miner, 1984).

Even if one has access to past performance, the sample may not be large enough to allow a valid inference of stable ability. If you track the best performers in *The Wall Street Journal* data from one period to the next, they are no more accurate than the average judge in later periods (Mannes et al., 2011). Why? Performance is a function of both skill and luck. More formally, apparent experts in one period of time regress to the mean of performance in the next period (for a discussion of regression to the mean, see Chap. 10 by Fiedler & Krueger in Krueger, 2011).[3] As a result, one is better off using the average of the whole sample of economists in the current period than to bet on the winner from the last survey.

Whether one should pick a single expert or rely on a crowd depends not just on access to valid evidence about the ability of judges, but also the presence of a large difference between the best judge and other judges. The benefits of diversity are so strong that one can combine the judgments from individuals who differ a great deal in their individual accuracy and still gain from averaging. In a two judge case, one judge can be 50% more accurate than another judge and averaging will still outperform the better judge with realistic rates of bracketing (Soll & Larrick, 2009). For example, if over many prediction periods one economist tends to miss true GNP (gross national product) increases by $50 billion on average and a second economist tends to miss by $75 billion, there is still a benefit to combining their judgments. It takes a large difference in ability to justify choosing one judge instead of averaging.

In sum, there are many advantages to averaging a crowd over choosing single experts. First, when judges are similar in ability, it allows their errors to cancel. Second, when judges differ in ability but differences are hard to detect, an averaging strategy is sure to give at least some weight to the best performers; by contrast, trying to pick a single expert based on available cues could put all the weight on a less accurate judge. Finally, an averaging strategy can be implemented even in the absence of evidence about relative expertise.

Types of Crowd Judgments

Most of the examples offered so far have focused on quantitative judgments under uncertainty. But the benefits of crowds can apply to many tasks. When choosing among options, majority rule performs well compared to more complex approaches

---

[3] Denrell and Fang (2010) showed that when a *Wall Street Journal* economist "wins" one period with more extreme judgments—that is, judgments that are outliers compared to the rest of the group—they are actually less accurate than the average judge in subsequent periods.

(Hastie & Kameda, 2005; Sorkin et al., 2004). In the popular game show *Who Wants to be a Millionaire?* the studio audience answered the trivia questions correctly 91% of the time (Surowiecki, 2004). More qualitative tasks also benefit from crowds. Research on creativity has shown that once a person has pursued one approach to solving a problem, it is hard for the person to generate other approaches. Brainstorming overcomes this problem by tapping the diverse perspectives of a group to generate a larger and more complete pool of ideas (Girotra et al., 2010; Paulus & Yang, 2000). Bond et al. (2008) asked business students to generate objectives for their summer job (e.g., pay level, location, growth opportunities, relevance to future career plans, and so forth). They found that students listed about seven objectives on average. However, when students were then presented with both their own objectives along with a list of objectives generated by others, they tended to find another seven objectives that were as important as the ones they had generated on their own. Groups are smarter than individuals in creating a wider range of creative ideas, objectives, and alternatives.

Technology has made it easier to draw on the wisdom of crowds. Some tools are as simple as aggregating average ratings on consumer Web sites. Others are more complex, such as prediction markets, in which people wager real or pretend money to bet on future events, such as sports. (A famous but short-lived Department of Defense market had people betting for and against the timing of future terrorist attacks; betting "for" an attack was perceived as distasteful.) Similarly, corporations have used internal "idea jams" to tap employee perspectives on innovation opportunities and have used external "crowd sourcing" to reach a broad pool of diverse entrepreneurs to address unsolved technological problems they currently face.

The Individual as a Crowd

Research on the wisdom of crowds supports the old saying that two heads are better than one. It is interesting that the insights from this literature have also been used to show that one head can be nearly as good as two (Herzog & Hertwig, 2009; Vul & Pashler, 2008), as long as a judge follows the principles of relevant knowledge and diverse perspectives. The key insight is that people typically rely on only a sample of the evidence available to them at any given time. But what if people had a reset button, so that they could retrieve facts from memory anew or handle the same facts in a new way?

One way to free people from their original answers is to delay a second answer (Vul & Pashler, 2008) so that people forget their initial perspectives and think about the problem differently the second time around. Another way to free people is to have them try to construct a fresh perspective. To demonstrate this possibility, Herzog and Hertwig (2009) had participants make estimates about quantitative values they did not know with certainty (specifically, dates in history). All participants gave two answers to the same question, and the authors constructed an average of the first and second judgments for each individual. In one condition, participants simply gave a second estimate following their first estimate. This condition did little to increase diversity—people simply anchored on their initial opinions—and there was no benefit from averaging. In a second condition, participants were told to assume that their first answer was incorrect, think of some reasons it might be wrong, and then "based on this new perspective, make a second, alternative estimate" (p. 234). This process of *second guessing* increased bracketing; as expected, the average of the first and second judgments was significantly more accurate than the first estimate. A lesson of Herzog and Hertwig's study is that we each carry around our own crowd, but we gain the wisdom only if we ask different members of the crowd.

How Well Do People Use Crowds?

Strategies for Combining Judgments

Given that crowds are often wise, an important question for social psychology is whether people understand the value of combining knowledge across people. How well do people use judgments of others? This has become a growing area of research in recent years. Most research has focused on a very simple version of a crowd: two-person collectives involving the self (Sniezek & Buckley, 1995; Yaniv & Kleinberger, 2000). In these studies, people make estimates and then learn actual, representative estimates of others. The source of estimates is often called an *advisor* and the literature as a whole has come to be known as "advice taking." The advice-taking literature has used a wide range of quantitative stimuli, including estimating ages or weights of people from photographs, years in which historical events occurred, temperatures of cities, and so on. Studies that have focused on accuracy then compare initial and revised estimates to the truth and typically pay subjects for the closeness of their judgment. A smaller amount of research has looked at how people use the estimates of larger collectives of which they might or might not be members. We consider these two areas of research separately.

Using Advice from Another Person

One of the most robust findings in the advice-taking literature is that people underweight advice from another and overweight their own opinions (see Bonaccio & Dalal, 2006, for a review). A common result is that, on average, people tend to adjust their estimates 20% to 30% of the way toward advice (Harvey & Fischer, 1997; Soll & Larrick, 2009; Yaniv, 2004), a phenomenon that Yaniv and Kleinberger (2000) labeled *egocentric discounting*. For example, imagine estimating the age of someone from a photograph. You might make an initial estimate of 42 years old, see an advisor's estimate of 50, and adjust your answer to 44. The initial estimate and advice in this example are 8 years apart. The revised answer of 44 reflects a movement of 2/8, which translates to putting 25% weight on advice (WOA) and keeping 75% weight on your initial answer.

Subsequent research has found that 20% to 30% weight on advice is not descriptive of how people actually revise their judgments. The common pattern of 20% to 30% weight on advice is an average result of more extreme underlying behavior. Soll and Larrick (2009) showed that people often either choose one of the two answers (typically their own) or use an equal-weighted average. In their studies, the 30% mean weight on advice reflected a pattern of frequently ignoring advice entirely (0% WOA), sometimes averaging their initial estimates with advice (50% WOA), and occasionally ignoring their own initial estimates and fully accepting advice (100% WOA). The most common response in these studies was 0% weight on advice. Such an extreme strategy takes no advantage of the error canceling benefits of a two-person crowd and significantly hurts final accuracy. Subjects would have formed more accurate final estimates if they had given *equal* weight to their own estimates and advice (Soll & Larrick, 2009).[4]

Why do people put so much weight on their own estimates? Several explanations have been offered. First, many people have an incorrect theory of combining judgments (Larrick & Soll, 2006), believing that averaging leads to mediocrity. Specifically, they incorrectly believe that the average judgment in a crowd is no more accurate than the average judge. Holding this incorrect belief is significantly related to ignoring advice (Larrick & Soll, 2006).

Other explanations for ignoring advice have focused on more psychological assumptions. Harvey and Harries (2004) proposed that people believe that the advisor is substantially less accurate than oneself. Yaniv and his colleagues (Yaniv, 2004; Yaniv & Kleinberger, 2000) proposed that people weight their own answers more highly because they know the reasons for their own judgments but not those behind the judgments of others. Soll and Mannes (2011) tested both explanations by directly measuring subjects' perceptions of their accuracy relative to their advisor and by systematically providing or withholding cues at the time of revision (where seeing cues can remind subjects of their reasons for their initial answer).

They found some evidence for inflated perceptions of the self, but not enough to explain the frequent use of 0% WOA. Moreover, they found no effect of having access to reasons on WOA. They proposed that the tendency to hold on to one's judgment may be less cognitive and more motivational: One's judgments are part of oneself and, like possessions, letting go of them is painful. Moreover, there may be an asymmetry in the regret of changing one's mind. Actively giving up an initially accurate answer for a worse one may lead to more regret than passively holding on to an inaccurate answer and foregoing improvement (see Chap. 15 by Baron in Krueger, 2011).

The advice-taking literature has found that a number of factors affect the weight placed on advice. Some factors are rational: Subjects weight advice more heavily

[4] In these studies, subjects made judgments independently (yielding bracketing rates of 30% to 40%), were randomly assigned advisors from their own subject population (yielding small average differences in expertise between judges), and given cues to expertise such as self-expressed confidence or a small sample of past performance (which are weak cues). All of these features, which favor averaging, were known by subjects.

when advisors are more experienced or knowledgeable (Harvey & Fischer, 1997; Soll & Larrick, 2009), when advisors express greater confidence in the quality of their advice (Sniezek & Buckley, 1995; Sniezek & Van Swol, 2001; Soll & Larrick, 2009), and when the subject finds the task difficult (Gino & Moore, 2007). As long as people use these advisor characteristics according to their validity, shifting weight to more expert advisors is an effective response to these cues. Other factors are more psychological: Decision makers weight advice less heavily when they feel powerful (See et al., 2011) and when they experience emotions that increase feelings of certainty, such as anger (Gino & Schweitzer, 2008). This research identifies a practical set of factors that reduces the use of advice and can help practitioners in different fields, such as business and medicine, recognize when egocentric discounting will be at its greatest.

Combining Judgments from a Collective

A smaller stream of research has focused on how people combine the opinions of multiple others. Most studies in this area have looked at how people combine judgments across a panel of experts. In these studies, subjects have not made their own initial judgment but are neutral arbiters deciding how to balance the judgments of others (Budescu, 2006; Harvey et al., 2000; Yaniv, 1997). Budescu and colleagues (Budescu, 2006; Budescu et al., 2003) have found that people tend to weight expert judgments in proportion to the expertise of different judges.

Two studies in this area have looked at advice taking from a group. As in the two-person advice research, these studies involve having people make an initial judgment and then revise it after seeing the estimates of a group (Mannes, 2009; Yaniv & Milyavsky, 2007). Yaniv and Milyavsky (2007) found that people cherry-pick the advice from a larger crowd, focusing on the judgments most consistent with their own. Subjects effectively use their first guess as a standard of accuracy and dismiss discrepant advice. From a wisdom-of-crowds perspective, this is dangerous: It ignores the benefits of incorporating diverse perspectives to cancel error. Mannes (2009) explored the extent to which people listen to the average judgment from crowds of different sizes. Normatively, subjects would be wise to put less weight on themselves and more weight on the crowd as the crowd grows in size (reflecting a basic principle in statistics known as the *law of large numbers*). In addition, if all judges are expected to be equally accurate in advance, subjects would be wise to put the same weight on themselves as they do on each member of the crowd (i.e., a $1/n$ weight on their own judgment and a $(n-1)/n$ weight on the crowd's advice). Mannes found that people put more weight on larger crowds, as they should from a normative perspective, but not enough weight. They put only 60% weight on advice from a nine-person crowd where equal weighting would require more than 90% weight. The consequence of egocentric weighting is that subjects paid a significant price in the accuracy of their final judgments.

Future Directions for the Psychology of the Wisdom of the Crowds

The main conclusion from existing research is that people use crowds too little: They put too much weight on their own judgment and thereby miss out on the benefit of diverse perspectives for reducing error. This is a young and growing area of research. What are some of the unanswered questions? Perhaps a key issue that arises in the existing work is that advice is quantitative, impersonal, and unsolicited—it consists of seeing numerical estimates made by others (including group averages) and making conscious decisions about how best to combine them with one's own independent estimates. The use of crowd judgments should be explored in other ways.

First, advice *seeking* could be an important variable to study. How often do people seek advice? Perhaps the easiest way to reduce error in judgment is to seek other's opinions, and the failure to do so has the same negative consequences as ignoring advice. We suspect people seek advice less often than they should. How does seeking advice affect its use? The act of seeking advice is likely to increase the extent to which advice is used (Gino, 2008) and thereby improve judgment. It is also possible that seeking advice will lead people to pick a single expert and put too much faith in that single piece of advice.

Second, other advice-taking contexts may change openness to advice, such as face-to-face interactions or interactions with richer information sharing. Richer information sharing may lead to deeper information processing. Face-to-face interactions may evoke processes such as empathy and mimicry that produce greater yielding to others.

Third, the benefits of independence should be carefully examined. Earlier we argued that independence increases diversity of perspective and thereby makes a crowd more accurate. Asch captured this idea when writing that "consensus, to be productive, requires that each individual contribute independently out of his experience and insight" (1955, p. 34). In this view, individual judgments are "inputs" to a combination process and they are more valuable if they are independent. However, individual judgments can also be "outputs" from exposure to the judgments of collectives. Egocentric discounting of advice is an example of an inferior output. In output situations there may be a benefit if the individual does *not* have an independent opinion: Anchoring on a crowd may actually yield more accurate judgments because it ensures that individual judges are using a larger sample—even if unwittingly.

Consider a study that predates Asch. Jenness (1932) asked students to estimate the number of beans in a jar. They made their estimates in a prescribed sequence: first individually, then by consensus in a three-person group, and then individually again. The initial individual guesses missed the true value (811) by 305 on average. The group consensus answers missed the value by just 91, producing a substantial improvement over their initial individual guesses. Strikingly, however, their final individual guesses missed by 122 on average—worse than the group answers. What went wrong? By reasserting their independence and deviating from the group answer, the subjects in Jenness's study were less accurate than if they had simply placed their faith in the crowd.

Thus, we can think of crowd processes as having two stages. Independence is important at Stage 1, the input stage, because the effective sample size is increased when different judges make different errors. However, independence may be unimportant or even detrimental at Stage 2, the output stage, when a decision maker uses others' judgments to form a final opinion that he or she is going to act on. Campbell adopted the Stage 2 perspective when he argued that, "[I]n Asch's famous situation, the single true subject might rationally decide that, since everybody's eyes are imperfect, and since it would be so extremely infrequent that so many Swarthmore students would deliberately lie in a situation like this, it is more probable that his own eyes are wrong than that all of the others are wrong. He might, therefore, rationally decide that, if asked to bet, he would bet with the majority" (1961, p. 123). In contrast to the view inherited from the Asch tradition, social influence may actually be beneficial. Normative and informational influence may serve as a *cognitive repair* (Heath et al., 1998) that mitigates depending too much on one's own judgments. Influence ensures that people incorporate the wisdom of the crowd in their own judgments.

Update 2024: A Decade of Discovery

We appreciate the opportunity to reflect on where the field has come since this chapter was first published. And we are delighted to see how academic interest in the Wisdom of Crowds has grown in the years, meriting a variety of special issues and reviews (e.g., Budescu et al., 2024; Kameda et al., 2022; Mellers et al., 2023). The original chapter used a social psychology lens to think about when crowds are likely to be most accurate and the degree to which people are willing to use aggregated judgments. Given the exciting growth in WoC research over the past decade, a number of the ideas in the original chapter merit updating with new insights. We organize these updates around two general themes. First, to what degree is discussion helpful or harmful to the wisdom of crowds? Second, to what extent can experts be identified and how should their judgments be used in crowds?

The Benefits and Costs of Discussion

Our original chapter took a largely pessimistic view of discussion. In classic social psychology research (and much forecasting research) the concern is that sharing information leads people to share error, reducing the benefits of aggregating judgments at the crowd level (e.g., through averaging). Newer research, however, has made clear that the actual impact of discussion is contingent and requires a deeper analysis. At the heart of this insight is the fact that discussion not only transmits error between individuals but also knowledge. There is a "horse race" between the two and whether harm or benefit "wins" depends on other factors. This horse race is captured in Scott Page's (2007) diversity prediction theorem where discussion lowers diversity but increases individual accuracy at the same time.

The original chapter concluded on the possibility that, at the individual level, it is important to distinguish whether an individual's judgment is an input to a collective judgment (termed "Stage 1") or an output of an information sharing process is a final judgment that will inform action (termed "Stage 2"). In some situations, individuals may benefit tremendously from copying the opinions of others (a Stage 2 process), even though crowd wisdom may have benefited most from individuals ignoring others and reporting their own, independent Stage 1 opinions.

A number of studies have shown how discussion leads individuals to become more accurate. Thomas Schultze and colleagues found evidence that individuals improve their individual judgments after group discussion (which they term group-to-individual transfer) because they gain a better understanding of both the range in which outcomes occur (a metric benefit) and the relationship between cues and outcomes—a mapping benefit (Schultze et al., 2012; Lippold et al., 2021). In this work, averages based on Stage 1 estimates were similarly accurate with and without discussion, so individual gains and diversity losses offset each other. Discussion often helps *individuals* get better, which may, or may not, help the crowd (Farrell, 2011).

Individuals can also benefit from information exchange and debate. This was shown by the Good Judgment Project (GJP), a team of researchers that convincingly won a multi-year geopolitical forecasting competition sponsored by IARPA (Mellers et al., 2014). The GJP researchers recruited laypeople to participate as their resident forecasters, tracked their forecasting performance over time, and tested various interventions, one of which had forecasters collaborate in teams that could engage on an electronic chat platform at their own discretion. This set-up appears to have encouraged independent research and thought, but also allowed for team members to share information and challenge each other's positions (Tetlock & Gardner, 2016). The aggregated judgments from interacting teams outperformed those from teams in which members worked alone. Further analysis showed that interacting teams benefited from information exchange, bias reduction, and noise reduction. In contrast, non-interacting teams benefited only from noise reduction (Satopää et al., 2023). These results show that a system that includes discussion, within the context of an information-rich environment and an appropriate process and platform for exchanging ideas, has the potential to outperform the mechanical aggregation of purely independent judgments.

We emphasize that the benefits of discussion are contingent upon both context and process. For example, Minson et al. (2018) explored the effect of discussion in dyads on problems that have bounded errors (such as guessing the percentage of Philadephians who have no health insurance, where all answers fall between 0% and 100%) or relatively unbounded errors (such as guessing the number of Philadelphians who have no health insurance, where answers must be above 0 but for the unknowledgeable could plausibly be in the low thousands or more than a million). In their studies, dyad members went into discussions cold without any individual preparation. Also, relatively speaking, there were few new facts that they could share with one another, so discussion largely consisted of stating estimates as opposed to gathering and interpreting information. Minson et al. (2018) found that discussion prior to forming initial individual judgments hurt final dyadic judgments on bounded problems due to anchoring and lower rates of bracketing (Larrick & Soll, 2006). In this case, discussion harmed diversity more than it increased individual accuracy. But for unbounded questions, discussion was beneficial because it reduced the occurrence of extreme errors (paralleling the metric benefit observed by Lippold et al., 2021).

Other recent work has investigated how the structure of social networks impacts the tradeoff between accuracy and diversity. In this work, individuals learn the opinions of their neighbors in a network, which they can use to update their own opinions. In many of these studies, only numerical estimates are observed (often just an average estimate) without additional explanation or performance feedback, so there is limited opportunity for knowledge sharing. The research found that exposure to the estimates of others enhanced crowd wisdom when the network was decentralized as opposed to having a single well-connected actor, with the caveat that there has to be an inverse relationship between a person's susceptibility to social influence and their ability to produce accurate estimates (Becker et al., 2017; see also Mason et al., 2008). Furthermore, exposure to others' estimates also helps when individuals can "rewire" their social connections based on accuracy feedback on crowd members to which they are connected, affording an opportunity to explore the network to seek out the most informed individuals (Almaatouq et al., 2020). In contrast, when individuals are all connected to the same actor or cannot rewire, accuracy gains might not overcome the loss of diversity, and thus sharing information can potentially harm crowd wisdom (see review by Centola, 2022).

The Identification and Use of Experts in Crowds

Our original chapter also described the difficulty of identifying experts in crowds (a factor that argues for averaging the whole crowd rather than trying to weight individuals differentially). Historically, social psychology research focused on comparing group performance to a "best member" identified after an outcome is known. But the challenge in devising WoC strategies for identifying experts is that they must work prospectively under uncertainty.

In the original chapter, we briefly reviewed findings in the group decision making literature and concluded that interacting groups rarely show a reliable ability to intuitively give more weight to the judgments of their best performing member on quantitative tasks. The reason is that cues to stable underlying ability are hard to detect, and other factors (such as frequency of speaking or confidence) often are used as imperfect cues to expertise. We think our original conclusion that it is hard to identify experts intuitively continues to be a reasonable one.

Yet the field has made progress in developing tools that *analysts* can use when identifying and weighing superior knowledge in crowds. Prelec et al. (2017) proposed a mechanism for identifying experts in a crowd choice task by having judges answer two questions: their own choice of a correct answer and their prediction of the answer most commonly given by others. They argue that there is a metacognitive asymmetry that helps reveal true experts. More ignorant individuals will tend to give the same answer for both questions (e.g., that the capital of Illinois is Chicago) and those more expert will give different answers (e.g., that the capital of Illinois is Springfield but that other people will frequently give the answer Chicago); as a result, the true answer (Springfield) is surprisingly popular as a guess compared to what is predicted. Surprisingly popular answers then receive more weight in a final answer which improves crowd accuracy.

Palley and Soll (2019) developed a similar technique for quantity estimates that utilizes two separate average opinions—the average estimate of the truth and the average estimate of others' guesses. To fully incorporate information distributed across crowd members, the algorithm *pivots* away from the average estimate of the truth in the direction *away from* the average estimate of others. This maneuver has the effect of deweighting commonly held information, and puts more weight on the opinions of those who know something more or different (see Lichtendahl et al., 2013, for yet a different approach to upweighting private information in a crowd).

Budescu and Chen (2015) and Mannes et al. (2014) propose mechanisms for identifying experts drawing on each judge's past performance. Budescu and Chen (2015) measure the degree to which individual judge's answer contributed unique incremental accuracy to past crowd judgments. Judges who provided the most valuable contributions then receive more weight in the calculation of subsequent crowd judgments. Mannes et al. (2014) use small samples of past performance in a judgment domain to identify the judges who had the smallest errors, and then construct a smaller crowd of the most accurate five or ten judges to provide estimates that are averaged on new judgment items. These "select" crowds perform well across a wide range of circumstances because when there are large differences in ability, a short history is sufficient for the best judges to be identified; and when there are not large differences in ability, a crowd of 5 to 10 provides most of the accuracy benefits of larger crowds (due to diminishing returns to crowd size).

Another approach to identifying the best performers relies on the observation that the most knowledgeable judges are often (but not always) near the crowd average. This *intersubjective* result suggests that judges near the crowd average on past judgments should get more weight in new judgment tasks (Batchelder & Anders, 2012), and recent work bears out this prediction (Himmelstein et al., 2023; Atanasov & Himmelstein, 2023).

Finally, the success of the Good Judgment Project was in part due to the identification of the top 2% of forecasters from previous rounds of the tournament (Mellers et al., 2015). These *superforecasters* were drawn from the general population and had access only to public information. Yet interacting teams composed of superforecasters were able to outperform professional intelligence analysts in forecasting geopolitical events (Tetlock & Gardner, 2016). This finding is impressive, and it also provides additional support for select crowds, broadly construed. As we noted in the original chapter, when the comparison is between crowds and single experts, the crowd typically wins. However, select crowds that are chosen based on a valid cue to expertise (such as in the GJP), can enhance accuracy without too much harm to diversity. Moreover, aggregates of superforecasters in the GJP performed best when they could engage in discussion. We believe that this idea of "interacting select crowds" represents a promising area for future research.

Conclusion

We close with the following the reflection on the original chapter. The chapter argued that certain aspects of social influence—such as having an individual learn someone else's judgment before making their own—will lead to anchoring-induced shared error that harms the quality of an input ("Stage 1") judgment. In retrospect, social influence also conveys useful knowledge about a task (how to use cues, what is a reasonable range of answers, etc.) and therefore discussion prior to a Stage 1 input can both help and hurt the collective quality of Stage 1 judgments. We believe the distinction between Stage 1 and Stage 2 is still a useful framework for clarifying "what role is the individual playing in a collective judgment process?" Many findings in the literature suggest that the race between loss of diversity and gain in individual accuracy often have an offsetting effect on crowd accuracy, yielding neither a net gain nor net loss.

There are times when it is important to be individually accurate, and other times when it is important to provide the most useful input to a group. Because of the tradeoff between accuracy and diversity, it turns out that an individual should provide different estimates in the two cases. We suspect that most people do not fully understand this difference and may confuse which type of judgment they are seeking and offering. What are the implications of this for individual and collective decision making? And what are the implications for decision analysis when individual judgments are elicited and used?

References

Allen, V. L. (1965). Situational factors in conformity. *Advances in Experimental Social Psychology, 2*, 133–175.

Almaatouq, A., Noriega-Campero, A., Alotaibi, A., Krafft, P. M., Moussaid, M., & Pentland, A. (2020). Adaptive social networks promote the wisdom of crowds. *Proceedings of the National Academy of Sciences, 117*(21), 11379–11386.

Armstrong, J. S. (2001). *Principles of forecasting: A handbook for researchers and practitioners*. Kluwer Academic.

Armstrong, J. S. (2006). Should the forecasting process eliminate face-to-face meetings? *Foresight: The International Journal of Applied Forecasting, 5*, 3–8.

Asch, S. E. (1955). Opinions and social pressure. *Scientific American, 193*, 31–35.
Atanasov, P., & Himmelstein, M. (2023). Talent spotting in crowd prediction. In *Judgment in predictive analytics* (pp. 135–184). Springer International Publishing.
Baron, J. (2011). Where do nonutilitarian moral rules come from? In J. I. Krueger (Ed.), *Social judgment and decision making* (1st ed.). Psychology Press. https://doi.org/10.4324/9780203854150
Batchelder, W. H., & Anders, R. (2012). Cultural consensus theory: Comparing different concepts of cultural truth. *Journal of Mathematical Psychology, 56*(5), 316–332.
Becker, J., Brackbill, D., & Centola, D. (2017). Network dynamics of social influence in the wisdom of crowds. *Proceedings of the National Academy of Sciences, 114*(26), E5070–E5076.
Bell, D., Raiffa, H., & Tversky, A. (1988). *Decision making: Descriptive, normative, and prescriptive interactions*. Cambridge University Press.
Bonaccio, S., & Dalal, R. S. (2006). Advice taking and decision-making: An integrative literature review, and implications for the organizational sciences. *Organizational Behavior and Human Decision Processes, 101*, 127–151.
Budescu, D. V., & Chen, E. (2015). Identifying expertise to extract the wisdom of crowds. *Management Science, 61*(2), 267–280.
Budescu, D. V., Grushka-Cockayne, Y., & Soll, J. B. (2024). Introduction to the special issue on judgment and decision research on the wisdom of the crowds. *Decision, 11*(1), 1.
Bond, S. D., Carlson, K. A., & Keeney, R. L. (2008). Generating objectives: Can decisión makers articulate what they want? *Management Science, 54*, 56–70.
Brunswik, E. (1955). Representative design and probabilistic theory in a functional psychology. *Psychological Review, 62*, 193–217.
Budescu, D. V. (2006). Confidence in aggregation of opinions from multiple sources. In K. Fiedler & P. Juslin (Eds.), *Information sampling and adaptive cognition* (pp. 327–352). Cambridge University Press.
Budescu, D. V., Rantilla, A. K., Yu, H.-T., & Karelitz, T. M. (2003). The effects of asymmetry among advisors on the aggregation of their opinions. *Organizational Behavior and Human Decision Processes, 90*, 178–194.
Burson, K. A., Larrick, R. P., & Klayman, J. (2006). Skilled or unskilled, but still unaware of it: How perceptions of difficulty drive miscalibration in relative comparisons. *Journal of Personality and Social Psychology, 90*, 60–77.
Burt, R. S. (1992). *Structural holes*. Harvard University Press.
Burt, R. S. (2004). Structural holes and good ideas. *American Journal of Sociology, 110*, 349–399.
Campbell, D. T. (1961). Conformity in psychology's theories of acquired behavioral dispositions. In I. A. Berg & B. M. Bass (Eds.), *Conformity and deviation* (pp. 101–142). Harper & Brothers.
Centola, D. (2022). The network science of collective intelligence. *Trends in Cognitive Sciences, 26*(11), 923–941.
Chapman, G. B., & Johnson, E. J. (1999). Anchoring, activation and the construction of values. *Organizational Behavior and Human Decision Processes, 79*, 115–153.
Clemen, R. T. (1989). Combining forecasts: A review and annotated bibliography. *International Journal of Forecasting, 5*, 559–609.
Clemen, R. T., & Winkler, R. L. (1986). Combining economic forecasts. *Journal of Business and Economic Statistics, 4*, 39–46.
Cronin, M. A., & Weingart, L. R. (2007). Representational gaps, information processing, and conflict in functionally diverse teams. *Academy of Management Review, 32*, 761–773.
Denrell, J., & Fang, C. (2010). Predicting the next big thing: Success as a signal of poor judgment. *Management Science, 56*, 1653–1667.
Deutsch, M., & Gerard, H. B. (1955). A study of normative and informational social influences upon individual judgment. *Journal of Abnormal and Social Psychology, 51*, 629–636.
Dhami, M. K., Hertwig, R., & Hoffrage, U. (2004). The role of representative design in an ecological approach to cognition. *Psychological Bulletin, 130*, 959–988.
DiDonato, T. E., Ullrich, J., & Krueger, J. I. (2011). Social perception as induction and inference: An integrative model of intergroup differentiation, ingroup favoritism, and differential accuracy. *Journal of Personality and Social Psychology, 100*, 66–83.

Epley, N., & Gilovich, T. (2001). Putting adjustment back in the anchoring and adjustment heuristic: Differential processing of self-generated and experimenter-provided anchors. *Psychological Science, 12*, 391–396.

Farrell, S. (2011). Social influence benefits the wisdom of individuals in the crowd. *Proceedings of the National Academy of Sciences, 108*(36), E625–E625.

Festinger, L. (1954). A theory of social comparison processes. *Human Relations, 7*, 117–140.

Fiedler, K., & Krueger, J. (2011). More than an artifact: Regression as a theoretical construct. In J. I. Krueger (Ed.), *Social judgment and decision making* (1st ed.). Psychology Press. https://doi.org/10.4324/9780203854150

Gino, F. (2008). Do we listen to advice just because we paid for it? The impact of cost of advice on its use. *Organizational Behavior and Human Decision Processes, 107*, 234–245.

Gino, F., & Moore, D. A. (2007). Effects of task difficulty on use of advice. *Journal of Behavioral Decision Making, 20*, 21–35.

Gino, F., & Schweitzer, M. (2008). Blinded by anger or feeling the love: How emotions influence advice taking. *Journal of Applied Psychology, 93*, 1165–1173.

Girotra, K., Terwiesch, C., & Ulrich, K. T. (2010). Idea generation and the quality of the best idea. *Management Science, 56*, 591–605.

Harvey, N., & Fischer, I. (1997). Taking advice: Accepting help, improving judgment, and sharing responsibility. *Organizational Behavior and Human Decision Processes, 70*, 117–133.

Harvey, N., & Harries, C. (2004). Effects of judges' forecasting on their later combination of forecasts for the same outcomes. *International Journal of Forecasting, 20*, 391–409.

Harvey, N., Harries, C., & Fischer, I. (2000). Using advice and assessing its quality. *Organizational Behavior and Human Decision Processes, 81*, 252–273.

Hastie, R., & Kameda, T. (2005). The robust beauty of majority rules in group decisions. *Psychological Review, 112*, 494–508.

Heath, C., Larrick, R. P., & Klayman, J. (1998). Cognitive repairs: How organizations compensate for the shortcomings of individual learners. *Research in Organizational Behavior, 20*, 1–37.

Herzog, S. M., & Hertwig, R. (2009). The wisdom of many in one mind: Improving individual judgments with dialectical bootstrapping. *Psychological Science, 20*, 231–237.

Himmelstein, M., Budescu, D. V., & Ho, E. H. (2023). The wisdom of many in few: Finding individuals who are as wise as the crowd. *Journal of Experimental Psychology: General.*

Jenness, A. (1932). The role of discussion in changing opinion regarding a matter of fact. *Journal of Abnormal and Social Psychology, 27*, 279–296.

Kameda, T., & Tindale, R. S. (2006). Groups as adaptive devices: Human docility and group aggregation mechanisms in evolutionary context. In M. Schaller, J. Simpson, & D. Kenrick (Eds.), *Evolution and social psychology* (pp. 317–341). Psychology Press.

Kameda, T., Toyokawa, W., & Tindale, R. S. (2022). Information aggregation and collective intelligence beyond the wisdom of crowds. *Nature Reviews Psychology, 1*(6), 345–357.

Koehler, D. J., & Beauregard, T. A. (2006). Illusion of confirmation from exposure to another's hypothesis. *Journal of Behavioral Decision Making, 19*, 61–78.

Krueger, J. I., & Massey, A. L. (2009). A rational reconstruction of misbehavior. *Social Cognition, 27*, 785–810.

Larrick, R. P., & Soll, J. B. (2006). Intuitions about combining opinions: Misappreciation of the averaging principle. *Management Science, 52*, 111–127.

Lichtendahl, K. C., Jr., Grushka-Cockayne, Y., & Pfeifer, P. E. (2013). The wisdom of competitive crowds. *Operations Research, 61*(6), 1383–1398.

Lippold, M., Schulz-Hardt, S., & Schultze, T. (2021). GI transfer in multicue judgment tasks: Discussion improves group members' knowledge about target relations. *Journal of Experimental Psychology: Learning, Memory, and Cognition, 47*(3), 532.

Littlepage, G. E., Robison, W., & Reddington, K. (1997). Effects of task experience and group experience on group performance, member ability, and recognition of expertise. *Organizational Behavior and Human Decision Processes, 69*, 133–147.

Luan, S., Katsikopolous, K. V., & Reimer, T. (2012). The "less-is-more" effect in group decision making. In R. Hertwig, U. Hoffrage, & The ABC Research Group (Eds.). *Simple heuristics in a social world* (pp. 319–342). Oxford University Press.

Mannes, A. E. (2009). Are we wise about the wisdom of crowds? The use of group judgments in belief revision. *Management Science, 55*, 1267–1279.

Mannes, A. E., Soll, J. B., & Larrick, R. P. (2011). The wisdom of small crowds. Unpublished manuscript.

Mannes, A. E., Soll, J. B., & Larrick, R. P. (2014). The wisdom of select crowds. *Journal of Personality and Social Psychology, 107*(2), 276.

Mason, W. A., Jones, A., & Goldstone, R. L. (2008). Propagation of innovations in networked groups. *Journal of Experimental Psychology: General, 137*(3), 422.

Mellers, B., Stone, E., Murray, T., Minster, A., Rohrbaugh, N., Bishop, M., Chen, E., Baker, J., Hou, Y., Horowitz, M., & Ungar, L. (2015). Identifying and cultivating superforecasters as a method of improving probabilistic predictions. *Perspectives on Psychological Science, 10*(3), 267–281.

Mellers, B., Ungar, L., Baron, J., Ramos, J., Gurcay, B., Fincher, K., Scott, S. E., Moore, D., Atanasov, P., Swift, S. A., & Murray, T. (2014). Psychological strategies for winning a geopolitical forecasting tournament. *Psychological Science, 25*(5), 1106–1115.

Mellers, B. A., McCoy, J. P., Lu, L., & Tetlock, P. E. (2023). Human and algorithmic predictions in geopolitical forecasting: Quantifying uncertainty in hard-to-quantify domains. *Perspectives on Psychological Science*, 17456916231185339.

Miner, F. C. (1984). Group versus individual decision making: An investigation of performance measures, decision strategies, and process losses/gains. *Organizational Behavior and Human Performance, 33*, 112–124.

Minson, J. A., Mueller, J. S., & Larrick, R. P. (2018). The contingent wisdom of dyads: When discussion enhances vs. undermines the accuracy of collaborative judgments. *Management Science, 64*(9), 4177–4192.

Mussweiler, T., & Strack, F. (1999). Hypothesis-consistent testing and semantic priming in the anchoring paradigm: A selective accessibility model. *Journal of Experimental Social Psychology, 35*, 136–164.

Page, S. E. (2007). *The difference: How the power of diversity creates better firms, schools, groups, and societies*. Princeton University Press.

Palley, A. B., & Soll, J. B. (2019). Extracting the wisdom of crowds when information is shared. *Management Science, 65*(5), 2291–2309.

Paulus, P. B., & Yang, H. C. (2000). Idea generation in groups: A basis for creativity in organizations. *Organizational Behavior and Human Decision Processes, 82*, 76–87.

Prelec, D., Seung, H. S., & McCoy, J. (2017). A solution to the single-question crowd wisdom problem. *Nature, 541*(7638), 532–535.

Satopää, V. A., Salikhov, M., Mellers, B., & Tetlock, P. (2021). Bias, information, noise: The BIN model of forecasting. *Management Science, 67*, 7599–7618.

Satopää, V. A., Salikhov, M., Tetlock, P., & Mellers, B. (2023). Decomposing the effects of crowd wisdom aggregators: The bias-information-noise (BIN) model. *International Journal of Forecasting, 39*(1), 470–485.

Schultze, T., Mojzisch, A., & Schulz-Hardt, S. (2012). Why groups perform better than individuals at quantitative judgment tasks: Group-to-individual transfer as an alternative to differential weighting. *Organizational Behavior and Human Decision Processes, 118*(1), 24–36.

See, K. E., Morrison, E. W., Rothman, N. B., & Soll, J. B. (2011). Powerful and unpersuaded: The implications of power for confidence, advice-taking, and accuracy. *Organizational Behavior and Human Decision Processes, 116*, 272–285.

Sniezek, J. A., & Buckley, T. (1995). Cueing and cognitive conflict in judge-adviser decision making. *Organizational Behavior and Human Decision Processes, 62*, 159–174.

Sniezek, J. A., & Van Swol, L. M. (2001). Trust, confidence, and expertise in a judge-advisor system. *Organizational Behavior and Human Decision Processes, 84*, 288–307.

Soll, J. B., & Larrick, R. P. (2009). Strategies for revising judgment: How (and how well) people use others' opinions. *Journal of Experimental Psychology: Learning, Memory and Cognition, 35*, 780–805.

Soll, J. B., & Mannes, A. E. (2011). Judgmental aggregation strategies depend on whether the self is involved. *International Journal of Forecasting, 27*, 81–102.

Sorkin, R. D., Luan, S., & Itzkowitz, J. (2004). Group decision and deliberation: A distributed detection process. In D. Koehler & N. Harvey (Eds.), *Handbook of judgment and decision making* (pp. 464–484). Oxford University Press.

Surowiecki, J. (2004). *The wisdom of crowds: Why the many are smarter than the few and how collective wisdom shapes business, economies, societies, and nations*. Little, Brown.

Tetlock, P. E., & Gardner, D. (2016). *Superforecasting: The art and science of prediction*. Random House.

Tversky, A., & Kahneman, D. (1974). Judgment under uncertainty: Heuristics and biases. *Science, 185*, 1124–1131.

Vul, E., & Pashler, H. (2008). Measuring the crowd within: Probabilistic representations within individuals. *Psychological Science, 19*, 645–647.

Watson, G. B. (1928). Do groups think more efficiently than individuals? *Journal of Abnormal and Social Psychology, 23*, 328–336.

Yaniv, I. (1997). Weighting and trimming: Heuristics for aggregating judgments under uncertainty. *Organizational Behavior and Human Decision Processes, 69*, 237–249.

Yaniv, I. (2004). Receiving other people's advice: Influence and benefit. *Organizational Behavior and Human Decision Processes, 93*, 1–13.

Yaniv, I., & Kleinberger, E. (2000). Advice taking in decision making: Egocentric discounting and reputation formation. *Organizational Behavior and Human Decision Processes, 83*, 260–281.

Yaniv, I., & Milyavsky, M. (2007). Using advice from multiple sources to revise and improve judgments. *Organizational Behavior and Human Decision Processes, 103*, 104–120.

Predicting Behavior in Games: Loss Aversion vs. Rank Dependent Utility vs. Range Utility Theory

Manel Baucells, Philip Leclerc, Michał Lewandowski, and Jason Merrick

Abstract Rank dependent probability weighting—an integral part of cumulative prospect theory—has come to dominate the behavioral modeling of risk preferences in non-strategic settings over the last 40 years. We draw attention to some serious limitations of rank dependence when it comes to game-theoretic settings. First, in strategic settings where the probability of payoffs may be determined by the joint choice of all players, ranking outcomes (in a matrix) from lowest to highest becomes psychologically unnatural. Second, existence and interpretation of equilibrium when players possess rank-dependent preferences is problematic. Third, rank dependent models are notoriously complex to compute. In contrast, we argue that an alternative model, range utility theory, preserves much of the descriptive realism of rank-dependent utility, while sharing the theoretical and computational advantages of expected utility. We compare the two models using simple games of strategy as examples, and discuss the importance of accounting for loss aversion.

Keywords Risk preference · Expected utility · Rank dependent utility · Range utility · Loss aversion · Strategic games

---

M. Baucells (✉)
Darden School of Business, University of Virginia, Charlottesville, VA, USA
e-mail: BaucellsM@darden.virginia.edu

P. Leclerc
U.S. Census Bureau, Washington, DC, USA
philip.leclerc@census.gov

M. Lewandowski
Department of Quantitative Economics, Warsaw School of Economics, Warsaw, Poland
e-mail: michal.lewandowski@sgh.waw.pl

J. Merrick
Supply Chain Management and Analytics, Virginia Commonwealth University, Richmond, VA, USA
e-mail: jrmerric@vcu.edu

F. M. Federspiel et al. (eds.), *Behavioral Decision Analysis*, International Series in Operations Research & Management Science 350,
https://doi.org/10.1007/978-3-031-44424-1_8

Introduction

Decision analysis's main focus is on individual decision making, with risk and uncertainty being a major consideration. Uncertainty, however, could be strategic in nature, reflecting the inability to predict what other actors may do (Luce & Raiffa, 1957). Our starting point is to introduce four models for decision under risk that we seek to compare when it comes to 'solving' a game situation. In game theory payoffs are given in utility terms, i.e. they are assumed to reflect player preferences over strategy profiles. Because we are interested in predictions based on observables, we assume that payoffs are observable monetary payments. Then, we focus on the descriptive power of different preference models in the context of strategic uncertainty.

The first model is expected utility of wealth, the normative benchmark. The second model adds the behavioral aspect of reference dependence and loss aversion, with a choice of reference point tailored to game situations. Loss aversion is eminently descriptive, but could have a normative stand (e.g., it is easy to spend more, but cutting on expenses may be hard). The last two models are purely descriptive, and seek to capture the four-fold pattern of risk preferences (i.e., that a 1% chance of $1000 is preferable to at 10% chance of $100) in two alternative ways. We will discuss some of the advantages and limitations of each model, and illustrate the general issues using two relatively simple examples.

Our goal is not to delve on transitory phases of how boundedly rational individuals learn to play a game (Camerer et al., 2004; Ho & Su, 2013), but on the static notion of equilibrium: given some player's preferences, a set of strategies for each player such that no one player would have an incentive to unilaterally deviate.

Expected Utility

To set things up, a *prospect* is a finite lottery, denoted by σ, yielding outcomes $x_1, \ldots, x_K \in R$ with probabilities $p_1, \ldots, p_K$. Under expected utility (EU), there is a cardinally unique utility function, $u : R \to R$, defined over absolute levels of wealth, and preferences over prospects are represented by:

$$U^{\mathrm{EU}}(\sigma) = \sum_{k=1}^{K} p_k u(x_k). \tag{1}$$

Expected utility obeys the rational axioms of Von-Neumann and Morgenstern (1944) and so is the foundation for prescriptive decision analysis (what the decision maker (DM) should do), but does a poor job in predicting observed behavior, making it a poor model for descriptive decision analysis (what the decision-maker would do without decision support). The following three sub-sections introduce leading models for descriptive decision analysis.

We will assume the utility of wealth is linear in the range of payoffs we consider (i.e., the gains and losses involved represent a small fraction of the DM's current wealth), or

$$u(x) = x. \tag{1b}$$

Loss Aversion

One standard tweak to expected utility is to introduce reference dependence (Markowitz, 1952; Kahneman & Tversky, 1979) and loss aversion. Instead of preferences being defined over levels of wealth, they are defined over changes of wealth relative to some reference wealth level. Here, we choose the standard formulation of comparing each outcome to one reference point.[1] Moreover, rather than taking the reference point as exogenously given, we follow Schneider and Day (2016) and set the reference point at the maxmin point that each player could have guaranteed for himself. That is, the decision maker evaluates every outcome relative to what he would have obtained, if he played with extreme caution. Evidence supporting the maxmin reference point is provided by Baillon et al. (2020).

For a decision maker with reference point r, wealth levels above r are perceived as gains, and those below r as a loss. A simple way to account for loss aversion (LA) is to replace u by a value function defined over gains and losses relative to a reference point, and that introduces a kink at the reference point, as follows:

$$U^{\mathrm{LA}}(\sigma) = \sum_{k=1}^{K} p_k v(x_k), \text{where } v(x) = \begin{cases} u(r+x) - u(r), x \geq 0, \\ \lambda\left[u(r+x) - u(r)\right], x < 0. \end{cases} \tag{2}$$

In models of this form, values of λ between 1.5 and 3 are commonly inferred from experiments (Wakker, 2010). If u is linear, then the loss averse value function takes the piece-wise linear form

$$v(x) = \begin{cases} x, x \geq 0, \text{and} \\ \lambda x, x < 0. \end{cases} \tag{2b}$$

[1] Alternative formulation include regret models, where a list of outcomes is compared to another reference list of outcomes (Bell, 1985), or stochastic reference points whereby all outcome pairs are cross compared (Delquié & Cillo, 2006).

Rank-Dependent Utility

Loss aversion cannot explain the four-fold pattern of risk preferences (Kahneman & Tversky, 1979). One way to remedy this shortcoming is by introducing non-linear probability weighting (Edwards, 1954) through a strictly increasing and surjective function $w : [0,1] \rightarrow [0,1]$. In the original development of prospect theory (Kahneman & Tversky, 1979), the weighting function was directly applied to probabilities of individual consequences, but doing so may cause violations of stochastic dominance. Rank-dependent formulations, in which cumulative probabilities of consequences are sorted by their value, provide a natural way of restoring compliance (Tversky & Kahneman, 1992; Quiggin & Wakker, 1994).

Let $x_{(1)}, \ldots, x_{(K)}$ denote the list of potential outcomes ordered from lowest to highest, and $p_{(1)}, \ldots, p_{(K)}$ denote their associated probabilities. Using the convention $\sum_{k=1}^{0} = 0$ and $v(x_{(0)}) = 0$, and assuming $w(p) = 1 - w(1 - p)$ (for the second expression), we can write the rank-dependent utility (RDU) of a prospect as:

$$\begin{aligned} U^{\mathrm{RDU}}(\sigma) &= \sum_{k=1}^{K}\left[w\left(\sum_{l=1}^{k} p_{(l)}\right) - w\left(\sum_{l=1}^{k-1} p_{(l)}\right)\right] v\left(x_{(k)}\right) \\ &= \sum_{k=1}^{K} w\left(\sum_{l=k}^{K} p_{(l)}\right)\left[v\left(x_{(k)}\right) - v\left(x_{(k-1)}\right)\right]. \end{aligned} \tag{3}$$

Experimental behavior is well expressed by an inverse-S shaped probability weighting function. One commonly used parameterization with this form is

$$w(p) = \frac{p^{\gamma}}{p^{\gamma} + (1-p)^{\gamma}}, 0 < \gamma \leq 1. \tag{3b}$$

Values of γ between 0.3 and 0.9 best fit experimental evidence (Gonzalez & Wu, 1999, Table 3).

Range Utility Theory

RDU cannot explain context-dependent phenomena such as the preference reversal phenomena in choice between simple prospects (Lichtenstein & Slovic, 1971). The recently introduced range utility theory, which evaluates each prospect relative to the range of consequences in a given decision context, can address this challenge (Baucells et al., 2020). Let G and L denote the highest and lowest consequence in the menu of alternatives. The relative value of any consequence $x \in [L, G]$ is given by $\frac{v(x) - v(L)}{v(G) - v(L)}$. To this relative value, we apply a range distortion $D : [0, 1] \rightarrow [0, 1]$, strictly increasing and surjective, and satisfying $D(z) = 1 - D(1 - z)$, $z \in [0, 1]$.

Finally, we take the expected utility of this transformation of outcomes. Thus, under range utility theory (RUT) a prospect is evaluated as

$$\begin{aligned} U^{\mathrm{RUT}}(\sigma) &= \sum_{k=1}^{K} p_k u_{[L,G]}(x_k), \text{ where} \\ u_{[L,G]}(x) &= D\left(\frac{v(x)-v(L)}{v(G)-v(L)}\right). \end{aligned} \tag{4}$$

Experimental behavior is well expressed by an S-shaped distortion function, which can be parametrically captured by the inverse of (3b), given by

$$D(z) = \frac{z^{\frac{1}{\gamma}}}{z^{\frac{1}{\gamma}} + (1-z)^{\frac{1}{\gamma}}}, 0 < \gamma \le 1. \tag{4b}$$

The role of D in RUT is occasionally similar to that of w^{-1} in RDU. For example, consider the certainty equivalent of a binary prospect yielding G with probability p and L otherwise. Under RDU, we have that $v(ce) = w(p)v(G) + (1 - w(p))v(L)$, which rearranges to $w^{-1}\left(\frac{v(ce)-v(L)}{v(G)-v(L)}\right) = p$. Under RUT, the certainty equivalent (CE) solves $D\left(\frac{v(ce)-v(L)}{v(G)-v(L)}\right) = pu(G)+(1-p)u(L) = p$. Thus, if $D = w^{-1}$ then both models express the same certainty equivalents. In particular, RUT can successfully explain the four-fold pattern of risk preferences observed using binary gambles. For more than two outcomes, or when a binary gamble is compared to another one with wider range, RDU and RUT are no longer equivalent. Henceforth, and to compare both models on an equal footing, we assume $D = w^{-1}$. In our parametric forms, values of $\gamma < 1$ indicate an inverse S-shape form for w in RDU, as well as an S-shaped form for D in RUT.

RUT can explain the original Allais paradoxes by invoking certainty effects (in line with Schneider & Day, 2016). Being linear in probabilities, however, RUT cannot explain the common ratio effect for prospects inside the Marschak-Machina triangle, i.e. with probabilities strictly less than 1 (for which the empirical support is much weaker, see Harless, 1992).

A Simultaneous 2 × 2 Inspection Game

We now examine how models (1) to (4) treat mixed strategies in games. To illustrate the key issues, it suffices to consider a concrete 2×2 inspection game played between a company (C) and a regulator (R). The regulator can choose to inspect (I) or not, and the company can choose to disobey (D) with some onerous regulation or to comply. A compliant company is indifferent to the regulator's choice, yielding a normalized payoff of 0. The company's preferred outcome is to disobey without being inspected, yielding a payoff of 1. If the company disobeys and gets caught, however, he incurs a fine of f.

The regulator's preferred outcome is to not inspect and have the company comply, which we normalize to 1. If he inspects and the company complies, then the regulator incurs an inspection cost $0 < c < 1$. If he inspects and catches the company the regulator obtains a normalized payoff of 0. And not inspecting while the company disobeys yields a loss for the regulator of ℓ. We assume that the regulator does not directly benefit from the fine the company may pay. That is, if we vary f, the payoffs to the regulator remain unaltered. The payoff matrix is given by:

W M	Inspect		Not Inspect	
Disobey	$-f$	0	1	$-\ell$
Obey	0	$1-c$	0	1

The company could choose a pure strategy $S_c \in \{\text{Comply, Disobey}\}$, or a mixed strategy σ_c where Disobey is chosen with probability p_D. Similarly, the regulator could choose a pure strategy $S_R \in \{\text{Inspect, Not Inspect}\}$, or a mixed strategy σ_R, where Inspect is chosen with probability p_I.

Equilibrium Under Expected Utility

This game has no equilibrium in pure strategies, hence even under common knowledge of rationality among the players it is uncertain what the opponent will do. A mixed strategy profile (σ_C, σ_R) is a Nash equilibrium if σ_C is the company's best response to the regulator choosing mixed strategy σ_R and vice versa. Formally, Nash equilibrium requires

$$\sigma_i \in \arg\max_{\sigma_i'} \left\{ U_i^{\text{EU}} \left(\sigma_i' | \sigma_{-i} \right) \right\}, i \in \{\text{C,R}\} \tag{5}$$

If preferences are linear in probabilities, then a mixed strategy σ_i is a best response if and only if player i is indifferent to all pure strategy in the support of σ_i. Thus, if one correctly guesses the support of the mixed-strategy equilibrium, then one can solve for the equilibrium by finding the probabilities in σ_{-i} that make player i indifferent between all pure strategies in the support of σ_i.

In the case of the inspection game where full support is obvious, and assuming utility is linear in the payoffs, we obtain

$$U_{\text{C}}^{\text{EU}} \left(\text{Obey} | \sigma_{\text{R}} \right) = U_{\text{C}}^{\text{EU}} \left(\text{Disobey} | \sigma_{\text{R}} \right): \qquad 0 = -p_I f + (1 - p_I), \text{and}$$
$$U_{\text{R}}^{\text{EU}} \left(\text{Inspect} | \sigma_{\text{C}} \right) = U_{\text{R}}^{\text{EU}} \left(\text{Not Inspect} | \sigma_{\text{C}} \right): \quad (1 - p_D)(1 - c) = -p_D \ell + (1 - p_D).$$

Solving for the equilibrium probabilities produces

$$p_I^{\mathrm{EU}} = \frac{1}{1+f} \text{ and } p_D^{\mathrm{EU}} = \frac{c}{c+\ell}.$$

At the Nash equilibrium, the company is more likely to disobey if the cost of inspection is high or if the regulator's loss from missing their disobedience is low; and the regulator is more likely to inspect if the company's fine from getting caught is low.

Equilibrium Under Loss Aversion

The first behavioral aspect we ought to consider is loss aversion. In our game, we assume the linear utility exhibits a kink at the reference point, with λ_{R} and λ_{C} denoting the regulator's and the company's loss aversion, respectively. We assume the normalized payoff of 0 is the reference point, which is also the maxmin for each player in this game. Thus, the company fine now counts as $\lambda_{\mathrm{C}} f$, and the regulator's loss in case of not inspecting when the company is disobeying now counts as $\lambda_{\mathrm{R}}\ell$. The rest of payoffs in the matrix remain the same.

Equilibrium can be defined as in (5), but using U^{LA} instead of U^{EU}, and calculated as:

$$U_{\mathrm{C}}^{\mathrm{LA}}(\text{Obey}|\sigma_{\mathrm{R}}) = U_{\mathrm{C}}^{\mathrm{LA}}(\text{Disobey}|\sigma_{\mathrm{R}}): \quad 0 = -p_I \lambda_{\mathrm{C}} f + (1-p_I), \text{and}$$
$$U_{\mathrm{R}}^{\mathrm{LA}}(\text{Inspect}|\sigma_{\mathrm{C}}) = U_{\mathrm{R}}^{\mathrm{LA}}(\text{Not Inspect}|\sigma_{\mathrm{C}}): \quad (1-p_D)(1-c) = -p_D \lambda_{\mathrm{R}} \ell + (1-p_D).$$

The equilibrium becomes

$$p_I^{\mathrm{LA}} = \frac{1}{1+\lambda_{\mathrm{C}} f} \text{ and } p_D^{\mathrm{LA}} = \frac{c}{c+\lambda_{\mathrm{R}}\ell}.$$

If the regulator knows that the company is highly averse to getting a fine, then he will be less likely to inspect. And if the company knows that the regulator is highly loss averse, then he will be less likely to disobey.

Equilibrium Under Rank-Dependent Utility

In game situations, there are three sources of randomness: nature, what the opponents might do, and one's own mixing among pure strategies. Clearly, the rank dependent model must deal with nature and what the opponents might do. What is more delicate is the treatment of one's mixing. Here, the literature has considered two possibilities.

The first possibility assumes players do choose mixed strategies, hence their preferences are driven by the joint distribution of payoffs determined by nature and the mixing of all players, including themselves. According to this view, the rank dependent equilibrium must satisfy:

$$\sigma_i \in \arg\max_{\sigma_i'} \left\{ U_i^{\mathrm{RDU}} \left(\sigma_i' | \sigma_{-i} \right) \right\}, i \in \{\mathrm{C,R}\}.$$

Here, players would sort the outcomes in the support of the joint distribution from lowest to highest, and apply a transformation of cumulative probabilities. In the case of the inspection game, rank-dependent preferences over the joint distribution of mixed strategies are represented by:

$$\begin{aligned} U_{\mathrm{C}}^{\mathrm{RDU}} (\sigma_i | \sigma_{-i}) &= -w(p_D p_I)\lambda_{\mathrm{C}} f + 1 - w(p_D p_I + 1 - p_D), \text{and} \\ U_{\mathrm{R}}^{\mathrm{RDU}} (\sigma_i | \sigma_{-i}) &= -w(p_D(1-p_I))\lambda_{\mathrm{R}} \ell + \left(w(p_D + (1-p_D)p_I) - w(p_D) \right) \\ &\quad (1-c) + 1 - w(p_D + (1-p_D)p_I). \end{aligned}$$

Using these preferences, the left panel of Fig. 1 depicts the best response curves for the company as a function of p_I, and for the regulator as a function of p_D. The company's best response is to disobey (by setting $p_D = 1$) if $p_I \leq 0.1$, and to comply (by setting $p_D = 0$) if $p_I \geq 0.1$. For $p_I = 0.1$, the company is indifferent between these two pure strategies. In contrast to EU, and as shown in the middle panel of Fig. 1, the company is no longer indifferent to mixing. In fact, the best response is convex in p_D, so that the company strictly prefers either pure strategy, $p_D \in \{0, 1\}$, to choosing a mixture $p_D \in (0, 1)$. This corresponds to the broken horizontal line in the left panel of Fig. 1.

The best response segment for the regulator is more intricate. The regulator's best response is not to inspect (by setting $p_I = 0$) if $p_D \leq 0.75$, and to inspect (by setting $p_I = 1$) if $p_D \geq 0.93$. As p_D runs from 0.75 to 0.93, the regulator's best response has a unique hilltop that runs from $p_I = 0$ to $p_I = 0.65$. For $p_D = 0.93$, as shown in the right panel, the regulator is indifferent between inspecting with 0.65 probability, or inspecting with probability 1, and either of these choices is preferred to any mixture of them. The broken vertical line in the left panel at $p_D = 0.93$ connects these two choices.

A candidate for equilibrium could be $(p_I, p_D) = (0.1, 0.79)$, where the regulator's best response line meets the broken horizontal line for the company. As we have seen, however, disobeying with a 0.79 chance is not a best response from the company's viewpoint. If preferences are not quasi-concave—which can be the case for rank-dependent preferences with a probability weighting function containing strictly convex portions—and players choose mixed strategies, then equilibrium may fail to exist (Crawford, 1990, pp. 137–138), (Dekel et al., 1991, p. 234), (Ritzberger, 1996, Prop. 1). If w were (strictly) concave, a player facing two equally preferred pure strategies would (strictly) prefer some interior mixing. Hence, $U_{\mathrm{C}}^{\mathrm{RDU}}$

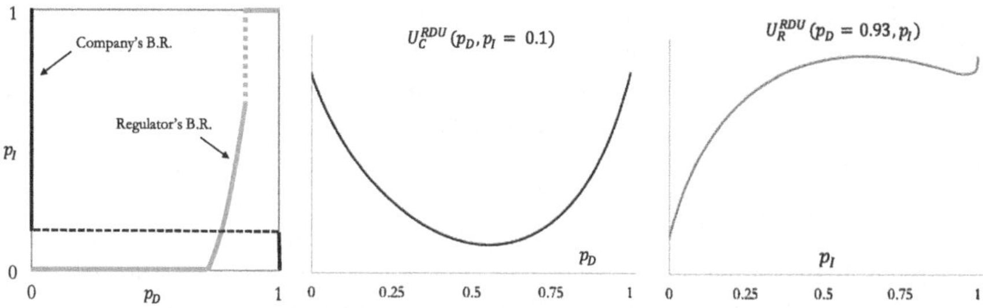

Fig. 1 Left: Best response curves over the joint distribution of mixed strategies. Middle: company's utility for different choices of probability of disobeying (fixing the opponent's probability at $p_I = 0.1$). Right: regulator's utility for different choices of probability of inspecting (fixing the opponent's probability at $p_D = 0.93$). Parameters are set to $(f,c,\ell) = \left(\begin{array}{c}\frac{2,1}{\frac{2,1}{6}}\end{array}\right)$, $(\lambda_C, \lambda_R) = (1.5, 1)$, and $(\gamma_C, \gamma_R) = (0.5, 0.5)$

would be concave in p_D, U_R^{RDU} concave in p_I, the best response hilltop would not be flat (as in EU), but trace a continuous best response curve as a function of the opponents' choice of probability. Consequently, equilibrium would be guaranteed (Ritzberger, 1996, Theorem 1).

Crawford (1990) introduced a straightforward mathematical fix for equilibrium non-existence using a convexification operator $\sigma_i \in co\left(\arg\max_{\sigma_i'}\left\{U_i^{RDU}\left(\sigma_i'|\sigma_{-i}\right)\right\}\right)$, so that all mixed strategies between any two maxima are also regarded as acceptable. In Fig. 1, this identifies $(p_I, p_D) = (0.1, 0.79)$ as the unique equilibrium. The justification for such a fix invokes subjective probabilities of what the opponent will do when choosing at random between a pure strategy and a mixed strategy. In addition to being psychologically contrived, finding an equilibrium under Crawford's definition is computationally expensive (Leclerc, 2014). In 2×2 games, the equilibrium could involve the crossing of two broken lines, and each broken line could connect a mixed strategy with a pure strategy. Describing Crawford's equilibrium in our inspection game for all values of (f, ℓ, c) would comprise of a long list of cases.

As an an alternative to Crawford's approach, Leclerc (2014) stipulates that the choice set of each player consist solely on pure strategies (see also Keskin, 2016 for a recent paper also advocating for this approach). This view is psychologically plausible (people do not seem to randomize in practice) and consistent with the idea of population dynamics, or purification of mixed equilibrium (Harsanyi, 1973).[2] When

[2] According to this interpretation each player is uncertain about the precise nature of their opponent's preferences, and privately observes an (arbitrarily small) payoff shock depending on the action they choose. Harsanyi (1973) proved that for almost all Nash equilibria of the original game of complete information there is a pure strategy Bayesian-Nash equilibrium of the perturbed (incomplete-information) game.

indifferent between two or more pure strategies, a player chooses one of them arbitrarily; they do not randomize. They do still, however, recognize strategic uncertainty. Thus, the probability p_D describes the regulator's subjective probability as for what the company will do; and p_I describes the company's subjective probability as for what the regulator will do (a perspective with close ties to Aumann (1974)'s foundational work on correlated equilibria).

Thus, a pair of beliefs, (σ_C, σ_R), is a mixed-strategy equilibrium if each player i is indifferent between the pure strategies in the support of σ_i, chooses one such arbitrarily, and believes the opponent will choose according to σ_{-i} when indifferent to the pure strategies in the support. Formally, Leclerc's proposed rank-dependent equilibrium is defined as

$$s_i \in \arg\max_{s'_i} \left\{ U_i^{\text{RDU}}\left(s'_i|\sigma_{-i}\right)\right\}, s_i \in supp\left(\sigma_i\right), i \in \{\text{C,R}\}.$$

Player i still has the same rank-dependent preferences, but the component σ_i is always a pure strategy. Computationally, Leclerc's equilibrium is calculated as usual by making players indifferent to the pure strategies in the support of equilibrium, as follows:

$$U_{\text{C}}^{\text{RDU}}\left(\text{Obey}|\sigma_{\text{r}}\right) = U_{\text{C}}^{\text{RDU}}\left(\text{Disobey}|\sigma_{\text{r}}\right):\ 0 = -w_{\text{C}}\left(p_I\right)\lambda_{\text{C}} f + 1 - w_{\text{C}}\left(p_I\right), \text{and}$$
$$U_{\text{R}}^{\text{RDU}}\left(\text{Inspect}|\sigma_{\text{c}}\right) = U_{\text{R}}^{\text{RDU}}\left(\text{Not}|\sigma_{\text{c}}\right):\ \left(1 - w_{\text{R}}\left(p_D\right)\right)$$
$$\left(1 - c\right) = -w_{\text{R}}\left(p_D\right)\lambda_{\text{R}}\ell + 1 - w_{\text{R}}\left(p_D\right).$$

Solving for equilibrium gives

$$p_I^{\text{RDU}} = w_{\text{c}}^{-1}\left(\frac{1}{1+\lambda_{\text{C}} f}\right) \text{ and } p_D^{\text{RDU}} = w_{\text{R}}^{-1}\left(\frac{c}{c+\lambda_{\text{R}}\ell}\right).$$

In what follows, we adopt Leclerc's equilibrium notion because its existence is guaranteed, is computed as usual, and is psychologically more plausible than Crawford's.[3] In Fig. 2, the equilibrium is found where the broken lines in the left panel meet. As shown in the middle and right panels, the company and the regulator are indifferent between their pure strategies. Mixtures are not in their choice set, hence the fact that they may strictly prefer such mixtures is irrelevant.

[3] An alternative approach which is operationally equivalent to Leclerc's is to allow players to choose mixtures, assume utility is rank-dependent with respect to nature and the opponent's play, but *linear* in one's own probability (Dekel et al., 1991; Metzger & Rieger, 2010). However, this latter fix feels somewhat arbitrary and inconsistent with rank-dependent preferences.

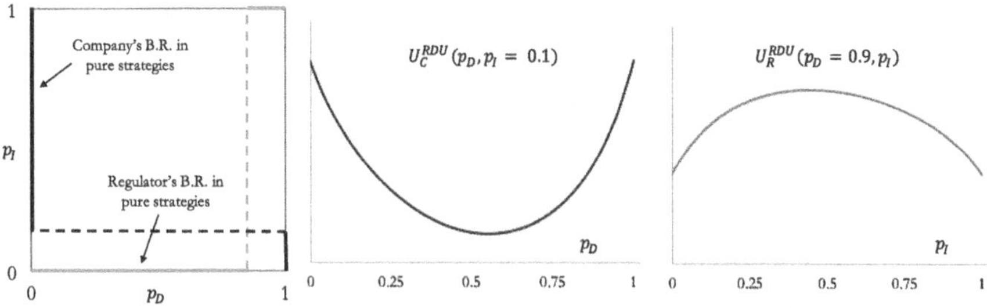

Fig. 2 Left: Best response curves when players choose only pure strategies. Middle: The company is indifferent between disobeying and not when he believes the regulator will inspect with $p_I = 0.1$. Right: The regulator is indifferent between inspecting and not when he believes the company will disobey with probability $p_D = 0.9$. Parameters are set to $(f,c,\ell) = \begin{pmatrix} 2,1 \\ \frac{2,1}{6} \end{pmatrix}$, $(\lambda_c, \lambda_r) = (1.5, 1)$, and $(\gamma_C, \gamma_R) = (0.5, 0.5)$

Equilibrium Under Range Utility Theory

To apply range-dependent utility to games, it is useful to assume the range of outcomes for a given player is given by the best and worst payoffs for that player that can happen in the game. A natural justification for this choice of range is the notion of a trembling-hand, i.e., all pure strategy have some chance, albeit small, of being chosen. In our 2×2 example, the equilibrium has full support, so that it is uncontroversial that the payoff range for the company is $[-f, 1]$, and the range for the regulator is $[-\ell, 1]$. Because range utility theory is linear in probabilities, mixed-strategy equilibria can again be found by making players indifferent to their pure strategies in the support. Thus, equilibrium can be defined and found as in (5) but using U^{RUT} instead of U^{EU}.

For the inspection game, we let

$$u_{\text{c}}^{\text{RUT}}(x) = D_{\text{c}}\left(\frac{v_{\text{c}}(x) - v_{\text{c}}(-f)}{v_{\text{c}}(1) - v_{\text{c}}(-f)}\right) \text{and}\, u_{\text{R}}^{\text{RUT}}(x) = D_{\text{R}}\left(\frac{v_{\text{R}}(x) - v_{\text{R}}(-\ell)}{v_{\text{R}}(1) - v_{\text{R}}(-\ell)}\right),$$

for any outcome x in the respective ranges, and solve

$$\begin{aligned} U_{\text{c}}^{\text{RUT}}(\text{Obey}|\sigma_{\text{R}}) = U_{\text{c}}^{\text{RUT}}(\text{Disobey}|\sigma_{\text{R}}) &: u_{\text{c}}^{\text{RUT}}(0) \\ &= p_I u_{\text{c}}^{\text{RUT}}(-f) + (1 - p_I) u_{\text{c}}^{\text{RUT}}(1), \text{and} \\ U_{\text{R}}^{\text{RUT}}(\text{Inspect}|\sigma_{\text{c}}) = U_{\text{R}}^{\text{RUT}}(\text{Not}|\sigma_{\text{c}}) &: p_D u_{\text{R}}^{\text{RUT}}(0) + (1 - p_D) u_{\text{R}}^{\text{RUT}}(1 - c) \\ &= p_D u_{\text{R}}^{\text{RUT}}(-\ell) + (1 - p_D) u_{\text{r}}^{\text{rut}}(1). \end{aligned}$$

Solving for the equilibrium probabilities, and applying $D(z) = 1 - D(1 - z)$, we obtain

$$p_I^{\mathrm{RUT}} = D_{\mathrm{c}}\left(\frac{1}{1+\lambda_{\mathrm{c}} f}\right) \text{ and } p_D^{\mathrm{RUT}} = \frac{D_{\mathrm{r}}\left(\frac{c}{1+\lambda_{\mathrm{R}}\ell}\right)}{D_{\mathrm{r}}\left(\frac{c}{1+\lambda_{\mathrm{R}}\ell}\right)+D_{\mathrm{r}}\left(\frac{\lambda_{\mathrm{R}}\ell}{1+\lambda_{\mathrm{R}}\ell}\right)}.$$

Summary of Each Equilibrium

Under all our four models, we have been able to define and guarantee existence of equilibrium. For EU, LA, and RUT, players can have mixed strategies as their objects of choice or, alternatively, only select pure strategies and choose arbitrarily when indifferent. In the latter case, probability mixtures represent subjective uncertainty about what the opponent will do. In the case of RDU, only the latter interpretation guarantees existence of equilibrium. As seen in Table 1, the four models generally produce different equilibrium predictions.

Note that if $D_{\mathrm{c}} = w_{\mathrm{c}}^{-1}$, then the equilibrium probabilities of inspection under RDU and RUT are identical. The equilibrium probabilities of disobeying under RDU and RUT are slightly different, but not by much. The similarity between RDU and RUT extends to all 2×2 games, as equilibrium probabilities have the same first-order Taylor expansion with respect to game payoffs. Thus, for 2×2 games, RUT makes qualitatively similar predictions, without the conceptual baggage required for RDU. For larger games, RDU and RUT differences are more nuanced, as we shall now see.

Table 1 Equilibrium probabilities for the inspection game under each decision model. For the numerical column, parameters are set to $(f,c,\ell) = \left(\frac{2,1}{\frac{2,1}{6}}\right)$, $(\lambda_{\mathrm{C}},\lambda_{\mathrm{R}}) = (1.5,1)$, and $(\gamma_{\mathrm{C}},\gamma_{\mathrm{R}}) = (0.5,0.5)$

Model	p_I		p_D	
Expected Utility	$\frac{1}{(1+f)}$	0.33	$\frac{c}{(\ell+c)}$	0.75
Loss Averse	$\frac{1}{(1+\lambda_{\mathrm{c}} f)}$	0.25	$\frac{c}{(\lambda_{\mathrm{R}}\ell+c)}$	0.75
Rank-Dependent Utility	$w_{\mathrm{c}}^{-1}\left(\frac{1}{(1+\lambda_{\mathrm{c}} f)}\right)$	0.10	$w_{\mathrm{R}}^{-1}\left(\frac{c}{(\lambda_{\mathrm{R}}\ell+c)}\right)$	0.90
Range Utility Theory	$D_{\mathrm{c}}\left(\frac{1}{(1+\lambda_{\mathrm{c}} f)}\right)$	0.10	$\frac{D_{\mathrm{R}}\left(\frac{c}{(1+\lambda_{\mathrm{R}}\ell)}\right)}{D_{\mathrm{R}}\left(\frac{c}{(1+\lambda_{\mathrm{R}}\ell)}\right)+D_{\mathrm{r}}\left(\frac{\lambda_{\mathrm{R}} l}{(1+\lambda_{\mathrm{R}}\ell)}\right)}$	0.93

Table 2 R&D investment game: Payoffs for the row player as a function of his investment and the column player's investment [$e = 5$]

	0	1	2	3	4	5
0	0	0	0	0	0	0
1	$z-1$	-1	-1	-1	-1	-1
2	$z-2$	$z-2$	-2	-2	-2	-2
3	$z-3$	$z-3$	$z-3$	-3	-3	-3
4	$z-4$	$z-4$	$z-4$	$z-4$	-4	-4
5	$z-5$	$z-5$	$z-5$	$z-5$	$z-5$	-5

A Simultaneous 6 × 6 Investment Game

Consider the R&D investment game examined by Rapoport and Amaldoss (2000) whereby two firms invest from their endowments to win a reward, z. The firm with the higher investment wins, and if the firms tie on their investments then neither wins the reward. We assume identical endowments $e = e_1 = e_2$, and that $z > e$. Table 2 describes the payoff matrix for the row player for $e = 5$. The column player faces a symmetric set of payoffs. Note that by investing nothing, $j = 0$, the row player can maintain its initial endowment, whereas any positive investment has risk. Hence, we set the reference point at the maxmin point associated with keeping the endowment, and assuring a normalized payoff of 0. If a firm invests $j > 0$, then it receives a payoff of $z - j > 0$ whenever it invests more than the competitor, and loses the investment otherwise.

This game has a unique symmetric equilibrium, which has full support.[4] Because of symmetry, we will obtain the equilibrium probabilities for the column player, which will depend on the preference parameters (utility, loss aversion, probability weighting, or range distortion) of the row player. For our empirical analysis, we will assume players have identical preferences. Hence, we will omit player subscripts, and compute the equilibrium strategies for just the row player.

It is convenient to allow investment to take continuous values in $[0, e]$. Suppose the column player chooses a mixed strategy with full support on $[0, e]$, described by $P(k < j)$, the probability that the column player investment, k, is strictly less than some given level $j \in [0, e]$. Next, we evaluate the row player's pure strategies under the different models, whose payoff is given by:

[4]The game admits two non-symmetric equilibria, given by $(\sigma_1, \sigma_2) = (1/2, 0, 1/4, 0, 1/4, 0; 0, 1/4, 0, 1/4, 0, 1/2)$ and its flipped version, with expected payoffs of $(8, 5)$ and $(5, 8)$. These equilibria are more efficient, as they avoid matching the investments. As such, they require some degree of coordination as for which player takes odd investments vs. even investments. Empirically, it is implausible that individuals paired anonymously would attempt to play one of the two non-symmetric equilibria.

$$\begin{aligned} U^{\text{EU,LA,RUT}}(j|k) &= P(k \geq j)u(-j) + P(k < j)u(z-j) \\ &= u(-j) + P(k < j)\left[u(z-j) - u(-j)\right], \text{and} \\ U^{\text{RDU}}(j|k) &= v(-j) + w(P(k < j))\left[v(z-j) - v(-j)\right]. \end{aligned}$$

By appropriately defining u as in (1), (2) or (4), the first expression incarnates into EU, LA or RUT. The second expression corresponds to RDU, and it is relatively simple because in this game each investment level has at most two potential outcomes. In all cases, we find the equilibrium probabilities for the column firm by making the row firm indifferent to all investment levels (i.e., for RDU, we adopt Leclerc's equilibrium notion). In particular, and for all models, because $U(0|k) = u(0)$, the equilibrium probabilities result from solving $U(j|k) = u(0)$, $j \in [0, e]$. Rearranging this equality we obtain that the distribution function of the equilibrium play is given by:

$$\begin{aligned} P^{\text{EU,LA,RUT}}(k < j) &= \frac{u(0) - u(-j)}{u(z-j) - u(-j)}, \text{and} \\ P^{\text{RDU}}(k < j) &= w^{-1}\left(\frac{-v(-j)}{v(z-j) - v(-j)}\right). \end{aligned}$$

By symmetry, these probabilities also apply to the solution for the row player; hence, together, they form a symmetric Nash equilibrium. The cdf is strictly increasing in j, hence the mixed strategy has full support on $[0, e)$. Because $P(j < e) < 1$, the mixed strategy possesses a point mass or atom at $j = e$, indicating that the full investment must be played with positive probability. Finally, we can express the equilibrium in discrete probability terms by letting, for each model $* \in \{EU, LA, RDU, RUT\}$,

$$\begin{aligned} q_j^* &= P(j \leq k < j+1) = P(k < j+1) - P(k < j), j \in \{0, \ldots, e-1\} \text{ and} \\ q_e^* &= 1 - P^*(k < e). \end{aligned}$$

Setting linear utility, we obtain that the risk-neutral symmetric Nash equilibrium distributes a probability mass of $\frac{e}{z}$ uniformly over $[0, e)$, yielding the discrete distribution:

$$\begin{aligned} q_j^{\text{EU}} &= \frac{1}{z}, j \in \{0, \ldots, e-1\}, \text{and} \\ q_e^{\text{EU}} &= 1 - \frac{e}{z}. \end{aligned}$$

Thus, the baseline equilibrium is that all strategies $j < e$ will be played with *equal* probability, and investing the full endowment is played with a higher probability. Moreover, the probability of investing the full endowment increases with the reward. We now compare these predictions with observation.

Table 3 First three columns: Observed frequencies of play for the high ($z = 20$) and low ($z = 8$) conditions of the investment game (Rapoport & Amaldoss, 2000). Next seven columns: equilibrium predictions of the different models after minimizing the mean absolute error

z	j	q^{obs}	q^{EU}	q^{LA}	$q^{RDU}_{\lambda=1}$	q^{RDU}	$q^{RDU}_{\lambda\geq 1,\gamma\leq 1}$	$q^{RUT}_{\lambda=1}$	q^{RUT}
20	0	0.141	0.050	0.086	0.141	0.141	0.086	0.054	0.141
	1	0.055	0.050	0.079	0.065	0.075	0.079	0.062	0.096
	2	0.053	0.050	0.074	0.050	0.059	0.074	0.069	0.066
	3	0.053	0.050	0.069	0.043	0.051	0.069	0.078	0.044
	4	0.069	0.050	0.064	0.038	0.045	0.064	0.108	0.025
	5	0.628	0.750	0.628	0.662	0.628	0.628	0.628	0.628
λ			1	1.78	1	1.41	1.78	1	2.61
γ			1	1	1.63	1.44	1	1.40	0.67
MAD			0.243	0.121	0.088	0.052	0.121	0.174	0.106
8	0	0.169	0.125	0.107	0.181	0.169	0.125	0.129	0.169
	1	0.116	0.125	0.111	0.118	0.114	0.125	0.119	0.128
	2	0.088	0.125	0.116	0.103	0.102	0.125	0.114	0.105
	3	0.118	0.125	0.121	0.098	0.098	0.125	0.111	0.093
	4	0.090	0.125	0.127	0.098	0.099	0.125	0.109	0.087
	5	0.418	0.375	0.418	0.402	0.418	0.375	0.418	0.418
λ			1	0.84	1	0.92	1	1	1.22
γ			1	1	1.29	1.28	1	0.87	0.71
MAD			0.175	0.135	0.073	0.045	0.175	0.094	0.056

Table 3 reports the observed frequencies of play by Rapoport and Amaldoss (2000, Table 3), who assigned 18 subjects to play a high-reward ($z = 20$) and a low-reward ($z = 8$) version of the game over 160 trials in randomized pairs with $e = 5$. The column next to q^{obs} is q^{EU}, the prediction of EU with linear utility. Expected utility correctly predicts that players will randomize will full support, that the frequency with which they invest the full endowment ($j = 5$) is higher than any other intermediate investment, and that such probability increases with the reward. Indeed, as $z : 8 \rightarrow 20$ we predict $q^{EU} : 0.375 \rightarrow 0.750$, and we observe $q^{obs} : 0.418 \rightarrow 0.628$. EU, however, fails to predict over-play of the safe strategy ($j = 0$), and is a bit off in predicting the frequency of the full investment ($j = e$).

We now examine whether LA, RDU, or RUT can pick up on these behavioral inclinations. To apply RUT, note that the range of outcomes in the continuous version of this game is given by $[-e, z]$. Hence, we set $u(x) = D\left(\frac{v(x)-v(-e)}{v(z)-v(-e)}\right)$. For convenience, D will denote both the inverse of w in RDU, as well as the range distortion function in RUT.

In the data, we observe that subjects over-play the safe strategy relative to the EU prediction. As we shall now see, loss aversion is the most parsimonious way to account for this deviation. Surprisingly, rank-dependent utility (with loss aversion) is incompatible with this deviation, whereas range utility theory remains agnostic.

To see this, it is useful to calculate the density function of the equilibrium play across the four models, and examine its height at zero. For $j \in [0,e)$, we have that[5]

$$p^{EU}(j) = \frac{1}{z},$$

$$p^{LA}(j) = \left.\frac{z\lambda}{\left(z+j(\lambda-1)\right)^2}\right|_{j=0} = \frac{\lambda}{z},$$

$$p^{RDU}(j) = D'\left(\frac{\lambda j}{z+j(\lambda-1)}\right)\left.\frac{z\lambda}{\left(z+j(\lambda-1)\right)^2}\right|_{j=0} = D'(0)\frac{\lambda}{z}, \text{and}$$

$$p^{RUT}(j) = \left.\frac{D'\left(\frac{(e-j)\lambda}{z+e\lambda}\right)\frac{\lambda}{z+e\lambda}\left[D\left(\frac{z-j+e\lambda}{z+e\lambda}\right)-D\left(\frac{e\lambda}{z+e\lambda}\right)\right] + D'\left(\frac{z-j+e\lambda}{z+e\lambda}\right)\frac{1}{z+e\lambda}\left[D\left(\frac{e\lambda}{z+e\lambda}\right)-D\left(\frac{(e-j)\lambda}{z+e\lambda}\right)\right]}{\left[D\left(\frac{z-j+e\lambda}{z+e\lambda}\right)-D\left(\frac{(e-j)\lambda}{z+e\lambda}\right)\right]^2}\right|_{j=0}$$

$$= \frac{D'\left(\frac{e\lambda}{z+e\lambda}\right)\frac{\lambda}{z+e\lambda}}{1-D\left(\frac{e\lambda}{z+e\lambda}\right)}.$$

Loss aversion alone predicts that individuals will overplay the safe strategy relative to EU by a factor λ. In the high condition, the safe strategy is over-played by a factor 0.141/0.05 = 2.82, and in the low condition by a factor 0.169/0.125 = 1.35. Thus, loss aversion does an excellent job in explaining the deviation in the high condition, and can also do so in the low condition, albeit with a relatively low estimate of λ. As for RDU, all parametric forms of the weighting function used in practice possess infinite slope at 0, hence the inverse exhibits $D'(0) = 0$. Thus, the prediction of RDU with an inverse S-shape weighting function is that the safe strategy will be under-played, and loss aversion cannot really compensate for that. For this reason, the best fit of the data will yield an S-shape weighting function.

[5] The density on $[0,e)$, given by $p(k=j) = dP(k<j)/dj$, is:

$$p^{\text{EU,LA,RUT}}(j) = \frac{u'(-j)\left[u(z-j)-u(0)\right]+u'(z-j)\left[u(0)-u(-j)\right]}{\left[u(z-j)-u(-j)\right]^2}, \text{and}$$

$$p^{\text{RDU}}(j) = D'\left(\frac{-v(-j)}{v(z-j)-v(-j)}\right)\frac{v'(-j)v(z-j)-u'(z-j)v(-j)}{\left[v(z-j)-v(-j)\right]^2}.$$

Finally, RUT's prediction for playing safe can go both ways. If the ratio $\frac{e\lambda}{z+e\lambda}$ is less than 0.5 (i.e., $z \geq e\lambda$) and falls on the steep middle portion of the range distortion function (i.e., $D'() > 1$), then $p^{\text{RUT}}(0)$ is guaranteed to be higher than $p^{\text{la}}(0)$. If z takes much lower or much higher values than $e\lambda$, then $D'()$ can become small, and produce $p^{\text{RUT}}(0) < p^{\text{LA}}(0)$. Hence, RUT adds little to loss aversion to explain this first deviation.

Next, we examine the probability of investing the full endowment. In the data, such risky strategy is slightly under-played in the high condition, and slightly over-played in the low condition. According to our models, the equilibrium probabilities of investing the full endowment are:

$$\begin{aligned}
q_e^{\text{EU}} &= 1-\frac{e}{z}, \\
q_e^{\text{LA}} &= 1-\frac{e\lambda}{z+e(\lambda-1)}, \\
q_e^{\text{RDU}} &= 1-D\left(\frac{e\lambda}{z+e(\lambda-1)}\right), \text{and} \\
q_e^{\text{RUT}} &= 1-\frac{D\left(\frac{e\lambda}{z+e\lambda}\right)}{D\left(\frac{z+e(\lambda-1)}{z+e\lambda}\right)}.
\end{aligned}$$

Loss aversion always makes players shy about investing the full amount, as $q_e^{\text{LA}} < q_e^{\text{EU}}$ for $\lambda > 1$. Thus, LA cannot possibly explain the over-play of the full endowment in the low condition. Both RDU and RUT predict that if the reward is sufficiently large, $z > e(\lambda + 1)$ in RDU or $z > e\lambda$ in RUT, then the full investment will be over-played relative to q_e^{LA}. Intuitively, individuals are attracted to the small chance of a large reward, and both models equally capture such attraction.

Table 3 shows the available parameters chosen to minimize the mean absolute deviation, $\text{MAD} = \frac{1}{e}\sum_{j=1}^{e}\left|q_j^{\text{obs}} - q_j^{\text{PRED.}}\right|$, between each equilibrium solution and the experimentally observed results for each condition. We observe the following:

- Loss Aversion does a nice job over expected utility in improving the fit with the data observed in the high condition. In the low condition, however, we obtain a loss aversion parameter less than 1. A broad literature shows that decision makers commonly weigh losses more than gains, and values of λ below 1 would indicate a rare loss-seeking behavior.
- Rank-Dependent Utility yields $(\lambda, \gamma) = (1.41, 1.44)$ in the high condition, and $(\lambda, \gamma) = (0.92, 1.28)$ in the low condition. A curvature parameter higher than 1 in

both cases goes with an S-shaped probability weighting. This indicates higher likelihood sensitivity near 0.5 probabilities, which is rarely observed in experiments elsewhere. Setting $\lambda = 1$ still yields a curvature parameter larger than 1 in both conditions. In the low condition, RDU increases the estimate of λ, but loss aversion still falls short of 1. Finally, constraining the RDU parameters to $\lambda \geq 1$ and $\gamma \leq 1$ produces $\gamma = 1$ in the high condition, and $\lambda = \gamma = 1$ in the low condition, so that traditional RDU adds little to LA or EU to explain this data.

- Range Utility Theory yields very credible parameter estimates in the high condition, namely $(\lambda, \gamma) = (2.61, 0.67)$. In the low condition, RUT increases the estimate of loss aversion as compared to RDU, this time to an acceptable value of $(\lambda, \gamma) = (1.22, 0.71)$. Thus, RDU fixes the low estimate of λ in the low condition, and improves the fit over LA in the two conditions. Hence, RUT with loss aversion is the only model delivering satisfactory parameter estimates for both conditions: one that is not specific only to the current data, but is consistent with data in other contexts as well.

Conclusions

We consider four models of risk preferences and their application to modeling player behavior in games, namely expected utility, loss aversion, rank-dependent utility, and range utility theory. We first demonstrate the steps to find an equilibrium for a 2 × 2 inspection game using each approach, illustrating that an equilibrium is guaranteed to exist under expected utility, loss aversion, and range utility theory. We show why such existence guarantees cannot be made for rank-dependent utility, and discuss alternative definitions of an equilibrium that guarantee existence.

We also find the equilibrium under each decision approach for a 6 × 6 investment game and show how well each can match the experimental results reported in Rapoport and Amaldoss (2000). The equilibrium under rank-dependence and loss aversion can closely match the experimental results for certain parameter values, but the parameter estimates contradict the standard values (a loss aversion parameter less than one, which represents loss seeking behavior; and a probability weighting curvature parameter larger than one, which represents insensitivity to probabilities near zero and one, and increased sensitivity to intermediate probabilities). On the other hand, the equilibrium under range utility theory and loss aversion yields a reasonable fit, and produces parameter values typically observed in single decision maker experiments (loss aversion larger than one, curvature parameter less than one).

In summary, we provide a proof of concept that range utility theory can represent player preferences in games, guarantee the existence of an equilibrium without complicating its definition, and predict observed player behavior with similar parameter values that represent single decision-maker behavior. While further research and experimental verification is required, we propose that range utility theory with a loss averse value function should be considered a leading descriptive model of risk preferences for player behavior in games.

Disclaimer and Acknowledgments The views and opinions expressed in this paper are those of the authors and not the U.S. Census Bureau.

References

Aumann, R. J. (1974). Subjectivity and correlation in randomized strategies. *Journal of Mathematical Economics, 1*(1), 67–96.

Baillon, A., Bleichrodt, H., & Spinu, V. (2020). Searching for the reference point. *Management Science, 66*(1), 93–112.

Baucells, M., Lewandowski, M., & Kontek, K. (2024). A contextual range-dependent model for choice under risk. *Journal of Mathematical Psychology, 118*, 102821.

Bell, D. (1985). Putting a premium on regret: Reply. *Management Science, 31*(1), 117–120.

Camerer, C. F., Ho, T.-H., & Chong, J.-K. (2004). A cognitive hierarchy model of games. *The Quarterly Journal of Economics, 119*(3), 861–898.

Crawford, V. P. (1990). Equilibrium without independence. *Journal of Economic Theory, 50*(1), 127–154.

Dekel, E., Safra, Z., & Segal, U. (1991). Existence and dynamic consistency of Nash equilibrium with non-expected utility preferences. *Journal of Economic Theory, 55*(2), 229–246.

Delquié, P., & Cillo, A. (2006). Disappointment without prior expectation: A unifying perspective on decision under risk. *Journal of Risk and Uncertainty, 33*(3), 197–215.

Edwards, W. (1954). The theory of decision making. *Psychological Bulletin, 51*(4), 380.

Gonzalez, R., & Wu, G. (1999). On the shape of the probability weighting function. *Cognitive Psychology, 38*(1), 129–166.

Harless, D. W. (1992). Predictions about indifference curves inside the unit triangle: A test of variants of expected utility theory. *Journal of Economic Behavior and Organization, 18*(3), 391–414.

Harsanyi, J. C. (1973). Games with randomly disturbed payoffs: A new rationale for mixed-strategy equilibrium points. *International Journal of Game Theory, 2*(1), 1–23.

Ho, T.-H., & Su, X. (2013). A dynamic level-k model in sequential games. *Management Science, 59*(2), 452–469.

Kahneman, D., & Tversky, A. (1979). Prospect theory: An analysis of decision under risk. *Econometrica, 47*(2), 263–292.

Keskin, K. (2016). Equilibrium notions for agents with cumulative prospect theory preferences. *Decision Analysis, 13*(3), 192–208.

Leclerc, P. (2014). *Prospect theory preferences in noncooperative game theory*. PhD thesis, Virginia Commonwealth University.

Lichtenstein, S., & Slovic, P. (1971). Reversals of preference between bids and choices in gambling decisions. *Journal of Experimental Psychology, 89*(1), 46.

Luce, R. D., & Raiffa, H. (1957). *Games and decisions*. Wiley.

Markowitz, H. (1952). The utility of wealth. *Journal of Political Economy, 60*, 151–156.

Metzger, L. P., & Rieger, M. O. (2010). *Equilibria in games with prospect theory preferences*. Preprint.

Quiggin, J., & Wakker, P. (1994). The axiomatic basis of anticipated utility: A clarification. *Journal of Economic Theory, 64*(2), 486–499.

Rapoport, A., & Amaldoss, W. (2000). Mixed strategies and iterative elimination of strongly dominated strategies: An experimental investigation of states of knowledge. *Journal of Economic Behavior and Organization, 42*(4), 483–521.

Ritzberger, K. (1996). On games under expected utility with rank dependent probabilities. *Theory and Decision, 40*(1), 1–27.

Schneider, M., & Day, R. (2016). Target-adjusted utility functions and expected-utility paradoxes. *Management Science, 64*(1), 271–287.
Tversky, A., & Kahneman, D. (1992). Advances in prospect theory: Cumulative representation of uncertainty. *Journal of Risk and Uncertainty, 5*(4), 297–323.
Von-Neumann, J., & Morgenstern, O. (1944). *Theory of games and economic behavior*. Princeton University Press.
Wakker, P. P. (2010). *Prospect theory: For risk and ambiguity*. Cambridge University Press.

Consequences of Missing Objectives in Applications of Multiattribute Utility Analysis

Sarah A. Kusumastuti and Richard S. John

Abstract Multiattribute decision analysis allows decision makers to identify their objectives as a critical part of constructing a prescriptive model for decision making. Failure to consider all relevant objectives is one of the leading causes of poor decision outcomes (Keeney & Raiffa, Decisions with multiple objectives: Preferences and value trade-offs. Cambridge University Press, 1976). However, studies have shown that decision makers are often ill-equipped to identify objectives and may generate less than half of the objectives they later recognize as important (Bond et al., Management Science, 54(1), 56–70, 2008; Bond et al., Decision Analysis, 7(3), 238–255, 2010). The present study examines the consequences of incomplete objective sets in a broad range of multiattribute utility analysis applications from various fields such as energy planning, conservation, and disaster management. We compare agreement between models that use the originally identified objectives with models constructed from only a subset of objectives using performance metrics related to the top choice, value loss, and rank ordering of alternatives. Analyses of the MAU applications considered suggest that the consequences of missing objectives depend primarily on three factors: (1) the direction and magnitude of the relationships (correlations) between attributes defining the objectives, (2) the decision space of the alternatives considered, i.e., the competitiveness and spread of the alternatives, and (3) the steepness of the assessed scaling parameters (weights). Our analysis demonstrates in actual MAU applications that the magnitude of negative consequences associated with missing objectives is highly variable.

S. A. Kusumastuti (✉)
Faculty of Behavioural, Management and Social Sciences (BMS), Department of Learning, Data analytics and Technology (LDT), Section Cognition, Data and Education (CoDE), University of Twente, Enschede, The Netherlands
e-mail: s.a.kusumastuti@utwente.nl

R. S. John
Department of Psychology, University of Southern California (USC), Los Angeles, CA, USA
e-mail: richardj@usc.edu

F. M. Federspiel et al. (eds.), *Behavioral Decision Analysis*, International Series in Operations Research & Management Science 350,
https://doi.org/10.1007/978-3-031-44424-1_9

Keywords Multiattribute utility · Objective identification · Missing objectives · Objective correlation · Hit rate · Value loss

Introduction

Any prescriptive approach to analyzing decision problems with conflicting objectives involves identifying the decision maker's objectives and constructing measures that capture the extent to which an option fulfills each objective (Keeney & Raiffa, 1976). One critical component of structuring any decision problem with multiple and conflicting objectives is identifying objectives. Specifying objectives reflects the decision maker's values by structuring the decision maker's values relevant to the decision at hand. Articulating one's objectives is considered a critical step in structuring any decision problem, and making poor decisions is associated with not having a clear awareness of relevant objectives (Nutt, 1998; Payne et al., 1999; Bond et al., 2008). Therefore, making better decisions in a multiattribute context can be aided by having a more comprehensive set of objectives. However, studies by Bond et al. (2008, 2010) have suggested that decision makers are ill-equipped to generate their objectives. These studies reported that decision makers could identify only 30–50% of objectives they consider important, indicating that their initial structuring process is flawed for not considering all values relevant to the decision.

Objectives in Multiattribute Decision Modeling

Practitioners of multiattribute methods consider the structuring of a decision problem to be as important as the modeling, and it is essential to understand how to structure the decision maker's values to produce meaningful results (Keeney, 2007; Keeney & Raiffa, 1976, pp. 31–65; Montibeller & von Winterfeldt, 2015; von Winterfeldt, 1980; von Winterfeldt & Edwards, 1986, pp. 26–62; von Winterfeldt & Edwards, 2007; von Winterfeldt & Fasolo, 2009). A common approach in identifying and structuring the decision maker's concerns is Value Focused Thinking (VFT). Structuring decision problems through VFT encourages broader thinking that genuinely reflects what the decision maker wants, as opposed to alternative-focused thinking, which works within the boundaries of the identified available options (Keeney, 1996, pp. 29–30). VFT facilitates the identification of relevant values that can be operationalized in the form of objectives and attributes.

Objectives are derived from values expressed directionally, such as maximizing or minimizing a characteristic of the alternatives. Objectives are operationalized using attributes, a metric used to quantify each alternative's performance vis-à-vis each objective. For example, in choosing a city in which to live, one may value security, which can be expressed as the objective of maximizing safety and operationalized using a metric such as current crime rates, e.g., homicides per 100,000 people. The consequences of not having a comprehensive list of objectives in a decision problem have not been explored adequately despite being a critical foundation for structuring decision problems.

Current Literature on Missing Objectives/Attributes

Previous research examining the effects of missing objectives is limited and has yielded mixed results (Aschenbrenner, 1977; Barron & Kleinmuntz, 1986; Barron, 1987; Fry et al., 1997; Barron & Barrett, 1999; Fasolo et al., 2007). However, substantial methodological variation among these studies makes it difficult to interpret or explain the mixed results. More importantly, the Bond et al. studies challenge many of the assumptions implicit in these studies.

One of the main assumptions in the studies examining the effect of missing attributes is that the omitted objectives are likely to be those with the smallest weights. However, Bond et al. (2008, 2010) discovered that this might not be the case, as they found that objectives that are initially identified and those that are later selected from a master list are ranked similarly in terms of importance to the decision maker.

Some other potential sources of inconsistency across studies include the scope and complexity of the MAU models in terms of the number of attributes and the number of alternatives considered, as well as performance metrics used to compare models. Some measures, such as hit rate and value loss, focus on the top choice of the models, while others, such as model convergence, consider the overall rank order of alternatives indicated by the models. The results produced from these measures may not always lead to the same conclusions (Barron, 1987). Utility loss and hit rate are more appropriate for decision problems that require the selection of a single alternative, while convergence is more suitable for selecting a subset of alternatives (pick K of N options).

Brief Overview of Multiattribute Modeling

The applications evaluated in this study used additive models, the most commonly used multiattribute model. The additive model assumes the strength of preference for various levels of each attribute is independent of levels of the other attributes. The multiattribute model is expressed in Eq. (1).

$$v(X_i) = w_1 v_1(x_{i1}) + w_2 v_2(x_{i2}) + \ldots + w_m v_m(x_{im}) = \sum_{j=1}^{m} w_j v_j(x_{ij}) \tag{1}$$

where $\sum_{j=1}^{m} w_j = 1$ and $0 < w_j < 1$. An alternative X_y is preferable to an alternative X_z if and only if $v(X_y) > v(X_z)$.

The weights, wj, serve as scaling parameters to specify the exchange rate between attribute units. Thus, weights define the trade-offs between attribute metrics and are at the core of the decision maker's values. Various methods are available for eliciting weights from decision makers, including swing weighting, direct trade-offs, lotteries, etc. (Keeney & Raiffa, 1976; von Winterfeldt & Edwards, 1986). Because the additive model (Eq. 1) requires independence, weight ratios are preserved for reduced models with missing attributes. Weights for a reduced model can be calculated by dividing the weights from the original model by the sum of the weights in the reduced model. This renormalization calculation assures that the weights in the reduced model sum to 1.0 and preserves weight ratios from the original model. Various weight approximations using only the rank order of the wj are commonly used. Rank order weighting methods, such as Rank Order Centroid (ROC), are typically used because they require less time and effort, especially for group decision making (Barron & Barrett, 1996; Jia et al., 1998).

Methods

The analysis of each application begins with a review of the decision problem, followed by a summary of the model, including objectives, alternatives, weight elicitation, and relevant stakeholders involved. A brief description of each application's results is also provided. The model used in the original analysis is referred to as the full model and serves as a baseline for comparison. We acknowledge that the full models used in these applications are likely missing relevant objectives that were omitted; however, we treat the published models as ground truth since there is no way of identifying missing objectives from these published applications.

For the present study, new multiattribute models are constructed by omitting some of the objectives included in the full model. MAU scores are calculated for each alternative using the new reduced model, and the reduced model results are compared to results from the full model. Differences in the utility of the best options using the full and reduced model measure loss from omitting objectives for the "select the best" decision problem. Differences in the rank ordering of alternative scores are a measure of incongruence for the "select k-of-n" decision problem.

Selection of Cases

The analysis procedures described in the previous section will be applied to seven applications of multiattribute methods to actual decision problems to better understand the potential impact of missing objectives in practice. The applications were selected from published journal articles demonstrating the use of multiattribute methods in various decision contexts.

Four criteria were applied for selecting cases included in the study:

1. The application consisted of an additive multiattribute utility or value model.
2. The published paper provided a complete description of the objectives, attribute measures for each objective, and weights utilized in the model.
3. The paper described the set of alternatives considered in the problem, along with the alternatives by attributes consequence matrix and either value or utility scores or raw scores and the single-attribute value or utility functions.
4. The results of the multiattribute analysis presented in the paper are reproducible from the required model information described in 1–3.

We purposely intended to sample applications from various fields that span multiple interdisciplinary journals. The academic search engine Google Scholar, complemented by the ProQuest journal database, was utilized for the search process. The search used the keywords "multi-attribute," "application," "model," as well as "weights" and "table" to identify papers that satisfied the inclusion criteria 1–4 listed above.

There were 100 abstracts examined during the search process. The most common reason a study was excluded was not presenting all the required data for the analysis. For example, a study may not show the full set of alternatives and their attribute values. Some of the studies are eliminated due to being more theoretical and lacking applicable decision contexts.

The seven applications of multiattribute value or utility models selected for the present study are shown in Table 1, listed alphabetically by application name.

Properties of Decision Problems

Table 2 provides more details on the characteristics of the decision context of the applications in this study. It includes information about the number of objectives and alternatives, the decision makers, the weighting methods used, and some parameters describing the distribution of correlations between attribute values or utilities in the decision problem. A more detailed description of how each application addressed objectives generation and a broader description of the decision structuring process is provided in the appendix.

Analysis Procedures

Previous research indicates that decision makers typically fail to identify about half of the relevant objectives; hence, reduced models will be constructed by omitting subsets of (approximately) 1/3, 1/2, and 2/3 of objectives included in the full model. Suppose for a reduced model there are ℓ attributes to be omitted from the full

Table 1 Published multiattribute applications included in the analysis

Application name	Decision context	Citation
Airline competitiveness	Evaluating airline competitiveness	Chang, Y. H., & Yeh, C. H. (2001). Evaluating airline competitiveness using multiattribute decision making. *Omega, 29*(5), 405–415.
Cargo delivery	Planning of cargo delivery in a disaster aftermath	Cavalcanti, L. B., Mendes, A. B., & Yoshizaki, H. T. Y. (2017). Application of multi-attribute value theory to improve cargo delivery planning in disaster aftermath. *Mathematical Problems in Engineering, 2017*.
Climate change policy	Evaluation of climate change mitigation policy	Konidari, P., & Mavrakis, D. (2007). A multi-criteria evaluation method for climate change mitigation policy instruments. *Energy Policy, 35*(12), 6235–6257.
Container ports	Selection of container ports in the gulf coast for shipping lines	De Icaza, R. R., Parnell, G. S., & Pohl, E. A. (2019). Gulf Coast Port Selection Using Multiple-Objective Decision Analysis. *Decision Analysis, 16*(2), 87–104.
Historical buildings	Choice of historical buildings to repurpose	Ferretti, V., Bottero, M., & Mondini, G. (2014). Decision making and cultural heritage: An application of the Multi-Attribute Value Theory for the reuse of historical buildings. *Journal of Cultural Heritage, 15*(6), 644–655.
Power plant	Options for power plant development	Jacobi, S. K., & Hobbs, B. F. (2007). Quantifying and mitigating the splitting bias and other value tree-induced weighting biases. *Decision Analysis, 4*(4), 194–210.
Radioactive waste	Immobilizing radioactive liquid waste	Brothers, A. J., Mattigod, S. V., Strachan, D. M., Beeman, G. H., Kearns, P. K., Papa, A., & Monti, C. (2009). Resource-limited multiattribute value analysis of alternatives for immobilizing radioactive liquid process waste stored in Saluggia, Italy. *Decision Analysis, 6*(2), 98–114.

multiattribute model with a total of m attributes. Select m-ℓ attributes from the full attribute set such that we have the reduced model for each alternative X_i. This model has a reduced set of weights $W = \{w'_1, w'_2, \ldots, w'_{m-l}\}$, which would be a normalization of the selected l weights.

$$v_{reduced}\left(X_i\right) = \sum_{m-l}^{j=1} w'_j v_j\left(x_{ij}\right) \tag{2}$$

Previous empirical findings show little difference in the importance of objectives identified from recall (self-generated) compared to objectives recognized from a master list (Bond et al., 2008, 2010). Therefore, multiple reduced models will be sampled from each possible subset of objectives of a given size. For example, for a model with a full set of 12 objectives, the 1/3 reduced model will include a subset of 8 objectives. All $\binom{12}{8} = 495$ possible reduced models are considered in the present analysis.

Table 2 Summary of application characteristics

Application name	Number of objectives	Number of alternatives	Decision makers	Weighting method	Median and IQR for attribute intercorrelation
Airline competitiveness	11	4	Airline passengers	Ratio	Median = 0.26, IQR = −0.09 – 0.47
Cargo delivery	5	6	Humanitarian/ peacekeeping experts	Rank order centroid (ROC)	Median = 0.53, IQR = 0.29 – 0.74
Climate change policy	11	8	Climate policymakers	Ratio	Median = 0.13, IQR = −0.19 – 0.37
Container ports	18	5	Industry expert	Ratio	Median = −0.02, IQR = −0.51 – 0.49
Historical buildings	5	7	Experts from four different fields: history of architecture, spatial planning, restoration, and economics	Ratio	Median = −0.32, IQR = −0.56 – −0.17
Power plant	13	15	Energy management executives	Ratio	Median = −0.08, IQR = −0.31 – 0.27
Radioactive waste	11	3	Policymakers	Ratio	Median = 0.71, IQR = 0.15 – 0.91

For all possible reduced models of a given size, the hit rate is simply the proportion of reduced models with the same best alternative as the full model. Value loss is the difference in value (using the full model) between the best option identified in the full model and the best alternative determined by the reduced model. Finally, the convergence value is the rank order correlation (Spearman's ρ) between aggregate model scores for all options using the full and reduced model. The three performance parameters are collected for every decision maker in each case at every level of reduction, with value loss and convergence values averaged across models within each reduction level.

Results

The results are partitioned into two sections: (1) a detailed description of calculations of one of the seven applications analyzed in the study, and (2) the aggregated parameter results from all seven applications.

Selected Application Analysis: Container Ports (De Icaza et al., 2019)

This section presents a detailed analysis of selecting a container port on the gulf coast for shipping lines as an example of the qualitative and quantitative analysis performed on all seven applications. According to the full model applied to the ports considered, the best container port on the gulf coast is Houston, with a value of 0.356, and the worst is Gulfport, with a value of 0.169. Therefore, the value range for the alternatives considered is 0.187. Due to the large number of objectives (18), this analysis provides the greatest number of possible reduced models. The full model and complete list of attribute values for each alternative are displayed in Table 3.

Table 4 summarizes reduced model performance for each level of model reduction across all possible reduced models. Remarkably, reduced models with only 12

Table 3 Full model and a complete list of attribute values for port selection application

Objective	Houston	New Orleans	Mobile	Gulfport	Tampa	Weights
Maximize potential of bigger ships	0.47	0.47	0.47	0.00	0.37	0.110
Maximize vessel arrival	0.38	0.05	0.05	0.38	0.00	0.077
Maximize berth capacity	0.05	0.00	0.00	0.15	0.00	0.105
Maximize cargo handling performance	0.29	0.06	0.03	0.00	0.00	0.099
Maximize port capacity	0.21	0.00	0.04	0.10	0.03	0.050
Maximize refrigerated containers capacity	0.23	0.14	0.03	0.26	0.00	0.006
Maximize market/cargo volume	0.28	0.05	0.02	0.02	0.00	0.094
Maximize ship calls	0.87	0.44	0.10	0.05	0.00	0.083
Maximize container handling capacity	0.34	0.34	0.34	0.00	0.28	0.061
Maximize shipping lines serviced	0.42	0.16	0.19	0.00	0.02	0.066
Maximize intermodal service	0.25	0.01	0.56	0.10	0.79	0.055
Maximize rail connectivity	0.20	1.00	0.80	0.20	0.00	0.039
Minimize landside congestion	0.00	0.82	0.97	1.00	0.66	0.033
Maximize environmental protection	0.75	0.25	0.00	0.36	0.50	0.022
Minimize severe weather	1.00	1.00	0.00	0.60	0.20	0.044
Minimize disasters situation	0.00	0.59	0.46	0.38	0.71	0.017
Minimize tornadoes presence	0.00	0.82	0.78	0.78	0.62	0.011
Minimize precipitation condition	0.00	0.24	0.30	0.49	0.61	0.028
Alternative value	0.356	0.277	0.233	0.167	0.182	

Table 4 Performance parameters at each level of reduction for port selection application

Parameter	Reduced model		
	1/3 reduced	1/2 reduced	2/3 reduced
Number of objectives (out of 18)	12	9	6
Number of possible reduced models	18,564	48,620	18,564
Hit Rate	0.916	0.806	0.682
Average Value Loss	0.0082	0.0207	0.0377
Convergence Values (ρ)			
Median	0.90	0.90	0.70
Mean	0.87	0.76	0.61
IQR	0.90–1.00	0.70–1.00	0.40–0.90

of the 18 objectives (1/3 reduction), 91.6% select the same best port (Houston), yield an average value loss of less than 0.01, and produce a median rank order correlation across all alternatives of 0.90. As expected, the hit rate for the best container port and the rank order correlation across container ports decreases as more objectives are removed; likewise, utility loss (for the best port) increases as more objectives are omitted.

In order to interpret the utility loss metric, we translated utility loss into equivalent losses on each of the attributes. Many attributes in the port evaluation application utilized natural measures; hence, value loss is easily interpretable equivalent attribute units on a natural scale. The complete list of value losses translated to equivalent units on each attribute is displayed in Table 5.

Attribute weights with the largest values indicate the biggest gap between the best and worst attribute levels; thus, value loss affects these attributes more than those with smaller weights. For example, consider the attribute with the greatest weight, maximizing the potential of bigger ships, defined by depth in feet. The real unit equivalent of the value loss for 1/3, 1/2, and 2/3 reduction corresponds to 0.16, 0.39, and 0.72 feet, respectively, which may not be a substantially large difference when considering the sizes of ships harboring in such ports. The attribute with the next largest weight is maximizing berth capacity, defind as the length of the berths in feet. The real unit equivalent of the value loss for 1/3, 1/2, and 2/3 reduction corresponds to 227.38, 573.99, and 1045.38 feet. Differences in berth length affect the size of ships that can dock in the harbor. These differences could mean that the port would have to reject vessels too long to dock reasonably at the harbor; hence, this value loss may have a larger impact than the value loss from the objective with the largest weight. The attribute with the third-largest weight is the maximizing cargo handling performance, defined by the number of cranes. The real unit equivalent of the value loss for 1/3, 1/2, and 2/3 reduction corresponds to 0.57, 1.45, and 2.64 cranes. The real unit equivalence for value losses represents differences in actual units of cranes, which directly impacts the throughput of the port operation.

Table 5 Value loss real unit equivalence for port selection application

Objective	Attribute	Attribute range	Linearized real unit difference from 1/3 model reduction value loss	Linearized real unit difference from 1/2 model reduction value loss	Linearized real unit difference from 2/3 model reduction value loss
Maximize potential of bigger ships	Depth (feet)	19	0.16	0.39	0.72
Maximize vessel arrival	No. of berths	21	0.17	0.43	0.79
Maximize berth capacity	Berth length (feet)	27,729	227.38	573.99	1045.38
Maximize cargo handling performance	No. of cranes	70	0.57	1.45	2.64
Maximize port capacity	Port capacity (acres)	1608	13.19	33.29	60.62
Maximize refrigerated containers capacity	No. of refrigerated slots	3414	28	70.67	128.71
Maximize market/cargo volume	Container traffic (TEUs)	5,874,366	48,169.8	121,599.38	221,463.6
Maximize ship calls	Ship calls (no.)	1099	9.01	22.75	41.43
Maximize container handling capacity	Maximum ship capacity call (TEUs)	16,877	138.39	349.35	636.26
Maximize shipping lines serviced	No. of shipping lines calling at Terminal	43	0.35	0.89	1.62
Maximize intermodal service	% of intermodalism used for shipments in state	15	0.12	0.31	0.57
Maximize rail connectivity	No. of class 1 railroads	5	0.04	0.1	0.19
Minimize landside congestion	Landside annual traffic delay (hours)	199,173	1633.22	4122.88	7508.82

(continued)

Table 5 (continued)

Objective	Attribute	Attribute range	Linearized real unit difference from 1/3 model reduction value loss	Linearized real unit difference from 1/2 model reduction value loss	Linearized real unit difference from 2/3 model reduction value loss
Maximize environmental protection	No. of environmental protection Policies	8	0.07	0.17	0.3
Minimize severe weather	Severe weather data inventory (no.)	5	0.04	0.1	0.19
Minimize disasters situation	Billion-dollar weather and climate disasters events (no.)	56	0.46	1.16	2.11
Minimize tornadoes presence	Average annual no. of tornadoes	144	1.18	2.98	5.43
Minimize precipitation condition	Precipitation ranks	70	0.57	1.45	2.64

Aggregated Results

This section describes the aggregated evaluation metrics across all application model. A total of ten decision models were analyzed from the seven applications, as one involved multiple decision makerswith different model parameters. (The historical buildings restoration application featured four decision models constructed from the judgment of different experts to evaluate the same set of alternatives.)

Hit Rate

Figure 1 shows the hit rates for the best alternative identified by the reduced model matching the full model for each application and all three reduction levels. As anticipated, hit rates decrease as more objectives are omitted from the full model. Hit rates vary dramatically across applications for the same proportion of omitted objectives. For example, for 1/3 omission rate, hit rates vary from below 40% to nearly 100%. This suggests that some applications, defined by the attributes X alternatives matrix, weight parameters, and single attribute value or utility functions, are more robust to omitted objectives than others.

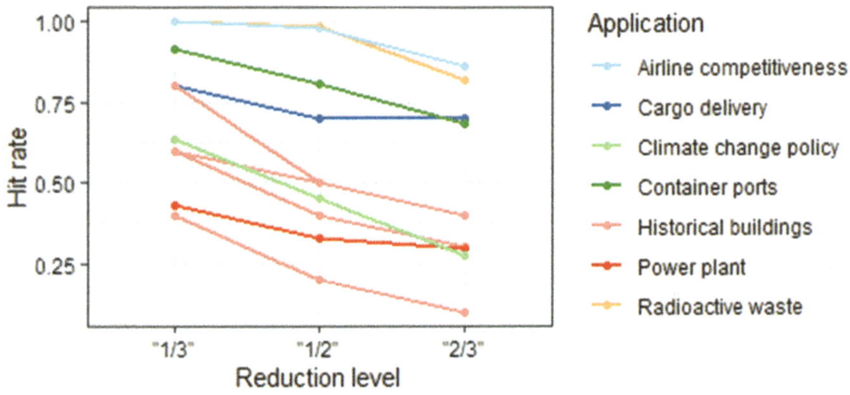

Fig. 1 Hit rate for each application by the proportion of attribute reduction

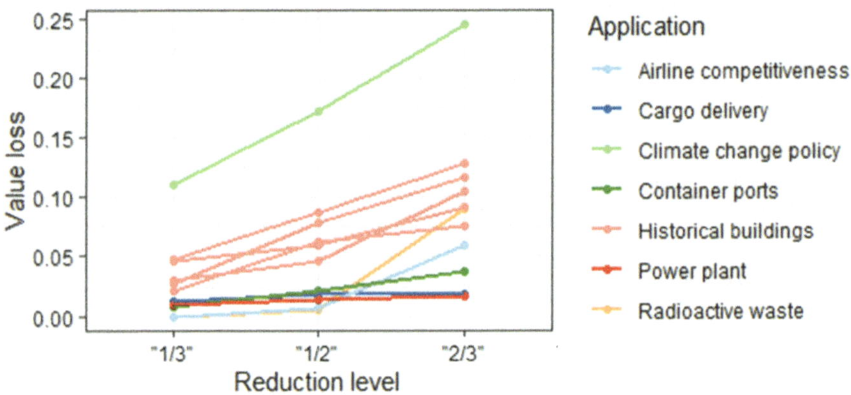

Fig. 2 Mean value loss for each application by the proportion of attribute reduction

Value Loss

Figure 2 plots the mean value loss for each application at all three levels of omitted objectives. As expected, value loss increases as more objectives are omitted and is inversely related to the hit rate. Value loss is a more sensitive measure than hit rate due to attribute omission since it considers the utility or value differences between best alternatives for reduced and full models. [By definition, there is no value loss if the reduced model selects the same best alternatives as the full model.] Like the hit rate, value loss is nearly linear in the proportion of objectives omitted for many applications, but for some applications value loss accelerates in a nonlinear manner as more objectives are omitted. As for hit rate, the magnitude of value losses varies considerably across applications for the same proportion of missing objectives. In particular, value losses in the climate change policy case are notably higher than the other cases, possibly due to the level of competitiveness of alternatives and the greater variance in alternative values.

Translating Value Loss into a Real Unit Equivalent to Cost

Several applications aim to minimize cost, measured in U.S. dollars or euros. The real unit value loss equivalent can be obtained by multiplying the value loss by the dollar range for the cost objective. Table 6 displays value loss for four applications that included a cost objective that could be converted to currency equivalents. Note that for airline competitiveness, the original cost attribute is the cost per available seat-kilometer in $, which is converted to the total operating cost of a 100-seat plane for each 1000 km flown. For the applications of climate change policy and radioactive waste, the original currency was stated in euros (€), so we converted it to U.S. dollars using the exchange rate as of September 2021, where 1 € equals US$1.18. Table 6 describes in very concrete terms the costs of omitting objectives from the MAU model for four real-world applications. For the climate change application, utility losses from missing objectives are in the hundreds of millions of dollars. However, in the airline and power plant cases, missing objectives have very little real financial impact.

Mean Convergence for Ordering Alternatives

Figure 3 summarizes the mean convergence (rank order correlation) for each application for all three levels of objectives reduction. As anticipated, mean rank order correlations across alternatives for the reduced and full models decreases for increased levels of attribute omission. Mean convergence is the most sensitive performance measure, especially in smaller alternative sets with limited possible rank order combinations. Mean convergence values express a more consistent pattern of decreasing values between each level of model reduction than hit rate or value loss. As for hit rates and value loss, the magnitude of convergence varies dramatically across the ten applications for the same proportion of missing objectives. For

Table 6 Mean value losses translated to equivalent currency

				Mean value loss cost equivalent to millions of US$		
Application	Objective	Attribute	Range	1/3	1/2	2/3
Airline competitiveness	Minimizing unit operation cost	Total operating cost of a 100-seat plane for a flight for every 1000 km flown	0.105	0	0.0006	0.0006
Climate change policy	Maximizing cost efficiency	Difference in savings	1354.76	149.16	234.11	332.05
Power plant	Minimizing total cost	Average capital expenditures year 0–20/year	306	3.24	4.16	5.17
Radioactive waste	Minimizing total cost	Mid-value total cost	60.20	0	34.92	54.30

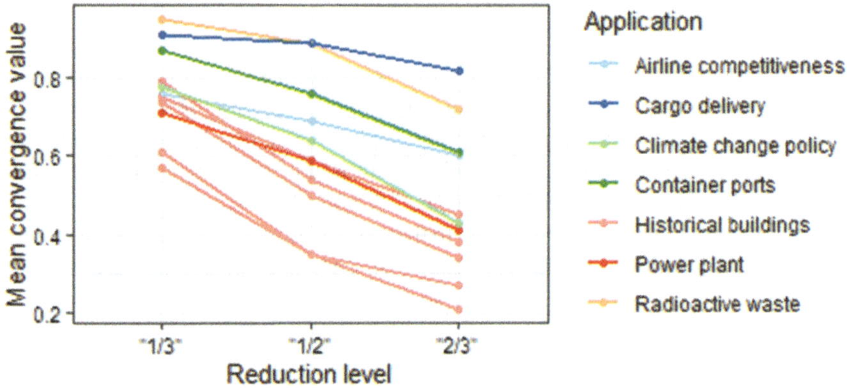

Fig. 3 Mean convergence value for each application at every reduction level

example, when half of the objectives are missing, the rank order correlation between scores in the reduced and full model ranges from 0.35 to 0.90, depending on the application. Selcting K of N with a rank order correlation of 0.90 would be quite similar for the full and reduced models; in contrast, with a correlation of 0.35 the K selected from a reduced model would be quite different from the K alternatives selected from the full model.

Discussion

The analysis of this diverse sample of MAU applications demonstrates that the effects of missing objectives vary considerably. Results from the missing objectives analyses suggest a range of impacts on MAU model performance. The analyses of the seven applications lead to several conclusions:

1. *The relationship (correlations) between attribute values may matter more than the number of attributes/objectives in the model*

   Cases with many attributes do not necessarily lead to a high reduction in model performance. For example, the application with the largest number of objectives (container ports) still shows a relatively high hit rate for reduced models with missing objectives compared to other cases with a smaller number of objectives. Similarly, applications with a small number of identified objectives result in relatively lower performance in hit rate and convergence values for reduced models (historical buildings).

   Besides the number of alternatives considered, one possible factor related to reduced model performance from missing objectives is the correlation between attribute values. As discussed in previous studies (Aschenbrenner, 1977; Fasolo et al., 2007), reduced models with inverse relationships between objectives, e.g., cost and quality, are more sensitive to omitting attributes.

2. *Distributional properties of the set of alternatives are important when measuring the impact of missing objectives*

   While missing objectives generally lead to different results in multiattribute models, there is substantial variability in how severe this impact is on the model. One factor apparent in decision problems, particularly when observing problems with the same number of objectives in the model (meaning that it experiences the same level of reduction), is the space of alternatives considered. The missing objectives analyses suggest characteristics of attribute distributions that may lead to more pronounced losses from missing objectives:

   (a) Competitive set of alternatives

   The competitiveness of alternatives is inversely related to the variability in the desirability (i.e., the value) of the alternatives considered, as smaller differences in alternative value result in lower convergence of reduced models with the full model. In addition, more competitive alternatives at the top may also lead to lower performance in hit rate for reduced models, as small changes in the model are more likely to change the alternative with maximum value.

   (b) Alternative set size

   The size of the alternative set also affects the performance of reduced objectives models. This characteristic mainly affects the measure of convergence value since a long list of alternatives leads to more order combinations of alternatives. However, if the alternative set contains dominated alternatives, it does not adversely affect model performance.

3. *The magnitude of the impact of missing objectives may dramatically vary between models for different stakeholders for the same decision problem.*

   As demonstrated in the applications with multiple decision makers, the extent to which the parameter change varies across decision makers. Some reduced models still perform close to the full model even after a substantial reduction in the number of objectives. In contrast, others dramatically deviate from the full model, even with a relatively small omissions of objectives. The effect of missing objectives in a decision problem is not independent of the set of weights used in the model, even for the same consequence matrix.

All of the factors above work in conjunction with each other. The effect of missing objectives in a multiattribute value problem is highly dependent on multiple properties of the decision model, including the set of objectives identified and the set of alternatives considered. While it is better to have a complete set of objectives for an MAU model, the impact of missing objectives on decision quality is not always severe. In cases with many objectives and few negative correlations among attribute values (utilities), the impact of missing objectives on decision quality may be negligible.

Limitations and Future Research

While this study attempts to include a variety of application contexts and decision spaces, it is still a limited sample of applications with fairly broad selection criteria. It may be useful to systematically investigate reduced model performance in specific decision contexts, e.g., siting problems. The relationship between reduced model performance from missing objectives and attribute correlations warrants further investigation. For example, the distribution of positive and negative correlations within the objective set may change for reduced models with missing objectives. Examining how attribute correlations affect reduced model performance could provide more insight into the likely consequences of missing objectives.

The current study computed reduced model performance by aggregating over models with synthetically omitted objectives. To fully understand the consequences of missing objectives in the way they occur during the decision structuring process, research should go beyond analysis of excluding objectives already generated in the structuring process. One possible approach is to extend the paradigm introduced by Bond et al. (2008, 2010) by including the additional steps of eliciting an attributes by alternatives matrix and weighting parameters. This would allow for the same model comparisons as described in this paper for models with truly missing objectives based on the initial objectives identification process.

In conclusion, the current study examined the consequences of omitted objectives in a multiattribute model. We discover a variety of factors that influence the extent to which missing objectives affect model results, including the correlations between attribute values and the competitiveness of the set of alternatives. However, we also observed a broad range of magnitudes in costs due to missing objectives. It is not always the case that missing objectives lead to losses in utility; a decision maker can still arrive at a good choice, consistent with a full model, even when objectives are not identified and hence not included in the model. The cost of missing objectives is heavily depending on the structure of decision space of alternatives, including number of objectives, number of alternatives, attribute intercorrelations, single attribute value distributions, and trade-off parameters (weights).

Appendices

Decision Problem Description

Airline Competitiveness Chang and Yeh (2001)

Chang and Yeh (2001) examine the performance of four domestic air carriers in Taiwan. The goal of this study is not to choose among airlines but to compare the performance of different domestic airlines and evaluate the strength and weaknesses of each airline based on the distribution of attribute values that contribute to the evaluation of airline quality. This analysis was designed to guide airline companies in determining strategies to improve their competitiveness. The application uses 11 performance measures as attributes related to cost, productivity, service quality, price, and management. The performance measures are based on airline performance records during 1992–1997. The study used surveys to obtain an aggregated judgment from various participants, then refined through the fuzzy weight algorithm to obtain the model. The attributes are mostly positively correlated with each other.

Cargo Delivery (Cavalcanti et al., 2017)

The specific decision context for this study is to choose among portfolios of disaster aid strategies. The alternatives compared involve directing the strategy's focus to various critical factors, given time and resource constraints. The objectives in the problem were extensively elicited from multiple experts with experience in humanitarian aid or peacekeeping and utilized available literature on the topic. They produced five objectives that are included in the analysis: (1) safety of the cargo and workers, (2) stability with local communities, (3) quantity delivered proportional to needs, (4) speed of urgent cargo delivery, and (5) demand fulfillment of priority cargo. The attributes to measure performance were also elicited from the decision maker. The weights for the attributes were elicited using the rank order centroid (ROC) method. The alternatives were selected through a Value Focused Thinking (VFT) approach, where options are formulated based on the type of aid deployment strategies that would fulfill one objective at a time. The vast majority of correlation values among attributes are positive.

Climate Change Policy (Konidari & Mavrakis, 2007)

This application is an example of multiattribute methods to compare alternatives rather than selecting the best. Konidari and Mavrakis (2007) utilized various MCDA methods, including MAUT, to evaluate climate change mitigation policies from eight European nations. The researchers gathered policies from the nations and judged them based on criteria selected from objectives identified in previous studies concerning energy policymaking. They organized the criteria into three main objectives: (1) environmental performance, (2) political acceptability, and (3) feasibility of implementation. Several lower-level objectives are developed from the three main objectives, resulting in a total of 11 objectives utilized in the multiattribute model. The attribute weights are based on three stakeholders: policymakers, researchers, and target groups. As a result, most of the attribute intercorrelation values are positive.

Container Ports (De Icaza et al., 2019)

De Icaza et al. (2019) evaluated and compared five ports across the U.S. Gulf Coast in this study. The analysis incorporated 18 objectives and corresponding attribute measures gathered from previous studies of port selection literature and input from subject matter experts. Utility functions were used to obtain a normalized attribute value where 0 represents the worst case, and one represents the best (for this study's analysis, the utility functions are linearized for simplicity).

The researchers elicited weights from experts using the swing weighting matrix (Parnell & Trainor, 2009). Three levels of importance were used to classify the value measures: critical, moderate, and minor, while three levels of attribute value measure variations were used to classify variation: small, medium, and large. As a result, there are about equal amounts of positive and negative correlations among the 18 attributes.

Historical Buildings (Ferretti et al., 2014)

This study applies multiattribute value modeling to selecting buildings for preservation. In this decision problem, four decision makers from different specialties (history, planning, restoration, and economics) are asked to evaluate seven different historical buildings and determine the building most suitable for restoration for tourism. There were five objectives considered in the selection: (1) quality of the context, (2) economic activities, (3) flexibility of the building, (4) accessibility, and (5) conservation level. The objectives were chosen based on the recommendation of a panel of experts. The weights utilized in the model were elicited using swing weighting methods which explicitly require the stakeholders (represented by the experts) to consider attribute ranges from worst to best in determining weights. In addition to the expert models, a model that uses the mean of the attribute weights from all the experts is also constructed. The correlation values among attributes are notably primarily negative.

Power Plant (Jacobi & Hobbs, 2007)

The decision problem in this study involves energy management executives choosing among long-term plans for energy generation and conservation. The initial decision structuring process involved a group of eleven experts (mostly planners or midlevel executives) brainstorming to identify plan alternatives for the expansion of the energy company. The alternatives consisted of various changes and improvements that could be made to the current power plant operations, such as focusing more on renewable energy or improving the efficiency of current generators. As a result, 14 proposed plans, in addition to the status quo, totaled 15 alternatives.

The researchers provided a set of objectives and attributes. Examples of the objectives used in the study include minimizing 20-year capital expenditures, minimizing carbon dioxide emissions, and minimizing regional job loss. There are 15 alternatives in total. The primary purpose of this particular study was to examine the presence of splitting biases during the weight elicitation process. The splitting bias occurs when the model weights elicited from the decision maker are influenced by the structure of the objectives hierarchy (or value tree) used to represent the set of objectives/attributes. The researchers compared the weights elicited from eleven decision makers who were presented with different forms of value trees for the same problem. For this analysis, the set of weights from Decision Maker #5 was chosen because every weight in the model is nonzero. There are about equal numbers of positive and negative correlations among attributes in the decision problem.

Radioactive Waste (Brothers et al., 2009)

This study examines the decision problem of evaluating options in the processing and disposing of liquid radioactive waste in Saluggia, Italy. The three alternatives were proposed by an expert in the design and management of nuclear waste. They presented three waste disposal plans to consider: (1) vitrification and cementation at the site, (2) cementation at the site, and (3) transport abroad. There are eleven objectives included in the analysis, many of which relate to the risks involved in the consequences of each alternative, e.g., technical risk and schedule risk. Thus, this decision problem would be classified as a multiattribute utility problem. The objectives were outlined to account for concerns from various stakeholders, such as management, technicians, and the public. The attribute values used to measure the objectives included engineering data and expert judgments.

The attribute values are then converted using a value or utility function bounded on [0,1], where 0 represents the worst value, and 1 represents the best value. The attributes are mostly positively correlated with each other, except for one objective, final product confinement, which negatively correlates with all remaining attributes. The weights for this model were elicited from a modified simple multiattribute rating technique (SMART) devised by Edwards and Barron (1994). Again, the attribute intercorrelation values are primarily positive.

References

Aschenbrenner, K. M. (1977). Influence of attribute formulation on the evaluation of apartments by multi-attribute utility procedures. In *Decision making and change in human affairs* (pp. 81–97). Springer.

Barron, F. H. (1987). Influence of missing attributes on selecting a best multiattributed alternative. *Decision Sciences, 18*(2), 194–205.

Barron, F. H., & Barrett, B. E. (1996). Decision quality using ranked attribute weights. *Management Science, 42*(11), 1515–1523.

Barron, F. H., & Barrett, B. E. (1999). Linear inequalities and the analysis of multi-attribute value matrices. In *Decision science and technology* (pp. 211–225). Springer.

Barron, F. H., & Kleinmuntz, D. N. (1986). Sensitivity in value loss of linear models to attribute completeness. In B. Brehmer, H. Jungermann, P. Lorens, & G. Sevon (Eds.), *New directions in research on decision making*. Elsevier.

Bond, S. D., Carlson, K. A., & Keeney, R. L. (2008). Generating objectives: Can decision makers articulate what they want? *Management Science, 54*(1), 56–70.

Bond, S. D., Carlson, K. A., & Keeney, R. L. (2010). Improving the generation of decision objectives. *Decision Analysis, 7*(3), 238–255.

Brothers, A. J., Mattigod, S. V., Strachan, D. M., Beeman, G. H., Kearns, P. K., Papa, A., & Monti, C. (2009). Resource-limited multiattribute value analysis of alternatives for immobilizing radioactive liquid process waste stored in Saluggia, Italy. *Decision Analysis, 6*(2), 98–114.

Cavalcanti, L. B., Mendes, A. B., & Yoshizaki, H. T. Y. (2017). Application of multi-attribute value theory to improve cargo delivery planning in disaster aftermath. *Mathematical Problems in Engineering, 2017.*

Chang, Y. H., & Yeh, C. H. (2001). Evaluating airline competitiveness using multiattribute decision making. *Omega, 29*(5), 405–415.

De Icaza, R. R., Parnell, G. S., & Pohl, E. A. (2019). Gulf coast port selection using multiple-objective decision analysis. *Decision Analysis, 16*(2), 87–104.

Edwards, W., & Barron, F. H. (1994). SMARTS and SMARTER: Improved simple methods for multiattribute utility measurement. *Organizational behavior and human decision processes, 60*(3), 306–325.

Fasolo, B., McClelland, G. H., & Todd, P. M. (2007). Escaping the tyranny of choice: When fewer attributes make choice easier. *Marketing Theory, 7*(1), 13–26.

Ferretti, V., Bottero, M., & Mondini, G. (2014). Decision making and cultural heritage: An application of the Multi-Attribute Value Theory for the reuse of historical buildings. *Journal of Cultural Heritage, 15*(6), 644–655.

Fry, P. C., Rinks, D. B., & Ringuest, J. L. (1997). Comparing the predictive validity of alternatively assessed multi-attribute preference models when relevant decision attributes are missing. *European Journal of Operational Research, 94*(3), 599–609. https://doi.org/10.1016/0377-2217(95)00142-5

Jacobi, S. K., & Hobbs, B. F. (2007). Quantifying and mitigating the splitting bias and other value tree-induced weighting biases. *Decision Analysis, 4*(4), 194–210.

Jia, J., Fischer, G. W., & Dyer, J. S. (1998). Attribute weighting methods and decision quality in the presence of response error: A simulation study. *Journal of Behavioral Decision Making, 11*(2), 85–105.

Keeney, R. L. (1996). *Value-focused thinking*. Harvard University Press.

Keeney, R. L. (2007). Developing objectives and attributes. In W. Edwards, R. F. Miles Jr., & D. Von Winterfeldt (Eds.), *Advances in decision analysis: From foundations to applications* (pp. 81–103). Cambridge University Press.

Keeney, R. L., & Raiffa, H. (1976). *Decisions with multiple objectives: preferences and value trade-offs*. Cambridge University Press.

Konidari, P., & Mavrakis, D. (2007). A multi-criteria evaluation method for climate change mitigation policy instruments. *Energy Policy, 35*(12), 6235–6257.

Montibeller, G., & Von Winterfeldt, D. (2015). Cognitive and motivational biases in decision and risk analysis. *Risk Analysis, 35*(7), 1230–1251.

Nutt, P. C. (1998). Evaluating alternatives to make strategic choices. *Omega, 26*(3), 333–354.

Parnell, G. S., & Trainor, T. E. (2009). 2.3. 1 using the swing weight matrix to weight multiple objectives. In *INCOSE International Symposium 19*(1), 283–298.

Payne, J. W., Bettman, J. R., Schkade, D. A., Schwarz, N., & Gregory, R. (1999). Measuring constructed preferences: Towards a building code. In *Elicitation of preferences* (pp. 243–275). Springer.

von Winterfeldt, D. (1980). Structuring decision problems for decision analysis. *Acta Psychologica, 45*(1-3), 71–93.

von Winterfeldt, D., & Edwards, W. (1986). *Decision analysis and behavioral research*. Cambridge University Press.

von Winterfeldt, D., & Edwards, W. (2007). Defining a decision analytic structure. In W. Edwards, R. F. Miles Jr., & D. Von Winterfeldt (Eds.), *Advances in decision analysis: From foundations to applications* (pp. 81–103). Cambridge University Press.

von Winterfeldt, D., & Fasolo, B. (2009). Structuring decision problems: A case study and reflections for practitioners. *European Journal of Operational Research, 199*(3), 857–866.

When Are We Willing to Wait? Prescriptive Challenges in Evaluating Intertemporal Outcomes

Jeffery L. Guyse, Candice H. Huynh, L. Robin Keller, and Jay Simon

Abstract The classic normative model for intertemporal preferences uses a constant discount rate, but behavioral experiments have shown that people do not tend to make choices consistent with a constant discount rate. We first present normative models for time preferences, then discuss descriptive results for choices between single outcomes occurring at different times. People often have different implicit discount rates for different types of scenarios, and several anomalies arise consistently. We contrast those results with findings for preferences for sequences of multiple outcomes over time. People tend to prefer increasing or constant sequences of outcomes over time, especially when the outcomes are non-monetary in nature. This suggests a willingness to wait for improvement, but not in the way that classical discounting would prescribe. We end with prescriptive nudges to improve dynamic consistency and pose questions still to be resolved about how decisions involving outcomes over time can be improved prescriptively.

Keywords Intertemporal preferences · Normative model · Descriptive models · Prescriptive interventions

---

J. L. Guyse (✉) · C. H. Huynh
Technology and Operations Management, College of Business Administration, California State Polytechnic University, Pomona, CA, USA
e-mail: JLGuyse@cpp.edu; CandiceHuynh@cpp.edu

L. R. Keller
The Paul Merage School of Business, University of California, Irvine, CA, USA
e-mail: LRKeller@uci.edu

J. Simon
Kogod School of Business, American University, Washington, DC, USA
e-mail: JaySimon@American.edu

F. M. Federspiel et al. (eds.), *Behavioral Decision Analysis*, International Series in Operations Research & Management Science 350,
https://doi.org/10.1007/978-3-031-44424-1_10

Introduction

Intertemporal decisions have been studied for centuries. Long before the modern fields of decision theory or economics, Smith (1759), for instance, discussed the idea that positive outcomes in the future are far less appealing than positive outcomes in the present. Rae (1834) examined the idea that differences in wealth may partly be attributed to differences in people's desires to accumulate; that is, to sacrifice in the present to increase future prosperity. Ramsey (1928) developed a maximin prescriptive theory of saving that maximized the welfare of the generation that would be the worst off. A detailed history is beyond the scope of this article but suffice it to say that the topic is not exclusive to recent scholars.

Modern approaches to intertemporal decision making, however, owe their origins in large part to the foundational work of Samuelson (1937). Samuelson gives an overview of how present and future outcomes can be compared and introduces the concept of a *discount rate*: a parameter capturing the degree to which we are willing to accept an inferior outcome that occurs sooner.

It is widely (but not universally) accepted that a rational decision maker should have a constant discount rate, *e.g.*, the relative desirability of receiving $1100 in 1 year vs. receiving $1000 today should be the same as that of receiving $1100 in 5 years vs. receiving $1000 in 4 years. However, countless empirical studies have found evidence that people do not exhibit constant discount rates. A few early examples are Ainslie (1975), Solnick et al. (1980), and Thaler (1981).

The concept of discounting arose from monetary outcomes that can grow over time with investment. However, it is also applied to non-monetary outcomes that cannot similarly grow over time. It is not merely a way to capture investment returns or interest; it reflects the normative preference for experiencing positive outcomes sooner (and negative outcomes later).

A constant discount rate is one of many normative properties we might expect a rational decision maker to follow. In this chapter, we first discuss what those normative properties are. We then explore several specific ways in which they tend to be violated. Some of these deviations from the normative approach involve comparisons between individual outcomes at different times, while others involve sequences of outcomes.

Next, we offer some prescriptive recommendations for how these behavioral challenges can be overcome. We also provide several open research questions on decision making with intertemporal outcomes.

How Should We Evaluate Intertemporal Outcomes?

To appreciate the challenges of decision making with intertemporal outcomes, it is important first to discuss how those decisions *should* be made. This section explores the normative piece of the puzzle: how would a perfectly rational individual behave?

Unfortunately, that question does not have a simple satisfying answer. There are properties that it is clear a rational decision maker should follow, and we will begin by presenting those before moving on to others on which there is not universal agreement.

First, we can adopt all of the more general normative properties of decision making. We can assert that the decision maker's preferences over a set of intertemporal outcomes should be complete, transitive, and continuous. The decision maker's preferences should be based only on the outcomes and their timing, and should be immune to framing effects (*i.e.*, changes in how the outcomes are described or presented). If these properties, and one or two more technical conditions, are met then the decision maker's preferences over the outcomes can be represented by an ordinal *value function*, where a larger value indicates a more preferred outcome. For further details on representing preferences with ordinal value functions, see Debreu (1954, 1964), Rader (1963), Fishburn (1970), and Krantz et al. (1971).

In this chapter, we consider decisions for which there is no uncertainty; for any possible choice, it is known what will occur and when. If there is uncertainty, then additional rationality conditions, such as those provided by Savage (1954), would apply, and preferences would be represented by a cardinal *utility function* rather than a value function. The differences between value and utility are tangential to this chapter, and thus we will not discuss them further here.

Now, we can move on to normative ideas that are unique to an intertemporal setting. Perhaps the earliest established approach is given by Samuelson (1937), who asserts: "*the individual behaves so as to maximise the sum of all future utilities, they being reduced to comparable magnitudes by suitable time discounting*" (p. 156). In many ways, this is similar to additive multiattribute value or utility (Debreu, 1960; Keeney & Raiffa, 1976); the overall value/utility function involves converting each individual component of the outcome into a value/utility, and then calculating a weighted sum. However, in an intertemporal setting, there are additional properties that are normatively appealing.

To simplify assessment and understanding, a homogeneity condition is usually assumed, either implicitly or explicitly. Roughly, homogeneity means that the shape of the value/utility function does not change over time. This leads to the form:

$$V(x) = w_1 v(x_1) + w_2 v(x_2) + \cdots + w_n v(x_n) \tag{1}$$

where the subscripts denote periods of time. While this function imposes no restrictions on the weights, note that v does not have a subscript; each single-period outcome is converted to a value in the same way. An infinite-period version of this function is presented by Harvey (1986). This homogeneity condition is also used for outcomes dispersed spatially rather than temporally; see, *e.g.*, Simon et al. (2014) and Keller and Simon (2019).

The specification of the weights in an intertemporal value/utility function is often referred to as *discounting*. The simplest and most common approach is to use a constant discount rate r, where a value/utility experienced t periods into the future is equivalent to a value/utility of $1/(1 + r)^t$ immediately. (This can also be extended to a continuous discounting function; see, *e.g.*, Weibull (1985).) While Samuelson (1937) did present this model of exponential discounting, it is worth noting that he did not argue for its normative or descriptive validity. Rather, he includes it as one of several assumptions that lead to a tractable utility function for income over time. Samuelson does mention a desirable consequence of a constant discount rate (which we will discuss shortly), but the only explicit justification he gives is its simplicity. However, as Frederick et al. (2002, p. 356) explain:

> the simplicity and elegance of this formulation was irresistible, and <it> was rapidly adopted as the framework of choice for analyzing intertemporal decisions.

Indeed, much of the prior work discussed in the following section treats exponential discounting as the standard normative model for intertemporal decisions and contrasts it with descriptive findings.

Note that all of the literature on discounting cited here specifies that it is values or utilities that should be discounted, not monetary outcomes or other physical quantities. In practice, this is often ignored, and a discounting function is applied directly to monetary outcomes or other quantities. Doing so makes an implicit assumption that value/utility is linear over money in the range of outcomes involved.

Whether applied to value/utility or to money, a constant discount rate implies that the tradeoffs a decision maker should be willing to make between time t and time $t + \Delta$ do not depend on t. That is, if the decision maker prefers \$1000 today to \$1050 in 1 week, then the decision maker will also prefer \$1000 in 52 weeks to \$1050 in 53 weeks. But why should a decision maker obey such a rule? A simple exercise reveals its benefit:

Imagine that the decision maker prefers \$1000 today to \$1050 in 1 week but prefers \$1050 in 53 weeks to \$1000 in 52 weeks. (As we will explore later in the chapter, this pair of preferences arises frequently in descriptive studies.) We ask the decision maker to choose immediately between \$1000 in 52 weeks and \$1050 in 53 weeks, and to sign a contract committing to her choice. This decision maker will choose \$1050 in 53 weeks. However, if we then wait 52 weeks and give her the option to change her choice, she may prefer to do so. She might even be willing to pay for that privilege! A constant discount rate ensures that these kinds of *preference reversals* cannot happen, and a person cannot be turned into a money pump (Ramsey, 1931).

This is the desirable normative property mentioned by Samuelson. It is called *dynamic consistency*: if a rational decision maker makes a choice between alternatives whose outcomes will be realized in the future, she should not want to change that choice in the interim simply due to the passage of time. (Of course, even a rational individual may still wish to change her choice if more information becomes available or her tastes change.)

Some researchers have argued that dynamic consistency is too restrictive as a normative condition and may not make sense in every decision setting. Harvey (1986), for instance, uses the example of decisions whose consequences are not fully realized for hundreds of years. There are two problems with requiring dynamic consistency for such decisions. First, the decision makers will be gone long before the outcomes are realized, so their eventual preferences are irrelevant. Second, any constant discount rate that involves a non-trivial amount of discounting will end up almost completely dismissing the distant future. At a modest yearly discount rate of 5%, one billion dollars in 500 years is equivalent to three cents today. Even accounting for inflation, most of us would be quite eager to donate three cents to give our 500-year descendants a billion dollars' worth of benefit!

Decisions in the public sector can present another challenge: the decision makers change frequently. While elected government officials should certainly care about outcomes that occur after they leave office, it is less clear that their preferences over those outcomes should satisfy dynamic consistency. Again, their eventual preferences when those outcomes are realized are irrelevant. A similar challenge arises in any organization where intertemporal decisions are made by individuals in short-term roles.

In summary, a constant discount rate does have normative appeal, and clearly will improve a class of flawed decision processes. In particular, for individual decision makers considering monetary outcomes such as possible cash flows or investment choices, it is a useful property. However, there are settings in which it is less clear that there is anything inherently irrational or undesirable about a non-constant discount rate. For example, for outcomes over multiple decades, such as with climate change, some have recommended a decreasing discount rate over time (Arrow et al., 2014).

When both monetary and non-monetary outcomes (such as health outcomes) are possible, one approach is to price the non-monetary amounts out in money, then discount both (largely monetary) costs and (largely non-monetary) benefits to net present value using the same discount rate. Keeler and Cretin (1983) present a philosophical perspective on the benefit of using the same discount rate across outcome types, when health can be traded for money.

Descriptive Results of Time Preference Experiments

Much experimental research has been dedicated to the study of intertemporal choice; for a detailed review, see Frederick et al. (2002). Standard economic models expect people to behave rationally, by making choices that are deemed stable with well-defined preferences that follow discounting models. In sections "Impatience: Preferring a Smaller Positive Outcome Sooner" and "Patience: Preferring a Constant or Increasing Sequence of Outcomes", we discuss studies that are dedicated to finding anomalies that are difficult to "rationalize" mathematically when evaluating (a) isolated outcomes at two points in time or (b) sequences of outcomes over time. Participants in experiments have had scenarios presented to them that would lead individuals to exhibit behaviors categorized as irrational. Such behaviors are termed *anomalies* when decisions do not follow the standard normative discounting model.

It is important first to note a related fundamental challenge: decision makers might not understand the basic mathematics behind interest and inflation that sometimes underlie intertemporal decisions. For instance, Lusardi and Mitchell (2011) found that only 67.1% of their sample of Americans over 50 were able to answer an extremely simple question about compound interest correctly. Similar results have been obtained by Lusardi (2008a, b) and Binswanger and Carman (2010). When such financial literacy is germane to a decision, it is important prescriptively to make sure that the decision maker is comfortable with these concepts before addressing the other anomalies presented in this section.

Impatience: Preferring a Smaller Positive Outcome Sooner

The standard normative discounting model uses a constant discount rate across all scenarios, but studies have found that participants systematically display differing discount rates in different scenarios. There are three main anomalies found in decision making under certainty when a participant chooses between receiving two isolated outcomes: one inferior but sooner versus one superior but later. They are (1) *short/long-term asymmetry* (also called dynamic inconsistency), (2) *the absolute magnitude effect*, and (3) *gain/loss asymmetry* (also known as the sign effect).

The most widely cited empirical study on these three anomalies is that of Thaler (1981). This study used volunteer university undergraduate students recruited through a paper advertisement to participate in a survey. A questionnaire designed to estimate implicit discount rates based on a variety of situations was incorporated. Students were asked to fill in the blank for scenarios such as winning a lottery prize (or paying a traffic ticket fine) that is paid (due) today with the value that they would be indifferent to receiving (paying) at a prescribed time in the future. The prize money (ticket fines) and time delays were varied and incorporated into four different forms of the questionnaire.

In an ideal situation, studies would analyze events where actual money was involved. Unfortunately, this is difficult to achieve; would volunteers really believe that they would receive payment in 6 months, 1 year or 3 years from now? Therefore, most studies have relied on hypothetical scenarios described in a survey questionnaire. Fortunately, there are studies to verify that choices based on hypothetical survey questionnaires are indeed consistent with choices made with actual real money outcomes (Holcomb & Nelson, 1992).

Thaler (1981) found that participants were impatient to receive a positive smaller single outcome sooner rather than waiting to receive a larger outcome later, as demonstrated by quite large implicit discount rates across the scenarios presented. The implicit discount rates dropped sharply (but still stayed relatively high) as the size of the prize, or the time delay increased. For example, when asked to fill in the blank for receiving $15 today or a _____ amount in 3 months to be indifferent between the two outcomes, the median response corresponded to a continuously compounded annual discount rate of 277%, but when 3 months was changed to 1 year it was 139% and then for 3 years it was 64%. When the prize money was a larger magnitude of $250 today or a _____ amount, the discount rate for 3 months was 73%,

1 year was 34%, and 3 years was 23%. As the time delay was increased, the discount rate dropped significantly exhibiting the short/long-term asymmetry anomaly. The paper offers a possible theory to explain why the relative marginal price of waiting for rewards declines as the wait time increases: the psychophysics of time suggests that the difference between today and tomorrow will seem greater than the difference between a year from now and a year plus one day. Subjects may view the difference in delay time as a percentage difference instead of an absolute difference. Relatively speaking, the difference between a year and a year plus one day is only 0.27% more time, while the difference between today and tomorrow is significantly more. But the standard normative discounting model requires these differences to be viewed as the same. This dilemma serves as motivation for the formulation of descriptive discounting models such as *hyperbolic discounting* (Ainslie & Haslam, 1992) or a hybrid approach, mating exponential and hyperbolic discounting models together (Adamou et al., 2021), to capture such behavior.

The absolute magnitude effect refers to the anomaly when decision makers apply a different discount rate based on the reward amount. Gaining larger prize money suffers from lower proportional discounting than gaining smaller monetary prizes. Subjects were indifferent between receiving $15 now and $60 in 1 year but were also indifferent between receiving $250 now and $350 in a year, as well as between $3000 now and $4000 in a year. Subjects may consider that waiting for a reward requires effort. For small rewards such as $15, a substantial (proportional) return is required to consider the wait worthwhile.

For the loss domain, the cover story in Thaler's study portrayed a scenario in which the participant must pay a traffic ticket fine either now or later. The continuously compounded annual discount rate for a $15 fine was 26% for 3 months, 29% for 1 year, and 20% for 3 years. While for the $100 fine, it was 6% for 3 months, 16% for 1 year, and 15% for 3 years. Lastly, for the $250 fine, it was 1% for 3 months, 8% for 1 year, and 7% for 3 years. There were startling differences in discount rates between gains and losses. This is known as gain/loss asymmetry. The paper finds that the implicit discount rates based on the responses for fines (losses) are much lower than ones when the outcome was a positive prize amount. Analogous to the results in the gains domain, the discount rates decline as the size of the fine increases.

To summarize, Thaler (1981) concludes that the discount rates vary with the size and sign of the reward, as well as the length of the time delay. Of course, this is not the only paper to explore these behavioral phenomena. For a comprehensive review of early works on anomalies for decisions under certainty with monetary outcomes, see Loewenstein and Thaler (1989) and Frederick et al. (2002).

There have been many research studies dedicated to finding viable explanations for the behaviors deviating from the standard normative discounting model. Loewenstein and Prelec (1992) proposed a descriptive model that defined intertemporal choice with respect to deviations from an anticipated status quo (or point of "reference"). Their model relates to the financial markets' behavior of individuals tending to hold onto losing stocks and to real estate that has dropped in value but to quickly sell assets that have gained in value. Wang et al. (2015) theorize that the absolute magnitude effect is due to subjective time perception. Based on a survey questionnaire completed by undergraduate students, they found that the magnitude of the outcome affects the participants' perception of the temporal durations. The survey asked: "How long does this time period until you get the winnings seem to you?" with participants responding to the question based on a 7-point scale from 1 ("seems very short") to 7 ("seems very long"). This survey question was adapted from Bilgin and LeBoeuf (2010). When the hypothetical lottery prize money was $4000, the perception of temporal duration was significantly shorter than for the $20 scenario, even though the waiting time for both prize money values was 3 months. Overall, Wang et al. (2015) showed that incorporating subjective time perception mitigated two of the anomalies discussed (short/long-term asymmetry and the absolute magnitude effect) but not gain/loss asymmetry.

Some differences in participants' implicit discount rate estimations have appeared when considering monetary versus non-monetary outcomes at two points in time. Chapman and Elstein (1995, Experiment 2) found average discount rates for health to be generally higher than rates for money, and Chapman (1996a) found that discount rates depended on the domain (monetary or health), with rates not being correlated between the domains. In contrast, Attema et al. (2018) found more discounting for money than for health in a sample of French participants interviewed in their homes, using a method that measures discounting independent of utility. With their method, they found median discount rates to be close to market interest rates (6.5% for money and 2.2% for health). The standard normative discounting model with a constant discount rate fit better than hyperbolic discounting models, which use lower discount rates in later periods.

Related to perceptions of time, but beyond the scope of this chapter, is work on the neural underpinnings of delay discounting (Frost & McNaughton, 2017; McClure et al., 2004), how teenagers are impatient and do not think much about future consequences (Bishai, 2004; Chesson et al., 2006), or how people react to time pressure (*e.g.*, Payne et al., 1996). In a non-discounting approach, Construal Level Theory (Trope & Liberman, 2010) experiments examine reactions to "near" vs. "distant" outcomes. Items or events seen as far away in time or space or personal relations are dealt with more rationally, while close things are dealt with more emotionally.

Patience: Preferring a Constant or Increasing Sequence of Outcomes

The beforementioned anomalies regarding single outcomes have predominantly been investigated using an elicitation procedure that involved some type of matching task. This matching technique usually required participants to make a set of judgements that set their personal (subjective) equivalences to different quantity-timing pairs that they were presented. For example, participants were told that they had won some money in a lottery that was being held for them by their bank. Then the participants were asked "how much they were required to make waiting just as attractive as getting the money now". The lottery winnings ranged from $15 to $3000, the timing ranging from 1 month to 10 years. Relatedly, a fine from a ticket was used to investigate these subjective matching equivalents in the domain of monetary losses (Thaler, 1981). The subsequent research into the anomalies that followed predominantly focused on this type of elicitation procedure, which has been termed *pairwise matching* (Guyse & Simon, 2011).

An alternate approach to investigating choice over time involves participants rating (or ranking) different sequences of outcomes, a task known as the *relative valuation of sequences* (Guyse & Simon, 2011). When this elicitation procedure was incorporated, a different set of (seemingly) contradictory results to the normative exponential discounting model was revealed that differed from those reported as anomalies. The two primary deviations found in this stream of literature are *negative time discounting* and a *preference for spreading* (Frederick & Loewenstein, 2008). Negative time discounting surfaces when participants display the preference for an increasing (improving) sequence over a decreasing (deteriorating) one with an equal mean (Read & Powell, 2002; Schmitt & Kemper, 1996). This preference can be revealed by more highly rating (or ranking) the improving sequence, or by choosing it over the deteriorating one. For example, participants in a seminal study generally gave higher rankings to sequences of monetary streams of income that started relatively low in value and increased in magnitude over time than to sequences that started at a relatively high value and then subsequently decreased in magnitude over time, even though the net present values of the latter streams were clearly greater than the former (Loewenstein & Sicherman, 1991). This may be thought of as a willingness to wait for improvement. This revealed preference could only be explained (when using the standard normative discounting model) by an interest rate that was negative, indicating a preference to wait for the larger (improved) outcome instead of receiving it earlier.

The second main deviation from the normative exponential discounting model, a preference for spreading, occurs when participants prefer a moderate sequence with a flatter, more horizontal, slope to a sequence that has a much steeper slope even when both sequences have equal means (Chapman, 1996b; Guyse et al., 2002; Loewenstein & Prelec, 1993). The standard normative discounting model predicts a preference for complete consolidation of the outcomes in the extremes of the time horizon; all as soon as possible if the discount rate is positive (no or minimum waiting for improvement) and all as far into the future as possible if the discount rate is negative (extreme or maximum waiting for improvement). Preferring a moderate sequence to one with a steeper slope indicates a desire to incorporate some amount of waiting, but not necessarily to the extreme. The research has shown that preferences can be influenced by the shape of the sequence, whether it is increasing, decreasing, or constant. Studies have further shown that it is not only this shape, but also the peak and endpoint of the sequence that can also influence its subjective valuation, especially when done retroactively (Ariely, 1998; Fredrickson & Kahneman, 1993; Kahneman et al., 1993; Redelmeier & Kahneman, 1996; Ross &

Simonson, 1991; Varey & Kahneman, 1992). These gestalt features are absent from the pairwise matching task used to investigate the presence of the anomalies as well as inconsistent with the predictions made by the standard normative discounting model. They can incorporate a sense of waiting that is at a more moderate level than positive or negative time discounting would predict.

Therefore, it appears that subjective temporal preferences for sequences can include some amount of moderate waiting for improvement that tends to contradict the predictions of the standard normative discounting model, regardless of the sign of the discount rate. In addition, these temporal preferences may differ for sequences versus the isolated outcomes from the previous subsection used predominantly in the pairwise matching task. In the monetary domain, the possible relationship between the latter two divergent streams of research has been investigated by Guyse and Simon (2011). In general, their study modified sets of monetary sequences to include factors that have led to the anomalies found in the pairwise matching task used previously. The findings did reveal a propensity for all three anomalies in the ranking of the sequences (with an indication of gain/loss asymmetry being the strongest of the three) along with a preference for the spreading of losses. Consistency, as measured through the implied sign of the implicit discount rate, between the two procedures was poorest when losses were involved, since the moderate waiting associated with the participants' preference of spreading found in the sequences results could not materialize in the pairwise matching task.

Up to this point, the descriptive research on sequences discussed has focused primarily on monetary outcomes, though a preference for spreading has been formulated for different sequences of dinner meals (Loewenstein & Prelec, 1993). When expanding the research into another domain, such as health, there are additional indications that temporal preferences differ from those of monetary outcomes. One study (Chapman, 1996b) transferred the shapes of monetary sequences (Loewenstein & Sicherman, 1991) into the health domain. It was found that when the time horizon was relatively short (12 days or 1 year), three consecutive experiments across health and money indicated that they were both discounted negatively, displaying a strong preference to wait for improvement. In contrast, another study found that decreasing sequences of money (indicating an aversion to waiting for improvement) were rated much higher than corresponding decreasing sequences of health (Guyse et al., 2002). In general, sequences of health that either remained the same or improved over time were more highly rated than those that decreased even though they had equal means. This same preference pattern was also found in that study for both air quality and near-shore ocean water quality, holding for both a short term (5 year) as well as a long term (50 year) time horizon. It was found that individuals in general are more willing to wait for the better outcome of health, the better outcome of air quality and the better outcome of near-shore water quality than they are for better monetary outcomes. Also, this waiting wasn't necessarily to the extreme. Moderate waiting in the form of spreading (the constant sequence shape being regarded as ideal) was the modal response for these three domains.

Sequences of another non-monetary outcome, lives over time, have also been investigated. In one study during what was labelled a "sequence" task, the participants chose between an increasing and a decreasing sequence of lives saved over the next three decades (Frederick, 2003). The increasing sequence shape (negative time discounting or strong desire to wait for improvement) was preferred by 71% of the participants. An "equity" task was also performed which had participants choose between saving all of the lives in this generation versus spreading out the lives saved uniformly over three generations (this generation and the next two). 80% of the participants preferred the uniform (constant) sequence in this scenario, displaying preference for waiting for improvement by spreading the lives instead of saving them all "up front". Only lives saved were investigated in this study though. When including the loss of the life in the scenarios, results indicate less preference for waiting for improvement when the lives were lost compared to when they were saved: 47% vs. 69% (Guyse et al., 2021). Furthermore, in the "equity" task, the majority in that study preferred the spreading of saved lives but the lost lives' complement revealed a different result; a preference to lose the lives now in this generation instead of delaying the loss of lives uniformly over three generations. So, when the loss of lives across generations was involved, people chose not to spread them but take the losses all up front so that the future would show maximum improvement (negative time discounting).

Guyse et al. (2020) extended the results of the binary choice scenarios discussed above between two different sequences to include a choice among three sequence shapes of lives saved or lost: (1) all now, (2) equal amounts over time, and (3) all later. Their within-subjects design allowed them to observe if negative time discounting (a strong desire to wait for improvement), preference for spreading (a moderate preference for waiting), as well as the three anomalies present in the monetary studies using pairwise matching surfaced when valuing sequences of lives. Only 2% of the participants were fully consistent with the standard normative discounting model with a positive discount rate, preferring not to wait for the better lives outcome. In addition, just 3% of all participants preferred the extreme waiting for improvement associated with negative time discounting. Indifference to waiting or not would be associated with zero discounting. No participant provided such ratings. Therefore 95% of the participants had some mix of waiting that tended to be on the more moderate side, a displayed preference for spreading for both lives saved as well as lives lost, with its strength growing when moving 15 years into the future. In addition, there was the presence of the absolute magnitude effect and short/long-term asymmetry occurring *simultaneously* for lives saved. These two anomalies happening at the same time indicates more willingness to wait (*i.e.*, lower discounting) for larger magnitudes of lives saved at the later point in time.

To account for the inability of the standard normative discounting model to account for a preference associated with moderate waiting, a descriptive model that incorporates the "uniformness" of the sequence is necessary. Loewenstein and Prelec (1993) provide such a model. It takes the form:

$$Sequence\,Value = \sum_{n}^{t=1} u_t + \beta \sum_{n}^{t=1} d_t + \sigma \sum_{n}^{t=1} |d_t| \tag{2}$$

The formulation includes two distinct parameters, β and σ. The parameter β can be thought to capture the preference for improvement over time, or waiting, with a positive β indicating a desire to wait for improvement, a negative β indicating no desire to wait for improvement. This parameter though cannot capture the moderate form of waiting that is implied by a preference for spreading, the attractiveness of the uniform or constant sequence shape. This aspect is captured by the parameter σ. If $\sigma < 0$ then there is a preference for uniformity (spreading or moderate waiting). If $\sigma > 0$ then there is a preference for non-uniformity (no waiting at all, or extreme waiting only). For each time period t, the utility of receiving the outcome at that point is u_t. The term d_t is a preceding calculation that accounts for the difference between the cumulative utility received up to time t and the cumulative utility that would have been received had the sequence shape been uniform across all periods ($t = 1$ to n). This term takes the following form:

$$d_t = \frac{t}{n} \sum_{n}^{i=1} u_i - \sum_{n}^{i=1} u_i \tag{3}$$

Loewenstein and Prelec applied this model at the individual participant level for sequences of ways to spend a weekend which ranged from "very pleasurable" to "boring and not at all fun" in which 75% of the participants exhibited a willingness to wait for improvement. When applied to the mean ratings for scenarios associated with income, health, air quality, and water quality, all 4 domains revealed a preference for spreading ($\sigma < 0$) on average with a desire for waiting for improvement in all but the monetary domain (Guyse et al., 2002). This model was also applied at the participant level to the rating of sequences of lives saved or lost over time (Guyse et al., 2020). There, 77% of the participants revealed a desire to spread the lives over time, with 67% "liking uniform" as their primary motive behind their ratings. The spreading of outcomes, away from the consolidated extremes in both directions, shows a preference to moderately wait, even for those who do prefer deteriorating sequences where the best outcome is realized earlier rather than later.

Prescriptive Guidance for Evaluating Intertemporal Outcomes

The standard normative discounting model is a theoretically clear roadmap on how to proceed to analyze decisions with intertemporal outcomes. But the descriptive results that people disobey the normative model present a challenge.

Do the anomalies reflect true preferences? Which deviations from the standard normative discounting model should a person try to "correct", and which ones are true preferences to use in decision making? Section "Future Research" covers open research questions still to be resolved about how decisions involving outcomes over time can be improved prescriptively.

Decisions involving outcomes over time can range from personal decisions to decisions by business executives or government policy makers impacting others, including future generations. In this section we prescribe two main prescriptive ways for decision makers to consider decisions containing outcomes received over time, informed by the descriptive results that people do not generally conform to discounting models without decision aids.

In section "Nudges", we consider nudges that help a person make more dynamically consistent choices involving outcomes over time. In such cases, in general, no single number would be computed to represent how good an alternative is, but the decision maker would directly consider sequences of outcomes over time on relevant dimensions and make a choice. In section "Using a Discount Rate or Other Model to Compute a Single Number Representing How Good an Option Is", we compute a single number to represent how good an alternative is. The way that standard normative models would prescribe is to convert all monetary and non-monetary outcomes to money and use a constant discount rate to discount the resulting monetary outcomes (or the value/utility of the outcomes) to the net present value using a suitable discount rate. In the middle between these two extreme approaches, one could portray choices with some summary numbers (such as annual averages) as well as graphs of outcome patterns over time.

Nudges

Thaler and Sunstein (2008) promoted the use of nudges to help yourself or others make better decisions. Their paternalistic libertarian idea is that while you still have all the choices available to you, the default option is set to be the one "best" for you. While the term paternalistic libertarianism appears to be an oxymoron, the two terms can exist together. First, the choice of the default option to be presented to people should be the one that a paternalistic person believes is best for people. Simultaneously, the libertarian idea of letting people choose what they want mandates that a range of choice options should be available to people. Following the philosophy in behavioral economics of examining degrees of conformity with economic norms and exploring ways to enhance conformity, interventional nudges by institutions often rely on changes in choice architecture (for example, what is the default choice vs. another possible choice that takes more steps to opt into it). Mertens et al. (2022) conducted a meta-analysis of over 450 behavioral interventions and found that changing the choice architecture promotes small to medium positive personal and societal behavioral changes, in health, food, environment, finance, and pro-social domains. Such institutional nudges can be seen as the more traditional nudges, having been investigated earlier than the more recently studied self-nudges.

While many personal decisions will not require formal decision analysis modeling, some insights may be drawn in light of the normative models and the experimental results in the previous sections. For example, in the face of the intertemporal biases of (1) impatience in the present but more patience in the future and (2) the tendency to not take action, people may want to find ways to exert self-control to be more patient or want institutions to nudge them towards self-control. For example, Laibson et al. (1998) cite results on the gap between consumer intentions and actions from a number of public surveys in the introduction to their hyperbolic consumer modeling paper, including from Farkas and Johnson (1997) that most Americans prefer to keep restrictions on retirement plans in place for more self-control. Future research should be conducted to explore people's preferences for their own temporal behavior, as well as preferences for receiving nudges from institutions or via self-control nudges.

Table 1 displays behavioral tendencies related to temporal preferences, along with self-nudges or interventional nudges by institutions to achieve greater dynamic consistency when facing intertemporal choices.

Self-Nudges

Since decision analysis research and practice aims to improve decision making, the notion of self-nudging to make better decisions is a natural area to explore. Self-nudges are habits and other self-initiated actions a person can establish to enhance self-control, for example in monetary or health behaviors (Keeney, 2020). Foreshadowing the self-nudge literature, Thomas Schelling (1985) presented a structured way to think about how people can enforce rules on themselves. Reijula and Hertwig (2020) promote the use of self-nudges, under which people construct their own decision architectures, for example, to avoid self-control problems. They label people using self-nudges as "citizen choice architects" and argue that this avoids paternalism or manipulation from institutional interventions. They identify four types of self-nudges: reminders, framing changes, making it easier (harder) to do what we want (don't want), and social pressure or personal commitments. In another self-nudge paper, Torma et al. (2016) interview consumers choosing a self-nudging strategy of signing up for an organic box scheme subscription, making that one larger decision replace many small grocery store choices. Siebert and Hannes (2021) gathered empirical evidence on the effectiveness of self-nudges, finding "individuals facing decision opportunities are more satisfied in their decision situations throughout the decision-making process than individuals facing decision problems".

Sometimes, establishing separate mental accounts (Thaler, 1985) and maintaining artificial limits on transactions within accounts may help a person augment self-control in spending and health behaviors over time. For example, within a credit card account, a person could set a habit to pay off the credit card bill in full each month to avoid interest charges. Similarly, in a mental account of recreation activities, a person could set a habit to exercise daily. A person could set mental budgets for spending or food consumption.

However, sometimes, those habits for separately handling heuristically set categories (*e.g.*, for spending on recreation vs. meals vs. clothing, etc.) may be suboptimal. A person can examine whether consistent decisions are being made across

Table 1 Nudges for Outcomes over Time

Behavioral Tendencies	Self-Nudges	Interventional Nudges by Institutions
Underestimating the effect of compound interest	Set habit to pay off credit card in full each month to avoid interest charges. Explore means for spending self-control, like using a debit card and reserving the credit card just for emergencies. Explore taking out a lower-rate car or house loan rather than not paying credit card off each month at a higher rate.	CARD Act mandates credit card companies to display how total owed on credit card grows if not paid off monthly. EPA Guidance: Display graphs with outcomes over time (to visually display exponential growth).
Impatience in the present but more patience in the future (short/long-term asymmetry)	Put some money from each paycheck immediately in savings. Dip into savings only in emergencies. Set habit to exercise daily.	Save More Tomorrow™: Pre-commit to invest later out of raises.
Status quo bias (Tendency to not take action to change)	Form habits to overcome avoidance of change. Set up a personal budget and stick to planned spending within categories. Stick to a diet: Place part of a restaurant order in a takeout box at the beginning of the meal.	Save More Tomorrow™: Automatically enrolled in 401 K Investment when hired, can opt out. Pay-later scheme for crop insurance.
Preference for constant or increasing or moderately spreading out sequences (Inconsistent with standard normative discounting)	When considering fixed rate or variable rate house loans, think about how your income and other expenses may change your available cash flow over time.	EPA Guidance: Display graphs with outcomes over time (to enable choice of a constant or increasing sequence).
Gain/loss asymmetry The absolute magnitude effect	Do not overreact to daily changes (seeing gains/losses) in investments/personal weight by not resetting reference point frequently. Bundle income so magnitude appears larger, more willing to wait for future payouts.	Save More Tomorrow™: Take first 401 K contribution out of future raise, so it is not seen as a loss from take-home pay.

physical or mental accounts. For example, a person could explore means for increasing self-control across spending accounts, like using a debit card and reserving the credit card just for emergencies or explore taking out a lower-rate car or house loan rather than not paying the entire balance of a credit card off each month at a higher rate.

Interventional Nudges by Institutions

Interventional nudges are designed by institutions to overcome behavioral tendencies.

CARD Act

U. S. President Obama signed the Credit Card Accountability, Responsibility, and Disclosure (CARD) Act in May 2009, requiring credit card companies to disclose terms in plain language in plain sight and provide real information about financial consequences.[1] They are now required to display how many months it will take to pay off the current balance if the patron pays only the required monthly minimum, plus what the total payments would add up to. As a nudge to try to convince patrons to pay more than the monthly minimum, they also must display how much a patron would have to pay monthly to pay off the total balance in 36 months, if no added purchases were made on the card, plus what the total payments would add up to. No visual displays are required, but one idea that was proposed was to show shopping bags of different sizes to emphasize that a patron will pay more if only the minimum monthly payment is made.

Save More Tomorrow™

Thaler and Benartzi (2004) and Benartzi and Lewin (2012) introduced and promoted the Save More Tomorrow™ nudge to help employees save for retirement using their company's 401 K savings plan. The U. S. Pension Protection Act of 2006 encouraged companies to adopt the core principles of Save More Tomorrow™. To avoid myopia from present bias, employees are asked to commit now to save more later once a future pay raise is received. Thus, the payroll deduction would not be seen as a loss in take-home pay since it would come out of the increment from the raise. Taking advantage of inertia after being in the program, to stop the program the employee would have to take action to opt out.

Crop Insurance

Casaburi and Willis (2017) present a pay-later scheme for crop insurance in Kenya taking advantage of farmers' greater willingness to spend in the future and overcoming cash flow constraints at the beginning of planting season.

[1] https://www.ftc.gov/enforcement/statutes/credit-card-accountability-responsibility-and-disclosure-act-2009-credit-card;https://www.usnews.com/opinion/economic-intelligence/2014/05/20/card-act-and-the-cfpb-are-protecting-consumers-from-credit-card-deception. Accessed 21 Dec 2021.

EPA Guidance: Display Graphs with Outcomes over Time

We were invited to present our work on preferences for constant or increasing sequences (Guyse et al., 2002) to the EPA, giving suggestions on how the EPA should consider outcomes over time (monetary, health, lives lost, etc.). Since such preferences do not conform with standard normative discounting, we suggested in our EPA talk that decision makers be presented with graphs of the outcomes over time for each possible policy.

Chapter 6 of the EPA Guidelines for Preparing Economic Analyses (2010) covers discounting future benefits and costs. EPA recommends (EPA Guidelines, 2010, page 6–18) that the time paths of benefits and costs be displayed as they are projected to occur over the time horizon of the policy, *i.e.*, without discounting (before subsequent discounting calculations are made). An advantage of this graphical approach is that the decision maker will understand what the pattern of outcomes will be. (Since no discount rate ≥ 0 can represent preferences for increasing sequences found in the experiments done with sequences, this graphing approach has prescriptive appeal for those who choose to express a preference for an increasing sequence.)

Using a Discount Rate or Other Model to Compute a Single Number Representing How Good an Option Is

Now assume we compute a single number to represent how good an alternative is. Usually this will be computed using a discount rate. However, in principle, there could also be a single number resulting from a value function which does not explicitly discount outcomes over time but considers patterns of outcomes over time and directly places value on different sequence shapes. This might be akin to a multiple attribute value function calculation, where one of the evaluation attributes captures preferences over sequence patterns (constant, decreasing, increasing, etc.). A similar approach could be used for equity considerations, where the fairness of the distribution of health across people could be considered as one attribute in a multiple attribute preference function.

If you use a discount rate to compute a single number, a modeling decision is needed on what discount rate to use. The way that standard economic models would prescribe is to convert the sequences of all monetary and non-monetary outcomes to money and use a constant discount rate to discount the resulting monetary outcomes (or, more generally, the value/utility of the outcomes) to the net present value using a suitable discount rate. The option with the highest net present value would be preferred, assuming risk neutrality. (Sometimes the sequence of costs is discounted separately from the series of benefits and a cost/benefit ratio is computed.)

For personal decisions, some financial decisions will include an externally provided interest rate such as for auto loan payback or interest-bearing savings accounts.

For company decisions, standard procedures may prescribe guidelines for discounting a cash flow of revenues and expenses to the net present value and set thresholds for required returns to fund a new project.

Public policy options involving impacts over generations (such as global climate change) in both monetary and non-monetary (*e.g.*, morbidity, mortality, environmental) pose challenges in discounting calculations. The typical practice in U. S. government agencies is to convert health outcomes (morbidity and mortality) or environmental outcomes to money and discount back to the present with a constant discount rate.

EPA Guidelines (2010) recommend computing discounted net present value twice using (1) a 7% rate as the rate of return to private capital for regular regulatory analyses and (2) a 3% rate as a consumption rate of interest, generally recommended for long term policies as the social discount rate. This follows the U.S. Office of Management and Budget Circular A-4 guidelines (OMB, 2003). The EPA guidelines also note that other (generally lower) discount rates (for "social discounting" considered as the rate at which society is willing to trade consumption in one period for consumption in the next period) may be considered for policies with long time horizons. The guidelines state that both costs and benefits should be discounted at the same rate.

If the decision includes non-monetary outcomes, a question is whether to use the same discount rate as used for monetary outcomes. Descriptive results show that people may use different implied discount rates for money and health. However, EPA Guidance (2010) recommends using the same discount rate for both monetary and non-monetary outcomes in each year. Beyond the scope of this paper is how non-monetary outcomes are assigned equivalent monetary values. EPA's Chapter 7 addresses how benefits are monetized and Chapter 10 addresses Environmental Justice, Children's Environmental Health and Other Distributional Considerations.

The surprising Stern Review (Stern, 2007) from the United Kingdom government authored by Lord Stern recommended a low pure rate of time preference of 0.1% for climate change policy analysis, which is effectively an equilibrium real interest rate of 1.4% once added economic assumptions are added in such as the 1.3% annual growth rate, using the Ramsey discounting equation. The Stern Review was controversial at the time (see, *e.g.*, the critique in Nordhaus, 2007) since its low interest rate allowed benefits far in the future to be counted relatively more than in others' analyses since they were discounted less than prevailing recommendations with higher interest rate assumptions. This approach was used to justify greater expenses now to avoid potential climate change damage in the future. See also Text Box 6.6 in the EPA Guidelines (2010) on "What's the Big Deal with the Stern Review?".

There is increasing support for using declining discount rates for decisions with intergenerational discounting over more than 50 years (Arrow et al., 2014; Section 6.3.3 Declining Discount Rates in EPA Guidelines (2020) draft revised Guidelines for Preparing Economic Analyses, updated from a small section in the 2010 guidelines, Section 6.3.3.3 Declining or Non-Constant Discount Rate.)[2] In such a non-constant discount case approach, for example, the discount rate from year 101 to year 100 would be lower than the one from year 1 to year 0.

Future Research

Several research questions remain to be answered. As mentioned previously, it is not clear the extent to which some of the anomalies may reflect true preferences (as opposed to short-cut heuristics or even simply mistakes). Whether these anomalies should or can be corrected is an open question.

What do people want their temporal behavior to be?
More needs to be known about what people want their behaviors over time to be. Will people say they want to adhere to the normative discounting model, or will they say some of the descriptive anomalies match their desired temporal behavior? Are the anomalies with single outcomes more or less realistic as true preferences than the anomalies seen in preferences for sequences? In daily life, people will likely want to set habits to be more consistent in money management and eating, for example. Survey research can be conducted to discover consumers' intentions.

Ken MacCrimmon's dissertation work provides an example of a way to challenge people to consider whether they wish to conform with a normative model or deviate from it. After mid- to upper-level executives participating in a training program had answered questions which showed descriptive violations of utility axioms, MacCrimmon (1968) found that in oral interviews presenting the difference between their answers and the axioms, many said their responses had been mistakes and chose to correct them, but some continued to say they had not made mistakes and that the axioms did not match their true preferences.

Similar research could be done for temporal anomalies. Normative model guidance along with prior contrasting results from descriptive research on discounting anomalies (for paired comparisons vs. sequences) can be presented to respondents and they can be asked what they would like to choose.

Do people's temporal behaviors match their intentions?
We know that temporal behaviors do not always match the normative discounting model. But more needs to be known about whether people's behavior is actually matching their intentions, rather than the normative model.

---

[2] When considering societal decisions over many lifetimes, much will change in the future. Discounting future outcomes may be a way to adjust for some potential changes without more detailed modeling. For example, as population grows, the impact of 1000 deaths now is a smaller proportion of a population than it is of a larger population later. When considering future cancer deaths, discounting them could also partly account for the chance that cancer will be cured by the time in the future that the cases would have shown up.

Do people want help to achieve their desired behaviors over time?
We suspect that people will often want help to correct dynamically inconsistent preferences. People may want to find ways to exert self-control to be more patient or want institutions to nudge them towards self-control. For example, in a consumer survey to create a status report on Americans' plans for retirement, Farkas and Johnson (1997) found that most Americans prefer to keep restrictions on retirement plans in place for more self-control.

Should advisors/institutions paternalistically attempt to change intentions or temporal behaviors?
This question raises philosophical issues. The behavior a paternalistic institution pushes for may not match what people would choose for themselves now or even for their future selves. Reijula and Hertwig (2020) promote the use of self-nudges and argue that this avoids paternalism or manipulation from institutional interventions.

A key tenet in decision analysis is that any decision aid should be consistent with a person's preferences/objectives. But, if a decision analyst is aiding a decision maker, how should temporal preferences be assessed? A general philosophy in decision analysis is that decisions are challenging, so helping a decision maker "divide and conquer" by assessing preferences about smaller components of a decision can overcome the challenging complexity. But in the temporal preference setting, comparing pairs of single outcomes can lead to different discount rates (if outcomes are gains vs. losses, large vs. small, or short term vs. long term) and sequences will have even more different results. The typical decision analytic advice is to ask in different ways and discuss with the person to resolve inconsistencies. The resulting agreed upon temporal preferences may not be a good reflection of what a person would truly prefer while experiencing life in a sequence of outcomes. Some may see the decision analytic advice as paternalistic?

Propose new ways to aid decision makers
Future studies could examine how to aid decision makers via institutional nudges, in decision analytic assessments, or via self-nudges without a decision analyst. There is a related stream of experimental literature that examines how to aid other components of decision making, such as Siebert (2016) on generating alternatives by looking at objectives and Siebert et al. (2021) on the effects of decision training on proactivity.

Do nudges work?
For existing and proposed nudges, it is important to evaluate their success and investigate whether the methods help people to achieve better outcomes and to better understand (a) outcome patterns over time and (b) how to improve decisions. In particular, research should examine whether the proposed self-nudges in section "Self-Nudges" will succeed in making choices over time lead to better outcomes and/or be more consistent with people's preferences.

When the chosen sequences of outcomes are eventually experienced over time, research should check what the experienced utility turns out to be. When sequences are viewed in isolation, perceiving marginal improvements from a reference point in the first period may make an increasing sequence seem particularly appealing. Also, it may be that preferences for moderately spreading outcomes, such as in constant or increasing sequences, could be found to mitigate recognized impatience.

How long do the effects of nudges last?
Do externally supplied nudges become a natural part of future decisions without further interventions? After being exposed to externally supplied nudges, will people be able to develop and implement self-nudges for future intertemporal behavior? Will self-nudges form long lasting good habits?

For pension investment decisions (between stocks and bonds, for example), a person may make a choice when hired at a company and never change the allocation. If a nudge is applied at the time of hiring, its effects can be long lasting since the new employee may not change the planned action over time. But, for behaviors that are repeated often, such as daily (healthy or not) food choices, the effects of a nudge may at first lead to a good habit but decay over time as a person falls back into bad habits.

Conclusion

We presented the normative exponential discounting model in section "How should We Evaluate Intertemporal Outcomes?". As shown in section "Descriptive Results of Time Preference Experiments", people do not understand compound interest, and display descriptively anomalous temporal preference behavior violating the normative discounting model. Section "Prescriptive Guidance for Evaluating Intertemporal Outcomes" covered prescriptions to nudge people into desired behaviors considering the anomalies in section "Nudges" as well as prescribed discount rates in section "Using a Discount Rate or Other Model to Compute a Single Number Representing How Good an Option Is". Finally, open research questions are in section "Future Research".

References

Adamou, A., Berman, Y., Mavroyiannis, D., & Peters, O. (2021). Microfoundations of discounting. *Decision Analysis, 18*(4), 257–272.

Ainslie, G. (1975). Specious reward: A behavioral theory of impulsiveness and impulse control. *Psychological Bulletin, 82*(4), 463–496.

Ainslie, G., & Haslam, N. (1992). Hyperbolic discounting. In G. Loewenstein & J. Elster (Eds.), *Choice over time* (pp. 57–92). Russell Sage Foundation.

Ariely, D. (1998). Combining experiences over time: the effects of duration, intensity changes and on-line measurements on retrospective pain evaluations. *Journal of Behavioral Decision Making, 11*, 19–45.

Arrow, K. J., Cropper, M. L., Gollier, C., Groom, B., Heal, G. M., Newell, R. G., Nordhaus, W. D., Pindyck, R. S., Pizer, W. A., Portney, P. R., & Sterner, T. (2014). Should governments use a declining discount rate in project analysis? *Review of Environmental Economics and Policy, 8*(2), 145–163.

Attema, A. E., Bleichrodt, H., L'Haridon, O., Peretti-Watel, P., & Seror, V. (2018). Discounting health and money: New evidence using a more robust method. *Journal of Risk and Uncertainty, 56*, 117–140.

Benartzi, S., & Lewin, R. (2012). *Save more tomorrow: Practical behavioral finance solutions to improve 401(k) plans*. Penguin.

Bilgin, B., & LeBoeuf, R. A. (2010). Looming losses in future time perception. *Journal of Marketing Research, 47*(3), 520–530.

Binswanger, J., & Carman, K. G. (2010). *The miracle of compound interest: does our intuition fail?* Netspar Discussion Paper, No. 12/2010-079.

Bishai, D. M. (2004). Does time preference change with age? *Journal of Population Economics, 17*, 583–602.

Casaburi, L., & Willis, J. (2017). *Increasing crop insurance adoption among smallholder farmers with pay-at-harvest premium payment*. VoxDev. Accessed December 21, 2021, from https://voxdev.org/topic/finance/increasing-crop-insurance-adoption-among-smallholder-farmers-pay-harvest-premium-payment

Chapman, G. B. (1996a). Expectations and preferences for sequences of health and money. *Organizational Behavior and Human Decision Processes, 67*(1), 59–75.

Chapman, G. B. (1996b). Temporal discounting and utility for health and money. *Journal of Experimental Psychology: Learning, Memory, and Cognition, 22*(3), 771–791.

Chapman, G. B., & Elstein, A. S. (1995). Valuing the future: discounting health and money. *Medical Decision Making, 15*, 373–386.

Chesson, H. W., Leichliter, J. S., Zimet, G. D., Rosenthal, S. L., Bernstein, D. I., & Fife, K. H. (2006). Discount rates and risky sexual behaviors among teenagers and young adults. *Journal of Risk and Uncertainty, 32*(3), 217–230.

Debreu, G. (1954). Representation of a preference ordering by a numerical function. In R. M. Thrall, C. H. Coombs, & R. L. Davis (Eds.), *Decision processes* (pp. 159–165). Wiley.

Debreu, G. (1960). Topological methods in cardinal utility theory. In K. J. Arrow, S. Karlin, & P. Suppes (Eds.), *Mathematical methods in the social sciences* (pp. 116–126). Stanford University Press.

Debreu, G. (1964). Continuity properties of Paretian utility. *International Economic Review, 5*(3), 285–293.

EPA Guidelines. (2010). *Guidelines for preparing economic analyses*. Accessed December 21, 2021, from https://www.epa.gov/environmental-economics/guidelines-preparing-economic-analyses

EPA Guidelines. (2020). *Guidelines for preparing economic analyses, April 3, 2020, Review copy prepared for EPA's Science Advisory Board's Economic Guidelines Review Panel*. A final revised version is not yet available to the public of EPA's draft recommended revised: https://sab.epa.gov/ords/sab/f?p=100:18:17480157678849:::RP,18:P18_ID:2545, list of SAB reports with link to 2020 draft guidelines. The Jan. 6, 2021 review (EPA-SAB- 21-002) by the Science Advisory Board review panel of the draft revision is at https://yosemite.epa.gov/sab/sabproduct.nsf/LookupWebProjectsCurrentBOARD/61C74C0E14BD5956852586550071E058/$File/EPA-SAB-21-002.pdf and at Advisory Reports | US EPA = https://sab.epa.gov/ords/sab/f?p=100:12:17480157678849:::12::. Accessed 21 December 2021.

Farkas, S., & Johnson, J. (1997). *Miles to go: A status report on Americans' plans for retirement*. Public Agenda.

Fishburn, P. C. (1970). *Utility theory for decision making*. Wiley.

Frederick, S. (2003). Measuring intergenerational time preference: Are future lives valued less? *Journal of Risk and Uncertainty, 26*(1), 39–53.

Frederick, S., & Loewenstein, G. (2008). Conflicting motives in evaluations of sequences. *Journal of Risk Uncertainty, 37*(2), 221–235.

Frederick, S., Loewenstein, G., & O'Donoghue, T. (2002). Time discounting and time preference: A critical review. *Journal of Economic Literature, 40*(2), 351–401.

Fredrickson, B. L., & Kahneman, D. (1993). Duration neglect in retrospective evaluations of affective episodes. *Journal of Personality and Social Psychology, 65*, 45–55.

Frost, R., & McNaughton, N. (2017). The neural basis of delay discounting: A review and preliminary model. *Neuroscience and Biobehavioral Reviews, 79*, 48–65.

Guyse, J. L., & Simon, J. (2011). Consistency among elicitation techniques for intertemporal choice: A within-subjects investigation of the anomalies. *Decision Analysis, 8*(3), 233–246.

Guyse, J. L., Keller, L. R., & Eppel, T. (2002). Valuing environmental outcomes: Preferences for constant or improving sequences. *Organizational Behavior and Human Decision Processes, 87*(2), 253–277.

Guyse, J. L., Keller, L. R., & Huynh, C. H. (2020). Valuing sequences of lives lost or saved over time: Preference for uniform sequences. *Decision Analysis, 17*(1), 24–38.

Guyse, J. L., Huynh, C. H., & Keller, L. R. (2021). Lives saved vs. lives lost in survey research: Investigating methodological consistency. *Proceedings of the 2021 Northeast Decision Sciences Institute Annual Conference*. Accessed December 21, 2021, from https://nedsi.decisionsciences.org/wp-content/uploads/2021/06/NEDSI-2021-Proceedings.pdf

Harvey, C. M. (1986). Value functions for infinite-period planning. *Management Science, 32*(9), 1123–1139.

Holcomb, J. H., & Nelson, P. S. (1992). Another experimental look at individual time preference. *Rationality and Society, 4*(2), 199–220.

Kahneman, D., Fredrickson, B. L., Schreiber, C. A., & Redelmeier, D. A. (1993). When more pain is preferred to less: Adding a better end. *Psychological Science, 4*, 401–405.

Keeler, E. B., & Cretin, S. (1983). Discounting of life-saving and other nonmonetary effects. *Management Science, 29*(3), 300–306.

Keeney, R. L. (2020). *Give yourself a nudge: Helping smart people make smarter personal and business decisions*. Cambridge University Press.

Keeney, R. L., & Raiffa, H. (1976). *Decisions with multiple objectives: Preferences and value trade-offs*. Wiley and Cambridge University Press.

Keller, L. R., & Simon, J. (2019). Preference functions for spatial risk analysis. *Risk Analysis, 39*(1), 244–256.

Krantz, D. H., Luce, R. D., Suppes, P., & Tversky, A. (1971). *Foundations of measurement. additive and polynomial representations* (Vol. 1). Academic.

Laibson, D. I., Repetto, A., & Tobacman, J. (1998). Self-control and saving for retirement. *Brookings Papers on Economic Activity, 1998*(1), 91–196.

Loewenstein, G., & Prelec, D. (1992). Anomalies in intertemporal choice: Evidence and an interpretation. *The Quarterly Journal of Economics, 107*(2), 573–597.

Loewenstein, G., & Prelec, D. (1993). Preference for sequences of outcomes. *Psychological Review, 100*(1), 91–107.

Loewenstein, G., & Sicherman, N. (1991). Do workers prefer increasing wage profiles? *Journal of Labor Economics, 9*(1), 67–84.

Loewenstein, G., & Thaler, R. H. (1989). Anomalies: Intertemporal choice. *Journal of Economic Perspectives, 3*(4), 181–193.

Lusardi, A. (2008a). *Financial literacy: An essential tool for informed consumer choice?* Working Paper Series no. 14084. National Bureau of Economic Research.

Lusardi, A. (2008b). *Household saving behavior: The role of financial literacy, information, and financial education programs*. Working Paper Series no. 13824. National Bureau of Economic Research.

Lusardi, A., & Mitchell, O. S. (2011). *Financial literacy and planning: Implications for retirement wellbeing*. Working Paper Series no. 17078. National Bureau of Economic Research, .

MacCrimmon, K. R. (1968). Some normative and descriptive aspects of the decision theory postulates. In K. Borch & J. Mossin (Eds.), *Risk and uncertainty* (pp. 3–23). Macmillan.

McClure, S. M., Laibson, D. I., Loewenstein, G., & Cohen, J. D. (2004). Separate neural systems value immediate and delayed monetary rewards. *Science, 306*(5695), 503–507.

Mertens, S., Herberz, S. M., Hahnel, U. J. J., & Brosch, T. (2022). The effectiveness of nudging: A meta-analysis of choice architecture interventions across behavioral domains. *Proceedings of the National Academy of Sciences, 119*(1).

Nordhaus, W. D. (2007). A review of the Stern Review on the economics of climate change. *Journal of Economic Literature, XLV*, 686–702.

OMB. (2003). *Circular A-4, Regulatory Analysis*, Sept. 17.

Payne, J. W., Bettman, J. R., & Luce, M. F. (1996). When time is money: Decision behavior under opportunity-cost time pressure. *Organizational Behavior and Human Decision Processes, 66*(2), 131–152.

Rader, T. (1963). The existence of a utility function to represent preferences. *The Review of Economic Studies, 30*(3), 229–232.

Rae, J. (1834). *The sociological theory of capital*, reprint 1834th edition. Macmillan.

Ramsey, F. P. (1928). A mathematical theory of saving. *Economic Journal, 38*(4), 543–549.

Ramsey, F. P. (1931). *The foundations of mathematics and other logical essays*. Routledge.

Read, D., & Powell, M. (2002). Reasons for sequence preferences. *Journal of Behavioral Decision Making, 15*(5), 433–460.

Redelmeier, D. A., & Kahneman, D. (1996). Patients' memories of painful medical treatments-real time and retrospective evaluations of two minimally invasive procedures. *Pain, 66*, 3–8.

Reijula, S., & Hertwig, R. (2020). Self-nudging and the citizen choice architect. *Behavioural Public Policy, 6*(1), 119–149.

Ross, W. T., & Simonson, I. (1991). Evaluations of pairs of experiences: A preference for happy endings. *Journal of Behavioral Decision Making, 4*, 273–282.

Samuelson, P. A. (1937). A note on measurement of utility. *The Review of Economic Studies, 4*(2), 155–161.

Savage, L. J. (1954). *The foundations of statistics*. Wiley.

Schelling, T. C. (1985). Enforcing rules on oneself. *Journal of Law, Economics and Organization, 1*(2), 357–374.

Schmitt, D. R., & Kemper, T. D. (1996). Preference for different sequences of increasing or decreasing rewards. *Organizational Behavior and Human Decision Processes, 66*(1), 89–101.

Siebert, J. U. (2016). Can novices create alternatives of the same quality as experts? *Decision Analysis, 13*(4), 278–291.

Siebert, J. & Hannes, C. (2021). Empirical evidence on the effectiveness of "giving oneself a nudge": The relative benefits of pursuing decision opportunities and solving decision problems, Presented at the *31st EURO Conference (Virtual)*, https://www.euro-online.org/conf/admin/tmp/program-euro31.pdf, in MD-21 session, Accessed 2/27/2022.

Siebert, J. U., Kunz, R., & Rolf, P. (2021). Effects of decision training on individuals' decision-making proactivity. *European Journal of Operational Research, 294*(1), 264–282.

Simon, J., Kirkwood, C. W., & Keller, L. R. (2014). Decision analysis with geographically varying outcomes: Preference models and illustrative applications. *Operations Research, 62*(1), 182–194.

Smith, A. (1759). *The theory of moral sentiments*. Printed for A. Millar, A. Kincaid, & J. Bell.

Solnick, J. V., Kannenberg, C. H., Eckerman, D. A., & Waller, M. B. (1980). An experimental analysis of impulsivity and impulse control in humans. *Learning and Motivation, 11*(1), 61–77.

Stern, N. (2007). *The economics of climate change: The Stern Review*. Cambridge University Press.

Thaler, R. H. (1981). Some empirical evidence on dynamic inconsistency. *Economics Letters, 8*(3), 201–207.

Thaler, R. H. (1985). Mental accounting and consumer choice. *Marketing Science, 4*(3), 199–214.

Thaler, R. H., & Benartzi, S. (2004). Save More Tomorrow™: Using behavioral economics to increase employee saving. *Journal of Political Economy, 112*(S1), S164–S187.

Thaler, R. H., & Sunstein, C. (2008). *Nudge: Improving decisions about health, wealth, and happiness*. Yale University Press.

Torma, G., Aschelmann-Witzel, J., & Thøgersen, J. (2016). I nudge myself: Exploring 'self-nudging' strategies to drive sustainable consumption behaviour. *International Journal of Consumer Studies, 42*(1), 141–154.

Trope, Y., & Liberman, N. (2010). Construal-level theory of psychological distance. *Psychological Review, 117*(2), 440–463.

Varey, C., & Kahneman, D. (1992). Experiences extended across time: Evaluation of moments and episodes. *Journal of Behavioral Decision Making, 5*(3), 169–185.

Wang, Y., Wang, L., & Keller, L. R. (2015). Discounting over subjective time: Subjective time perception helps explain multiple discounted utility anomalies. *International Journal of Research in Marketing, 32*(4), 445–448.

Weibull, J. W. (1985). Discounted-value representations of temporal preferences. *Mathematics of Operations Research, 10*(2), 244–250.

The Near-Miss Bias

Florian M. Federspiel, Robin Dillon-Merrill, Matthias Seifert, and Sofía Rodriguez

Abstract Near-miss events are a topic of increasing interest, motivated by a growing body of literature showing that these events are often not perceived as a sign of warning, but may lead to unwarranted increases in risk taking behavior in similar future situations. However, still fairly little is known about the bias and its behavioral underpinnings. What defines a near-miss event and how does it influence risk taking behavior? What triggers the near-miss bias, and under which conditions does it manifest itself? And what kind of decision support can be provided to counteract the bias?

Keywords Near-miss bias · Risk perception · Risk taking behavior · Definition · Measurement · Debiasing · Prescriptive interventions

This chapter is based in part on Florian Federspiel's (2016) Ph.D. Dissertation "The experience of near miss events and their influence on risk taking behaviors", IE University. Madrid, Spain.

F. M. Federspiel (✉) · S. Rodriguez
INCAE Business School, La Garita, Costa Rica
e-mail: Florian.Federspiel@incae.edu; Sofia.Rodriguez@incae.edu

R. Dillon-Merrill
McDonough School of Business, Georgetown University, Washington, DC, USA
e-mail: Robin.DillonMerrill@georgetown.edu

M. Seifert
Operations and Technology, IE Business School, IE University, Madrid, Spain
e-mail: Matthias.Seifert@ie.edu

F. M. Federspiel et al. (eds.), *Behavioral Decision Analysis*, International Series in Operations Research & Management Science 350,
https://doi.org/10.1007/978-3-031-44424-1_11

Introduction

> [...] Neither Thiokol [the contractor for the O-ring seals] nor NASA expected the rubber O-rings sealing the joints to be touched by hot gases of motor ignition, much less to be partially burned. However, as tests and then flights confirmed damage to the sealing rings, the reaction by both NASA and Thiokol was to increase the amount of damage considered "acceptable" [emphasis added]. At no time did management either recommend a redesign of the joint or call for the Shuttle's grounding until the problem was solved. (Presidential Commission on the Space Shuttle Challenger Accident, 1986, p. 120)

The accident of the Challenger spacecraft—caused by a failure of the joint of the rocket motor—was as such not merely due to technical matters but equally so due to a questionable pattern in the decision makers' assessment of the risk. Disaster finally strikes, despite the fact of plenty of previous *near misses* preceding the 1986 Challenger spacecraft disaster. Engineers had repeatedly reported damaged O-ring seals after previous missions, noting that with lower outside temperatures damage tended to worsen. Despite a particularly low temperature on the day of the launch NASA decided to proceed, eventually leading to the loss of the Challenger and its crew. There was, and in fact engineers had known about it, a chance that O-ring seals could be damaged during lift-off and that this damage could result in the loss of the spacecraft. Damaged O-ring seals had not been a single occurrence and yet up until the day of the disaster the space shuttles had completed their missions and returned to earth. Unresolved problems related to O-ring seal erosion and blow-by dated back to 1977. In 1985, the 15th flight of NASA's Space Shuttle program and the third flight by the Discovery, significant erosion and blow-by discovered. In fact a total of 42 cases of either erosion or blow-by had been recorded prior to the Challenger's disaster. The loss of the Challenger and its crew could indeed have occurred during previous missions. The fact that it did not happen was notably not due to prevention (with regards to the O-ring seal issue) but merely due to *chance*. Ironically, given several seemingly successful tests and missions the O-ring seal issue became what was eventually called an 'acceptable flight risk' (Presidential Commission on the Space Shuttle Challenger Accident, 1986: 120).

Strikingly, the Challenger was not going to remain NASA's only major victim where the near-miss bias likely played a role. The loss of the Columbia occurred only 15 years later. Again, engineers were indeed well informed about the phenomenon of foam strikes upon re-entry based on previous missions and went as far as to model the potential danger (Dillon & Tinsley, 2005a). 300 tiles had to be replaced after Colombia's very first mission in 1981. In 2002, the Atlantis sustained the most severe foam strikes compared to any prior missions. At least 14 significant foam-shedding events were recorded between 1981 and 2003. Yet after many missions from which space shuttles returned with tile damage, the risk became accepted, and space shuttles were continually allowed to embark on further missions. The behavior surrounding foam strikes, thus, is strikingly similar to that of the O-ring seal issues. One may ask the question of what has led such an unquestionably professional organization to fail so dramatically twice in recent history?

Notably, the events leading up to these high-profile examples share a common characteristic and are only among many possible cases to be told: Near-miss events are plentiful and naturally occurring events that often receive little attention and at times may lead to disaster. Remarkably, both tragedies, and likely many others, could have been avoided if these events would have been properly recognized and measures taken to prevent them. Instead, by now we know that the experience of near-miss events, which only recently began to receive attention in the domain of decision analysis (Dillon & Tinsley, 2008; Phimister et al., 2003; Tinsley et al., 2012), is effectively associated with an increase in risk taking behavior, leading to potentially disastrous outcomes as just outlined (Dillon & Tinsley, 2008).

Near-miss events are ubiquitous and relevant for many professional domains including medicine, aviation, firefighting, counterterrorism, natural disaster management, engineering, and risk mitigation (Bier & Mosleh, 1990; Dillon & Tinsley, 2008; Dillon et al., 2011, 2014; Federal Aviation Administration, 2022; Phimister et al., 2003).

Provided the inter-disciplinary nature of research into the phenomenon, what precisely defines near-miss events relevant to behavioral decision analysis? What triggers the near-miss bias in different settings, and what can be done to de-bias undesired behavior? This chapter seeks to provide answers to these questions.

Near-Miss Events: A Definition

In addition to the field of decision analysis, near misses have been the subject of study across several academic disciplines. Researchers in pediatric medicine (Kelly & O'Connell, 1978), for instance, have examined the occurrence and implications of near-miss events such as near infant death, whereas others have studied near misses in the context of road (Hayward, 1972) and air traffic safety and at the interfaces of decision analysis with engineering and risk analysis (Bier & Mosleh, 1990). A result of this widespread examination of near-miss events across fields is a diverse range of definitions, as showcased in Table 1.

Notably, the existing definitions differ in what is considered a near miss versus an actual miss. In other words, the reference points implied in the different definitions, which qualify what is seen as a near miss as opposed to a miss, are not identical. For instance, while Phimister et al. (2003) suggest that near misses as seen by some may involve small losses experienced by the decision maker most other definitions qualify those events as near misses that came close to a loss but were effectively still a gain. These differences, however, are likely to have an important impact on how near-miss situations are generally perceived and acted upon (Dillon et al., 2014). In other words, what constitutes a near miss resides along a continuum with the decision maker determining where the line is drawn between what is perceived to be gain or a loss. We offer an overarching definition of a near miss:

Table 1 Near-miss definition in different fields

Authors	Field	Definition
Federal Aviation Administration.	Aviation	"… an incident associated with the operation of an aircraft in which a possibility of collision occurs as a result of proximity of less than 500 feet to another aircraft" (p. 772).
Tinsley, Dillon & Cronin (2012).	Decision Analysis & Management	"When people escape an impending disaster by chance, they have experienced a "near miss." more precisely, a near miss is an event that has some nontrivial expectation of ending in disaster but because of luck did not." (p. 1)
Goldenhar, L. M., Williams, L. J., & Swanson, N. G. (2003).	Industry & Workplace safety	"An incident that could have resulted in an injury but did not" (p. 228).
Phimister, J. R., Oktem, U., Kleindorfer, P. R., Kunreuther, H. (2000).	Risk & decision analysis	"An opportunity to improve safety practice based on a condition, or an incident with potential for more serious consequence" (p. 11).
Mantel, G. D., Buchman, E., Rees, H., Pattinson, R. C. (1998).	Medicine	"A patient with an acute organ system dysfunction, which if not treated appropriately, could result in death" (p. 985).
Bier, V., & Mosleh, A. (1990).	Risk & decision analysis	"Accident precursors" (p. 91).

A near miss is a probabilistic event nearly resulting in a reference dependent loss that does not materialize due to chance circumstances.

However, another important difference relates to the underlying assumption of causality, or in other words, regarding probabilistic (in-)dependence. For instance, Bier and Mosleh (1990) explicitly call near misses 'accident precursors', which implies that they form part of a causal chain of events and provide useful signals for decision makers regarding future decisions. A similar assumption is true for Mantel et al.'s (1998) definition. These are examples of where near misses are seen through a lens of probabilistic dependence. That is, an accident may well be more (or less) likely following the experience of a near miss. On the other hand, the other definitions such as the one offered by Tinsley et al. (2012) is either silent about this aspect or assumes probabilistic independence. In the latter case, a prior near miss does not change the future likelihood of particular hazard at all.

This distinction of course is of great importance when interpreting subsequent behavior to near miss in order to compare it to normative standards and guide prescriptive efforts. Importantly, the current literature in the domain of behavioral decision analysis, focuses entirely on the type of events best described by probabilistic independence when investigating near-miss events. Consequently, before discussing behavioral insights describing behavior following near misses, it is important to consider the normative perspective.

Before considering both normative and descriptive perspectives on near misses we believe that it is useful to first outline a general framework to operationalize near misses following the definitional discussion.

Operationalizing Near-Miss Events

Related to the issue of definitional scope and clarity, previous studies investigating near misses often lack a precise and bounded measure and operationalization of these events. That is, near misses are often defined merely as probabilistic events in which some outcome *nearly*, but lastly did *not* occur (Dillon & Tinsley, 2008; Sundali et al., 2012; Tinsley et al., 2012). In other words, it lacks a definition of the notion of near, which if left undefined could mean that *any* event with some non-trivial probability of failure which lastly did not materialize would constitute a near miss.

To address this, we may broadly operationalize near-miss events in terms of a probabilistic target event (x), which is represented by a given probability distribution ($f(x)$) over a range of possible outcomes (Fig. 1). We may further assume that the target event follows a normal distribution with mean $\overline{x}$ and standard deviation σ_x. Let the decision maker's utility function associated with the outcome of the target event be denoted as $u(x)$, whereby $u(x) = 1$, if the event outcome can be classified as successful. In addition, let x_r denote a reference point for the decision maker, below which the decision maker's perceived utility would start to decrease due to an experienced loss in the sense that $u(x) < 1$.

A near miss is experienced if target event x is located *close* to reference point x_r. Taking this into account, the important question relates to what can be considered to be *near*. Without the restriction of a threshold at which an outcome is no longer perceived to be near a potential loss, any successful outcome could effectively be considered a near miss. We therefore assume the existence of threshold value x_m, which delineates an upper limit of the range of possible near-miss outcomes. There are many possible heuristics a decision maker may employ to lastly decide on what

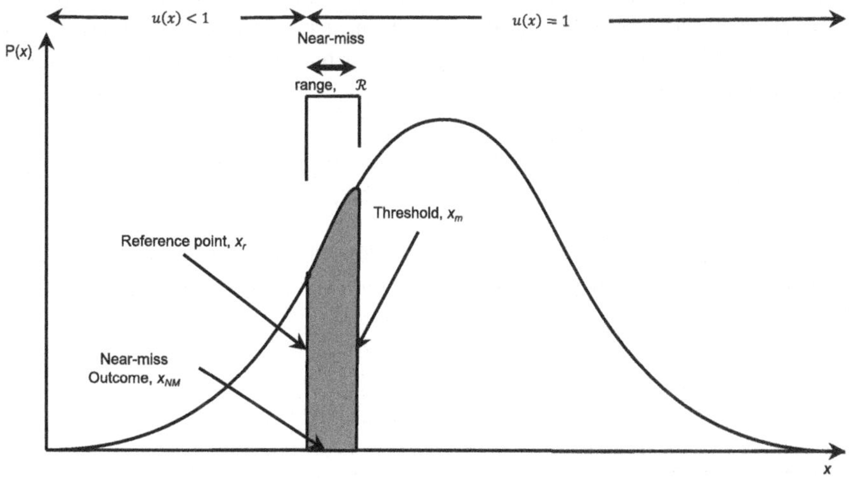

Fig. 1 A representation of a near-miss event

is "near". Here we propose for a simple one: In order to decide on what is considered near, a decision maker considers the assumed range, h_x, of possible outcomes of target event (x), $h_x = \max(x) - \min(x)$,[1] and applies a certain fraction, f_d, which may vary by decision domain, d, of the range to her reference point as a threshold value. This captures the notion that for large values of f_d, the resulting range the decision maker may consider as near can be rather small, and vice versa for small values of f_d. The location of x_m depends on whether the experienced loss is associated with values for x that lie on the right or left side of the distribution. Analytically, we define the threshold value x_m as:

Definition 1 If $u(x) < 1 \ \forall\, x < x_r$, $x_m = x_r + \frac{h_x}{f_d}$. If $u(x) = 1 \ \forall\, x < x_r$, $x_m = x_r - \frac{h_x}{f_d}$.

This allows us to express x_m as

$$x_m = x_r \pm \frac{h_x}{f_d}, \tag{1}$$

where x_r denotes the decision maker's reference point, h_x the range of target event (x) and f_d a factor capturing a decision maker's near-miss range for decision domain d.

We will hereafter refer to the range $\mathcal{R}$ as the near-miss range, where

$$\begin{cases} u(x) < 1 \forall x < x_r; \mathcal{R} = x_m - x_r \\ u(x) = 1 \forall x < x_r; \mathcal{R} = x_r - x_m \end{cases}. \tag{2}$$

In the example in Fig. 1 we assume that the experienced loss is associated with values for x that lie on the left side of the distribution and the decision maker's utility domain is denoted on the top bar. The y-axis displays the probability of respective outcomes of the target event (x), whereas the x-axis captures possible outcome values for the target variable (x). Moreover, the near-miss range $\mathcal{R}$ is represented by the grey shaded area, whereby an exemplary near-miss event is illustrated by event outcome x_{NM}, where

$$\begin{cases} u(x) < 1 \forall x < x_r; x_r \le x_{NM} \le x_m \\ u(x) = 1 \forall x < x_r; x_r \ge x_{NM} \ge x_m \end{cases}. \tag{3}$$

Lastly, if we consider that target event (x) follows a univariate distribution with a probability density function $f(x)$, the near-miss range $\mathcal{R}$ can be expressed as

[1] We may assume that in the case of a normal distribution, a decision maker's range could be expressed as $h_x = \max\left(CI_{.99}(\bar{x})\right) - \min\left(CI_{.99}(\bar{x})\right)$.

$$\begin{cases} u(x) < 1 \forall x < x_r; \mathcal{R} = \mathrm{P}(\mathrm{x_r} \le \mathrm{x_{NM}} \le \mathrm{x_m}) = \int_{\mathrm{x_r}}^{\mathrm{x_m}} \mathrm{f}(\mathrm{x})\mathrm{dx} \\ u(x) = 1 \forall x < x_r; \mathcal{R} = \mathrm{P}(\mathrm{x_r} \ge \mathrm{x_{NM}} \ge \mathrm{x_m}) = \int_{\mathrm{x_m}}^{\mathrm{x_r}} \mathrm{f}(\mathrm{x})\mathrm{dx} \end{cases}. \tag{4}$$

Figure 1 shows a corresponding representation of an exemplary near-miss event.

Note that while this example uses a continuous probability distribution, the framework applies equally to dichotomous outcomes. This formal description of near-miss events allows for a clearer definition and conceptualization of near-miss events and comparability across studies and can be used in accordance with decision theoretic theories such as expected utility theory. The framework's parameters such as a decision maker's reference point as well as threshold values raise important considerations for the manipulation and measurement in investigative settings of near misses. Lastly, the addition of a threshold value closes a previously unspecified loop-hole without which anything but disaster could be considered a near miss.

Moreover, we know from extant studies that decision makers' perception of near misses is the deciding factor determining future behavior. Formally, the notion of perceived nearness as part of what constitutes a *near* miss has not yet received much attention. Our framework relates the near-miss range, *R*, to the perception of how close of a call the near miss represents to the decision maker. Tinsley et al. (2012) showed that depending on whether decision makers' perceive a near miss as a sign of system vulnerability vs. system resilience drives either future risk aversion or risk taking, respectively. A perception of vulnerability (resilience) following a near miss may well be associated with an outcome that in terms of perceived nearness came very close (not too close) to the decision maker's reference point, x_r. However, this proposed connection remains to be tested empirically.

A recent working paper by Permut et al. (2021) investigates how varying proximity to losses affects decision makers' reactions to near misses and finds that closeness determines later risk taking. After what they call 'far misses' based on linear distance decision makers' increase risk taking whereas 'near misses' lead to risk aversion. Here, too, our framework provides a conceptual and formal way to capture the measurement of closeness, while once more drawing attention to the importance of the threshold, x_m, and consequent near-miss range, *R*, within which we could expect differing perceptions akin to what Permut et al. (2021) called far- and near misses.

The Normative Perspective on Near Misses

Classical approaches such as expected and subjective expected utility (Savage, 1954) stipulate that a decision maker faced with risky or uncertain prospects should assess these based on their (subjective) expected utility. The expected utility $\mathbb{E}U(\varsigma)$

(Savage, 1954), of a given option, ς, is found by multiplying the option's possible outcome utilities, $U(O_i)$, with their respective probabilities, p_i:

$$\mathbb{E}U(\varsigma) = \sum_{n=1}^{i} p_i U(O_i). \tag{5}$$

From a normative perspective, a risk neutral rational agent provided with several options should choose the option with the highest expected utility. As such, a decision maker's expected utility depends on two crucial aspects regarding the possible outcomes: First, the subjective value the decision maker places on the different possible outcomes, conceivable as the overall benefit she derives from an outcome, denoted as utilities, $U(O_i)$, and second, her subjective belief regarding the likelihood of the different possible outcomes, p_i.

For example, think of a simplified situation in which NASA has to choose between the safe option of keeping its spacecraft aground or the risky option of launching it into space. The potential outcomes of both options (using arbitrary outcome utilities as an example) as well as NASA's assumed probabilistic estimates regarding their occurrence are shown in Table 2.

If the potential rewards of a space mission, adjusting them for the likelihood of success or failure exceed those of keeping it aground, NASA's expected utility will be higher if deciding to launch. In the exemplary case shown in Table 2, such is the case. In that sense, if we think of differences in risk taking behaviors associated with the experience of near misses we may initially relate them to changes in how decision makers assess either the value of different outcomes, or their expectations regarding those values.

From what we may call an *updating perspective*, decision makers may revise their subjective likelihoods of possible success, p, or failure, $1 - p$, after the experience of one or several near misses (i.e. lastly a success, O_1) in a Bayesian fashion. That is, decision makers may use Bayes rule, which generally states that the posterior likelihood of an event of interest is proportional to its likelihood function provided the evidence at hand, times the general prior likelihood before having seen the evidence:

$$\textit{Posterior} \propto \textit{Likelihood} * \textit{Prior}. \tag{6}$$

Here, we may use a binomial distribution for the chances of success (versus failure) and use a uniform prior (e.g. before the first mission the chances of success or

Table 2 Example: NASA's options

Option, ς	Launch spacecraft		Keep spacecraft aground
Possible outcomes, O_i	Success, O_1	Failure, O_2	Status quo
Utility, $U(O_i)$	1	0	0.3
Probability, p_i	$p = 0.5$	$1 - p = 0.5$	1
Expected utility, $\mathbb{E}U(\varsigma)$	$1 \times 0.5 + 0 \times 0.5 = 0.5$		$0.3 \times 1 = 0.3$

failure are unknown or pretty even as stated above). This allows us to express the likelihood function as:

$$L(p) = p^{Y}(1-p)^{n-Y}, \tag{7}$$

where Y equals the number of successes (including near misses) over n experiences. For the uniform prior we may use a beta distribution, $p \propto beta(1,1)$, allowing us to express the prior as

$$p^{1-1}(1-p)^{1-1}, \tag{8}$$

which then lastly allows us to express the posterior simply as:

$$p^{Y+1-1}(1-p)^{n-Y+1-1}. \tag{9}$$

In practice, much of course depends on the particular choice of the prior. Taking the above example, if NASA decided to launch and experienced a near miss in which the spacecraft however returned successfully, NASA may revise its prior likelihood of the mission's failure, continuing its assessment for future missions using a new posterior likelihood in its decision calculus.

Given for instance that the spacecraft did make it back, NASA may revise its subjective likelihood of a catastrophic failure occurring slightly downwards, i.e., lower than the exemplary 50% to 44%. Because of this, the decision to launch would seem more attractive to NASA in the future, given that a lower estimate of the likelihood of failure would increase the expected utility of the action to launch compared with keeping the spacecraft on the ground. The result is that NASA would now be less likely to keep the spacecraft on the ground in the future, an action that is normatively warranted. This is because there exists an assumption of probabilistic dependence which describes many settings in which near misses are experienced.

Working under this assumption as mentioned, for instance, Bier and Mosleh (1990) and Yi and Bier offer Bayesian approaches of how to properly incorporate precursor data, in particular, near misses in a normative fashion. This is normatively warranted under an assumption of probabilistic dependence and seems descriptively plausible (if at least for the direction of an increased or lowered probability estimate) as an explanation for the effect of near-miss events on risk taking behaviors. However, this explanation has mostly been rejected from a behavioral perspective based on previous evidence in which decision makers did not seem to engage in any kind of updating process (Dillon & Tinsley, 2008; Tinsley et al., 2012). That is, prompting subjects that experienced a near miss for their subjective probabilities of the outcome associated with the near miss, Dillon & Tinsley (2008) found no difference in elicited probabilities compared to a control group. In a different setting, Permut et al. (2021) recently did find support for updating to occur and to drive differences in subsequent risk taking. This suggests that delineating under which settings or which kind of near misses a cognitive updating perspective may hold remains to be further investigated.

Alternatively, it is conceivable that through a process, which we may call the *value perspective*, the experience of a near miss affects the utility decision makers place on the different possible outcomes, i.e., $U(O_i)$. Taking the above example, the experience of a near failure may serve to increase the utility NASA places on the spacecraft successfully returning from a mission, i.e., $U\left(O_{t+1}|O_t\right) > U\left(O_{t+1}|\overline{O_t}\right)$. If this were to be the case, the decision to launch would now once more result in higher expected utility compared to before. Thus, once more NASA would be less likely to keep the spacecraft on the ground as opposed to before experiencing the near miss. Here, several studies (Dillon & Tinsley, 2008; Tinsley et al., 2012) have shown some support for this perspective, however it appears inadequate to fully explain subsequent behavior reliably.

In summary, if a decision maker were to change her evaluation of a possible outcome of interest in question, a near miss may well motivate a consistent change of behavior in accordance with maximizing her expected utility in a future similar situation. Likewise, without information about the probabilistic nature of the event in question or under the assumption of probabilistic dependence, a decision maker may also update her respective likelihoods following near misses and change her future behavior in a consistent fashion. Both examples constitute normatively warranted behaviors and a decision analyst is well equipped to assist a decision maker in this situation.

Unfortunately, what by now we know from several experimental studies in behavioral decision analysis is that support for these normative perspectives is at best mixed and they often appear inconsistent with or unable to explain witnessed behaviors reliably.

The Near-Miss Bias: Behavioral Insights

We will now explore different reactions to near misses based on empirical studies in behavioral decision analysis. We distinguish between results at the individual versus at the organizational level. Further we first discuss these at the descriptive level before discussing results regarding prescriptive interventions.

Individual Level

The main finding regarding the near-miss phenomenon based on numerous recent studies relates to an increase in risk taking behavior following near misses when making subsequent similar decisions (Dillon & Tinsley, 2005b, 2008, 2016a, b; Tinsley et al., 2012; Kirshner, 2021; Paine et al., 2020). This has been found repeatedly both under experimental conditions as well as using secondary field data (Table 3).

Table 3 Main findings at the individual level

Finding	Studies
Near misses lead to *increases* in risk taking when making similar decisions going forward	Experimental data: Dillon and Tinsley (2005b, 2008, 2016a, b), Tinsley et al. (2012), Kirshner (2020), Paine et al. (2020), Permut et al. (2021) Field survey data: Tinsley et al. (2012)
Decision makers perceive the outcome of a near miss as positively as they perceive successes, contrary to failures, disregarding the process that led to the outcome, suggesting an outcome bias	Experimental data: Dillon and Tinsley (2008, 2014)
The near-miss experience is associated with increased optimism	Experimental data: Dillon and Tinsley (2008, 2016a), Kirshner (2020)
Near misses that are perceived as *almost* resulting in a loss (highlighting *vulnerability*) attenuate risk taking behavior found after near misses that are perceived as those that merely *could have* resulted in a loss (highlighting *resilience*)	Experimental data: Tinsley et al. (2012), Dillon et al. (2014), Dillon and Tinsley (2016a)
Near misses that are *near* in terms of linear distance to the possible loss in question are attenuating the otherwise found increase in risk taking behavior	Permut et al. (2021)

A possible explanation relates to the associated finding that decision makers seem to fall prey to an outcome bias. That is, they judge near-miss outcomes as positively as they do successes, in clear contrast to failures (Dillon & Tinsley, 2008, 2014). This is notable despite a finding of surprise regarding the outcome shown in Dillon and Tinsley's (2008) early studies. Dillon and Tinsley (2008) argue that even though people understand that a near miss event outcome may be surprising and might not have been the result of intentional actions of the decision maker, they still regard and categorize it as a success. This also applies to judging decisions made by others.

What is concerning from a normative perspective is that decision makers do not seem to engage in conscious updating of likelihoods or other changes in their decision calculus that could justify changes in risk taking behavior (with the notable exception of Permut 2021, as previously mentioned). Instead, decision makers become more optimistic about the hazard category. Dillon and Tinsley (2014, 2016a) show that people's riskier behaviors when presented with near-miss information are mediated by an increase in dispositional optimism. When people are exposed to near-miss events, without an eventual loss, it results in an unfounded optimism of how the outcome came to be. Coupled with an outcome bias, the overall interpretation of the events is one that lowers how decision makers feel about the risk, and results in a willingness to take more risk in the future when in a similar situation. That is, near misses appear to affect how decision makers feel or perceive the hazard at hand which depends entirely on their interpretation of the near miss.

There are two attenuating findings that serve to reduce the otherwise found increases in risk taking. The first relates to the perception and counterfactual thoughts decision makers experience when the near miss occurs. Tinsley et al. (2012) categorize near misses in resilient versus vulnerable near misses. On the one hand, resilient near misses are those where people associate the experience with a loss that *could* have happened but was avoided. Vulnerable near misses, on the other hand, are those experienced as negative events that are interpreted as a loss that *almost* happened, but did not. When people experience a near-miss event as something that almost happened, they perceive the event on a more negative light, and therefore behave more cautiously in the future (Tinsley et al., 2012; Dillon et al. 2014; Dillon & Tinsley, 2016a).

Relatedly, Permut et al. (2021) show that only those near misses that in terms of linear distance are further away from a possible loss (consequently called far misses), for instance regarding a car crash, indeed lead to increases in risk taking. Here, the authors found a link to a cognitive updating perspective explaining said behavior. In that sense decision makers may think it less likely to experience a car crash after they had a 'close call' that was not too close after all. Vice versa, when in terms of linear distance the near miss comes close to the crash, the estimated likelihood of future occurrence increases and decision makers lowered their risk going forward.

Individual Differences

Paine et al. (2020) investigated how the role of a person's motivational system, specifically how a prevention motivation affects interpretation and decision making subsequent to near misses. The main finding here relates to not all decision makers responding alike to the near-miss bias. Regulatory focus theory (Higgins 19xx) distinguishes a prevention from a promotion motivation. Prevention is more concerned with maintaining the status quo and preventing losses, whereas promotion focuses on obtaining gains and is less sensitive to potential losses. Paine et al. (2020) find that those with high prevention focus interpret near misses more cautiously. That is, they increase their risk perception after a near miss and consequently take less risk in similar decisions going forward (Table 4).

In turn, Kirshner (2021) looks at a person's construal level and the effect it has on their behavior. He finds that higher levels of construal appear to lead to a higher perception of the risk following a near miss, resulting in more mitigation actions, i.e. less risky behavior, when compared to those with low construal levels (Kirshner,

Table 4 The role of individual differences regarding the near-miss bias

Finding	Studies
Those with a regulatory prevention focus will regard the risk as greater and take less risks following near-miss events	Experimental data: Paine et al. (2020)
Higher construal levels lead to less risky behavior following near misses, and vice versa for low construal levels	Experimental data: Kirshner (2021)

2021). The author proposes that the construal level mediates the effect of the near-miss event by affecting how the severity of the outcome is perceived. These findings relate to those found previously by Dillon et al. (2014), who show that people who experienced previous near misses in natural disaster situations are less likely to evacuate an area because the event results are familiar, which, according to Kirshner (2021), lowers the level of construal.

Organizational Characteristics

At the organizational level there are three different aspects that have proven to affect how people react to near-miss events. The first is related to project salience. If a project is perceived to be highly significant and costly, and decisions made during the implementation lead to a near-miss event, people are subsequently less optimistic compared to those without the near-miss experience (Dillon et al. 2014, 2016). It appears that the significance of the project leads decision makers to correctly focus not only on the outcome but notably the decision process leading to the outcome in the first place. The contrary is true for projects of low significance and cost, where decision makers evaluate the outcome of a near miss as more optimistically (Table 5).

Similarly, another organizational characteristic that changes the interpretation of near-miss events is the perceived importance of safety for the company. In organizations where safety is communicated clearly as an organizational value, decision makers value managers whose decisions result in a near miss as less highly compared to those whose decisions result in clear successes. Possibly adding to this is the finding that in organizations with a low safety climate, there is also less reporting of near misses (Dillon et al., 2016).

Finally, another important aspect is whether decision makers feel accountable for the decisions they make subsequent to near misses. According to Dillon et al.

Table 5 Findings related to organizational characteristics

Finding	Studies
When projects that are perceived as highly significant for the company suffer near misses, decision makers are less optimistic going forward	Experimental data: Dillon et al. (2014, 2016) Secondary data from NASA incident reports: Dillon et al. (2016)
An organizational climate that focuses on safety leads workers to place less value on decisions that led to near misses	Experimental data: Dillon et al. (2014, 2016) Secondary data from NASA incident reports: Dillon et al. (2016)
People will view decisions that lead to a near miss more negatively if they are held accountable for what they recommend based on that event	Experimental data: Dillon et al. (2014)

(2014), when people are told that they will be held accountable for their recommendations of who should get a promotion, they are less likely to recommend managers whose actions led to a near miss, even if the outcome is technically a desired one. It seems to be the case that accountability drives further attention to the process preceding near-miss events, and successfully differentiates them from clear successes.

Counteracting the Near-Miss Bias: Prescriptive Solutions

Given the often normatively unwarranted behaviors ensuing after the experience of near-miss events in terms of how these events are interpreted and reacted upon, various prescriptive solutions have been identified. The next section provides a brief review of successful interventions across the individual and organizational level.

Individual-Level Interventions

With the objective of identifying decision makers who are less likely to fall prey to the near-miss bias, Cui et al. (2017) have developed the Near-Miss Appraisal Scale (NMAS). The scale consists of 10 items that focus on personal, physical risks. The NMAS is able to identify a person's appraisal of near misses using their "willingness to take protective measure after experiencing the near miss" (Cui et al., 2017, p. 77). This scale provides an initial effort in providing a diagnostic measure, and can be a starting point for further diagnostic tools to be developed (Table 6).

Building on the insights related to different reactions to near misses based on a person's construal level, Kirshner (2021), shows that, by priming people towards a high construal level, you can effectively lower the risk that people take when making decisions following near misses.

Table 6 Findings regarding successful interventions of the near-miss bias at the individual level

Recommendation	Studies
The near-miss appraisal scale (NMAS) is able to gauge a person's near-miss appraisal	Scale development: Cui et al. (2017)
Decision makers can be primed towards a high construal level	Experimental data: Kirshner (2021)
Telling people how close a near-miss event was from an undesired outcome, changes their behavior towards a less risky option	Experimental data: Permut et al. (2021)

Permut et al. (2021) found yet another way of counteracting the near-miss bias. The authors focus on decisions following near misses and provide an explicit intervention by alerting decision makers to the risk. They show that once people are explicitly told and made aware of how close they came to an undesired event, decision makers decrease their risk taking going forward.

Organizational-Level Interventions

At the organizational level, the main recommendations fall in line with the results of Dillon et al.'s (2016) study. That is, the focus should lie on establishing a organizational safety climate that enhances people's attentiveness when presented with unexpected events, resulting on an increase in near-miss reporting. Following this recommendation, the authors place emphasis on how workers' behavior can be changed by increasing the salience of a project. As discussed, workers either perceiving a project to be highly significant for their company or safety being known to be an important value, caution and a process perspective will prevail (Table 7).

Further, providing a guide of best practices for organizations to follow, Tinsley et al. (2011) propose 7 strategies to recognize and avoid falling prey to the near-miss bias. While these recommendations are based both on industry best practices and previously cited research, not all strategies have yet been validated empirically. The recommendations consist of paying attention to high pressure, as high pressure likely provides the breeding ground for shortsighted decisions or biases to creep into the picture more than in any other situation, learning from deviations and uncovering root causes. Demanding accountability, considering worst-case scenarios, constant evaluation and follow up as well as rewarding owning up to failure are the additional strategies recommended.

Table 7 Findings regarding successful organization-level interventions of the near-miss bias

Recommendation	Studies
By highlighting a safety climate and significance of a specific project, workers pay more attention to near-miss evens and report them as such	Experimental data: Dillon et al. (2016) Secondary data from NASA incident reports: Dillon et al. (2016)
7 step process to recognize and prevent near misses	Industry best practices: Tinsley et al. (2011)

Conclusion

Near-miss events are ubiquitous, and with recent studies in behavioral decision analysis increasingly pointing towards systematically biased behavior, often resulting in increased risk-taking, a better understanding of near misses is both practically and theoretically needed. Why and under which circumstances do near-miss events lead to changes in risk taking behaviors—and what can be done to counteract it? This chapter sought to provide a thorough review of the near-miss phenomenon. As such it serves as a basis for further inquiry into the near-miss bias, both for theoretical developments, as well as effective managerial interventions.

References

Bier, V. M., & Mosleh, A. (1990). The analysis of accident precursors and near misses: Implications for risk assessment and risk management. *Reliability Engineering and System Safety, 27*, 91–101.

Cui, J., Rosof, H., & John, R. S. (2017). A polytomous item response theory model for measuring near-miss appraisal as a psychological trait. *Decision Analysis, 14*(2), 75–86.

Dillon, R. L., & Tinsley, C. H. (2005a). Whew that was close: How near-miss events bias subsequent decision-making under risk. Paper Presented at *Academy of Management Annual Meeting*, Honolulu, HI.

Dillon, R. L., & Tinsley, C. H. (2005b). Interpreting near-miss events. *Engineering Management Journal, 17*(4), 25–29.

Dillon, R. L., & Tinsley, C. H. (2008). How near-misses influence decision making under risk: A missed opportunity for learning. *Management Science, 54*(8), 1425–1440.

Dillon, R. L., Tinsley, C. H., & Cronin, M. (2011). Why near-miss events can decrease an individual's protective response to hurricanes. *Risk Analysis, 31*(3), 440–449.

Dillon, R. L., & Tinsley, C. H. (2016a). *How near-miss events can embolden or mitigate risky decision making*.

Dillon, R. L., & Tinsley, C. H. (2016b). Near-miss events, risk messages, and decision making. *Environment Systems and Decisions, 36*(1), 34–44.

Dillon, R. L., Tinsley, C. H., & Rogers, E. W. (2014, March). Using organizational messages to improve the recognition of near-miss events on projects. In *2014 IEEE aerospace conference* (pp. 1–10). IEEE.

Dillon, R. L., Tinsley, C. H., Madsen, P. M., & Rogers, E. W. (2016). Organizational correctives for improving recognition of near-miss events. *Journal of Management, 42*(3), 671–697.

FAA. (2022). *Aeronautical information manual*. Federal Aviation Administration.

Goldenhar, L. M., Williams, L. J., & Swanson, N. G. (2003). Modelling relationships between job stressors and injury and near-miss outcomes for construction labourers. *Work and Stress, 17*(3), 218–240.

Hayward, J. C. (1972). *Near miss determination through use of a scale of danger*.

Kelly, D. H., & O'Connell, K. (1978). Care of infants with near-miss sudden infant death syndrome. *Pediatrics, 61*(4), 511–514.

Kirshner, S. N. (2021). Construal level theory and risky decision making following near-miss events. *Journal of Behavioral Decision Making, 34*, 379–392.

Mantel, G. D., Buchmann, E., Rees, H., & Pattinson, R. C. (1998). Severe acute maternal morbidity: A pilot study of a definition for a near-miss. *BJOG: An International Journal of Obstetrics and Gynaecology, 105*(9), 985–990.

Paine, J. W., Federspiel, F., Seifert, M., & Zou, X. (2020). Take a risk or proceed with caution: Prevention motivation moderates responses to near-loss events. *Journal of Behavioral Decision Making, 33*, 505–522.

Permut, S., Downs, J. S., Saccardo, S., & Loewenstein, G. (2021). *How close is too close: The effect of near losses on subsequent risk taking*. Available at SSRN 3819009.

Phimister, J. R., Oktem, U., Kleindorfer, P. R., & Kunreuther, H. (2000). *Near-miss system analysis: Phase I.* Risk Management and Decision Processes Center, The Wharton School, University of Pennsylvania.

Phimister, J. R., Oktem, U., Kleindorfer, P. R., & Kunreuther, H. (2003). Near-miss incident management in the chemical process industry. *Risk Analysis, 23*(3), 445–459.

Presidential Commission on the Space Shuttle Challenger Accident. (1986). Report of the presidential commission on the space shuttle challenger accident. http://history.nasa.gov/rogersrep/genindex.htm. Accessed 11 May 2012.

Savage, L. J. (1954). *The foundations of statistics*. Dover Publications.

Sundali, J. A., Safford, A. H., & Croson, R. T. (2012). The impact of near-miss events on betting behavior: An examination of casino rapid roulette play. *Judgment and Decision Making, 7*(6), 768–778.

Tinsley, C. H., Dillon, R. L., & Madsen, P. M. (2011). How to avoid catastrophe. *Harvard Business Review, 89*(4), 90–97.

Tinsley, C. H., Dillon, R. L., & Cronin, M. A. (2012). How near-miss events amplify or attenuate risky decision making. *Management Science, 58*(9), 1596–1613.

Behavioral Challenges in Practice When Dealing with Public Environmental Decision Problems

Judit Lienert

Abstract Public policy and environmental decisions are complex. They comprise high uncertainty and affect many people with different interests. Making trade-offs between achieving environmental and socio-economic objectives is inevitable. I highlight recent research and the many interesting opportunities for behavioral decision analysis, hereby including some literature from other fields. Following a typical Multi-Criteria Decision Analysis (MCDA) process, we start with problem structuring, specifically by identifying stakeholders, generating objectives and reducing these to a viable set, and generating alternatives. I only shortly cover making predictions, and focus on preference elicitation, which is especially prone to biases. I introduce preference construction and behavioral issues related to eliciting marginal value and utility functions, and weights. I also introduce online preference elicitation and gamification. For MCDA modeling, we should check that stakeholders agree with model assumptions. To deal with uncertainty in practice, I propose stepwise interactive sensitivity analyses. Throughout, I reference application examples and summarize research opportunities. We need to understand preference construction processes in order to elicit preferences efficiently in real-world decisions. This requires experimental and process research across cases. We still lack proven approaches that are easily applicable by practitioners and that meet high standards of academic rigor and consistency.

Keywords Multicriteria decision analysis · Public policy · Environmental decisions · Preference elicitation · Biases · Stepwise interactive sensitivity analyses

---

J. Lienert (✉)
Eawag: Swiss Federal Institute of Aquatic Science and Technology, Dept. Environmental Social Sciences, Cluster Decision Analysis, Dübendorf, Switzerland
e-mail: judit.lienert@eawag.ch

F. M. Federspiel et al. (eds.), *Behavioral Decision Analysis*, International Series in Operations Research & Management Science 350,
https://doi.org/10.1007/978-3-031-44424-1_12

Introducing Environmental and Public Policy Decisions

Public policy and environmental decision problems share typical characteristics, which have been somewhat neglected in standard applications of Multi-Criteria Decision Analysis (MCDA). Societal and public policy problems were termed "wicked problems" half a century ago (Rittel & Webber, 1973). For a conceptual overview from the perspective of decision analysis see French and Geldermann (2005). In such problems, exhaustive problem formulation is not possible because there is always more information that could be added to the system description (unlike e.g., optimization problems). The solutions (i.e., alternatives) are not true or false, but—at the best—good or bad; and which it is can only be determined in the far future. Often many alternatives could be followed, which cannot be tested beforehand because wicked problems are typically unique. Moreover, actions may be irreversible. In societal contexts, we are confronted with a diversity of worldviews, and which values or objectives we should pursue is unclear.

The good news is that MCDA methods offer a systematic, structured approach for disentangling and addressing the complexities inherent to wicked problems. Such problems are receiving increased interest by the decision analysis community. However, many papers that focus on MCDA to support public environmental decisions were published in applied (environmental) journals rather than in the decision analysis and operational research (OR) literature (some recent exceptions are Cegan et al., 2017; Colapinto et al., 2020; Diaz-Balteiro et al., 2017; Kandakoglu et al., 2019; Kurth et al., 2017; Marttunen et al., 2018). Nevertheless, many reviews were published by decision analysts (e.g., Cinelli et al., 2014; Esmail & Geneletti, 2018; French & Geldermann, 2005; Gregory et al., 2012a; Huang et al., 2011; Mustajoki & Marttunen, 2017; Reichert et al., 2015; Walling & Vaneeckhaute, 2020). These authors usually agree on following properties of public environmental decisions:

- Social and environmental systems are highly complex and characterized by large uncertainty. The scientific evidence can be uncertain and difficult to establish.
- Many alternatives may be suitable. Predicting consequences of a decision is difficult and can have impacts far in the future, which further increases uncertainty.
- Sustainability issues span environmental, social, and economic dimensions, which requires interdisciplinary collaboration. Trade-offs between achieving objectives are unavoidable.
- Such decisions affect interests of the public and possibly of future generations. Many stakeholders should be included. Conflicts of interest are unavoidable.
- Preferences of stakeholders can be elicited. However, it may be difficult to include a broad range of people in decision-making. Lay people may not properly understand the complex problem, people may be uncertain about their own preferences, and preference elicitation methods are especially prone to biases.

Decision analysis, in whatever application context has been defined as *"(…) a formalization of common sense for decision problems which are too complex for informal use of common sense"* (Keeney, 1982; p. 806). Moreover, *"MCDA* [can be regarded] *as an umbrella term to describe a collection of formal approaches which seek to take explicit account of multiple criteria in helping individuals or groups explore decisions that matter"* (Belton & Stewart, 2002, p. 2).

In my own research, I use Multi-Attribute Value Theory (MAVT) and Multi-Attribute Utility Theory (MAUT). This is the perspective in the remainder of this chapter (Eisenführ et al., 2010; Keeney, 1982; Keeney & Raiffa, 1976). We have specified the reasons for using MAVT/MAUT to address environmental problems (Lienert et al., 2022; Reichert et al., 2015; Schuwirth et al., 2012). However, many of the behavioral issues discussed here equally concern other MCDA methods such as outranking (e.g., Brans et al., 1986; Roy & Bouyssou, 1993), or the popular AHP method (Saaty, 1990). Overviews of MCDA methods are given in textbooks (e.g., Belton & Stewart, 2002; Greco et al., 2016). Cinelli et al. (2014) reviewed properties of different MCDA methods for sustainability assessments, recently followed by a useful taxonomy of MCDA methods in application cases (Cinelli et al., 2020).

Whatever MCDA method is used, the problem should be structured into smaller steps to make it manageable. Different numbers of steps have been proposed, some authors emphasizing the cyclic nature of decision analysis (see Belton & Stewart, 2010, and references therein). Keeney (1982, p. 808) proposed four main steps:

(A) *Structure the decision problem,*
(B) *Assess possible impacts of each alternative,*
(C) *Determine preferences (values) of decision-makers, and*
(D) *Evaluate and compare alternatives.*

In this chapter, I focus on behavioral aspects, which are dominant for preference elicitation (step C). However, they are important in other steps as well.

Problem Structuring for Use in MCDA

In the field of "soft OR" or "soft systems" (Rosenhead & Mingers, 2001), a rich variety of problem structuring methods (PSMs) have evolved. Some methodologies were developed to address deficiencies of more technical approaches in mainstream "hard OR", specifically to address the complexities of real-world problems. Other PSMs emerged in various fields such as transdisciplinary research, policy analysis (e.g., social network analysis), management (e.g., SWOT analysis), or have simply been used in workshop settings as creativity techniques. Many PSM approaches and methodologies can be highly useful to inform the early stages of MCDA.

There has been important earlier research on problem structuring for decision analysis. Despite this, and as summarized below, there is a real need to develop further and systematize problem structuring methods for practical use in decision analysis. Descriptions of MCDA applications often start with a decision problem that is already structured or that does not need much structuring due to its straightforward nature (Belton & Stewart, 2010). However, public policy and environmental decisions are hardly ever simple; usually they are messy, complex, and can become overwhelmingly huge. If MCDA is applied to a problem that is not well structured, results will be incomplete as best outcome, or simply wrong.

Various biases occur in the problem structuring phase for MCDA (see Montibeller & von Winterfeldt, 2015; Morton & Fasolo, 2009; and references therein). Some are common and difficult to correct. Especially relevant is myopic problem representation and omitting important variables (e.g., hypotheses, objectives, alternatives). The confirmation bias is also problematic, whereby unconsciously evidence is acquired that confirms ones' beliefs (Montibeller & von Winterfeldt, 2015).

We recently reviewed articles that combined PSMs with MCDA (Marttunen et al., 2017). Although this combination is popular, we concluded that the benefits of PSMs are not fully utilized. Usually, a single and simple PSM was combined with MCDA in linear order. As illustration: 40% of the selected 68 papers that combined PSMs with MCDA used SWOT (Strengths, Weaknesses, Opportunities, Threats). If issues identified in SWOT are directly used as objectives in MCDA, problems can occur in later weight elicitation. Thus, post-processing is needed to build suitable objectives hierarchies. Moreover, we found that an intertwining of PSMs with MCDA was rare, and that more complex methodologies such as Soft Systems Methodology (SSM), Strategic Options Development and Analysis (SODA), or the Strategic Choice Approach (SCA) were rarely used (references and methods are given in Table 1 in Marttunen et al., 2017). In line with our observation, French (2021) emphasized that soft and hard OR, or qualitative and quantitative models, have developed in separate research "silos", and that an intertwined, cyclic understanding of OR processes is needed to address complex decision problems.

Researchers are increasingly emphasizing the need for systematization of soft OR and PSMs to increase the theoretic understanding of these processes and to allow for the generalization of observed phenomena. Yearworth and White (2014) postulated that it might be somewhat unclear what we are actually doing when applying PSMs. They proposed that non-codified PSMs from (usually one-off) case studies could be documented, which allows for a broader database and later axiomatic foundation of PSMs. Several researchers stressed the need for developing methods to evaluate PSMs and overcome the limitation of single case studies (e.g., Ackermann, 2012; Ackermann & Howick, 2021; Lami & Tavella, 2019; Midgley et al., 2013; White, 2006). Behavioral biases are not well understood in PSMs and qualitative model building (French, 2021). Indeed, a recent review of behavioral OR literature detected a serious lack of research that systematically examines the impact of PSMs on behavioral changes of participants (Franco et al., 2021). This is surprising, since it is claimed that PSMs increase the understanding and commitment of participants, which may lead to consensus finding and behavioral changes.

To conclude, despite decades of research and practice, we still require systematic and sound research that assesses the benefits and drawbacks of problem structuring for use in MCDA. Below, I cover main problem structuring steps at the beginning of a decision analysis process, pointing to insights from recent research and to open questions.

Identifying Stakeholders

In applied cases, we may assume that we "somehow" included the important decision-makers. This is often the case for smaller decision problems, e.g., at company level. However, for environmental and public policy decisions, deciding whom to involve is not straightforward (Gregory et al., 2020; Müller et al., 2012). Some reviews of MCDA applications to environmental problems found that around 40% to 50% of reviewed publications included stakeholders; but often only when assigning weights (Diaz-Balteiro et al., 2017; Kandakoglu et al., 2019; Marttunen et al., 2018). Several reviews concluded that there is a serious lack of stakeholder participation throughout the entire decision process, e.g., in flood risk management (de Brito & Evers, 2016), or in nature conservation (Esmail & Geneletti, 2018).

Different frameworks for stakeholder identification have been proposed in application fields of complex decisions including public policy (Hermans & Thissen, 2009), health care (Brugha & Varvasovszky, 2000), and environmental management (Gregory et al., 2020; Grimble & Wellard, 1997; Reed et al., 2009). As simplest approach, stakeholder analysis is useful to identify who has decision-making power and high influence, and who is affected once the decision is made (Grimble & Wellard, 1997). Interviews, surveys, snowball sampling, or focus groups are common methods. However, such processes may result in a long list of stakeholders, which cannot all be included in traditional decision-making workshops.

In a subsequent phase, the stakeholder list thus needs to be reduced to a manageable number. Stakeholder analysis allows doing so, e.g., by identifying those that are highly important for and/or highly affected by the decision, possibly including some outlier positions. Such approaches have been criticized for lack of analytic quality and academic rigor (Hermans & Thissen, 2009; Reed et al., 2009). Statistical methods are rigorous, but rarely used. In a case study about nutrient management in the San Francisco Bay Area, we used cluster analysis to select stakeholders for a second set of decision analysis interviews (Harris-Lovett et al., 2019). Social network analysis (SNA) is a systematic approach from the political sciences (Kenis & Schneider, 1991). To understand policy processes in environmental decisions, SNA can help analyzing, for instance, stakeholder interactions and collaborations in multi-level governance settings (Ingold et al., 2019). To the best of my knowledge, the decision analysis literature has largely neglected the integration of such methods. In a Swiss case about sustainable wastewater infrastructure management, we combined stakeholder analysis with SNA (Lienert et al., 2013). We found this useful for gaining a deeper understanding of the stakeholders' motivations and collaborations, and SNA enabled addressing concrete research hypotheses.

Stakeholder analysis methods have far more to offer than merely identifying workshop participants. A research question of practical relevance is, as example, how we can be confident that we have identified all stakeholders that could potentially block the decision once it is made. This question is related to the identification of decision objectives (see below). We might consider (quasi-) experimental approaches to determine how many stakeholders with outlier positions should be included. Process research could help understanding in which situations it would be beneficial to include marginalized stakeholders, and where stakeholders with rare outlier positions might disturb a constructive decision process (Franco et al., 2021 distinguish between variance research, e.g., experiments, and process methodologies as two main research approaches in behavioral OR). Moreover, collaborating with political scientists will open our research to new hypotheses, such as determining whether collaborations or conflicts among stakeholders are reflected in similar or opposing preferences regarding the importance of objectives.

Generating Decision Objectives

Decision analysis textbooks provide good rules that help generating decision objectives. A main rule is to use fundamental objectives (which are important "because" they are important to address this decision) rather than means objectives (means to achieve a more fundamental objective; see Keeney, 1992). Moreover: *"The system of (fundamental) objectives which are relevant in a given decision situation should fulfill a number of requirements: completeness, lack of redundancies, measurability, independence and conciseness"* (Eisenführ et al., 2010; p. 59). Such recommendations are useful and reasonable, but already Ralph Keeney emphasized that generating objectives is more art than science: *"Identifying a set of objectives does not involve anything quantitative although it may be the most important input to a quantitative value model. (…) Eliciting a set of objectives is an art. To begin, one wishes to stress that the decision makers or individuals specifying the objectives should think broadly about consequences of interest in order to make sure that all concerns with the decision problem are covered"* (Keeney, 1988; p. 151). However, later research indicated that people have difficulties in generating objectives (discussed below). A relevant bias is omitting objectives (Montibeller & von Winterfeldt, 2015). A reason can be the availability bias, whereby people mention only salient objectives readily available in the mind (Bond et al., 2008). In my opinion, more behavioral research is needed to advance the "art of generating objectives" to a systematic, scientifically validated procedure. I introduce some aspects below.

Diverging Phase: Capturing All Important Interests

Creating objectives for public environmental decisions means capturing very many interests. As example, a river management decision may affect local people and many species such as fish, algae, birds, or beetles. Ecologists use various indicators to measure impacts to a natural system. Ideally, we can use indicators as objectives, but there will likely be many overlaps and interactions (for a river rehabilitation example see Langhans & Lienert, 2016). Moreover, additional socio-economic objectives are required to address the needs and values of stakeholders, possibly including future generations. How can we best capture all these perspectives?

Traditionally, objectives are created in group workshops using creativity techniques such as cognitive mapping, a problem structuring method (PSM). For an example of combining cognitive mapping with MCDA see Franco and Lord (2011). An overview of different PSMs to generate objectives for MCDA is given in the review by Marttunen et al. (2017). Group workshops using PSMs are an excellent way for generating objectives, but the number of participants is limited. An obvious way to include many stakeholders and the public is with online surveys.

Online surveys come with the drawback that there is no guidance by a facilitator, and no exchange between participants. Research indicated that people have difficulties to generate objectives without assistance by a moderator, and individuals omitted about half of the objectives that were fundamentally important to them (Bond et al., 2008, 2010). Continuing this research, we conducted an experimental online survey in five Swiss wastewater management cases (Haag et al., 2019c). We first asked 70 stakeholders to brainstorm and list objectives important for making such a decision, then to choose the important objectives from a master list, among other interventions. The master list was by far the most effective intervention for generating a broad and distinct set of around 30–40 objectives. This approach should now be validated in other application cases and settings.

Converging Phase: Generating a Concise, Well-Structured Hierarchy

Once the stakeholders' objectives are collected, they need to be processed. Textbooks recommend reducing the number of objectives to a manageable set of around 10–15 distinctly different objectives, and to structure them in an objectives hierarchy (e.g., Eisenführ et al., 2010). An experienced facilitator will have acquired the expertise for doing this effectively, e.g., in group decision-making workshops.

We carried out a meta-analysis to understand how objectives are used in practical environmental and energy decisions, and how the structure of the objectives hierarchy may induce biases in later MCDA (Marttunen et al., 2018). We found that many of these applied projects used a high number of objectives, ranging from 3 to 51 (average 15). Other reviews also indicated that some environmental projects used too many objectives, potentially causing problems in later MCDA (Diaz-Balteiro et al., 2017; Esmail & Geneletti, 2018). Several problems may arise, not least that too many objectives will clutter the decision and hide main trade-offs between important objectives (Marttunen et al., 2018). This makes weight elicitation more laborious. Moreover, many objectives will receive very low weights, thus becoming irrelevant. Too many objectives also increases our workload for making estimations about the performance of the decision alternatives.

Furthermore, this meta-analysis indicated that the structure of the objectives hierarchy is relevant (Marttunen et al., 2018). Asymmetric hierarchies with a higher number of objectives in some branches, and a lower number in others, may induce biases in weight elicitation. This occurs if hierarchical weighting is used, i.e., when weights are assigned separately for each branch. We found statistically significantly lower weights in those branches with many objectives compared to those with few.

Across the many cases, this systematic effect is difficult to explain with the stakeholders' preferences alone. There are some indications that people tend to assign equal weights to objectives (equalizing bias; Montibeller & von Winterfeldt, 2015). However, our meta-analysis did not confirm this (Marttunen et al., 2018). The reasons for such observations are unclear and merit future investigation (also see Esmail & Geneletti, 2018; Walling & Vaneeckhaute, 2020).

Although textbooks provide recommendations, in my experience it can be puzzling for beginners to understand post-processing of objectives to create a meaningful hierarchy. The literature provides only limited support. We investigated known methods for reducing the number of objectives using data from two real-world environmental cases (Marttunen et al., 2019a). Qualitative methods include constructing a means-ends network. This graphical tool allows checking whether all objectives are needed by differentiating between means and fundamental objectives, and supports identifying alternatives (e.g., Gregory et al., 2012a; Keeney, 1996). Causal maps are more rigorous and have been combined with MCDA (e.g., Montibeller & Belton, 2009). Relevancy analysis uses questionnaires to separate the general importance of a concern from the extent to which an objective differentiates between alternatives, based on the problem-specific impact range. As discussed in Marttunen et al. (2019a), the method is related to a general "test of importance of an objective" (Keeney & Raiffa, 1976). Relevancy analysis can be useful for screening objectives and communicating their importance to stakeholders (Marttunen et al., 2019a). However, this should be studied in other cases, focusing on behavioral aspects (for a river rehabilitation example see Marttunen et al., 2019b).

A recent review of MCDA applied to sustainability problems indicated that statistical analyses were used in some cases to reduce the number of objectives (Diaz-Balteiro et al., 2017). These are for instance correlations and factor analysis, or principal components analysis (PCA). We discussed such methods in Marttunen et al. (2019a). As example, PCA or correlation analysis can help identifying overlapping objectives, of which some can be excluded. In contrast, distinctly different objectives should be included in the MCDA. Moreover, we encourage using sensitivity analyses early in the project to identify objectives that are especially sensitive to changed weight preferences.

As final step, we need to find attributes, which operationalize objectives. As examples, the objective "low costs" can be measured by the attribute "€/person/year", or the objective "high biodiversity" with a "biodiversity index", which is commonly used by ecologists. Finding a good attribute is not always straightforward, and I refer to recommendations (e.g., Eisenführ et al., 2010; Keeney & Gregory, 2005). Using natural units (e.g., €) is certainly preferred to using proxy or constructed attributes (e.g., a scale). Different ways of presenting an attribute may induce biases (i.e., framing or scaling biases). Moreover, several biases when weighting attributes are known, e.g., the proxy bias (proxy attributes receive higher weights than the respective fundamental objective), or the range insensitivity bias (for an overview see Montibeller & von Winterfeldt, 2015). However, how strongly the early choice of an attribute can influence the decision outcome is to date unclear and merits behavioral research: *"There is not, as far as we are aware, any descriptive research on the impact of this choice"* (Montibeller & von Winterfeldt, 2015, p. 1241).

Generating Decision Alternatives

The step of creating alternatives is subject to similar biases as generating objectives. A prominent bias is again myopic problem representation (Montibeller & von Winterfeldt, 2015). Many people have difficulties to think out of the box and tend to stick to known alternatives. Recent systematic research is in line with the mentioned research on objectives: In personal decisions, people omit about half of the important alternatives (Siebert & Keeney, 2015). This can strongly affect the MCDA result: *"Practically, the mainstream decision analysis literature focuses on how to 'choose' an alternative without considering where these alternatives come from and how they can be established. On the other hand, it should be obvious: if all the alternatives in the considered set are 'bad' we are going to choose a bad option even if it is the best one"* (Colorni & Tsoukias, 2020, p. 150).

As with objectives, traditionally creativity techniques are used in group decision-making workshops to create alternatives (see textbooks; e.g., Clemen & Reilly, 2001; Eisenführ et al., 2010). In our projects, we often used a strategy generation table to create alternatives together with stakeholders, for instance, for removing pharmaceuticals from hospital wastewater (Lienert et al., 2011), for Swiss water infrastructure management (Lienert et al., 2015), and for creating a flood early warning system in West Africa (Lienert et al., 2022). A strategy generation table is a systematic creativity method (Howard, 1988), which has been recommended for environmental decisions (Gregory et al., 2012a, b). The decision is structured into elements, each with different characteristics. Stakeholders choose a characteristic from each element, which in combination form a strategy (i.e., alternative). Many other creativity techniques help generating alternatives, including brainstorming methods and metaphorical thinking to stimulate people's imagination [for an overview see Clemen and Reilly (2001)]. Siebert and Keeney (2015) propose to first use a master list to generate objectives, and then use objectives to create alternatives. They provide some practical guidelines in this paper.

As for objectives, systematic research is needed that explores the creation of alternatives, thus allowing for generalization across single cases. A recent literature review indicated a serious lack of research concerning the generation of alternatives (Colorni & Tsoukias, 2020). Nevertheless, some concepts for creating alternatives are well-known in decision analysis, most prominently "value focused thinking" (Keeney, 1996). Hereby, decision-makers are encouraged to focus first on their fundamentally important values, which are captured as objectives, before focusing on alternatives. The review by Colorni and Tsoukias (2020) also mentions "real options theory" (Smit & Trigeorgis, 2004). In risky or uncertain decisions, decision makers might feel uncomfortable with the binary choice ("do/not do") when using decision trees. Real options theory increases flexibility by offering "intermediate decisions", which are an indirect exploration of new alternatives. Although the field of real options is expanding, generating alternatives has not been explicitly addressed to date by real options theory (Colorni & Tsoukias, 2020). In OR, "multi-objective programming" has been used to establish a large set of alternatives by exploring the pareto front (see Colorni & Tsoukias, 2020 for methods and references). According to these authors, the highest interest in designing alternatives stems from public policy decisions, but this literature lacks theory formulation (again, please see Colorni & Tsoukias, 2020 and references therein). These authors show that constructing a useful set of alternatives is in itself a decision problem, and formulate such a theory.

From a practical perspective, several authors confirmed that public policy decisions lack formalized approaches for generating alternatives (Ferretti et al., 2019; Pluchinotta et al., 2019). Interest in this issue is increasing. To generate alternatives, several authors draw on literature from "design thinking". Geldermann et al. (2018) explored the similarities and differences between design thinking and MCDA. Design thinking could be especially useful for creating alternatives as it focuses on innovatively creating a prototype. Design theory has also recently been used for creating a framework and a tool for generating alternatives in public policy decisions together with stakeholders (Pluchinotta et al., 2019). It was applied to a groundwater protection policy case in Southern Italy. Moreover, two territorial policy making processes in Italy were analyzed to understand why and how new alternatives arose in the design phase (Ferretti et al., 2019). These authors identified two main forces, namely dissatisfaction of people involved with the proposed alternatives, and opportunity for change in one of the variables. Obviously, these are issues of high interest, and they merit further exploration by behavioral research.

Conclusion: Problem Structuring

To conclude this section, sound problem structuring is of decisive importance for a decision analysis process. An unbalanced selection of stakeholders and an unstructured, biased selection of objectives or alternatives will inevitably cause problems in later MCDA stages. In the worst case, the resulting recommendations will be wrong because they are based on limited, biased, or false input data. Despite decades of research on problem structuring for decision analysis, we still require sound research addressing various open questions that are summarized in this chapter. Behavioral research seems especially appropriate to tackle many of these questions. We should aim at understanding where, when, how, and why the integration of problem structuring methods into an MCDA process is beneficial, and where this is not the case. On the other hand, our research could benefit soft OR and problem structuring, where a general need for theory development has been identified. This includes systematic evaluation of different PSMs using (semi-) experimental research and clever study designs.

Regarding objectives, and despite probably countless applications of MCDA that used an objectives hierarchy, the "art" of generating and post-processing objectives requires systematization in such a way that newcomers and practitioners can easily apply the methods. We face a serious trade-off between capturing a broad range of stakeholder interests and constructing a concise and balanced objectives hierarchy. Above, I proposed qualitative and quantitative methods that can be of practical help to decision analysts, and for interacting with stakeholders. However, we urgently need systematic guidance for constructing objectives hierarchies, which should be based on rigorous study designs. Such behavioral studies can apply both experimental (variance) and process methodologies, as proposed by Franco et al. (2021). In combination, the two complementary approaches will allow drawing solid conclusions about suitable PSMs across cases. The same applies to generating decision alternatives, an area that has been neglected even more strongly.

Recent research indicates that we can learn from literature outside decision analysis. For instance, using methods from the political sciences such as social network analysis (SNA) can stimulate new research ideas. SNA increases our understanding of the stakeholders' motivations, preferences, and interactions because it allows for testing hypotheses. As another example, the recent literature about generating alternatives demonstrates that design theory can inform and advance our own research.

From a practical perspective, we should aim at systematizing and developing efficient and fast methods. Many real-world cases have limited resources, and stakeholders are busy people. Future research for the first MCDA step could address integrating "decision sketching" (quickly running through the entire MCDA; Gregory et al., 2012a) with flexible, interactive problem structuring. The latter means that we interact with stakeholders only if desktop analyses indicate that it is necessary. Such an interactive approach was proposed for weight elicitation (de Almeida et al., 2016), but exploring its use for the early MCDA steps could also be interesting.

Predicting the Outcome of Decision Alternatives

Making predictions means determining how well each alternative performs regarding each objective. We can use data from literature, run models, or ask experts for best estimates (e.g., Eisenführ et al., 2010). This step is not trivial and can be highly important in environmental projects. The required resources often seem underestimated in decision analysis literature. In environmental decisions, we usually collaborate with experts, for instance ecologists, hydrologists, or wastewater engineers, and this interdisciplinary collaboration can be a challenge. On the other hand, it is daily work of natural scientists or engineers to model impacts of an intervention to a natural or technical system, and we can use their model results for predictions, or we can conduct expert interviews. In my experience, these experts tend to overemphasize making exact predictions and underestimate the importance of including preferences in the decision model (discussed in Gregory et al., 2012b).

From the point of view of behavioral decision analysis, using outputs from predictive modelling as input to the MCDA is not a highly relevant concern. However, for environmental decisions, it is of huge importance to include the uncertainty of predictions, and the main issues arise when using expert estimates as MCDA inputs. The many biases that can occur when "modeling uncertainty" and "assessing probabilities" are nicely summarized by Montibeller and von Winterfeldt (2015). As examples, these include the anchoring or overconfidence bias, or scaling biases. There are various de-biasing suggestions, including probability trainings, asking multiple experts, or using counterfactuals. For practice, good expert elicitation protocols are available (Burgman et al., 2011; Hemming et al., 2018; O'Hagan, 2019).[1]

Preference Elicitation

If we base decisions on "value focused thinking" (Keeney, 1996), the preferences of stakeholders are important. According to the structure of Keeney (1982), we determine preferences in step C. Of course, there are many methods to include peoples' values in decision processes. If we use MCDA, we need to capture preferences as numbers and represent them quantitatively. The data concerning the stakeholders' preferences enter the decision model on equal footing to the data about the performance of each alternative on each objective in step B. We use marginal value or utility functions to convert the attribute levels to a normalized value. Furthermore, we need to elicit the scaling constants of the MCDA model, the weights. These aspects are discussed below. We should also check that the model appropriately captures the main aspects; ideally together with stakeholders. In practice applications of MCDA, it is common to use the linear, additive aggregation model, the weighted sum of value scores (see textbooks, e.g., Eisenführ et al., 2010). If other aggregation models are used, we might need to elicit additional preference parameters (see later discussion of step D of the four steps proposed by Keeney (1982)).

Preference Construction

To start, I emphasize that preference elicitation is challenging. Preferences are often formed during decision-making processes rather than being readily available in our minds. Preferences are sensitive to the context (Warren et al., 2011) and are influenced by feelings and emotions (Angie et al., 2011; Slovic et al., 2007). The huge body of literature on "preference construction" stemming from psychologists in the field of descriptive decision analysis is described in the classic book by Lichtenstein and Slovic (2006). People use heuristics when making choices, and preference

[1] Also see http://tonyohagan.co.uk/shelf/

elicitation is especially sensitive to biases (Montibeller & von Winterfeldt, 2015; Morton & Fasolo, 2009).

Public and environmental decisions are often expensive and far-reaching; they affect the environment, many people, and future generations, and are difficult or impossible to reverse. We would certainly try to avoid using biased preferences in MCDA, which might produce wrong results and recommendations (French & Geldermann, 2005). However, as preference elicitation is highly sensitive to a wide array of internal or external factors, it will be impossible to avoid that such factors affect preferences. To cope with peoples' cognitive limitations, it is important to use debiasing methods during preference elicitation, where available (for an excellent overview see Montibeller & von Winterfeldt, 2015). Research is needed to further develop such debiasing approaches. We should aim at supporting people with the best available methods in forming their preferences. Additionally, we can overcome some limitations if we elicit preferences that are representative of the values and opinions of a broad range of stakeholders.

Moreover, in public policy and environmental decisions, ideally preferences are stable over some period of time. A recent review of 343 papers that used MCDA in sustainable development projects indicated that temporal aspects are rarely addressed (Kandakoglu et al., 2019). We have recently started exploring preference change over time in cases from wastewater management and flood risk research (Kuller et al., 2023; Lienert et al., 2016). To the best of my knowledge, behavioral decision analysis has not (yet) attempted to address this topic, for instance the underlying mechanisms of temporal preference construction processes. However, preference stability over time has received interest by various environmental economists. As examples, preference stability was studied in a stormwater pollution case, and concerning health risks related to bathing water quality after an extreme weather event (Brouwer, 2006; Jorgensen et al., 2004). These researchers have similar motivations as environmental decision analysts: in public decisions requiring large investments, it is not desirable that the public changes its willingness to pay for improving an environmental good or service.

Marginal Value Functions

Attributes operationalize objectives such as "low costs" and "high biodiversity". Because they have different units, we need a conversion to a common scale. In Multi-Attribute Value Theory (MAVT), marginal value functions transfer attribute levels (e.g., "€/person/year) to a normalized value between 0 and 1; where 0 is the worst-possible case across all alternatives considered in this decision, and 1 the best case (e.g., the lowest costs of all considered alternatives). I wish to emphasize that this attribute range is of highest importance in weight elicitation (see below).

In the simplest case, a linear conversion is used, but other shapes of a value function usually better capture preferences. As example, some stakeholders may find it more valuable to improve a river that is in a poor ecological state than a river in a good state. For others, improving a river in a good state to achieve an even better ecological state might be more valuable (such examples are given in Langhans & Lienert, 2016).

There are several methods for eliciting the shape of marginal value functions, but they are relatively time-consuming (Eisenführ et al., 2010). As shortcut in some practice projects, we roughly elicited shapes of marginal value functions only for objectives with the highest weights (e.g., Lienert et al., 2011; Scholten et al., 2015; Zheng et al., 2016). Even more timesaving is to assume linear value functions as first approximation, and test the sensitivity of results to other shapes in later analyses. Sensitivity analyses can also be time-consuming. We recently developed the online application ValueDecisions, which allows doing interactive sensitivity analyses of various parameters in an user-friendly interface (Haag et al., 2022). The shape of marginal value functions can be changed with one mouse-click, and an application example is given in this paper. The elicitation of value functions is to the best of my knowledge not much studied in behavioral decision analysis. In their review, Montibeller and von Winterfeldt (2015; see Table V) mentioned the occurrence of several biases such as the anchoring or gain-loss bias. However, most research addresses utility functions.

Risk, Uncertainty, and Marginal Utility Functions

Environmental and public policy decisions are full of uncertainty. People often prefer choices without uncertainty and try to avoid uncertain or "risky" decisions. Therefore, preference modelling should change, and Multi-Attribute Utility Theory then replaces MAVT (see textbooks, e.g., Eisenführ et al., 2010; Keeney & Raiffa, 1976). Like value functions, utility functions capture the stakeholders' preferences for outcomes. Additionally, the stakeholders' risk attitude may play a role, and the shape of the utility function will differ from the corresponding value function if a person is risk averse or risk seeking. In standard decision analysis, lotteries are used to elicit marginal utility functions, and several methods are available. However, these elicitation methods are cognitively demanding. The behavioral aspects of the elicitation of marginal utility functions has received more attention by research compared to value functions, and biases are summarized by Montibeller and von Winterfeldt (2015). When observing peoples' real choices under uncertainty, they often do not comply with the standard models of utility theory (Tversky & Kahneman, 1974). Several theories have been formulated to overcome obvious problems, most prominently "prospect theory" (Kahneman & Tversky, 1979). Much of this research was carried out some 30–40 years ago. From a practical, prescriptive view, applying standard MAUT may still be appropriate. On a side note, in environmental and public policy decisions, making hypothetical choices between lotteries—or gambles—may seem ethically suspect to some stakeholders. It could be interesting for behavioral decision analysis to study the large body of psychological literature concerning such "protected values" or "taboo trade-offs" (e.g., Baron & Spranca, 1997; Tetlock, 2003).

Because eliciting utility functions is demanding, simplifications have been proposed, including using linear or standard shapes of utility functions, or using value functions as proxy to utility functions (Montibeller & von Winterfeldt, 2015). Value functions can be converted to utility functions if the stakeholders' risk attitude is known (Dyer & Sarin, 1982). In principle, such a conversion would need to be done for each objective, as risk taking seems to be domain-specific rather than a stable trait, i.e., the risk attitude can differ for e.g., investment or gambling decisions, health/safety, recreational, ethical, or social decisions (Weber et al., 2002).

For environmental decisions, Reichert et al. (2015) proposed to first elicit marginal value functions, and after aggregating to an overall value for the entire set of objectives, convert the marginal value to a utility. This requires eliciting the stakeholders risk attitude at the highest level of the objectives hierarchy, taking into account all lower-level objectives. Obviously, this can be a difficult task. We used local sensitivity analyses to check the effect of this simplification on MCDA results in two wastewater management cases and found that eliciting the risk attitude in detail might not be worth the effort (Haag et al., 2019b; Zheng et al., 2016). On the other hand, global sensitivity analyses in a water supply case indicated that the results were very sensitive to the risk attitude (Scholten et al., 2015). Given the current state of research, I recommend to check the sensitivity of the results to risk attitudes.

Economists and psychologists are testing different approaches for eliciting utility functions. These include developing simpler methods, but this trend is to the best of my knowledge not visible in decision analysis. Some experiments are conducted in relatively artificial settings, and the risk attitude often relates to monetary gains or losses. As one example, using gambles in an experiment indicated that simpler methods could be better for people who exhibit low numeracy as they reduced noise, but complex elicitation was preferable due to greater predictive accuracy for people with higher numerical skills (Dave et al., 2010). An overview of the different methods discussed in this economic literature is provided by (Charness et al., 2013).

An interesting study indicated that differences in risk taking between individuals, gender, or content domains (financial, health/safety, recreational, ethical, and social decisions) do not seem to be primarily associated with the "conventional" risk attitude, but can be largely explained with perceived benefits or risks associated with an activity (Weber et al., 2002). These authors proposed a relatively simple scale for eliciting the perceived and conventional risk attitudes in the suggested six domains (financial was split into investment and gambling). As these domains concerned personal activities (such as asking your boss for a pay rise, buying illegal drugs, or never wearing a seatbelt), further development and testing for public policy and environmental decisions is needed. Psychologists are currently aiming to uncover whether peoples' different risk attitudes could be a stable personality characteristic (Mata et al., 2018). Despite some indications that this might be the case, these authors concluded that the measurement of risk preference requires more research. Pedroni et al. (2017) compared six different types of methods for eliciting risk preferences across 1507 respondents. They found a near-complete lack of consistency across methods. Moreover, results suggested that the choice of the method most strongly affects which decision strategies an individual uses. Consequently, these authors concluded that the concept of risk preference as a general trait-like, stable entity might be totally misguided. Moreover, it can hardly be elicited easily using a single method, and more research is needed. An important message for behavioral decision analysis is: *"What is clear, however, is that scientists' common practice, namely, measuring risk preferences with one simple behavioural elicitation method (for example, lotteries) and thus creating the fiction that they can capture consistent risk preferences, should stop"* (Pedroni et al., 2017; p. 807).

In which way the results of such research translates to public and environmental decisions that encompass many other non-monetary risks is unclear. Agricultural economists recently compared lottery-choice tasks with simplified tools for risk elicitation (Menapace et al., 2016). Although such farmer surveys are more realistic, the focus was again on monetary risks. More generally, Iyer et al. (2020) systematically reviewed risk preference measurement and decision-making of farmers across Europe. As in our case of public environmental decisions, these researchers are interested in improving tools in such a way that they are applicable in practice. As one example, different methods were compared with the actual behavior of farmers, i.e., buying a hail insurance (Menapace et al., 2016). The simplest method tested was one straightforward question: *"On a scale from 1 to 10 (...), how would you assess your personal inclination to take risks?"* (Menapace et al., 2016; p. 117). In earlier studies about general risk-taking behavior of individuals, this question provided satisfactory results when compared to risk elicitation with lotteries (Dohmen et al., 2011). However, in the farmer survey, the results differed between methods, and further research is needed (Menapace et al., 2016).

As conclusion, I suggest that contributions from behavioral decision analysis could be a rewarding research avenue; and especially in the context of public policy and environmental decisions, including non-monetary objectives. From a practical point of view, Gregory and Keeney (2017), recently addressed the treatment of uncertainty in stakeholder deliberations. They proposed using the certainty equivalent (CE) as a theoretically robust approach to incorporate the stakeholders' uncertainties when evaluating alternatives in public policy decisions. However, the CE needs to be elicited with lottery-questions, which brings us back to the above discussion. In my opinion, decision analysts should start with systematically scoping the literature introduced above from outside our own research field, including psychological, economic, and applied research in e.g., agricultural economics regarding risk attitudes, and the proposed elicitation methods for decision-making under uncertainty. From a practical perspective, because the elicitation of utility functions is demanding, behavioral research could focus on understanding the advantages and drawbacks of using simpler elicitation methods.

Weights

As additional preference parameters, we need the scaling constants, commonly called weights. Various methods are available to elicit weights from stakeholders (e.g., Eisenführ et al., 2010). Decision analysts have intensively studied weight elicitation. This is justified as MCDA results can be very sensitive to weights, and because preferences are often constructed during decision-making processes (Lichtenstein & Slovic, 2006). Therefore, it is not surprising that weight elicitation is subject to many biases (Montibeller & von Winterfeldt, 2015; Morton & Fasolo, 2009). For an overview of biases in practice applications see Riabacke et al. (2012).

It is out of scope of this book chapter to delve into details. I summarize some main research findings that should be considered in practical decision analysis. First, a number of studies indicate that the choice of the elicitation method can affect the weights (Belton, 1986; Borcherding et al., 1991; Lienert et al., 2016; Pöyhönen & Hämäläinen, 2001; Zheng & Lienert, 2018). An important recommendation is thus to always carry out consistency checks of the elicited weights, preferably using another elicitation method (Eisenführ et al., 2010). Ideally, strong weight deviations should be explored together with the stakeholder to understand reasons and to try reducing some of the uncertainty of the elicited weights. This interaction will likely be part of his or her preference construction process. For practice projects under time constraints, I recommend exploring with sensitivity analyses whether such weight deviations actually change the MCDA results. If not, the different weights do not matter much (examples from wastewater management and flood risk research see e.g., Lienert et al., 2016, 2022).

As introduced in the problem structuring section, the number of objectives and structure of the objectives hierarchy can affect the weights (Marttunen et al., 2018). The decision analyst can control these undesired side effects to some extent. The splitting bias has been well-studied (Hämäläinen & Alaja, 2008; Jacobi & Hobbs, 2007; Pöyhönen et al., 2001; Weber et al., 1988). It relates to the phenomenon that those branches of an objectives hierarchy systematically receive higher weights if the objectives are "split" into a larger number of sub-objectives, compared to branches with less objectives. In practice, this bias can be avoided by constructing more balanced objectives hierarchies, or by using hierarchical weighting. For the latter, the weights of the main objectives at the higher level can be elicited without presenting the lower-objectives. I point out that this requires explaining details and ranges concerning the lower-level objectives to stakeholders, which can be difficult at an aggregated level. In a second step, the weights for the lower-level objectives in each branch are elicited separately. A practical example for a case of removing pharmaceuticals from hospital wastewater is given in Schuwirth et al. (2012).

An important bias in practical weight elicitation that I find difficult to deal with is the range insensitivity bias. Weights depend on the range of the attribute, i.e., the worst and best case across all alternatives considered in the specific decision (e.g., the lowest and highest costs). If the range changes, the weights need to be adapted to reflect the presumably unchanged preferences of a stakeholder. Experimental research indicates that people do not sufficiently adapt weights to changed ranges (Fischer, 1995; von Nitzsch & Weber, 1993). This implies that people do not properly consider the attribute range when assigning weights, also in non-experimental settings. In practical weight elicitation, it is thus very important to emphasize the attribute ranges. Explicitly considering ranges is part of two common elicitation methods, "swing" and "trade-off" (methods see e.g., Eisenführ et al., 2010). Moreover, it is important to use consistency checks, and if possible multiple weighting methods (Montibeller & von Winterfeldt, 2015). Practical examples of how attribute ranges can be visualized for weight elicitation are presented in the supplementary information to Schuwirth et al. (2012) and Zheng et al. (2016).

Above, I introduced "relevancy analysis" to identify the most important objectives in the problem structuring phase (Marttunen et al., 2019a). Relevancy analysis can also be used to specify weights, as was demonstrated for Swiss river restoration measures (Marttunen et al., 2019b). Relevancy analysis is a relatively easy method based on questionnaires that emphasizes the range and provides a nice visualization. This method seems to mirror the thinking of practitioners by separating the "general importance of an objective" from the "problem-specific impact range" in the concrete decision. To give an example: the stakeholders or experts are allowed to specify that e.g., "flow dynamics" is a generally important objective in a river management decision. However, they can acknowledge that it is not important in the specific case, because the worst and best predicted outcomes/impacts across all considered alternatives are similar. This objective thus does not help decision-making because it does not discriminate between alternatives (Marttunen et al., 2019b). Relevancy analysis is conceptually similar to the "swing weight matrix" method (Ewing et al., 2006; Parnell & Trainor, 2014). Further systematic assessment of relevancy analysis including behavioral aspects could be a useful research avenue to find practicable methods that reduce biases in weight elicitation.

Generally, to date the reasons and underlying mechanisms of the observed phenomena are not well understood. This makes it difficult to pinpoint critical issues in weight elicitation and improve methods. Behavioral research could thus focus on systematic exploration of cognitive processes. Additionally, finding ways to elicit weights in a relatively simple and practical way without promoting wrong results is an important area of practice-oriented research.

Online Preference Elicitation and Gamification

In many fields such as economics and psychology, there is a trend to carry out online surveys. This enables collecting large datasets from a broad sample of people, thus allowing for e.g., experimental research and hypothesis testing. For decision analysis, online approaches are promising because the population can be included in decision processes, which is not possible in workshops where usually some 10 to 30 people are included. There are exceptions, as example, a community hospital project using soft OR methods included hundreds of participants, which were split into smaller working groups (White & Bourne, 2007). Enabling participation is of course especially relevant in public policy and environmental decisions.

However, online methods come with drawbacks. Lay people might be invited who have limited understanding of the complexity of the environmental problem. Therefore, they first need to learn about the facts and uncertainties. There is a recent trend to use serious games or game elements in such processes. Our review of serious games in the water sector indicated that many games are used to broadcast a message and could thus stimulate learning about the problem (Aubert et al., 2018). In a first survey, we found that game elements can indeed enhance learning about facts in the decision, but further research is needed (Aubert & Lienert, 2019).

Eliciting peoples' preferences online for later use in MCDA would be an interesting possibility. Our review indicated that there is a serious lack of research, and that there is no gamified procedure available for preference elicitation (Aubert et al., 2018). There have been a few earlier attempts to elicit weights online (e.g., Lienert et al., 2016). However, online preference elicitation has rightly been criticized because the risk of biases increases if there is no interaction with a facilitator (Marttunen & Hämäläinen, 2008). We proposed using learning loops with repeated elicitation to mimic consistency checks in live interactions with a facilitator (Aubert & Lienert, 2019). The concept is based on "transformational learning theory" (Mezirow, 2000). First results using online swing weighting in a wastewater case with 600 participants from the Paris region were somewhat disappointing (Aubert et al., 2020). Respondents learned about own preferences and about facts of wastewater management to some extent. However, they made methodological mistakes and obviously did not properly understand the swing weight elicitation method. We are now experimentally testing whether introducing game elements to the online survey could improve weight elicitation. One reason is that gamification can provide a positive experience, for instance because there is a narrative and an attractive interface. Other reasons are that critical learning can be enhanced by introducing win/fail situations, and guidance by the facilitator can be mimicked with a character who "interacts" with respondents and gives encouraging feedback. Research in this area is in its infancy, offering many opportunities for exciting behavioral studies.

Conclusion: Preference Elicitation

Preferences are constructed during decision-making processes, which has far-reaching practical consequences for behavioral decision analysis. There is ample earlier research uncovering the many biases that can occur during preference elicitation. Moreover, it is disturbing that research concerning the elicitation of risk attitudes or weights indicates that the choice of the method can result in different preferences. Although many phenomena have been detected, the underlying cognitive processes are often unclear. How to deal with them in practice remains a challenge. As starting point, I recommend gaining an overview of de-biasing methods in the review paper by Montibeller and von Winterfeldt (2015).

Theoretical contributions are important to research. Personally, I agree with authors who state that we need to understand what happens in real-world interventions, and in which way we can ensure that robust outcomes are produced. Such calls come from behavioral OR (Franco & Hämäläinen, 2016; Hämäläinen et al., 2013), environmental modelling (Hämäläinen, 2015; van Aken et al., 2016; Voinov et al., 2016), and environmental decision analysis (Gregory et al., 2012a). To understand behavioral processes in our interventions, we need both variance research that uses clever experimental and quasi-experimental designs as well as process research that uses a theoretical narrative to understand how a sequence of events leads to a certain outcome (Franco et al., 2021). I have given various examples above.

In practice, given the current state of research, ideally we would select a broad range of stakeholders from whom we elicit preferences using multiple methods, and maybe repeated over time. We should use consistency checks to verify with stakeholders that the elicited parameters are indicative of their true preferences. Such time-consuming procedures are hardly do-able in most practice applications. Thus, I strongly recommend carrying out careful sensitivity analyses to find out, where results are not robust if preferences would be different (see below).

MCDA Model, Uncertainty, and Sensitivity Analyses

In step D of the decision model (Keeney, 1982), we integrate the impacts of each alternative (step B) with the stakeholders' preferences (step C). This section merits an own book chapter. Here, I shortly cover aspects important from a behavioral perspective. For the theory and mathematical formula, I refer to literature.

Does the MCDA Model Match Stakeholder Preferences?

Additionally, to problem structuring and preference elicitation, the choice of the MCDA model can affect the result. In my experience, in applications of Multi-Attribute Value or Utility Theory (MAVT/MAUT), usually the linear additive aggregation model, the weighted arithmetic mean, is used (for the model see textbooks, e.g., Belton & Stewart, 2002; Eisenführ et al., 2010; Greco et al. 2016; Keeney & Raiffa, 1976). This is supported by reviews of environmental applications using MCDA (Diaz-Balteiro et al., 2017; Esmail & Geneletti, 2018; Kandakoglu et al., 2019). However, is the additive model a good choice? Choosing the wrong model to aggregate over the predictions and the stakeholders' preferences may produce wrong results. It is decisive to check that the model matches the stakeholders' preferences, which is however rarely done (see review by Esmail & Geneletti, 2018).

As theoretical requirement of the additive model, objectives need to be preferentially independent. As consequence, objectives that are on a poor level can be compensated by objectives that achieve a good level (Haag et al., 2019a; Reichert et al.,

2015). We found in several cases that stakeholders rarely agree with full compensation (Langhans & Lienert, 2016; Lienert et al., 2022; Reichert et al., 2019; Scholten et al., 2015; Zheng et al., 2016). Therefore, less extreme models that allow for interaction among objectives would be more appropriate. Some outranking methods are non-compensatory; and I refer to literature regarding properties of MCDA methods (Cinelli et al., 2014, 2020; Roy & Słowiński, 2013). Non-compensatory MAVT aggregation models such as multiplicative aggregation have been proposed for decades (Dyer & Sarin, 1979; Keeney & Raiffa, 1976). For a practice-oriented discussion of aggregation functions, see Rowley et al. (2012), and there is considerable theoretical development (e.g., Grabisch et al., 2008, 2009; Reichert et al., 2015). Practice applications that demonstrate how preferences can be elicited from stakeholders are rare, and the proposed approaches seem time-consuming (Argyris et al., 2014; Haag et al., 2019a; Reichert et al., 2019).

Future research in behavioral decision analysis could develop and improve methods for checking the validity of the MCDA aggregation model, and for inferring parameters of other models. In practice, we are currently using a few simple questions to ask whether stakeholders agree with full compensation, but this "method" is unsatisfactory. I recommend carrying out sensitivity analyses with other aggregation models, and we use the ValueDecisions app to do so (practical examples see Haag et al., 2022; Lienert et al., 2022).

Uncertainty and Sensitivity Analyses

As stated before, environmental decisions are full of uncertainty. Again, here I can only summarize main points important from a practical behavioral perspective. It is problematic that recent reviews indicate that uncertainty is often neglected in environmental applications of MCDA (de Brito & Evers, 2016; Esmail & Geneletti, 2018; Gregory & Keeney, 2017). Various authors emphasize the importance of including uncertainty in environmental decision analysis (French & Geldermann, 2005; Kandakoglu et al., 2019; Walling & Vaneeckhaute, 2020). Some provide overviews of the different types of uncertainties, and possible methods for dealing with these (e.g., Cinelli et al., 2014; Durbach & Stewart, 2012; Reichert et al., 2015).

To deal with the uncertainty of predictions, often probability theory is used in MAVT/MAUT. Monte Carlo simulations allow sampling from the distributions of the uncertain predictions, and propagating the input uncertainty to the results (for an application example, see e.g., Schuwirth et al., 2012). As discussed above, MAUT is appropriate for decisions with uncertain outcomes. However, it is demanding to elicit the utility function and behavioral research is needed.

Stakeholders can be uncertain about their preferences in elicitation processes. In my experience, it is often easier for people to define ranges rather than forcing them to give precise numbers, as discussed in literature on imprecise statements (e.g., Jessop, 2014; Mustajoki et al., 2006). The range can be tested in sensitivity analyses.

To deal with large uncertainty of the future, it is possible to combine scenario planning with MCDA. Treating this literature is out of scope here, but there are many interesting questions that could be tackled by behavioral decision analysis, as discussed in recent theory papers (Ram, 2020; Stewart et al., 2013; Wright et al., 2009, 2019). Moreover, a rich variety of practical applications for different environmental cases have been presented in literature (e.g., Harris-Lovett et al., 2019; Karvetski et al., 2011; Lambert et al., 2012; Montibeller et al., 2006; Ram & Montibeller, 2013; Trutnevyte et al., 2012; Witt et al., 2020; Zheng et al., 2016).

Sensitivity analyses are a good possibility to deal with the uncertainty of stakeholder preferences and for identifying where MCDA results are most sensitive to changed input data. In practical decision analysis, commonly local sensitivity analyses are used, but global sensitivity analyses (GSA) provide insights into all combined uncertainties (overviews see Borgonovo & Plischke, 2016; Saltelli et al., 2008). However, GSA proved to be computationally very demanding in an application case to water supply infrastructure management (Scholten et al., 2015).

In local sensitivity analyses, we change the input parameters, for instance the weights, calculate the MCDA for the changed setting, and compare the MCDA results with the original ones (for a good introduction see Eisenführ et al., 2010). We can then visually compare the different MCDA results, or statistically analyze the difference between results, for instance with Kendall's τ rank correlations (Kendall, 1938). Ideally, sensitivity analyses are done stepwise, systematically, and based on some ideas about the stakeholders' preferences. We might have elicited interval weights from stakeholders, or there might have been discussions, and we can later test the extremes. To give an example, when designing a flood early warning system for West Africa, stakeholders emphasized in plenary discussions that the system should be available in "several languages", but they gave relatively low weights to this objective in later weight elicitation (Lienert et al., 2022). Therefore, we tested whether higher weights would change results. We also found in some of our cases that the weight of "low costs" might have been underestimated, and we thus doubled the weight and checked whether this changed the ranking of alternatives. Underestimating the importance of economic objectives might actually be frequent: our meta-analyses of applied environmental cases using MCDA revealed a statistically significant lower weight of economic objectives ($w = 0.22$) compared to environmental objectives ($w = 0.38$; $N = 124$ cases; Marttunen et al., 2018). As discussed in this paper, the reasons are unclear, but could be related to taboo trade-offs (Baron & Spranca, 1997; Tetlock, 2003), which merits research. For examples of local, stepwise sensitivity analyses, I refer to some of our cases in urban water management (e.g., Scholten et al., 2017; Schuwirth et al., 2012; Zheng et al., 2016).

Additionally, other methods for integrating combined uncertainties have been tested in real cases and can be applied by practitioners. The family of SMAA methods (stochastic multi-criteria acceptability analysis) is certainly useful (e.g., Lahdelma & Salminen, 2001, 2012; Tervonen & Figueira, 2008). Recent developments are an integration of multi-dimensional sensitivity analyses and visualization of MCDA results in the tool SIMADA (Bertsch & Fichtner, 2016). SIMADA was combined with a natural language generator tool, which can be very interesting in stakeholder group deliberations (Geldermann et al., 2009; Wulf & Bertsch, 2017). We recently proposed using Expected Expected Utility theory (EEU), which is not well known in the decision analysis literature (Boutilier, 2003). EEU is an extension of MAUT and allows combining the uncertainty of predictions and of stakeholder preferences. We found EEU a useful, practicable method in a case of merging four wastewater treatment plants (Haag et al., 2019b). EEU provided clear results despite large uncertainty. However, the use of EEU including possible behavioral issues now needs to be explored in other cases.

Carrying out local sensitivity analyses for different preference parameters (value/utility functions, weights, and aggregation model) can be time-consuming. Standard MCDA software often incorporates sensitivity analyses of weights, but hardly ever of the aggregation model (e.g., Mustajoki & Marttunen, 2017). I thus wish to advertise our new open source application ValueDecisions, which has an intuitive interface and does not require programming skills (Haag et al., 2022). We specifically designed it to support public policy and environmental decision cases, and we incorporated important aspects treated in this chapter. ValueDecisions allows for sophisticated MCDA analyses for many alternatives and many stakeholders with different preferences. It can be run with or without uncertainty of predictions, and it can be used to explore the sensitivity of results to changed marginal value functions, weights, and different types of aggregation models. This can be done interactively for instance in stakeholder workshops, where results are visualized, explored, and discussed (examples of sensitivity analyses in two cases see Haag et al., 2022; Lienert et al., 2022). We hope that the development of such tools that are applicable in practice also supports applied research, e.g., in the exploration of some of the behavioral issues covered in this book chapter.

Conclusion: MCDA Model and Uncertainties

To conclude this section, uncertainties are prominent in public policy and environmental decision problems, but seem to be neglected in many applications. Moreover, the common additive MCDA model is rarely questioned, but the choice of the model in itself adds to the overall uncertainty. We require do-able ways to deal with uncertainties in applied decision analysis. Above, I have covered some aspects where behavioral research would be needed, not least to support practical cases.

In practice, there are usually time and resource constraints and we need to take a pragmatic view on what is realistically possible. "Decision sketching", a quick run through the entire decision problem with MCDA at the start of the project can support stakeholder deliberations (Gregory et al., 2012a). Additionally, desktop sensitivity analyses early in the project could help us determine where MCDA results are especially sensitive. de Almeida et al. (2016) proposed a stepwise, interactive procedure for weight elicitation. This requires interacting with stakeholders only if necessary to improve model results. At project start, we could use simplified assumptions, for instance very rough numbers for the predictions combined with large uncertainty ranges, and simplified assumptions about stakeholder preferences (e.g., linear value functions, equal vs. extreme weights, additive aggregation). We could use sensitivity analyses to determine which type of more-detailed data would change the results, and then collect these from experts or stakeholders to inform next sensitivity analyses. Such approaches, however, require further development, systematic analyses, and exploration of possible behavioral issues.

Conclusions

In this chapter, I argued that public policy and environmental decision problems offer many exciting opportunities for behavioral research. Such research is of great importance for decision-making in practice, where we need to structure messy problems and somehow include stakeholders' preferences.

I wish to point out that I have not covered several topics that can be important in public environmental decisions. Increasingly, Geographical Information Systems (GIS) are combined with MCDA to address "spatial environmental decisions" (e.g., Ferretti & Montibeller, 2019; Keenan & Jankowski, 2019; Malczewski & Jankowski, 2020). Interest in behavioral aspects seems to be increasing in this field (e.g., Ferretti & Geneletti, 2020; Harju et al., 2019; Keller & Simon, 2019; Simon, 2020; Simon et al., 2014). Moreover, "portfolio decision analysis" can be appropriate for tackling environmental decisions (e.g., Chacon-Hurtado & Scholten, 2021; Convertino et al., 2019; Lahtinen et al., 2017; Liesiö et al., 2021). Finally, there is a rich literature in group decision-making, and I refer to the classic textbook (Kilgour & Eden, 2010). Biases occurring in "group decision-making" processes have been reviewed (e.g., Kerr & Tindale, 2004; Kugler et al., 2012; Montibeller & von Winterfeldt, 2018; Quinn, 2008), but there is certainly room for behavioral research.

I also emphasize that we should consider what comes after MCDA. As final step, we should verify and discuss results with stakeholders. In some cases, we need to find compromise alternatives, or create new ones, for instance by combining best properties of existing alternatives. It would also be wise to discuss next steps with stakeholders, but implementation is usually out of the hands of decision analysis. We should at least be aware of the fact that even if good results are obtained by the MCDA, it is naïve to assume that they will be implemented, and additional activities are needed (Gregory et al., 2012a). *"(…) we need to realize that in many circumstances it* [decision analysis] *will only be one input to the political process that leads to the actual decision"* (French & Argyris, 2018; abstract).

To conclude, I summarize main insights from this chapter. Although there is a broad range of problem structuring methods (PSMs), we urgently require systematic behavioral research to understand and systematize the use of different PSMs in the early steps of MCDA. In many applied public policy and environmental decision cases, the selection of stakeholders, objectives, and alternatives has been neglected or carried out ad hoc. We need behavioral research that allows advancing the "art" of problem structuring, and we should develop scientifically validated procedures that are applicable in real-world decision-making. Research indicates that people have difficulties to identify objectives and alternatives, even in personal decisions, and methods to overcome such limitations have been proposed. Recent research also indicates that our choices, for instance regarding the structure of the objectives hierarchy, can systematically affect later MCDA phases such as weight elicitation. In the worst case, we will produce wrong results because we did not properly set up the decision problem. I suggest that we open up to fields outside decision analysis, including the political sciences or design theory. Our work can in turn enrich other fields, for instance by supporting systematization and theory building in soft OR.

I have treated the step of making predictions only superficially. Regarding behavioral decision analysis, this is only important if expert estimates are used.

There is huge evidence that preferences are constructed during decision-making processes and can be influenced by many factors. This is bad news for preference elicitation. Much behavioral research has focused on biases in weight elicitation. It is for instance disturbing that different elicitation methods can lead to different values (e.g., of weights or risk attitudes). There remain ample research opportunities for behavioral decision analysis. These include studying factors that influence preference change over time, developing simpler methods for eliciting utility functions and peoples' risk attitudes, finding ways to overcome the range insensitivity bias, or improving online preference elicitation. Again, we can learn a lot from literature in other fields such as environmental economics and psychology. We need research to understand cognitive processes and to develop de-biasing approaches. These procedures need to be applicable in practice; they should thus be simple and fast. As practical recommendation, we can overcome some problems by including a broad range of stakeholder perspectives, and by using different methods for preference elicitation and rigorous consistency checks.

In practical public environmental decisions, uncertainty is strongly neglected. I have summarized different types of uncertainty above, and methods for addressing these. I advocate systematic use of sensitivity analyses. Moreover, the popular additive MCDA model is widely applied in practice, even though it may not well capture the stakeholders' preferences. Behavioral research in this field is needed.

I am fully aware that my suggestions can lead to even more time-consuming procedures – which is unrealistic in practice projects. To save time, we can test the sensitivity of results to changed preferences with desktop modeling. This helps determining where it is worth investing efforts to improve predictions, or to interact with stakeholders. A rewarding research avenue could thus address combining simplified decision analysis methods with interactive, flexible decision processes.

References

Ackermann, F. (2012). Problem structuring methods 'in the Dock': Arguing the case for Soft OR. *European Journal of Operational Research, 219*, 652–658. https://doi.org/10.1016/j.ejor.2011.11.014

Ackermann, F., & Howick, S. (2021). Experiences of mixed method or practitioners: Moving beyond a technical focus to insights relating to modelling teams. *Journal of the Operational Research Society*. https://doi.org/10.1080/01605682.2021.1970486

Angie, A. D., Connelly, S., Waples, E. P., & Kligyte, V. (2011). The influence of discrete emotions on judgement and decision-making: A meta-analytic review. *Cognition and Emotion, 25*, 1393–1422. https://doi.org/10.1080/02699931.2010.550751

Argyris, N., Morton, A., & Figueira, J. R. (2014). CUT: A multicriteria approach for concavifiable preferences. *Operations Research, 62*, 633–642. https://doi.org/10.1287/opre.2014.1274

Aubert, A. H., & Lienert, J. (2019). Gamified online survey to elicit citizens' preferences and enhance learning for environmental decisions. *Environmental Modelling and Software, 111*, 1–12. https://doi.org/10.1016/j.envsoft.2018.09.013

Aubert, A. H., Bauer, R., & Lienert, J. (2018). A review of water-related serious games to specify use in environmental. *Multi-Criteria Decision Analysis Environmental Modelling and Software, 105*, 64–78. https://doi.org/10.1016/j.envsoft.2018.03.023

Aubert, A. H., Esculier, F., & Lienert, J. (2020). Recommendations for online elicitation of swing weights from citizens in environmental decision-making. *Operations Research Perspectives, 7*. https://doi.org/10.1016/j.orp.2020.100156

Baron, J., & Spranca, M. (1997). Protected values. *Organizational Behavior and Human Decision Processes, 70*, 1–16. https://doi.org/10.1006/obhd.1997.2690

Belton, V. (1986). A comparison of the analytic hierarchy process and a simple multi-attribute value function. *European Journal of Operational Research, 26*, 7–21. https://doi.org/10.1016/0377-2217(86)90155-4

Belton, V., & Stewart, T. S. (2002). *Multiple criteria decision analysis: An integrated approach*. Springer Science+Business Media Springer. https://doi.org/10.1007/978-1-4615-1495-4

Belton, V., & Stewart, T. J. (2010). Problem structuring and multiple criteria decision analysis. In M. Ehrgott, J. R. Figueira, & S. Greco (Eds.), *Trends in multiple criteria decision analysis* (Vol. 142, pp. 209–240). Springer. https://doi.org/10.1007/978-1-4419-5904-1

Bertsch, V., & Fichtner, W. (2016). A participatory multi-criteria approach for power generation and transmission planning. *Annals of Operations Research, 245*, 177–207. https://doi.org/10.1007/s10479-015-1791-y

Bond, S. D., Carlson, K. A., & Keeney, R. L. (2008). Generating objectives: Can decision makers articulate what they want? *Management Science, 54*, 56–70. https://doi.org/10.1287/mnsc.1070.0754

Bond, S. D., Carlson, K. A., & Keeney, R. L. (2010). Improving the generation of decision objectives. *Decision Analysis, 7*, 238–255. https://doi.org/10.1287/deca.1100.0172

Borcherding, K., Eppel, T., & Von Winterfeldt, D. (1991). Comparison of weighting judgments in multiattribute utility measurement. *Management Science, 37*, 1603–1619. https://doi.org/10.1287/mnsc.37.12.1603

Borgonovo, E., & Plischke, E. (2016). Sensitivity analysis: A review of recent advances. *European Journal of Operational Research, 248*, 869–887. https://doi.org/10.1016/j.ejor.2015.06.032

Boutilier, C. (2003). On the foundations of expected expected utility. In *18th International joint conference on artificial intelligence, IJCAI 2003* (pp. 285–290).

Brans, J. P., Vincke, P., & Mareschal, B. (1986). How to select and how to rank projects - the PROMETHEE method. *European Journal of Operational Research, 24*, 228–238. https://doi.org/10.1016/0377-2217(86)90044-5

Brouwer, R. (2006). Do stated preference methods stand the test of time? A test of the stability of contingent values and models for health risks when facing an extreme event. *Ecological Economics, 60*, 399–406. https://doi.org/10.1016/j.ecolecon.2006.04.001

Brugha, R., & Varvasovszky, Z. (2000). Stakeholder analysis: A review. *Health Policy and Planning, 15*, 239–246. https://doi.org/10.1093/heapol/15.3.239

Burgman, M., Carr, A., Godden, L., Gregory, R., McBride, M., Flander, L., & Maguire, L. (2011). Redefining expertise and improving ecological judgment. *Conservation Letters, 4*, 81–87. https://doi.org/10.1111/j.1755-263X.2011.00165.x

Cegan, J. C., Filion, A. M., Keisler, J. M., & Linkov, I. (2017). Trends and applications of multi-criteria decision analysis in environmental sciences: Literature review. *Environment Systems and Decisions, 37*, 123–133. https://doi.org/10.1007/s10669-017-9642-9

Chacon-Hurtado, J. C., & Scholten, L. (2021). Decisi-o-rama: An open-source Python library for multi-attribute value/utility decision analysis. *Environmental Modelling and Software, 135*, 104890. https://doi.org/10.1016/j.envsoft.2020.104890

Charness, G., Gneezy, U., & Imas, A. (2013). Experimental methods: Eliciting risk preferences. *Journal of Economic Behavior and Organization, 87*, 43–51. https://doi.org/10.1016/j.jebo.2012.12.023

Cinelli, M., Coles, S. R., & Kirwan, K. (2014). Analysis of the potentials of multi criteria decision analysis methods to conduct sustainability assessment. *Ecological Indicators, 46*, 138–148. https://doi.org/10.1016/j.ecolind.2014.06.011

Cinelli, M., Kadzinski, M., Gonzalez, M., & Slowinski, R. (2020). How to support the application of multiple criteria decision analysis? Let us start with a comprehensive taxonomy. *Omega-International Journal of Management Science, 96*. https://doi.org/10.1016/j.omega.2020.102261

Clemen, R. T., & Reilly, T. (2001) *Making hard decisions with decision tools®* (2nd rev edn). Duxbury, Brooks/Cole.

Colapinto, C., Jayaraman, R., Ben Abdelaziz, F., & La Torre, D. (2020). Environmental sustainability and multifaceted development: Multi-criteria decision models with applications. *Annals of Operations Research, 293*, 405–432. https://doi.org/10.1007/s10479-019-03403-y

Colorni, A., & Tsoukias, A. (2020). Designing alternatives in decision problems. *Journal of Multi-Criteria Decision Analysis, 27*, 150–158. https://doi.org/10.1002/mcda.1709

Convertino, M., Annis, A., & Nardi, F. (2019). Information-theoretic portfolio decision model for optimal flood management. *Environmental Modelling & Software, 119*, 258–274. https://doi.org/10.1016/j.envsoft.2019.06.013

Dave, C., Eckel, C. C., Johnson, C. A., & Rojas, C. (2010). Eliciting risk preferences: When is simple better? *Journal of Risk and Uncertainty, 41*, 219–243. https://doi.org/10.1007/s11166-010-9103-z

de Almeida, A. T., de Almeida, J. A., Costa, A., & de Almeida, A. T. (2016). A new method for elicitation of criteria weights in additive models: Flexible and interactive tradeoff. *European Journal of Operational Research, 250*, 179–191. https://doi.org/10.1016/j.ejor.2015.08.058

de Brito, M. M., & Evers, M. (2016). Multi-criteria decision-making for flood risk management: A survey of the current state of the art. *Natural Hazards and Earth System Sciences, 16*, 1019–1033. https://doi.org/10.5194/nhess-16-1019-2016

Diaz-Balteiro, L., Gonzalez-Pachon, J., & Romero, C. (2017). Measuring systems sustainability with multi-criteria methods: A critical review. *European Journal of Operational Research, 258*, 607–616. https://doi.org/10.1016/j.ejor.2016.08.075

Dohmen, T., Falk, A., Huffman, D., Sunde, U., Schupp, J., & Wagner, G. G. (2011). Individual risk attitudes: Measurement, determinants, and behavioral consequences. *Journal of the European Economic Association, 9*, 522–550. https://doi.org/10.1111/j.1542-4774.2011.01015.x

Durbach, I. N., & Stewart, T. J. (2012). Modeling uncertainty in multi-criteria decision analysis. *European Journal of Operational Research, 223*, 1–14. https://doi.org/10.1016/j.ejor.2012.04.038

Dyer, J. S., & Sarin, R. K. (1979). Measurable multiattribute value functions. *Operational Research, 27*, 810–822. https://doi.org/10.1287/opre.27.4.810

Dyer, J. S., & Sarin, R. K. (1982). Relative risk-aversion. *Management Science, 28*, 875–886. https://doi.org/10.1287/mnsc.28.8.875

Eisenführ, F., Weber, M., & Langer, T. (2010). *Rational decision making* (1st ed.). Springer.

Esmail, B. A., & Geneletti, D. (2018). Multi-criteria decision analysis for nature conservation: A review of 20 years of applications. *Methods in Ecology and Evolution, 9*, 42–53. https://doi.org/10.1111/2041-210x.12899

Ewing, P. L. J., Tarantino, W., & Parnell, G. S. (2006). *Use of decision analysis in the army base realignment and closure (BRAC) 2005 military value analysis vol 3. ABI/INFORM Collection*. doi:https://doi.org/10.1287/deca.1060.0062.

Ferretti, V., & Geneletti, D. (2020). Does the spatial representation affect criteria weights in environmental decision-making? Insights from a behavioral experiment. *Land Use Policy, 97*. https://doi.org/10.1016/j.landusepol.2020.104613

Ferretti, V., & Montibeller, G. (2019). An integrated framework for environmental multi-impact spatial risk analysis. *Risk Analysis, 39*, 257–273. https://doi.org/10.1111/risa.12942

Ferretti, V., Pluchinotta, I., & Tsoukias, A. (2019). Studying the generation of alternatives in public policy making processes. *European Journal of Operational Research, 273*, 353–363. https://doi.org/10.1016/j.ejor.2018.07.054

Fischer, G. W. (1995). Range sensitivity of attribute weight in multiattribute value models. *Organizational Behavior and Human Decision Processes, 62*, 252–266. https://doi.org/10.1006/obhd.1995.1048

Franco, L. A., & Hämäläinen, R. P. (2016). Behavioural operational research: Returning to the roots of the OR profession. *European Journal of Operational Research, 249*, 791–795. https://doi.org/10.1016/j.ejor.2015.10.034

Franco, L. A., & Lord, E. (2011). Understanding multi-methodology: Evaluating the perceived impact of mixing methods for group budgetary decisions. *Omega, 39*, 362–372. https://doi.org/10.1016/j.omega.2010.06.008

Franco, L. A., Hamalainen, R. P., Rouwette, E., & Leppanen, I. (2021). Taking stock of behavioural OR: A review of behavioural studies with an intervention focus. *European Journal of Operational Research, 293*, 401–418. https://doi.org/10.1016/j.ejor.2020.11.031

French, S. (2021). From soft to hard elicitation. *Journal of the Operational Research Society, 73*, 1–17. https://doi.org/10.1080/01605682.2021.1907244

French, S., & Argyris, N. (2018). Decision analysis and political processes. *Decision Analysis, 15*, 208–222. https://doi.org/10.1287/deca.2018.0374

French, S., & Geldermann, J. (2005). The varied contexts of environmental decision problems and their implications for decision support. *Environmental Science & Policy, 8*, 378–391. https://doi.org/10.1016/j.envsci.2005.04.008

Geldermann, J., Bertsch, V., Treitz, M., French, S., Papamichail, K. N., & Hamalainen, R. P. (2009). Multi-criteria decision support and evaluation of strategies for nuclear remediation management. *Omega-International Journal of Management Science, 37*, 238–251. https://doi.org/10.1016/j.omega.2006.11.006

Geldermann, J., Lerche, N., & Sepulveda, J. D. (2018). Combining multi-criteria decision analysis and design thinking. *European Journal of Industrial Engineering, 12*, 708–739. https://doi.org/10.1504/ejie.2018.10015684

Grabisch, M., Kojadinovic, I., & Meyer, P. (2008). A review of methods for capacity identification in Choquet integral based multi-attribute utility theory: Applications of the Kappalab R package. *European Journal of Operational Research, 186*, 766–785. https://doi.org/10.1016/j.ejor.2007.02.025

Grabisch, M., Marichal, J.-L., Mesiar, R., & Pap, E. (2009). *Aggregation functions* (Vol. 127). Cambridge University Press.

Greco, S., Ehrgott, M., & Figueira, J. R. (Eds.) (2016). Multiple criteria decision analysis. State of the Art Surveys. *International Series in Operations Research and Management Science* (2 edn). Springer. doi:https://doi.org/10.1007/978-1-4939-3094-4.

Gregory, R., & Keeney, R. L. (2017). A practical approach to address uncertainty in stakeholder deliberations. *Risk Analysis, 37*, 487–501. https://doi.org/10.1111/risa.12638

Gregory, R., Failing, L., Harstone, M., Long, G., McDaniels, T., & Ohlson, D. (2012a). *Structured decision making: A practical guide to environmental management choices*. Wiley-Blackwell.

Gregory, R., Long, G., Colligan, M., Geiger, J. G., & Laser, M. (2012b). When experts disagree (and better science won't help much): Using structured deliberations to support endangered species recovery planning. *Journal of Environmental Management, 105*, 30–43. https://doi.org/10.1016/j.jenvman.2012.03.001

Gregory, A. J., Atkins, J. P., Midgley, G., & Hodgson, A. M. (2020). Stakeholder identification and engagement in problem structuring interventions. *European Journal of Operational Research, 283*, 321–340. https://doi.org/10.1016/j.ejor.2019.10.044

Grimble, R., & Wellard, K. (1997). Stakeholder methodologies in natural resource management: A review of principles, contexts, experiences and opportunities. *Agricultural Systems, 55*, 173–193. https://doi.org/10.1016/S0308-521X(97)00006-1

Haag, F., Lienert, J., Schuwirth, N., & Reichert, P. (2019a). Identifying non-additive multi-attribute value functions based on uncertain indifference statements. *Omega-International Journal of Management Science, 85*, 49–67. https://doi.org/10.1016/j.omega.2018.05.011

Haag, F., Reichert, P., Maurer, M., & Lienert, J. (2019b). Integrating uncertainty of preferences and predictions in decision models: An application to regional wastewater planning. *Journal of Environmental Management, 252*, 109652–109652. https://doi.org/10.1016/j.jenvman.2019.109652

Haag, F., Zuercher, S., & Lienert, J. (2019c). Enhancing the elicitation of diverse decision objectives for public planning. *European Journal of Operational Research, 279*, 912–928. https://doi.org/10.1016/j.ejor.2019.06.002

Haag, F., Aubert, A. H., & Lienert, J. (2022). ValueDecisions, a web app to support decisions with conflicting objectives, multiple stakeholders, and uncertainty. *Environmental Modelling & Software, 150*, 105361. https://doi.org/10.1016/j.envsoft.2022.105361

Hämäläinen, R. P. (2015). Behavioural issues in environmental modelling – The missing perspective. *Environmental Modelling and Software, 73*, 244–253. https://doi.org/10.1016/j.envsoft.2015.08.019

Hämäläinen, R. P., & Alaja, S. (2008). The threat of weighting biases in environmental decision analysis. *Ecological Economics, 68*, 556–569. https://doi.org/10.1016/j.ecolecon.2008.05.025

Hämäläinen, R. P., Luoma, J., & Saarinen, E. (2013). On the importance of behavioral operational research: The case of understanding and communicating about dynamic systems. *European Journal of Operational Research, 228*, 623–634. https://doi.org/10.1016/j.ejor.2013.02.001

Harju, M., Liesio, J., & Virtanen, K. (2019). Spatial multi-attribute decision analysis: Axiomatic foundations and incomplete preference information. *European Journal of Operational Research, 275*, 167–181. https://doi.org/10.1016/j.ejor.2018.11.013

Harris-Lovett, S., Lienert, J., & Sedlak, D. (2019). A mixed-methods approach to strategic planning for multi-benefit regional water infrastructure. *Journal of Environmental Management, 233*, 218–237. https://doi.org/10.1016/j.jenvman.2018.11.112

Hemming, V., Burgman, M. A., Hanea, A. M., McBride, M. F., & Wintle, B. C. (2018). A practical guide to structured expert elicitation using the IDEA protocol. *Methods in Ecology and Evolution, 9*, 169–180. https://doi.org/10.1111/2041-210x.12857

Hermans, L. M., & Thissen, W. A. H. (2009). Actor analysis methods and their use for public policy analysts. *European Journal of Operational Research, 196*, 808–818. https://doi.org/10.1016/j.ejor.2008.03.040

Howard, R. A. (1988). Decision-analysis - Practice and promise. *Management Science, 34*, 679–695. https://doi.org/10.1287/mnsc.34.6.679

Huang, I. B., Keisler, J., & Linkov, I. (2011). Multi-criteria decision analysis in environmental sciences: Ten years of applications and trends. *Science of the Total Environment, 409*, 3578–3594. https://doi.org/10.1016/j.scitotenv.2011.06.022

Ingold, K., Driessen, P. P. J., Runhaar, H. A. C., & Widmer, A. (2019). On the necessity of connectivity: Linking key characteristics of environmental problems with governance modes. *Journal of Environmental Planning and Management, 62*, 1821–1844. https://doi.org/10.1080/09640568.2018.1486700

Iyer, P., Bozzola, M., Hirsch, S., Meraner, M., & Finger, R. (2020). Measuring farmer risk preferences in Europe: A systematic review. *Journal of Agricultural Economics, 71*, 3–26. https://doi.org/10.1111/1477-9552.12325

Jacobi, S. K., & Hobbs, B. F. (2007). Quantifying and mitigating the splitting bias and other value tree-induced weighting biases. *Decision Analysis, 4*, 194–210. https://doi.org/10.1287/deca.1070.0100

Jessop, A. (2014). IMP: A decision aid for multiattribute evaluation using imprecise weight estimates. *Omega, 49*, 18–29. https://doi.org/10.1016/j.omega.2014.05.001

Jorgensen, B. S., Syme, G. J., Smith, L. M., & Bishop, B. J. (2004). Random error in willingness to pay measurement: A multiple indicators, latent variable approach to the reliability of contingent values. *Journal of Economic Psychology, 25*, 41–59. https://doi.org/10.1016/s0167-4870(02)00167-8

Kahneman, D., & Tversky, A. (1979). Prospect theory - Analysis of decision under risk. *Econometrica, 47*, 263–291. https://doi.org/10.2307/1914185

Kandakoglu, A., Frini, A., & Ben Amor, S. (2019). Multicriteria decision making for sustainable development: A systematic review. *Journal of Multi-Criteria Decision Analysis, 26*, 202–251. https://doi.org/10.1002/mcda.1682

Karvetski, C. W., Lambert, J. H., Keisler, J. M., Sexauer, B., & Linkov, I. (2011). Climate change scenarios: Risk and impact analysis for Alaska coastal infrastructure. *International Journal of Risk Assessment and Management, 15*, 258–274. https://doi.org/10.1504/IJRAM.2011.042120

Keenan, P. B., & Jankowski, P. (2019). Spatial decision support systems: Three decades on. *Decision Support Systems, 116*, 64–76. https://doi.org/10.1016/j.dss.2018.10.010

Keeney, R. L. (1982). Decision-analysis - An overview. *Operations Research, 30*, 803–838. https://doi.org/10.1287/opre.30.5.803

Keeney, R. L. (1988). Building models of values. *European Journal of Operational Research, 37br*, 149–157. https://doi.org/10.1016/0377-2217(88)90324-4

Keeney, R. L. (1992). *Value-focused thinking. A path to creative decision making*. Harvard University Press.

Keeney, R. L. (1996). Value-focused thinking: Identifying decision opportunities and creating alternatives. *European Journal of Operational Research, 92*, 537–549. https://doi.org/10.1016/0377-2217(96)00004-5

Keeney, R. L., & Gregory, R. S. (2005). Selecting attributes to measure the achievement of objectives. *Operations Research, 53*, 1–11. https://doi.org/10.1287/opre.1040.0158

Keeney, R. L., & Raiffa, H. (1976). *Decisions with Multiple Objectives: Preferences and Value Tradeoffs*. Wiley.

Keller, L. R., & Simon, J. (2019). Preference functions for spatial risk analysis. *Risk Analysis, 39*, 244–256. https://doi.org/10.1111/risa.12892

Kendall, M. G. (1938). A new measure of rank correlation. *Biometrika, 30*, 81–93. https://doi.org/10.2307/2332226

Kenis, P., & Schneider, V. (1991). Policy networks and policy analysis: Scrutinizing a new analytical toolbox. In: *Policy networks: Empirical evidence and theoretical considerations* (pp. 25–59). Campus Verlag.

Kerr, N. L., & Tindale, R. S. (2004). Group performance and decision making. *Annual Review of Psychology, 55*, 623–655. https://doi.org/10.1146/annurev.psych.55.090902.142009

Kilgour, D. M., & Eden, C. (Eds.). (2010). *Handbook of group decision and negotiation, Vol. 4. Advance in group decision and negotiation*. Springer. https://doi.org/10.1007/978-90-481-9097-3

Kugler, T., Kausel, E. E., & Kocher, M. G. (2012). Are groups more rational than individuals? A review of interactive decision making in groups. *Wiley Interdisciplinary Reviews: Cognitive Science, 3*, 471–482. https://doi.org/10.1002/wcs.1184

Kuller, M., Beutler, P., & Lienert, J. (2023). Preference change in stakeholder group-decision processes in the public sector: Extent, causes and implications. *European Journal of Operational Research, 308*(3), 1268–1285. https://doi.org/10.1016/j.ejor.2022.12.001

Kurth, M. H., Larkin, S., Keisler, J. M., & Linkov, I. (2017). Trends and applications of multicriteria decision analysis: Use in government agencies. *Environment Systems and Decisions, 37*, 134–143. https://doi.org/10.1007/s10669-017-9644-7

Lahdelma, R., & Salminen, P. (2001). SMAA-2: Stochastic multicriteria acceptability analysis for group decision making. *Operations Research, 49*, 444–454. https://doi.org/10.1287/opre.49.3.444.11220

Lahdelma, R., & Salminen, P. (2012). The shape of the utility or value function in stochastic multicriteria acceptability analysis. *OR Spectrum, 34*, 785–802. https://doi.org/10.1007/s00291-011-0244-5

Lahtinen, T. J., Hämäläinen, R. P., & Liesiö, J. (2017). Portfolio decision analysis methods in environmental decision making. *Environmental Modelling & Software, 94*, 73–86. https://doi.org/10.1016/j.envsoft.2017.04.001

Lambert, J. H., et al. (2012). Prioritizing infrastructure investments in Afghanistan with multiagency stakeholders and deep uncertainty of emergent conditions. *Journal of Infrastructure Systems, 18*, 155–166. https://doi.org/10.1061/(asce)is.1943-555x.0000078

Lami, I. M., & Tavella, E. (2019). On the usefulness of soft OR models in decision making: A comparison of Problem Structuring Methods supported and self-organized workshops. *European Journal of Operational Research, 275*, 1020–1036. https://doi.org/10.1016/j.ejor.2018.12.016

Langhans, S. D., & Lienert, J. (2016). Four common simplifications of multi-criteria decision analysis do not hold for river rehabilitation. *PLoS One, 11*, e0150695. https://doi.org/10.1371/journal.pone.0150695

Lichtenstein, S., & Slovic, P. (Eds.). (2006). *The Construction of Preference*. Cambridge University Press.

Lienert, J., Koller, M., Konrad, J., McArdell, C. S., & Schuwirth, N. (2011). Multiple-Criteria Decision Analysis reveals high stakeholder preference to remove pharmaceuticals from hospital wastewater. *Environmental Science and Technology, 45*, 3848–3857. https://doi.org/10.1021/es1031294

Lienert, J., Schnetzer, F., & Ingold, K. (2013). Stakeholder analysis combined with social network analysis provides fine-grained insights into water infrastructure planning processes. *Journal of Environmental Management, 125*, 134–148. https://doi.org/10.1016/j.jenvman.2013.03.052

Lienert, J., Scholten, L., Egger, C., & Maurer, M. (2015). Structured decision-making for sustainable water infrastructure planning and four future scenarios. *EURO Journal on Decision Processes, 3*, 107–140. https://doi.org/10.1007/s40070-014-0030-0

Lienert, J., Duygan, M., & Zheng, J. (2016). Preference stability over time with multiple elicitation methods to support wastewater infrastructure decision-making. *European Journal of Operational Research, 253*, 746–760. https://doi.org/10.1016/j.ejor.2016.03.010

Lienert, J., Andersson, J. C. M., Hofmann, D., Silva Pinto, F., & Kuller, M. (2022). The role of multi-criteria decision analysis in a transdisciplinary process: Co-developing a flood forecasting system in western Africa. *Hydrology and Earth System Sciences*. https://doi.org/10.5194/hess-26-2899-2022

Liesiö, J., Salo, A., Keisler, J. M., & Morton, A. (2021). Portfolio decision analysis: Recent developments and future prospects. *European Journal of Operational Research, 293*, 811–825. https://doi.org/10.1016/j.ejor.2020.12.015

Malczewski, J., & Jankowski, P. (2020). Emerging trends and research frontiers in spatial multicriteria analysis. *International Journal of Geographical Information Science, 34*, 1257–1282. https://doi.org/10.1080/13658816.2020.1712403

Marttunen, M., & Hämäläinen, R. P. (2008). The decision analysis interview approach in the collaborative management of a large regulated water course. *Environmental Management, 42*, 1026–1042. https://doi.org/10.1007/s00267-008-9200-9

Marttunen, M., Lienert, J., & Belton, V. (2017). Structuring problems for Multi-Criteria Decision Analysis in practice: A literature review of method combinations. *European Journal of Operational Research, 263*, 1–17. https://doi.org/10.1016/j.ejor.2017.04.041

Marttunen, M., Belton, V., & Lienert, J. (2018). Are objectives hierarchy related biases observed in practice? A meta-analysis of environmental and energy applications of Multi-Criteria Decision Analysis. *European Journal of Operational Research, 265*, 178–194. https://doi.org/10.1016/j.ejor.2017.02.038

Marttunen, M., Haag, F., Belton, V., Mustajoki, J., & Lienert, J. (2019a). Methods to inform the development of concise objectives hierarchies in multi-criteria decision analysis. *European Journal of Operational Research, 277*, 604–620. https://doi.org/10.1016/j.ejor.2019.02.039

Marttunen, M., Weber, C., Åberg, U., & Lienert, J. (2019b). Identifying relevant objectives in environmental management decisions: An application to a national monitoring program for river restoration. *Ecological Indicators, 101*, 851–866. https://doi.org/10.1016/j.ecolind.2018.11.042

Mata, R., Frey, R., Richter, D., Schupp, J., & Hertwig, R. (2018). Risk preference: A view from psychology. *Journal of Economic Perspectives, 32*, 155–172. https://doi.org/10.1257/jep.32.2.155

Menapace, L., Colson, G., & Raffaelli, R. (2016). A comparison of hypothetical risk attitude elicitation instruments for explaining farmer crop insurance purchases. *European Review of Agricultural Economics, 43*, 113–135. https://doi.org/10.1093/erae/jbv013

Mezirow, J. A. (2000). *Learning as transformation: Critical perspectives on a theory in progress. The Jossey-Bass Higher and Adult Education Series* (1st ed.). Jossey-Bass Publishers.

Midgley, G., Cavana, R. Y., Brocklesby, J., Foote, J. L., Wood, D. R. R., & Ahuriri-Driscoll, A. (2013). Towards a new framework for evaluating systemic problem structuring methods. *European Journal of Operational Research, 229*, 143–154. https://doi.org/10.1016/j.ejor.2013.01.047

Montibeller, G., & Belton, V. (2009). Qualitative operators for reasoning maps: Evaluating multi-criteria options with networks of reasons. *European Journal of Operational Research, 195*, 829–840. https://doi.org/10.1016/j.ejor.2007.11.015

Montibeller, G., & von Winterfeldt, D. (2015). Cognitive and motivational biases in decision and risk analysis. *Risk Analysis, 35*, 1230–1251. https://doi.org/10.1111/risa.12360

Montibeller, G., & von Winterfeldt, D. (2018). Individual and group biases in value and uncertainty judgments. In L. Dias, A. Morton, & J. Quigley (Eds.), *Elicitation, vol 261. International series in operations research and management science*. Springer. https://doi.org/10.1007/978-3-319-65052-4_15

Montibeller, G., Gummer, H., & Tumidei, D. (2006). Combining scenario planning and multi-criteria decision analysis in practice. *Journal of Multi-Criteria Decision Analysis, 14*, 5–20. https://doi.org/10.1002/mcda.403

Morton, A., & Fasolo, B. (2009). Behavioural decision theory for multi-criteria decision analysis: A guided tour. *Journal of the Operational Research Society, 60*, 268–275. https://doi.org/10.1057/palgrave.jors.2602550

Müller, M. O., Groesser, S. N., & Ulli-Beer, S. (2012). How do we know who to include in collaborative research? Toward a method for the identification of experts. *European Journal of Operational Research, 216*, 495–502. https://doi.org/10.1016/j.ejor.2011.07.014

Mustajoki, J., & Marttunen, M. (2017). Comparison of multi-criteria decision analytical software for supporting environmental planning processes. *Environmental Modelling and Software, 94*, 78–91. https://doi.org/10.1016/j.envsoft.2017.02.026

Mustajoki, J., Hämäläinen, R. P., & Lindstedt, M. R. K. (2006). Using intervals for global sensitivity and worst-case analyses in multiattribute value trees. *European Journal of Operational Research, 174*, 278–292. https://doi.org/10.1016/j.ejor.2005.02.070

O'Hagan, A. (2019). Expert knowledge elicitation: Subjective but scientific. *American Statistician, 73*, 69–81. https://doi.org/10.1080/00031305.2018.1518265

Parnell, G. S., & Trainor, T. E. (2014). Using the swing weight matrix to weight multiple objectives. Paper presented at the *19th annual international symposium of the international council on systems engineering, INCOSE 2009*, 20–23 July 2009.

Pedroni, A., Frey, R., Bruhin, A., Dutilh, G., Hertwig, R., & Rieskamp, J. (2017). The risk elicitation puzzle. *Nature Human Behaviour, 1*, 803–809. https://doi.org/10.1038/s41562-017-0219-x

Pluchinotta, I., Kazakci, A. O., Giordano, R., & Tsoukias, A. (2019). Design theory for generating alternatives in public decision making processes. *Group Decision and Negotiation, 28*, 341–375. https://doi.org/10.1007/s10726-018-09610-5

Pöyhönen, M., & Hämäläinen, R. P. (2001). On the convergence of multiattribute weighting methods. *European Journal of Operational Research, 129*, 569–585. https://doi.org/10.1016/s0377-2217(99)00467-1

Pöyhönen, M., Vrolijk, H., & Hämäläinen, R. P. (2001). Behavioral and procedural consequences of structural variation in value trees. *European Journal of Operational Research, 134*, 216–227. https://doi.org/10.1016/S0377-2217(00)00255-1

Quinn, B. (2008). The psychology of group decision making in collection development. *Library collections, Acquisitions, and Technical Services, 32*, 10–18. https://doi.org/10.1016/j.lcats.2008.05.001

Ram, C. (2020). Scenario presentation and scenario generation in multi-criteria assessments: An exploratory study. *Technological Forecasting and Social Change, 151*. https://doi.org/10.1016/j.techfore.2019.119850

Ram, C., & Montibeller, G. (2013). Exploring the impact of evaluating strategic options in a scenario-based multi-criteria framework. *Technological Forecasting and Social Change, 80*, 657–672. https://doi.org/10.1016/j.techfore.2012.09.019

Reed, M. S., et al. (2009). Who's in and why? A typology of stakeholder analysis methods for natural resource management. *Journal of Environmental Management, 90*, 1933–1949. https://doi.org/10.1016/j.jenvman.2009.01.001

Reichert, P., Langhans, S. D., Lienert, J., & Schuwirth, N. (2015). The conceptual foundation of environmental decision support. *Journal of Environmental Management, 154*, 316–332. https://doi.org/10.1016/j.jenvman.2015.01.053

Reichert, P., Niederberger, K., Rey, P., Helg, U., & Haertel-Borer, S. (2019). The need for unconventional value aggregation techniques: Experiences from eliciting stakeholder preferences in environmental management. *EURO Journal on Decision Processes, 7*, 197–219. https://doi.org/10.1007/s40070-019-00101-9

Riabacke, M., Danielson, M., & Ekenberg, L. (2012). State-of-the-art prescriptive criteria weight elicitation. *Adv. Decis. Sci., 2012*, 1–24. https://doi.org/10.1155/2012/276584

Rittel, H. W. J., & Webber, M. M. (1973). Dilemmas in a general theory of planning. *Policy Sciences, 4*, 155–169. https://doi.org/10.1007/bf01405730

Rosenhead, J., & Mingers, J. (2001). *Rational analysis for a problematic world revisited: Problem structuring methods for complexity, uncertainty and conflict* (2nd ed.). Wiley.

Rowley, H. V., Peters, G. M., Lundie, S., & Moore, S. J. (2012). Aggregating sustainability indicators: Beyond the weighted sum. *Journal of Environmental Management, 111*, 24–33. https://doi.org/10.1016/j.jenvman.2012.05.004

Roy, B., & Bouyssou, D. (1993). *Aide multicritère à la décision: Méthodes et cas*. LAMSADE: Publications edn. London School of Economics and Political Science, Paris, London.

Roy, B., & Słowiński, R. (2013). Questions guiding the choice of a multicriteria decision aiding method. *EURO Journal on Decision Processes, 1*, 69–97. https://doi.org/10.1007/s40070-013-0004-7

Saaty, T. L. (1990). How to make a decision - The analytic hierarchy process. *European Journal of Operational Research, 48*, 9–26. https://doi.org/10.1016/0377-2217(90)90057-i

Saltelli, A., et al. (2008). *Global sensitivity analysis: The primer*. Wiley.

Scholten, L., Schuwirth, N., Reichert, P., & Lienert, J. (2015). Tackling uncertainty in multi-criteria decision analysis - An application to water supply infrastructure planning. *European Journal of Operational Research, 242*, 243–260. https://doi.org/10.1016/j.ejor.2014.09.044

Scholten, L., Maurer, M., & Lienert, J. (2017). Comparing multi-criteria decision analysis and integrated assessment to support long-term water supply planning. *PLoS One, 12*. https://doi.org/10.1371/journal.pone.0176663

Schuwirth, N., Reichert, P., & Lienert, J. (2012). Methodological aspects of multi-criteria decision analysis for policy support: A case study on pharmaceutical removal from hospital wastewater. *European Journal of Operational Research, 220*, 472–483. https://doi.org/10.1016/j.ejor.2012.01.055

Siebert, J., & Keeney, R. L. (2015). Creating more and better alternatives for decisions using objectives. *Operations Research, 63*, 1144–1158. https://doi.org/10.1287/opre.2015.1411

Simon, J. (2020). Weight approximation for spatial outcomes. *Sustainability, 12*. https://doi.org/10.3390/su12145588

Simon, J., Kirkwood, C. W., & Keller, L. R. (2014). Decision analysis with geographically varying outcomes: Preference models and illustrative applications. *Operations Research, 62*, 182–194. https://doi.org/10.1287/opre.2013.1217

Slovic, P., Finucane, M. L., Peters, E., & MacGregor, D. G. (2007). The affect heuristic. *European Journal of Operational Research, 177*, 1333–1352. https://doi.org/10.1016/j.ejor.2005.04.006

Smit, H., & Trigeorgis, L. (2004). *Strategic investment: Real options and games*. Princeton University Press.

Stewart, T. J., French, S., & Rios, J. (2013). Integrating multicriteria decision analysis and scenario planning – Review and extension. *Omega - International Journal of Management Science, 41*, 679–688. https://doi.org/10.1016/j.omega.2012.09.003

Tervonen, T., & Figueira, J. R. (2008). A survey on stochastic multicriteria acceptability analysis methods. *Journal of Multi-Criteria Decision Analysis, 15*, 1–14. https://doi.org/10.1002/mcda.407

Tetlock, P. E. (2003). Thinking the unthinkable: Sacred values and taboo cognitions. *Trends in Cognitive Sciences, 7*, 320–324. https://doi.org/10.1016/s1364-6613(03)00135-9

Trutnevyte, E., Stauffacher, M., & Scholz, R. W. (2012). Linking stakeholder visions with resource allocation scenarios and multi-criteria assessment. *European Journal of Operational Research, 219*, 762–772. https://doi.org/10.1016/j.ejor.2012.01.009

Tversky, A., & Kahneman, D. (1974). Judgment under uncertainty - Heuristics and biases. *Science, 185*, 1124–1131.

van Aken, J., Chandrasekaran, A., & Halman, J. (2016). Conducting and publishing design science research: Inaugural essay of the design science department of the Journal of Operations Management. *Journal of Operations Management, 47–48*, 1–8. https://doi.org/10.1016/j.jom.2016.06.004

Voinov, A., et al. (2016). Modelling with stakeholders – Next generation. *Environmental Modelling and Software, 77*, 196–220. https://doi.org/10.1016/j.envsoft.2015.11.016

von Nitzsch, R., & Weber, M. (1993). The effect of attribute ranges on weights in multiattribute utility measurements. *Management Science, 39*, 937–943. https://doi.org/10.1287/mnsc.39.8.937

Walling, E., & Vaneeckhaute, C. (2020). Developing successful environmental decision support systems: Challenges and best practices. *Journal of Environmental Management, 264*. https://doi.org/10.1016/j.jenvman.2020.110513

Warren, C., McGraw, A. P., & Van Boven, L. (2011). Values and preferences: Defining preference construction. *Wiley Interdisciplinary Reviews: Cognitive Science, 2*, 193–205. https://doi.org/10.1002/wcs.98

Weber, M., Eisenführ, F., & von Winterfeldt, D. (1988). The effects of splitting attributes on weights in multiattribute utility measurement. *Management Science, 34*, 431–445. https://doi.org/10.1287/mnsc.34.4.431

Weber, E. U., Blais, A.-R., & Betz, N. E. (2002). A domain-specific risk-attitude scale: Measuring risk perceptions and risk behaviors. *Journal of Behavioral Decision Making, 15*, 263–290. https://doi.org/10.1002/bdm.414

White, L. (2006). Evaluating problem-structuring methods: Developing an approach to show the value and effectiveness of PSMs. *Journal of the Operational Research Society, 57*, 842–855. https://doi.org/10.1057/palgrave.jors.2602149

White, L., & Bourne, H. (2007). Voices and values: Linking values with participation in OR/MS in public policy making. *Omega, 35*, 588–603. https://doi.org/10.1016/j.omega.2005.11.002

Witt, T., Dumeier, M., & Geldermann, J. (2020). Combining scenario planning, energy system analysis, and multi-criteria analysis to develop and evaluate energy scenarios. *Journal of Cleaner Production, 242*. https://doi.org/10.1016/j.jclepro.2019.118414

Wright, G., Cairns, G., & Goodwin, P. (2009). Teaching scenario planning: Lessons from practice in academe and business. *European Journal of Operational Research, 194*, 323–335. https://doi.org/10.1016/j.ejor.2007.12.003

Wright, G., Cairns, G., O'Brien, F. A., & Goodwin, P. (2019). Scenario analysis to support decision making in addressing wicked problems: Pitfalls and potential. *European Journal of Operational Research, 278*, 3–19. https://doi.org/10.1016/j.ejor.2018.08.035

Wulf, D., & Bertsch, V. (2017). A natural language generation approach to support understanding and traceability of multi-dimensional preferential sensitivity analysis in multi-criteria decision making. *Expert Systems with Applications, 83*, 131–144. https://doi.org/10.1016/j.eswa.2017.04.041

Yearworth, M., & White, L. (2014). The non-codified use of problem structuring methods and the need for a generic constitutive definition. *European Journal of Operational Research, 237*, 932–945. https://doi.org/10.1016/j.ejor.2014.02.015

Zheng, J., & Lienert, J. (2018). Stakeholder interviews with two MAVT preference elicitation philosophies in a Swiss water infrastructure decision: Aggregation using SWING-weighting and disaggregation using UTAGMS. *European Journal of Operational Research, 267*, 273–287. https://doi.org/10.1016/j.ejor.2017.11.018

Zheng, J., Egger, C., & Lienert, J. (2016). A scenario-based MCDA framework for wastewater infrastructure planning under uncertainty. *Journal of Environmental Management, 183*(Part 3), 895–908. https://doi.org/10.1016/j.jenvman.2016.09.027

Team Decision Making

Martin G. Kocher, Matthias Praxmarer, and Matthias Sutter

Abstract This chapter analyzes the role of teams in organizations and their potential for increasing productivity and profitability. In economics, the decision-maker is usually modeled as an individual, but most organizational and managerial decisions are taken at a team level, e.g. by committees, boards of directors, and work teams. In the past two decades, behavioral and experimental economics made substantial progress in documenting and understanding basic differences in decisions taken by individuals and teams. The bulk of this literature, in the tradition of social psychology, is based on laboratory studies, where differences in decisions by individuals and teams can be studied in a tightly controlled environment. This chapter reviews the literature on decisions in the context of uncertainty and time preferences, social preferences including bargaining and cooperation, in complex environments that require learning, and in moral dilemmas. In addition, this review discusses the important role of self-selection into teams and its potential consequences. Finally, the survey covers relevant field experiments that complement the

M. G. Kocher
Institute for Advanced Studies Vienna, Vienna, Austria

University of Vienna, Wien, Austria

University of Gothenburg, Göteborg, Sweden
e-mail: kocher@ihs.ac.at

M. Praxmarer
Max-Planck-Institute for Research on Collective Goods, Bonn, Germany
e-mail: praxmarer@coll.mpg.de

M. Sutter (✉)
Max-Planck-Institute for Research on Collective Goods, Bonn, Germany

University of Cologne, Cologne, Germany

University of Innsbruck, Innsbruck, Austria
e-mail: Matthias.Sutter@coll.mpg.de

F. M. Federspiel et al. (eds.), *Behavioral Decision Analysis*, International Series in Operations Research & Management Science 350,
https://doi.org/10.1007/978-3-031-44424-1_13

literature on decision-making by looking at how team-based incentive schemes influence productivity and output.

Keywords Uncertainty preferences · Intertemporal preferences · Social preferences · Complexity and learning · Morality and ethics · Self-selection · Incentives

Introduction

The answer to the question of how to structure and organize work within organizations and institutions is key to achieve efficiency. Deloitte's (2016) "Global Human Capital Trends" has ranked the organizational shift towards more teamwork, i.e. the "rise of teams", as the most important trend in human resources in 2016. Such a shift is based on the general assumption that teamwork is a potential success factor in modern organizations (e.g., Osterman, 1995; Lazear & Shaw, 2007; Bandiera et al., 2013), i.e. the benefits of teamwork outweighs its cost. Such presumptions raise the question of what makes teams different from individuals. Apart from analyzing information exchange in teams and synergies in production technologies, it calls for an examination of how teams make decisions—how they aggregate preferences and how they interact with other decision-makers. Over the past 20 years, behavioral and experimental economics has made considerable progress in understanding team decision-making and resulting differences in decisions taken by individuals and by teams. While in 2003, Colin Camerer (2003) listed a further inquiry into team decision-making as one of the top 10 open research questions in behavioral economics, today our profession has a much more improved understanding of the topic. This chapter summarizes the main insights from the past 20 years. This review uses the term "team" throughout, but some of the decision environments implemented in studies discussed below would rather fit the term "group". The difference in terminology is less important for economic analyses.

Naturally, a handbook chapter has to focus on a limited set of aspects. This survey concentrates mainly on unitary teams, i.e. on teams where members have to come up with a joint decision and face no internal conflicts of interest in terms of monetary payoffs. In such a setup, standard economic theory would often not predict any difference between an individual decision and the outcome of a team decision. However, if preferences of team members are heterogeneous, their aggregation might shift team decisions away from a simple average or median, once team members can interact, where all interaction formats from a simple voting mechanism to fact-to-face discussion have been addressed in the scholarly literature. In the following, this chapter reviews decision-making situations that involve uncertainty and time preferences, social preferences, including bargaining and cooperation, learning in complex environments, and moral aspects. The existing evidence on these topics is mainly based on laboratory studies that allow for a controlled comparison of individual and team decision-making [for previous surveys see Charness and Sutter (2012) and Kugler et al. (2012)].

Given the literature's focus on unitary teams so far, there is little experimental work in economics on team decision-making when team members face conflicts in terms of payoffs. Therefore, the last two sub-sections relax the restriction to unitary teams, because it seems to be relevant to include this emerging literature, as the setup is considered as a promising starting point for future research. To this end, this chapter concludes with sub-sections on self-selection into, i.e., adverse selection in, team environments, and on field experiments on how individual decision-making is affected when individual decisions have consequences for a team's outcome. The literature refers to payoff commonalities in this case (Charness et al., 2007), although individuals do not make a joint decision. This review discusses the case of payoff commonalities because it illustrates how individual behavior is affected by the prospect of a joint outcome, which complements the traditional case of team decision-making as the study of joint decisions.

Team vs. Individual Decision-Making

Uncertainty and Time Preferences

In the context of organizations, the majority of relevant decisions—be it investment decisions or more general managerial decisions—involve uncertainty and a time dimension. Hence, it is important to understand how individuals and teams decide in these contexts and whether there are differences in outcomes.

Uncertainty Preferences

Uncertainty involves situations in which decision-makers can assign probabilities to states of the world (risk) and cases in which probabilities cannot be assigned (ambiguity). Social and cognitive psychology has had a long-standing interest in investigating risk-taking decisions of individuals alone or as part of a team. In a seminal study, Stoner (1961) observes a risky shift when moving from individual to team decision-making. However, subsequent work in psychology has failed to establish a clear pattern of how teams behave in risky decisions compared to individuals (Kerr et al., 1996).

In economics, one of the first experiments comparing revealed risk attitudes of individuals and teams—here a team of three individuals—is Baker et al. (2008). They use a Holt and Laury Multiple-Price-List (MPL)-setup (e.g., Holt & Laury, 2002), where decision-makers have to decide in ten situations between a relatively safe lottery (with a small payoff difference between the two possible outcomes) and a risky lottery (with a larger payoff difference), with a chance to receive the higher payment ranging from 10% to 100%. Team members discuss face-to-face to reach unanimous decisions for each of the ten situations. The design includes both a between-subjects condition (subjects participate either in the individual or in the team task) and a within-subjects condition, where participants first decide individually, then as a member of a team, and finally individually again. The between-subjects design reveals that team decisions do not differ significantly from individual decisions in terms of risk attitudes; yet, teams make more choices in line with risk neutrality in lotteries with a relatively low or high chance to win the higher payoff. The within-subjects design highlights that teams of three make, on average, less risky choices and that team participation has spillover effects on individual decision-making in a subsequent individual task involving risk.

Masclet et al. (2009) use a similar Holt-Laury setup in a between-subjects design with students, salaried and self-employed workers. The focus of the study is on comparing risk-taking between individuals and three-person teams. The authors implement unanimity voting as the decision-making mechanism within the team. It turns out that teams of three choose the safe lottery significantly more often whenever the likelihood of winning the high amount is relatively low. Interestingly, an individual's occupation is correlated with her risk attitude, with self-employed workers being less risk averse than salaried workers. Moreover, the voting procedure allows assessing team decisions: relatively risk-averse subjects are less likely to change their mind in the team interaction, whereas less risk-averse subjects are the ones who give up their first preference more often. Harrison et al. (2013) investigate whether the knowledge on team members' risk attitudes matters. They show that without the knowledge of a teammate's risk attitude, subjects do not display different risk preferences in the team setting, while the common knowledge of other teammates' risk attitudes leads to more risk-averse choices.

Apart from the frequently used MPL-choices, there exist other simple methods to elicit risk attitudes. For instance, Shupp and Williams (2007) ask decision-makers to state their valuations for a given set of lotteries, involving a payment of either \$20 (\$60 in the team condition) or nothing and a variation in the likelihood of winning between 10% and 90% in steps of 10-percentage points. They find a smaller variance of risk preferences in teams and that teams are more (less) risk averse in high- (low-) risk situations than individuals. In terms of expected utility theory (EUT) neither Bone et al. (1999) nor Rockenbach et al. (2007) find a difference in choice consistency between individuals and teams, but Rockenbach et al. (2007) show that teams are more consistent with portfolio selection theory than individuals, which means that teams accumulate more expected value at a lower risk than individuals.

Time Preferences

Time preferences—measuring the tradeoff between a smaller, but earlier, and a larger, but later (monetary) reward—are another important dimension that is relevant in many organizational decisions. One of the first economic papers investigating differences in intertemporal decision-making between individuals and teams is Shapiro (2010). In the experiment, the author compares individual decision-making with joint decision-making in pairs and teams of four participants. The decision-making environment allows calculating a discount factor of the decisions-maker, and it varies the delay of the earlier payment by making it available either immediately or with an up-front delay, which allows assessing potential differences in time consistency and in discounting models. The data show that individuals and pairs do not differ significantly in their choices, but teams of four are significantly more patient than individuals, and team decisions seem to be less prone to time inconsistencies.

Denant-Boemont et al. (2017) elicit time preferences of individuals and teams of five in a within-subject design by using communication about the majority voting decision as a coordination mechanism. Similar to the findings of Shapiro (2010), the authors conclude that decisions taken at the team level are relatively more patient and more frequently time-consistent than individual choices.

Moving away from the usual paradigm in which team composition is determined randomly among (university) student participants, Carlsson et al. (2012) look at intertemporal decisions of real-life couples. After deciding at the individual level, wives and husbands take decisions together as a couple. The "team" decisions tend to be a compromise of the individual decisions, but they reflect more the wives' preferences when wives contribute more to the total household income. Focusing on the time preferences of married couples in Kenya, Schaner (2015) finds that the more heterogeneous the time preferences in a couple are, the more inefficient the savings decisions. The author elicits individual discount factors and gives both spouses the opportunity to open either several different individual savings accounts or a joint account. These accounts earn random interest rates, and thus it is possible to examine whether subjects put their money in dominated (with respect to interest rates) accounts. Spouses with more "heterogeneous" discount factors use dominated savings accounts much more often than spouses with more "homogeneous" discount factors.

Heterogeneity in discount factors seems to be particularly relevant for team decision-making in an organizational context, because team members might have different returns with respect to time due to, e.g., compensation schemes, seniority in the company/committee, and age among others. Therefore, Glätzle-Rützler et al. (2019) look at how differences in incentives to wait for higher payoffs in the future affect decisions, i.e., if and how differences in team members' incentive to wait affect the team choice and how this compares to individual decision-making. In the first part, all subjects complete a choice list with twenty binary choices to choose an immediate or a later payment. In the second part, subjects complete the same choice list in one of the following conditions. The authors implement four conditions, (i) an individual condition (same as in the first part), (ii) a team condition where all three team members have homogenous incentives to wait, (iii) a team condition where two out of the three members have higher incentives to wait than the other member, and (iv) a team condition where two out of the three members have lower incentives to wait than the other member. Team members must agree on whether to take the sooner payment or the later one (where the later one is much more favorable to some team members than others, while the earlier one is always identical for all team members). The comparison of individuals and teams with homogenous incentives to wait shows that teams are marginally more patient than individuals. Team decision-making with teams including at least one team member with higher incentives to wait leads to significantly more patient choices than individual decision-making.

This sub-section delivers the following insights: The studies on differences between individual and team decision-making with respect to decisions under uncertainty provide inconclusive evidence. Differences in the results of these studies could be rooted, for instance, in the elicitation method that was applied, differences in the team size, and differences in the team decision rules (unanimity versus majority). The majority of the results on time preferences suggest that team decision-making leads to more patient and time-consistent choices. Interestingly, heterogeneity in time preferences shifts decision-making towards the preferences of members with higher incentives to be patient.

Social Differences

The previous sub-section discussed differences in individual and team decision-making when decisions affect only the outcome for the relevant decision-maker, either individual or team. This sub-section focuses on decisions that do not only affect the monetary outcome of the decision-maker, but also the monetary outcome of others, i.e., other individuals or teams. The tradeoff between own and others' payoff is important in non-strategic situations, i.e., allocation decisions, as well as in strategic interactions such as bargaining and cooperation games.

Non-strategic Situations

The most prominent economic allocation task to study social preferences in a non-strategic environment is the so-called "dictator game". The standard version of this game involves two parties, i.e., a decision-maker who receives a certain monetary endowment and a recipient. In an anonymous setting, the decision-maker—the dictator—has to decide how to allocate her endowment between herself and the recipient. The money transferred to the recipient serves as a measure of a decision-maker's other-regarding preferences. As the recipient has no power in this situation, the standard solution based on money-maximizing decision-makers is to keep the whole endowment and give nothing to the recipient. However, a well-established finding in the economics literature is that people care about others and therefore deviate from this prediction and give a substantial fraction of the endowment to recipients (see, e.g., Engel, 2011 for a meta analysis).

The first experimental study that compares decisions of individuals and teams in a dictator game is by Cason and Mui (1997). In their design, subjects participate in an individual and in a team decision; in the latter, pairs are in the roles of dictators and recipients. In the aggregate, there are no significant differences in giving behavior of teams and individuals. Interestingly, team dictator giving is dominated by the more other-regarding team member.

Building on the findings of Cason and Mui (1997), Luhan et al. (2009) investigate team decisions in a slightly modified version. In the control condition, participants take the dictator decision individually for three times, while in the treatment condition subjects first make an individual decision, then a team decision in teams of three, and then an individual decision again. They show that teams send significantly smaller transfers—about 40% less—to recipients than individuals. The different findings in Cason and Mui (1997) and Luhan et al. (2009) could be, among other aspects, due to different team sizes, different communication mechanisms, and the anonymity of subjects. While Luhan et al. (2009) ensure complete anonymity among participants by implementing a real-time chat on the screen for team interaction, Cason and Mui (1997) ask team members to come to the front of the room to take the decision—a procedure that identifies team members. Kittel and Luhan (2013) highlight the importance of communication as a mean of coordination in a modified team dictator game with five individuals in each team. In this game, a team of five dictators have to allocate 50 Euros between themselves and a group of five anonymous receivers. A team dictator decision gets implemented when a majority agrees on implementing a certain allocation. If no agreement is reached, the dictators receive nothing and the recipients get an outside payment drawn from the distribution of all possible payments. In a baseline treatment, the five team members choose an amount individually, but have no means to coordinate their choices. If no majority is reached, team members can choose a second time without any information regarding the previous preferences within the team. The baseline treatment is contrasted to two conditions with a network structure (either star or circle) in which a team member's choice is revealed to connected members (who form a link in the network). Again, if there is no majority reached on the first attempt, team members can make a second proposal; yet this time they are informed about linked members' preferences in the first attempt. It turns out that this form of communication has a strong impact on team decisions. When information is revealed among linked members, teams reach a majority decision much more often. Moreover, team transfers in the network conditions are significantly lower than in the baseline condition, indicating that information flow within teams gears decisions towards more selfish actions (similar to the results in Luhan et al., 2009).

Strategic Situations

In the "ultimatum game" (Güth et al., 1982), best characterized by its take-it-or-leave-it property, a proposer has to decide about the distribution of a known endowment between herself and a recipient. The recipient (or responder) has the choice to accept the offer made by the decision-maker in order to implement it or to reject it so that both players receive nothing. Assuming payoff-maximization and common knowledge of rationality, the responder prefers any positive amount over nothing, for which reason the proposer offers the smallest possible positive amount, which gets accepted.

However, experimental evidence shows that this subgame perfect equilibrium is not a good predictor for individual behavior. Examining team decision-making, Bornstein and Yaniv (1998) find that teams of three (as proposers and responders) offer significantly less than individuals in the role of proposers, and teams are also willing to accept lower offers. Despite lower offers, teams reject as often as individuals (yet the number of observations is too small to draw robust conclusions on responder behavior). The strategic environment of senders does not allow for a "clean" inference on (advantageous) inequality aversion of teams and individuals in this role (the literature shows that teams send less than individuals in the ultimatum game, but this is also true in a non-strategic environment such as the dictator game), but teams seem to be less prone to disadvantageous inequality aversion as responders. Even though teams receive lower offers than individuals, teams implement the "disadvantageous" (for them), but at the same time more efficient allocations as often as individuals. Robert and Carnevale (1997) observe lower offers in a team-on-team ultimatum game driven by the strong influence of the most competitive team member, and Elbittar et al. (2011) show—even with restricted communication and different voting mechanisms to reach a team decision—similar results. Bradfield and Kagel (2015) find that two-person teams are closer to the standard game-theoretic benchmark than individuals. In their design, a legislative bargaining setting, three decision-makers (either individuals or pairs) bargain over the allocation of US$ 30. The authors argue that teams are more "rational" than individuals because their decisions are more sophisticated, rather than selfish or aggressive.

A further game that models a bargaining situation involves trust as its key aspect; hence it is commonly referred to as the "trust game" or "investment game" (Berg et al., 1995). This sequential game involves a first mover—called the trustor—and a second mover—called the trustee. Initially, the trustor receives an endowment and has to decide how much of this endowment she wants to invest in the trustee. The money the trustor sends to the trustee gets multiplied, usually by a factor of three. Thus, the amount the trustee receives is threefold the amount the trustor sent. Then, the trustee decides how much she wants to send back to the trustor (back-transfers are not tripled). Anticipating that the trustee (under standard assumptions) has no incentive to send any positive amount back to the trustor, the trustor initially has no incentive to send anything of her endowment to the trustee. The subgame perfect equilibrium solution entails an efficiency loss, since the multiplication of the transfer is forgone.

Kugler et al. (2007) find that three-person teams invest 20% less than individuals, i.e., teams are less trusting than individuals, but both individuals and teams return similar amounts, i.e., teams are not significantly different from individuals in their trustworthiness. The less trusting behavior by teams compared to individuals could be explained by a median voter approach in a model that accounts for inequality aversion, because senders infer that it is less likely to receive a positive amount when the responder is a team than an individual. However, the data shows that team responders are not significantly different from individual responders. Cox (2002) finds that team trustees send back significantly less, and Song (2009) finds that "representatives" (who make decisions on behalf of her 3-person team) invest 20% less as trustors, and return about 40% less as trustees than individual decision-makers who affect only their own outcome.

In a repeated version of the trust game known as the "centipede game", two decision-makers alternate over a finite number of rounds. They can stop the game at each of the decision nodes that they are active at and implement a certain allocation (with the higher payoff for the decision-maker who stops the game at a given node) or let the other player decide at the next node. The trade-off in this bargaining situation implies that the amount at stake increases over the rounds (in the standard increasing-sum centipede game), but that at the same time the negative consequences in relative payoffs become larger when the other player stops the game. The solution via backward induction predicts that the game stops at the initial node, which implies a huge welfare loss. Bornstein et al. (2004) provide evidence that teams stop the game significantly earlier than individuals.

In another bargaining game with a principal-agent setting called the "gift exchange-game", a principal first decides about the wage she offers to the agent, and then the agent, who knows the wage, chooses her costly effort level, which determines the profit of the principal, with a convex cost-effort function. The game captures a situation with incomplete contracts. Backward induction with standard assumptions predicts that the principal anticipates that the agent has no incentive to exert any effort other than the minimal effort due to the unconditional characteristic of the wage transfer; hence the principal chooses the lowest wage possible. The seminal paper by Fehr et al. (1993) shows that individuals significantly deviate from equilibrium play by offering high wage levels that are met with high levels of effort. Kocher and Sutter (2007) compare individuals in both roles and three-person teams in both roles who either communicate face-to-face within their teams or in a restricted and computerized way (a voting mechanism). Computerized decision-making in teams leads to lower wage offers than under individual play (face-to-face communication leads to results comparable to individual play), while in the role of agents, computerized communication in teams leads to similar effort levels as in individuals. Interestingly, face-to-face communication leads to significantly higher effort of teams compared to individual play. Another feature of the different team decision-making treatments of this experiment is that they give access to the black box of decision-making in unitary teams and document relevant insights on the importance of procedures for decision outcomes (e.g., communication: restricted and computerized compared to face-to-face discussions).

Cooperation

Findings from social psychology suggest that teams are less cooperative than individuals (see, for instance, the survey by Wildschut & Insko, 2007). In the psychology literature this is known as the discontinuity effect, and it describes the more competitive and selfish behavior of teams compared to individuals in social dilemmas. It is important to add that most of the relevant studies in social psychology not only allow within-team communication, but also across-team communication before team decisions.

In the economics literature, research on if and how teams and individuals differ in terms of cooperative behavior is relatively scarce and recent. Among the first studies on this topic is a paper by Kagel and McGee (2016) on individual versus team behavior in a finitely repeated prisoner's dilemma game. The authors implement a design with seven to ten super-games with ten rounds each. In each round agents can choose between cooperation and defection, with defection as the dominant strategy. Agents are either individuals or pairs, and individuals play with individuals and teams with teams. Members of a team can communicate with each other within the team about the team strategy. The results of the first super-game are consistent with the findings from psychology: Kagel and McGee (2016) observe a discontinuity effect in teams. However, in the subsequent super-games the data show the same or even higher cooperation rates in teams than in individuals. This shift is mainly motivated by taking some risk to increase payoffs. Teams expect opponents to realize the gains from cooperation as well and that opponents would reciprocate. Important differences between this paper and the psychology literature are that this experiment includes more than one super-game and that psychology uses a fixed matching with a single partner, while this paper uses repeated matching with different partners; hence, it becomes easier to restart cooperation. Yet, teams still anticipate the end-game effect, and this leads teams to choose the dominant strategy more often than individuals in the last super-game.

Cason and Mui (2019) implement a Prisoner's Dilemma (PD) with super-games as well, but they add uncertainty such that with a likelihood of 12.5% an action taken is switched to the other option. In three parts, they compare individuals and three-person teams. In the different parts, decision-makers either respond directly (round-by-round action choice) or choose plans (an extensive list of repeated game strategies). The main finding is that teams and individuals cooperate at similar levels. However, teams use tit-for-tat and forgiveness strategies more often than individuals, but always-defect is still the most popular strategy for both types of agents.

In a public goods experiment where people decide between how much of an endowment they want to contribute to a team account (that leads to socially optimal outcomes, i.e. is efficient) or leave in the private account (individually optimal),

Auerswald et al. (2018) examine individuals and three-person teams with and without the possibility to punish peers. First, all participants play a one-shot public goods game without feedback, and then a ten-period public goods game with or without punishment possibility in one of three conditions (individually, teams with majority rule, and teams with unanimity rule). In the absence of a punishment tool, unanimity teams cooperate significantly more than in both other conditions. With a punishment option, cooperation levels are not significantly different from each other across the three conditions, but teams with unanimity punish significantly less, i.e., unanimity eliminates extreme punishment behavior, which might be counterproductive in the given setup.

Inter-Group Competition

As elaborated above, the success of team work depends on the team members' willingness to cooperate. The presented evidence does not support the conclusion that teams are systematically different from individuals when it comes to make cooperative choices. However, solving the free-rider problem in situations where private and collective interests collide—i.e., people might rather choose to be selfish than to contribute to the socially optimal output—remains an important question. A potential mechanism to reduce free-riding in teams is to implement competition between teams as, for instance, Erev et al. (1993) show. In this field study with a within-subjects design, a team of four orange pickers work for (i) an individual reward, (ii) a team reward where all members receive a quarter of the reward, or (iii) an inter-group competition reward where the four subjects are divided into pairs and the more productive pair receives a bonus. Results show that competition between pairs within a team could alleviate (or eliminate) the productivity loss of the team reward (that originates from free-riding behavior of team members); an individual reward could not. In addition, the experiment provides evidence that this type of competition is more effective the more similar the competing teams are (in terms of ability).

A rather different view on competition between teams is revealed by Abbink et al. (2010). They look at individual and team behavior in repeated Tullock rent-seeking contests. In each round, two parties compete for a prize by buying lottery tickets. The likelihood of winning a round is determined by the amount of bought tickets by a party divided by the total amount of bought tickets by both parties. At the beginning of each round, each participant decides how much she wants to invest in the "conflict" (for herself or as part of a team) and how much she wants to keep for herself. The relevant treatments here are those where the authors vary the number of people per party (individuals and teams with four members), the nature of the competing parties (individuals vs. individuals, individuals vs. teams, and teams vs. teams), and the availability of costly (free-rider) peer punishment. Both individuals and teams invest more than prescribed in equilibrium, but team investments are substantially more inefficient. This is not driven by the nature of the competing party (individual or team). The availability of punishment in teams increases this inefficiency.

To sum up, in simple bargaining situations, teams seem to take decisions that are closer to standard theoretic equilibria, implying that their decisions are both more selfish and more rational than individual decisions. Interestingly, there seems to be at least some evidence that this conclusion depends on whether an efficiency gain is possible or not. In contrast to the findings associated with the discontinuity effect in social psychology, there are results in economics based on games with a substantial potential efficiency gain that find teams to be less selfish, i.e. more cooperative. However, the influence of efficiency on the discontinuity between individuals and teams seems to be context-specific, as well as the success of introducing competition between teams.

Complex Decision Environments and Learning

Demanding environments require decision-makers to understand new and complex situations rather fast, to use synergies in problem-solving, to think through problems from opposite perspectives, and, of course, to exhibit a steep learning curve when dealing with similar problems repeatedly.

A natural starting point is coordination in situations with multiple equilibria. Obviously, coordinating on an action or strategy is an important characteristic of a successful organization. Thus, understanding the coordination ability of individuals and teams seems relevant. In their experiment, Feri et al. (2010) aim to understand if and how individuals and teams differ in their coordination abilities by implementing six different coordination games (two weakest-link games and four average-opinion games). In their design, five decision-makers, either five individuals or five three-person teams, play the coordination games. The authors show that teams outperform individuals in terms of payoffs by earning about 20% more, that teams suffer less from mis-coordination, and that they settle more quickly in equilibrium, i.e., teams reach equilibrium more quickly and then repeat playing it more often than individuals. The data suggest that team behavior is much more strongly driven by payoff considerations. Moreover, teams learn differently than individuals. While individuals show typical patterns of reinforcement learning (where only taken actions are used to update probabilities of playing a particular action), team learning is better described by fictitious play (meaning that also unchosen strategies and their potential outcomes are used to update the probabilities for particular actions).

Another field of application is markets. Cheung and Palan (2012) provide data from a double-auction market which is intended to capture important aspects of a stock market. In their experimental asset market either individuals or two-person teams (the two team members sit next to each other) participate as traders. The data highlight that team traders are less likely to generate bubbles than individual traders, i.e., markets with teams instead of individual traders exhibit lower levels of mispricing. The precise mechanism driving the results in this direction remains an open question in this experiment, mainly because of the face-to-face communication of participants (i.e., missing chat protocols). On the one hand, team decision-making might simply eliminate, on average, extreme choices in buying behavior, i.e., team decision-making attenuates errors in the assessment of a stock's fundamental value. On the other hand, results could be driven by the fact that traders assume that other traders are less likely to engage in bubble-building (buying the good at a too high price) when the other traders are teams rather than individuals.

Moving away from a double-auction format, Cox and Hayne (2006) compare individual and team bidding in a sealed-bid common value auction, where bidders receive signals on the good's value. As long as all team members receive the same information, the team decisions outperform individual bidding (with respect to earnings and the likelihood of avoiding the winner's curse). However, when different team members receive different signals that would need to be shared in order to make the most out of them, teams do not outperform individual bidding. In a combination of a private and a common value auction format, Sutter et al. (2009) observe that three-person teams are more likely to overbid and thus experience the winner's curse more often than individuals due to a competitive shift from individual to team decision-making.

Casari et al. (2016) compare individuals and teams of size three in a game called "aquiring a company task". In this setting, bidders make a take-it-or-leave-it offer to a robot seller, and the seller accepts the offer only if it is at least as high as the value of the company. In an easy (difficult) version, the company's value could take on five (one-hundred) different values. In the within-subjects design, subjects first bid individually for six rounds and then individually or as a team member for twenty rounds. The authors provide evidence that teams outperform individuals in the easy version, but the result is the exact opposite in the difficult version. The mechanism that drives the result is that most teams solve a disagreement by choosing the median bid within the team. Taking into account that most participants are able to solve the easy version, but not the difficult one, can explain the, at first sight, contradictory result. Similar to the findings in Casari et al.'s (2016) easy version, Sheremeta and Zhang (2010) report that pairs place lower bids in a repeated (30 rounds) Tullock contest than individuals and that this is driven by making "better" decisions over time due to communication and learning within the team.

As learning is, more generally, an important feature of success in repeated interactions, it is important to discuss if and how teams could facilitate learning in new and complex environments with and without strategic components. Without strategic components, Slembeck and Tyran (2004) and Maciejovsky et al. (2013) examine behavior in the so-called Monty-Hall-problem. In this decision task, a decision-maker faces three doors. Behind one door is a prize, while behind both other doors there are blanks. First, the decision-maker chooses one door, but does not open it. Instead, the game master—who knows how prize and blanks are distributed—opens one of the unchosen doors which contains one of the two blanks. Then, the game master asks if the decision-maker wants to change her choice. While the dominant strategy is to switch, most individuals do not. Participants fail to update beliefs correctly. Slembeck and Tyran (2004) compare individual play and different institutions over 40 periods, i.e., competition among individuals (the prize depends on the ranking after all periods), communication (teams of three discuss the problem and decide), and communication and competition (a combination of both institutions). They show that all institutions help to perform better (between 75% and 87% switch in the last four rounds compared to 35% in the individual play), but that the combination of a rank-order tournament and team decision-making is superior in terms of learning transfer and information processing. Maciejovsky et al. (2013) are interested in how exposure to team decision-making influences subsequent individual decision-making. First, they show that teams switch more often than individual decision-makers. Second, exposure to team decision-making (compared to exposure to individual decision-making) has an impact on individual decision-making, with 60% versus 48% switching from their initial door. Third, this difference in decision-making is persistent and is observed also three weeks later.

The seminal paper by Cooper and Kagel (2005) compares individuals and pairs in signaling games that require strategic thinking and learning. The basic setup of this game is that a monopolist with either low or high costs faces a potential entrant with low or high costs. By observing a signal about the monopolist's output, the entrant has to decide whether to enter the market or not. In order to prevent the entrant from a market entry, a strategic monopolist should choose the "limit-pricing" output (e.g., choosing a pooling equilibrium instead of a separating equilibrium). The authors observe that teams act more sophisticatedly than individuals and were also able to transfer their knowledge to settings with different parameters, i.e., they were able to learn across setups.

In a similar vein, Kocher and Sutter (2005), Sutter (2005), and Kocher et al. (2006) analyze the "guessing game" (also known as the "beauty-contest game"). In this game, decision-makers choose simultaneously a number between zero and one-hundred. The winner of the game is the decision-maker whose submitted number is closest to p times the average (or median) choice by all participants, with $p < 1$ usually. The game can be solved by iterated elimination of weakly dominated strategies, with the equilibrium choice being zero. One of the attractive properties of this game is that the process of eliminating dominated strategies requires decision-makers using steps of reasoning about other' choices. Suppose a decision-maker thinks that people choose randomly over the interval, with the mean being 50. Then, choosing 50p is the winning choice. If, however, the decision-maker thinks that all people think along those lines, then she should choose p times 50p. A sophisticated decision-maker will think through all steps until the equilibrium of zero is reached. A k-level thinker would stop at k steps of reasoning. The papers on the game comparing individuals and teams find that, on average, teams are more sophisticated than individuals and use one more step of reasoning. However, teams are not more sophisticated than individuals per se (at the beginning), but they learn faster than individuals and thus converge more quickly to the equilibrium. If individuals and teams compete directly against each other in the game, teams of three members earn about 70% more than individuals, everything else kept constant. Finally, learning is positively correlated with the size of the team.

This sub-section points out that in complex decision environments, there is the potential for organizations to benefit significantly from team decisions compared to individual decisions, because teams coordinate faster, are more strategic, update their beliefs more quickly, have a steeper learning curve, and are better in predicting outcomes than individuals.

Morality and Ethical Decision Making

The results presented so far indicate that organizations could benefit from team decision-making in various dimensions. However, in their quest for maximizing payoffs and efficiency, there might be a tendency of teams to choose strategies that are less ethical as those taken by individuals. Organizations are aware of the general problem of unethical behavior, as the increasing share of organizations with a code of conduct suggests (Kaptein, 2004; ACFE, 2018). Recent evidence in economics has addressed the question of whether and, if yes, how (un-)ethical decision-making differs between individuals and teams.

The previous two chapters emphasized the superiority of teams in terms of strategically sophisticated decision-making compared to individuals. Sutter et al. (2009) builds on this finding and compares individual and team decision-making in a cheap-talk game, where a sender has to send one of two messages to a receiver who can choose one out of two options. The sender knows the payoff allocation for both options and could send either a true statement (that gives higher payoffs to the receiver) or a wrong statement that maximizes the sender's payoff. Senders who want to deceive the receiver in order to maximize their payoff could either send the wrong message with the expectation that the receiver follows their advice or send the true message with the expectation that the receiver does not trust the advice and goes for the other option. Sutter et al. (2009) observes slight differences between individuals and teams such that individual senders that want to deceive the receiver use more frequently (roughly 60%) the former strategy to deceive the sender, while team senders act more strategically when trying to deceive the receiver and use the latter strategy more often (roughly 68%).

Another relevant difference between individual and team decision-making is the feeling of responsibility, and perhaps accountability, for a taken decision. Conrads et al. (2013) examine this aspect in an adapted version of rolling a die (Fischbacher & Föllmi-Heusi, 2013). In this experiment, a decision-maker rolls a six-sided die in private (anonymously and unobserved), and she is then asked to report the outcome of the first die roll. The report determines the payment (for simplicity, assume that reporting a 1 results in a payment of 1 monetary unit, reporting a 2 results in a payment of 2 monetary units, and so on). The researchers implement three treatments. The first treatment is an individual decision-making treatment in which an individual rolls the die and then determines her payoff with the report. The second treatment is a team treatment in which each of two team members reports a number individually, and then the sum of both reported numbers determines the total payment which is shared evenly among team members. The third treatment is a mixed team treatment, and payment is identical to the team treatment only for one team member. The second team member receives a different payment. Her payment is half of the sum of the own report plus a random number drawn from the outcome space. Hence, a lie of the first player has no positive externality on the second player. The data show that teams are more likely to misreport the outcome of the die roll than individuals. Team dishonesty seems to be driven by diffusion of responsibility and not by "white lies", i.e., by lying because the other team member benefits as well.

Kocher et al. (2018) use a computerized version of the die-rolling experiment that allows them to assess lying inclination on the individual level in three within-subject treatments (an individual treatment, a team treatment with payoff commonality, and a team treatment without payoff commonality). The first and third stage in each treatment is an individual reporting stage. The second stage is the treatment stage. Subjects in the individual treatment perform the same task as in stage one and three, while participants in the team treatments can communicate via chat. In the treatment with payoff commonality, all team members have to report the same number to receive the payment indicated by the eyes on the die, while without payoff commonality payments are individual (after team members interacted in the real-time chat). The results confirm the hypothesis of a dishonesty shift from individuals to teams. Both teams with and teams without payoff commonality lie more than individuals. Teams use the chat as a coordination device, and the chat messages in both team treatments reveal that team members exchange significantly more often arguments in favor of dishonesty than for honesty. When team members talk about honesty with each other, dishonesty is reduced significantly. On average, however, team interaction leads to norm erosion, i.e., expectations about norm compliance is much lower after team interaction than after individual decision-making. In addition, dishonesty in stage 1 (individual decisions) of the experiment is, on average, not predictive of the behavior in the team environment, i.e., team interaction "overpowers" individual inclinations to be honest.

Summing up, team decision-making is associated with a stronger inclination to unethical behavior compared to individual decision-making. The main reasons are diffusion of responsibility, communication as a reinforcing process, and norm erosion.

Self-Selection into Teamwork

The previous sub-sections discussed teamwork as an organizational feature that is exogenously given. In other words, people are requested to work either in teams or individually, and institutions cannot be changed. Such an approach neglects the fact that some people might want to avoid one or the other working environment. What happens if people have the choice of whether they want to work in a team or alone? Who selects into teamwork and who opts out of teamwork? These questions are closely connected to free-riding behavior—or to the expectations about free-riding behavior—within teams. As already introduced in the parts on cooperation (2.2.3) and intergroup conflict (2.2.4), free-riding is—up to a certain extent—a problem when people are asked to "voluntarily" contribute to a team outcome. In this vein, Lazear and Shaw (2007) talk about "indolent" workers (one might think, among other reasons, of less motivated, less able/skilled or less educated workers). In a team environment, these workers would benefit from other team members. This could cause adverse selection if a system allows for self-selection into team work, i.e., indolent workers choose to work in teams, while more productive workers choose to escape the "free-riding trap".

The first study in this sub-section presents evidence from a field experiment by Hamilton et al. (2003) from a garment plant. The researchers observe and analyze weekly productivity data in the context of an organizational shift from individual piece rate incentives to team-based incentives, with six or seven workers per team. The workers could decide voluntarily whether to work under the new team-based incentive scheme or to stay with the individual piece rate. The main and most interesting result with respect to self-selection into teamwork is that workers with relatively high productivity chose the team-based incentive schemes at a very early stage. Although some of these high ability workers forwent profits compared to an individual incentive scheme, they did not display a greater likelihood to leave the firm than low ability workers. This suggests that besides monetary benefits, non-pecuniary motives such as status or warm glow from helping other team members might enter the utility function of workers. In addition, free-riding was not a big problem in the context of this study.

In a laboratory experiment, Cooper et al. (2019) investigate what motivates high ability workers to join a team with low ability workers. In their design, they can distinguish between pro-social motivations to join a team or long-term considerations, i.e., a pecuniary motivation to join a team by enhancing productivity of low ability workers via teaching and thus expecting higher financial gains in future collaborations. They investigate these two motivations by applying a three-stage design. First, participants solve nonograms (similar to Sudoku) individually and receive a piece rate for each correctly solved nonogram. In stage two, a high ability worker and a low ability worker are matched and then decide with common knowledge about the potential partner's ability to continue working under individual incentives or under team incentives. The team conditions in the second part mainly vary in the ability to chat and give hints, in the payoff dependence within a team, and in the tenure of the partnership (whether or not the partner from this stage is the same as in the third stage, which is important for whether teaching benefits could be expected and realized or not). The data reveal adverse selection when the revenue is shared within a team and when communication is not available. But whenever high ability workers could teach low ability workers and obtain a share of the monetary gains from their development, adverse selection is less pronounced.

A laboratory study on joint decision-making and without the strategic component of teaching by Kocher et al. (2006) analyzes self-selection into teams. In the beauty-contest games, the authors ask after an initial round of individual decision-making whether participants want to join a team of three subjects (with face-to-face discussion on the strategy) or continue individually to play another four rounds of a standard p-beauty-contest. The data reveal that approximately 60% of the participants, mainly low ability subjects, want to join a team and the remaining 40% prefer playing individually. The main driver behind team participation is the expectation that teams do "better" and thus increase potential individual earnings. The main reason for not joining a team is that people prefer having autonomy over their decisions. Despite earnings differences (being part of a team leads to higher profits), both types of participants are highly satisfied with their choice, even after the realization of payments.

The next study addresses the relationship between teamwork and gender. Kuhn and Villeval (2015) investigate if and how self-selection into individual- or team-based incentives schemes differs across genders in a real-effort laboratory experiment. Overall, they do not find a systematic difference between men and women joining team-based incentive schemes. Their data further display adverse selection in both genders—low ability workers select into teamwork—and upward-biased expectations about team mates' abilities (stronger for women). Among females, only high ability females increase their willingness to join a team-based incentive scheme when their performance has an impact on others' payoffs, while males are more prone to join team-based incentive schemes out of opportunistic reasons (when they receive efficiency gains from team work compared to an individual working environment).

Teamwork might be an instrument to mitigate the gender gap in competitiveness (e.g., Niederle & Vesterlund, 2007). Dargnies (2012) designs an experiment where a tournament is either team-based or individual. She finds no gender competition gap in the team-based tournament when the ability of the teammate is uncertain, because fewer men enter the team competition. This is especially driven by the fact that fewer men with above-median performance select into team competition when they fear to get caught in a free-riding trap. If men with above-median performance know that their teammate has a similar ability, the team tournament is also attractive for them. Team competition leads to more low ability women entering the contest (compared to a tournament on the individual level), but only if they are paired with similar others in terms of ability.

Cooper and Saral (2013) investigate whether being an entrepreneur or not is correlated with the preference to work alone. They do so by introducing a three-stage game in which participants have to solve questions. In the first stage, participants answer individually. In the second stage, pairs answer questions, but participants can ex-ante allocate questions to a team account or an individual account (similar to a social dilemma game with free-riding opportunities). In a third stage, participants pay for avoiding team production. The authors observe higher bids by full-time entrepreneurs for working alone in the third stage compared to all other participants, but they are not more likely to free-ride in the second stage. Working alone is less interesting for older participants, but it is more appealing to high-ability participants. The part on risk-taking already introduced the paper by Masclet et al. (2009). They also present findings from an experimental treatment in which participants have the possibility to pay for deciding alone, i.e., they elicit the willingness to pay for "escaping" teamwork. They observe, similar to Cooper and Saral (2013), that less risk averse people (who are typically more often self-employed) pay significantly more for avoiding to join the team.

This sub-section on self-selection into team work highlights that high-ability decision-makers and workers are willing to join teams and to create positive externalities (e.g., via teaching of low ability workers), but a threat of free-riding has detrimental effects on the high-ability workers' willingness to join work teams. Although based on different motivations, women and men seem similar in their tendencies to join a work team. In addition, preferring individual work does not necessarily imply free-riding in team settings.

Field Evidence on Working in Teams with Incentive Dependence

This sub-section on field evidence complements the other sub-sections with results on how payoff dependence within a team of workers—team incentives—shapes team composition, highlights social aspects of team incentives, and its impact on outcomes. Previous sub-sections, mainly based on laboratory experiments, were mainly concerned with how incentive structures affect decisions.

This sub-section continues discussing the paper by Hamilton et al. (2003) that was already discussed in the self-selection sub-section. Team incentives in their setting raised productivity by about 18% compared to individual incentives. The most productive teams were teams that formed earliest. The early presence of high ability workers in teams and the fact that some teams raised their productivity levels above the productivity level of the most able individual worker suggests that team incentives have an additional effect on productivity (e.g., through learning of worker's social skills in the team setting). Moreover, teams with more heterogeneity in team members' ability are also more productive when the average skill level within a team is held constant.

Along the lines of endogenous team formation—which can imply a trade-off between choosing fellow workers by ability or by social connections—Bandiera et al. (2013) present a field experiment with fruit pickers, where workers are organized in five-person teams within the company. The authors observe the impact of different payment schemes on team compositions. After spending the first week in a team, workers could form new teams each week, subject to the rule that all team members had to agree on a team's composition. In the first half of the fruit-picking season, workers got paid by team piece-rate incentives. After half of the season, teams still received team piece rates, but also received rank incentives (workers received information about their absolute and relative productivity in the total distribution on a daily basis). After three-quarters of the season, workers received an additional payment (on top of the team piece rate and the rank incentives) if they were team members of the most productive team, i.e., the tournament-winning team received a prize. The introduction of the two additional incentive schemes led to a change in team compositions such that workers focused more on co-workers' abilities than on existing social connections. In particular, workers formed teams with co-workers of similar ability. In terms of productivity, rank incentives decreased productivity by 14% compared to the team piece rate, while the tournament increased productivity by 24% compared to rank incentives. This is due to the heterogeneous impact of the two incentive schemes on teams at the bottom or at the top of the productivity distribution. Rank incentives decreased the productivity of teams at the bottom of the distribution, compared to a situation where workers work under team piece rates. In contrast, the tournament scheme increased the productivity of top teams compared to rank incentives.

Studying the same company, Bandiera et al. (2005) focus on the relationship between incentive schemes, with and without negative externalities on co-workers, and productivity, i.e., if and how social preferences influence the productivity of workers. The initial incentive scheme was a relative incentive scheme where workers got paid for their daily output compared to the average output of all workers who worked on the same day in the same field. During the season, the company switched to an individual piece rate incentive scheme. The authors used a daily change in team composition to investigate their research question. They find that the productivity of the average worker was approximately 1.5 times higher under individual piece rates than under the relative incentive scheme where the productivity of a given worker produced negative externalities on other workers. The lower productivity under the relative incentive scheme was due to the internalization of these negative externalities, especially if these externalities affected people with whom a worker had closer social ties. However, this result only holds as long as mutual monitoring is possible.

Friebel et al. (2017) present results from a field experiment in collaboration with a retail chain. They investigate the introduction of a team (store) bonus, additional to the usual salary, conditional on meeting a specific sales target in a randomly selected sample of all sales teams. The comparison between the control teams (no team bonus) and the treatment teams reveal that the team bonus is cost-effective, i.e., a dollar spent on the program increased sales by US$ 3.80 and resulted in an additional profit of US$ 2.10. The effect is driven by higher efforts of workers. The success of the experiment convinced the company to implement the bonus payment also in the control teams. The data show that the control teams experienced a similar productivity shift after introduction of the bonus, which suggests that this treatment effect of the bonus is robust.

This section concludes with a field experiment by Babcock et al. (2015) on educational (pay-for-studying) and health (pay-for-exercise) incentives. The focus lies on the comparison of their individual incentive treatment with the two team treatments, one without and one with social connections (and possibilities for repeated social interactions) between team members. The basic idea of the incentive is that participants received $2 per visit of the study room (gym) up to four (five) times, and they received a US$25 bonus (per person in the team treatment) if they visit the study room (gym) at least four (five) times. The requirement to receive the bonus in the team treatments is that both team members have to reach the minimum visits.

The only effective team treatment is the treatment with social connections. For instance, in the pay-for-study part, this team-based incentive scheme doubled the number of visits in the study room. However, team incentives only outperformed individual incentives if there was at least some social connection (e.g., knowing the other person) between team members. The mechanism behind the effects seems to be related to guilt aversion rather than to altruism.

This sub-section highlights the social, but sometimes also anti-social, effects of team incentives. The findings from field research show that team incentives and their effectiveness are sensitive to the social and organizational environment, but, in general, the social effect of team incentives can be very strong. Starting from increasing productivity via teaching, coordination or social skills, it could lead to team members putting more effort into their work to avoid the guilt from letting down their teammates.

Summary

Organizations steadily strive to improve decisions and thus to increase the productivity of their workers and profitability. Therefore, the choice of under which exact conditions and rules decisions are taken and how work is performed within the organization is of utmost importance. One key factor, as mentioned by Deloitte's (2016) "Human Capital Trends", might be the organization of work in teams. Indeed, teamwork is associated with organizations that are considered as high-performing (e.g., Ichniowski et al., 1997).

This chapter sheds light on evidence from the behavioral and experimental economics literature on teamwork and show that team decision-making can often be beneficial from an organization's point of view whenever decisions require strategic sophistication and learning. This is obviously particularly important in complex decision environments. Despite the greater strategic sophistication of teams compared to individuals, it is not clear whether team setups have a disadvantage in terms of caring for others. On the one hand, teams seem to be more selfish in simple allocation decisions, but they do not seem to be consistently less cooperative. Field experiments suggest that social motivations are an important aspect, and clever incentives that take these motivations into account have the opportunity to increase productivity of work teams.

However, individuals working in teams are also more likely than individual decision-makers to engage in dishonest behavior. Thus, compliance mechanisms within companies must take team-based working environments into account and create social architectures that are conducive to ethical decision-making. Another downside of work team environments may be potential adverse selection effects: high-ability workers tend to self-select into individual work modes; this is clearly not optimal from an organization's point of view.

Interesting topics for future research include, for instance, how the quality of the decision-making process, individual preferences, attitudes, and contributions affect the outcome of a team decision. Open questions remain on the development of expectations, beliefs, and moral norms during and after team interaction. Moreover, this review discussed some insights into how teams decide and how disagreements can be solved within teams, but further research on strategic decision-making is needed to understand how teams solve potential disagreements and come to joint decisions. Finally, methodologically there is still little knowledge on the specific effects of different forms of communication, decision-making rules, and in particular team size on team outcomes.

This chapter—investigating primarily team decision-making in controlled laboratory environments—covers studies with a broad variety of different communication mechanisms to coordinate decision-making in teams. Despite not being in the focus of the current chapter, this survey also highlights the importance of procedures (e.g., communication mechanisms, team size, coordination mechanisms) on decision outcomes in unitary teams. For further insights, the chapter on "Behavioral Aspects of Communication in Organizations" (see Cross-References) is highly recommended.

References

Abbink, K., Brandts, J., Herrmann, B., & Orzen, H. (2010). Intergroup conflict and intra-group punishment in an experimental contest game. *The American Economic Review, 100*(1), 420–447. https://doi.org/10.1257/aer.100.1.420

ACFE. (2018). *Report to the nations – 2018 global study on occupational fraud and abuse*. Technical report. Available at: https://www.acfe.com/report-to-the-nations/2018.

Auerswald, H., Schmidt, C., Thum, M., & Torsvik, G. (2018). Teams in public goods experiment with punishment. *Journal of Behavioral and Experimental Economics, 72*, 28–39. https://doi.org/10.1016/j.socec.2017.11.001

Babcock, P., Bedard, K., Charness, G., Hartman, J., & Royer, H. (2015). Letting down the team? Social effects of team incentives. *Journal of the European Economic Association, 13*(5), 841–870. https://doi.org/10.1111/jeea.12131

Baker, R. J., Laury, S. K., & Williams, A. W. (2008). Comparing small-group and individual behavior in lottery-choice experiments. *Southern Economic Journal, 75*(2), 367–382.

Bandiera, O., Barankay, I., & Rasul, I. (2005). Social preferences and the response to incentives: Evidence from personnel data. *Quarterly Journal of Economics, 120*(3), 917–962. https://doi.org/10.1093/qje/120.3.917

Bandiera, O., Barankay, I., & Rasul, I. (2013). Team incentives: Evidence from a firm level experiment. *The Journal of the European Economic Association, 11*(5), 1079–1114. https://doi.org/10.1111/jeea.12028

Berg, J., Dickhaut, J., & McCabe, K. (1995). Trust, reciprocity, and social history. *Games and Economic Behavior, 10*(1), 122–142. https://doi.org/10.1006/game.1995.1027

Bone, J., Hey, J., & Suckling, J. (1999). Are groups more (or less) consistent than individuals? *Journal of Risk and Uncertainty, 18*(1), 63–81. https://doi.org/10.1023/A:1007764411446

Bornstein, G., & Yaniv, I. (1998). Individual and group behavior in the ultimatum game: Are groups more "rational" players? *Experimental Economics, 1*(1), 101–108. https://doi.org/10.1023/A:1009914001822

Bornstein, G., Kugler, T., & Ziegelmeyer, A. (2004). Individual and group decisions in the centipede game: Are groups more "rational" players? *Journal of Experimental Social Psychology, 40*(5), 599–605. https://doi.org/10.1016/j.jesp.2003.11.003

Bradfield, A. J., & Kagel, J. H. (2015). Legislative bargaining with teams. *Games and Economic Behavior, 93*, 117–127. https://doi.org/10.1016/j.geb.2015.08.001

Camerer, C. F. (2003). *Behavioral game theory: Experiments in strategic interaction*. Princeton University Press.

Carlsson, F., He, H., Martinsson, P., Qin, P., & Sutter, M. (2012). Household decision making in rural China: Using experiments to estimate the influences of spouses. *Journal of Economic Behavior and Organization, 84*(2), 525–536. https://doi.org/10.1016/j.jebo.2012.08.010

Casari, M., Zhang, J., & Jackson, C. (2016). Same process, different outcomes: Group performance in an acquiring a company experiment. *Experimental Economics, 19*(4), 764–791. https://doi.org/10.1007/s10683-015-9467-7

Cason, T. L., & Mui, V. L. (1997). A laboratory study of group polarization in the team dictator game. *The Econometrics Journal, 107*(444), 1465–1483. https://doi.org/10.1111/j.1468-0297.1997.tb00058.x

Cason, T. L., & Mui, V. L. (2019). Individual versus group choices of repeated game strategies: A strategy method approach. *Games and Economic Behavior, 114*, 125–145. https://doi.org/10.1016/j.geb.2019.01.003

Charness, G., Rigotti, L., & Rusticchini, A. (2007). Individual behavior and group membership. *The American Economic Review, 97*(4), 1340–1352. https://doi.org/10.1257/aer.97.4.1340

Charness, G., & Sutter, M. (2012). Groups make better self-interested decisions. *The Journal of Economic Perspectives, 26*, 157–176.

Cheung, S. L., & Palan, S. (2012). Two heads are less bubbly than one: Team decision-making in an experimental asset market. *Experimental Economics, 15*(3), 373–397. https://doi.org/10.1007/s10683-011-9304-6

Conrads, J., Irlenbusch, B., Rilke, R. M., & Walkowitz, G. (2013). Lying and team incentives. *Journal of Economic Psychology, 34*, 1–7. https://doi.org/10.1016/j.joep.2012.10.011

Cooper, D. J., & Kagel, J. H. (2005). Are two heads better than one? Team versus individual play in signaling games. *The American Economic Review, 95*(3), 477–509. https://doi.org/10.1257/0002828054201431

Cooper, D. J., & Saral, K. J. (2013). Entrepreneurship and team participation: An experimental study. *European Economic Review, 59*, 126–140. https://doi.org/10.1016/j.euroecorev.2013.01.003

Cooper, D. J., Saral, K., & Villeval, M. C. (2019). *Why join a team?* Working paper (version: 13 July 2019).

Cox, J. C. (2002). Trust, reciprocity, and other-regarding preferences: Groups vs. individuals and males vs. females. In R. Zwick & A. Rapoport (Eds.), *Advances in experimental business research* (pp. 331–350). Kluwer Academic Publishers.

Cox, J. C., & Hayne, S. C. (2006). Barking up the right tree: Are small groups rational agents? *Experimental Economics, 9*, 209–222. https://doi.org/10.1007/s10683-006-9123-3

Dargnies, M. P. (2012). Men too sometimes shy away from competition: The case of team competition. *Management Science, 58*(11), 1982–2000. https://doi.org/10.1287/mnsc.1120.1542

Deloitte. (2016). *2016 Deloitte global human capital trends: The new organizational: different by design*. Deloitte University Press.

Denant-Boemont, L., Diecidue, E., & L'Haridon, O. (2017). Patience and time consistency in collective decisions. *Experimental Economics, 20*, 181–208. https://doi.org/10.1007/s10683-016-9481-4

Elbittar, A., Gomberg, A., & Sour, L. (2011). Group decision-making and voting in ultimatum bargaining: An experimental study. *The BE Journal of Economic Analysis and Policy, 11*(1). https://doi.org/10.2202/1935-1682.2631

Engel, C. (2011). Dictator games: A meta study. *Experimental Economics, 14*(4), 583–610. https://doi.org/10.1007/s10683-011-9283-7

Erev, I., Bornstein, G., & Galili, R. (1993). Constructive intergroup competition as a solution to the free rider problem: A field experiment. *Journal of Experimental Social Psychology, 29*, 463–478. https://doi.org/10.1006/jesp.1993.1021

Fehr, E., Kirchsteiger, G., & Riedl, A. (1993). Does fairness prevent market clearing? An experimental investigation. *Quarterly Journal of Economics, 108*, 437–459. https://doi.org/10.2307/2118338

Feri, F., Irlenbusch, B., & Sutter, M. (2010). Efficiency gains from team-based coordination – Large scale experimental evidence. *The American Economic Review, 100*(4), 1892–1912. https://doi.org/10.1257/aer.100.4.1892

Fischbacher, U., & Föllmi-Heusi, F. (2013). Lies in disguise – An experimental study on cheating. *Journal of the European Economic Association, 11*(3), 525–547. https://doi.org/10.1111/jeea.12014

Friebel, G., Heinz, M., Krueger, M., & Zubanov, N. (2017). Team incentives and performance: Evidence from a retail chain. *The American Economic Review, 107*(8), 2168–2203. https://doi.org/10.1257/aer.20160788

Glätzle-Rützler, D., Lergetporer, P., & Sutter, M. (2019). *Collective intertemporal decisions and heterogeneity in teams*. Working Paper.

Güth, W., Schmittberger, R., & Schwarze, B. (1982). An experimental analysis of ultimatum bargaining. *Journal of Economic Behavior and Organization, 3*(4), 367–388. https://doi.org/10.1016/0167-2681(82)90011-7

Hamilton, B. H., Nickerson, J. A., & Owan, H. (2003). Team incentives and worker heterogeneity: An analysis of the impact of teams on productivity and participation. *Journal of Political Economy, 111*(3), 465–497. https://doi.org/10.1086/374182

Harrison, G. W., Lau, M. I., Rutström, E. E., & Tranzona-Gómez, M. (2013). Preferences over social risk. *Oxford Economic Papers, 65*(1), 25–46. https://doi.org/10.1093/oep/gps021

Holt, C. A., & Laury, S. K. (2002). Risk aversion and incentive effects. *The American Economic Review, 92*(5), 1644–1655. https://doi.org/10.1257/000282802762024700

Ichniowski, C., Shaw, K., & Prennushi, G. (1997). The effects of human resource management practices on productivity: A study of steel finishing lines. *The American Economic Review, 87*(3), 291–313.

Kagel, J. H., & McGee, P. (2016). Team versus individual play in finitely repeated prisoner dilemma games. *American Economic Journal: Microeconomics, 8*(2), 253–276. https://doi.org/10.1257/mic.20140068

Kaptein, M. (2004). Business codes of multinational firms: What do they say? *Journal of Business Ethics, 50*(1), 13–31. https://doi.org/10.1023/B:BUSI.0000021051.53460.da

Kerr, N. L., MacCoun, R. J., & Kramer, G. P. (1996). Bias in judgment: Comparing individuals and groups. *Psychological Review, 103*, 687–719. https://doi.org/10.1037/0033-295X.103.4.687

Kittel, B., & Luhan, W. J. (2013). Decision making in networks: An experiment on structure effects in a group dictator game. *Social Choice and Welfare, 40*(1), 141–154. https://doi.org/10.1007/s00355-011-0594-6

Kocher, M. G., & Sutter, M. (2005). The decision maker matters: Individual versus group behaviour in experimental beauty-contest games. *The Econometrics Journal, 115*(500), 200–223. https://doi.org/10.1111/j.1468-0297.2004.00966.x

Kocher, M. G., & Sutter, M. (2007). Individual versus group behavior and the role of the decision making procedure in gift-exchange experiments. *Empirica, 34*, 63–88. https://doi.org/10.1007/s10663-006-9026-8

Kocher, M. G., Strauß, S., & Sutter, M. (2006). Individual or team decision-making – Causes and consequences of self-selection. *Games and Economic Behavior, 56*(2), 259–270. https://doi.org/10.1016/j.geb.2005.08.009

Kocher, M. G., Schudy, S., & Spantig, L. (2018). I lie? We lie! Why? Experimental evidence on a dishonesty shift in groups. *Management Science, 64*(9), 3971–4470. https://doi.org/10.1287/mnsc.2017.2800

Kugler, T., Bornstein, G., Kocher, M. G., & Sutter, M. (2007). Trust between individuals and groups: Groups are less trusting than individuals but just as trustworthy. *Journal of Economic Psychology, 28*(6), 646–657. https://doi.org/10.1016/j.joep.2006.12.003

Kugler, T., Kausel, E. E., & Kocher, M. G. (2012). Interactive decision making in groups. Are groups more rational than individuals? *Wiley Interdisciplinary Reviews: Cognitive Science, 3*, 471–482.

Kuhn, P., & Villeval, M. C. (2015). Are women more attracted to co-operation than men? *The Econometrics Journal, 125*(582), 115–140. https://doi.org/10.1111/ecoj.12122

Lazear, E. P., & Shaw, K. L. (2007). Personnel economics: The economist's view of human resources. *The Journal of Economic Perspectives, 21*(4), 91–114. https://doi.org/10.1257/jep.21.4.91

Luhan, W. J., Kocher, M. G., & Sutter, M. (2009). Group polarization in the team dictator game reconsidered. *Experimental Economics, 12*(1), 26–41. https://doi.org/10.1007/s10683-007-9188-7

Maciejovsky, B., Sutter, M., Budescu, D. V., & Bernau, P. (2013). Teams make you smarter: How exposure to teams improves individual decisions in probability and reasoning tasks. *Management Science, 59*(6), 1255–1270. https://doi.org/10.1287/mnsc.1120.1668

Masclet, D., Colombier, N., Denant-Boemont, L., & Loheac, Y. (2009). Group and individual risk preferences: A lottery-choice experiment with self-employed and salaried workers. *The Journal of Economic Behavior and Organization, 70*(3), 470–484. https://doi.org/10.1016/j.jebo.2007.11.002

Niederle, M., & Vesterlund, L. (2007). Do women shy away from competition? Do men compete too much? *Quarterly Journal of Economics, 122*(3), 1067–1101. https://doi.org/10.1162/qjec.122.3.1067

Osterman, P. (1995). How common is workplace transformation and who adapts it? *ILR Review, 47*, 173–187. https://doi.org/10.1177/001979399404700202

Robert, C., & Carnevale, P. J. (1997). Group choice in ultimatum bargaining. *Organizational Behavior and Human Decision Processes, 72*, 256–279. https://doi.org/10.1006/obhd.1997.2738

Rockenbach, B., Sadrieh, A., & Mathauschek, B. (2007). Teams take the better risk. *Journal of Economic Behavior and Organization, 63*(3), 412–422. https://doi.org/10.1016/j.jebo.2005.04.023

Schaner, S. (2015). Do opposites detract? Intrahousehold preference heterogeneity and inefficient strategic savings. *American Economic Journal: Applied Economics, 7*(2), 135–174. https://doi.org/10.1257/app.20130271

Shapiro, J. (2010). *Discounting for you, me, and we: Time preference in groups and pairs*. Working paper. Yale Department of Economics.

Sheremeta, R. M., & Zhang, J. (2010). Can groups solve the problem of over-bidding in contests? *Social Choice and Welfare, 35*, 175–197. https://doi.org/10.1007/s00355-009-0434-0

Shupp, R. S., & Williams, A. W. (2007). Risk preferences differentials of small groups and individuals. *The Econometrics Journal, 118*(525). https://doi.org/10.1111/j.1468-0297.2007.02112.x

Slembeck, T., & Tyran, J.-R. (2004). Do institutions promote rationality?: An experimental study of the three-door anomaly. *Journal of Economic Behavior and Organization, 54*(3), 337–350. https://doi.org/10.1016/j.jebo.2003.03.002

Song, F. (2009). Intergroup trust and reciprocity in strategic interactions: effects of group decision-making mechanism. *Organizational Behavior and Human Decision Processes, 108*, 164–173. https://doi.org/10.1016/j.obhdp.2008.06.005

Stoner, J. A. (1961). *A comparison of individual and group decisions involving risk*. Unpublished Master's thesis. Massachusetts Institute of Technology.

Sutter, M. (2005). Are four heads better than two? An experimental beauty-contest game with teams of different size. *Economics Letters, 88*(1), 41–46. https://doi.org/10.1016/j.econlet.2004.12.024

Sutter, M., Kocher, M. G., & Strauß, S. (2009). Individuals and teams in auctions. *Oxford Economic Papers, 61*, 380–394. https://doi.org/10.1093/oep/gpn037

Wildschut, T., & Insko. (2007). Explanations of interindividual-intergroup discontinuity: A review of the evidence. *European Review of Social Psychology, 18*(1), 175–211. https://doi.org/10.1080/10463280701676543

The manufacturer's authorised representative in the EU is Springer Nature Customer Service Centre GmbH, Europaplatz 3, 69115 Heidelberg, Germany. If you have any concerns regarding our products, please contact ProductSafety@springernature.com

Printed and bound by CPI Group (UK) Ltd, Croydon, CR0 4YY
28/09/2026
02224086-0009